Crime Scene Staging Dynamics in Homicide Cases

Crime Scene Staging Dynamics in Homicide Cases

Laura G. Pettler, PhD

Forensic Criminologist
Monroe, North Carolina, USA

CRC Press
Taylor & Francis Group
Boca Raton London New York

CRC Press is an imprint of the
Taylor & Francis Group, an **informa** business

CRC Press
Taylor & Francis Group
6000 Broken Sound Parkway NW, Suite 300
Boca Raton, FL 33487-2742

First issued in paperback 2020

© 2016 by Taylor & Francis Group, LLC
CRC Press is an imprint of Taylor & Francis Group, an Informa business

No claim to original U.S. Government works

ISBN-13: 978-1-4987-1118-0 (hbk)
ISBN-13: 978-0-367-70104-8 (pbk)

Library of Congress Cataloging-in-Publication Data

Pettler, Laura Gail. author.
    Crime scene staging dynamics in homicide cases / Laura Gail Pettler.
        pages cm
    Includes bibliographical references and index.
    ISBN 978-1-4987-1118-0 (hardcover : alk. paper) 1. Crime scenes. 2. Forensic sciences. 3. Homicide investigation. I. Title.

HV8073.P4455 2015
363.25'9523--dc23   2015026809

Visit the Taylor & Francis Web site at
http://www.taylorandfrancis.com

and the CRC Press Web site at
http://www.crcpress.com

For my Dad, without whom,
my life would not have been possible
and
In remembrance of the victims
In honor of their families
In partnership with colleagues
And in pursuit of truth and justice
This book is thereby dedicated

Contents

Section III: VICTIM-CENTERED
DEATH INVESTIGATION
METHODOLOGY

9   Crime Identification: Detecting Deception   219

List of Figures

Foreword

I grew up going to crime scenes. My dad was the county coroner and a founding member of our local volunteer rescue squad. Like many sons, I wanted to be just like my dad, so I went to crime scenes with him and joined the rescue squad at 13 years old. I would go with my dad to investigate local deaths and hang out at the morgue and the police departments—listening to cops and doctors talk about murder. We did not take many family vacations, so this was a way for us to spend time together.

In the 1970s, most families played board games on Saturday nights. Solving homicides was my family's Saturday night entertainment. My family cleared the kitchen table and spread out the evidence my dad had collected that week and we poured over it, devouring every new piece of evidence as if it alone held the answer to the mysteries each case posed. By asking questions, testing theories, and debating inferences, I began to learn the art of murder.

Sitting at the table staring intently into a bloody wallet, I often found myself asking, "Why are you this way?" I quickly learned that evidence, separated from the scene, is really only a thing—with little or no relevance by itself. "Things" cannot tell a story by themselves. It is only when you put them into the context of the entire crime that they begin to have meaning. And the most important question to ask? Not who, not what, not when, not where, but *why*! That is the question that brings understanding.

Evidence is important to have, but the investigator must strive to literally *see* the evidence in use during the crime to understand it. This is a hard concept to grasp when you are limited to the "sanitized" scene—a scene sanitized by the crime scene tape and devoid of the emotion involved in the crime. Absent the action of the attack and missing the last human drama played out by the victim and his or her murderer, we are often left guessing what happened. As a teenager riding in an ambulance, I got to see the crime scenes first hand. Responding to rescue calls gave me a taste of what the scenes looked like before they were "sanitized" by the crime scene tape.

The first murder that I remember being part of happened a mile from my home. I was 16 years old and responding to a "nature unknown" rescue call, and I was alone. I found myself in a house with a woman who had been shot seven times, her husband who had been stabbed, and their son who had committed the murders, as well as other family members who were telling the son he was crazy. From inside this scene, I could both see and understand the evidence my father would later collect. My father later found the murder weapon in my car. Why? Because I had to remove it from the killer's bedroom to protect us from him while we waited for the police to arrive. My father found a large butcher knife, bent at a 45° angle on an end table four feet from the murder victim and a room away from the kitchen. Why? The knife bent when the son stabbed his father in the back and struck a rib. Why was the knife 15 feet from the kitchen on an end table? That is where it landed when the dad wrestled the knife from his son and threw it across the house. Why was blood found running down the phone and the wall the phone was hanging on? That is where the father went to call for help after he was stabbed, and he leaned back against the wall so he could watch his son while dialing. Why was there a loaded shotgun found blocking the door to the father's bedroom? This was where the son placed it after his dad talked him into putting it down.

From this crime, I learned that it is not just the evidence that tells the story, but the placement and movement of the evidence that completes the picture. It is always the *why* that brings understanding.

Prosecution was an easy choice after law school. The DA's office soon learned that with a biological sciences degree, a medical background, and a coroner for a father I could read and understand autopsies. Over the next 25 years, I worked murder cases from investigation to trial. I quickly developed a love of circumstantial evidence cases. They were the hardest and most complicated cases to try—but like my granddaddy said, "If it ain't worth working for, it ain't worth having." Most circumstantial cases were domestic violence homicides, which I call "closed room" murders, and involved staging. Having now worked an estimated 800 homicides, I have gained a good bit of anecdotal evidence of homicide behavior.

I met Dr. Laura Pettler around 2005, before she was a "doctor." Initially, I hired her to help me on an unsolved child homicide. Although that case remains unsolved, she provided valuable insight into the murder weapon by employing scientific methods of trial and error until she identified the weapon used. I knew immediately that her scientific and academic skill set was very different from mine but could complement my field experience. I hired her full time at my first opportunity and immediately put her to work reviewing my pending cases and investigating new ones. Together, we learned from one another, spending countless hours standing in the cold, the heat, the rain, and the snow to work the never-ending stream of homicides we experienced in my district.

Those unfamiliar with rural southern counties may be deluded into thinking we are all like Mayberry, but not my four-county district. One particularly brutal month, Laura and I worked 17 homicides in 30 days. These numbers may not match Chicago standards, but they definitely are not "Mayberry" either. Between 1995 and 2003, my district handled more than 350 homicides. I estimate that my district handled at least that many from 2004 until 2010. Each county presented its own unique homicide pattern. One county seemed to specialize in murder for hire. Another county seemed to specialize in killing in packs or groups (they had no movie theater and what else do you do on a Saturday night?!). This county also killed a lot of women—it was their style of divorce—he gets the gold, she gets the lead. My third county had an assortment of homicides and a lot of mental health issues. But the fourth county was the most interesting. They had the fewest homicides, but it seemed every homicide was bizarre—almost as if they were ripped from the pages of a tabloid or a Hollywood movie—everything from torturing an 80-year-old woman with an electric carving knife to killing a city councilman to get control of a gospel radio station.

Ilsa Stark said, "When a person dies, a library burns." So, when I retired from prosecution in 2014, I was afraid that what I had learned from my father, what I had learned for myself, and what I had learned working long hours with Laura would be lost; I was thrilled to learn of her work on this book.

Laura works on scientific principles, looking for empirical evidence to support every assumption she makes, and I work on the premise investigators have used for centuries—have I seen this before and what did it mean then? When we combined these two approaches, we achieved great success.

Every killer has two motives: The first is their reason to kill; it is personal and varies from killer to killer. The second is the same in every criminal case, murder or not—not to get caught. After all, murder is not nearly as fun when you have to spend the rest of your life behind bars. In fact, if that were the guaranteed outcome for every killer, there would be fewer murderers who would take the chance. Each killer knows there is the chance that he might get away with it. Like thieves and burglars, murderers want to enjoy the fruits of their labors—or at the very least, their freedom. This second motive is the genesis of staging. It is essentially an effort to deflect suspicion from the true killer—by implicating an innocent person, by causing an investigator to question whether a crime has occurred at all, or by shifting the blame to the victim (e.g., suicide)—the goal is always the same: to make the investigator see only what the offender wants him to see.

Every killer is the author of his crime. To a prosecutor, staging is both a blessing and a curse. A staged crime scene calls into question every assumption a prosecutor would normally make about the placement and location of the evidence. In turn, the prosecutor can no longer build the trial story around the physical evidence—she cannot use the physical evidence to bring the victim's final moments to life for the jury—because it is all a lie. This should not be surprising, since murder requires a certain moral flexibility and lying is but a natural extension of the crime.

Conversely, staging is also a blessing, if the prosecutor knows how to use it. Why did the killer design the scene this way? Who is suspicion deflected from? Why go to all this trouble? What did the killer want me to see? What did he *not* want me to see? Why? Circumstantially, a staged crime scene is often manna from heaven—but it is like an oyster—it just takes a little more work to get to the meat of the matter.

Understanding staging and how it can help find your killer is the beauty of this book. I was surprised to learn that there had only been 11 studies on staging, involving only 340 offenders at the time of the writing of this book. Now, I want you to fully grasp these numbers. Do you realize that my small district had more killings between 1995 and 2003 than the number of staging offenders who have been studied globally in the history of the world? Yet, staging is an extremely important behavior to understand. It is a common behavior, it often misleads investigators, and, if not recognized, it thwarts justice.

Most homicide investigators do not get to start their careers at 8 years old like I did. So it is my hope that this book, the first one written on staging, will help investigators, prosecutors, and academicians to begin building a body of work that will bring more killers to justice. Laura has proposed new conceptual and practical theories here that I hope will get the readers' creative juices flowing and aid investigators in convicting more of the guilty and sending more of the innocent home. After all, the best predictor of future behavior is past behavior and the only way to predict behavior is to study and understand it. Godspeed, Laura; here is to praying this book will help more good men and women do justice. And Laura, I am proud to say, were my father still alive, he would be the first to read it!

Michael D. Parker, Esq.
Retired Former District Attorney
Prosecutorial District 20A of North Carolina

Preface

Crime scene staging is a problem. Staging can prevent victims from getting justice and leaves violent offenders roaming free in society with the opportunity to reoffend. The vision for this book was to provide an introduction to crime scene staging based on what is known at this very early stage in the research. Without the hard work and dedication of those who contributed to the literature to this profoundly underresearched topic, this book would not have been possible. To date, there have only been a handful of studies published on crime scene staging. Because so little is empirically known about the phenomenon of staging, writing a book about it at this point is a "first log on the fire" type of endeavor. Thus, this book comprises theoretical and conceptual information related to staging substantiated by the author's empirical crime scene staging research along with the other empirical literature published by Geberth, Turvey, Hazelwood, and Napier; Keppel and Weis; Eke, Ferguson, and Petherick; and Schlesinger, Gardenier, Jarvis, and Sheehan-Cook. Including the author, this list comprises 15 people in the world who have published studies on specifically staging. This trend cannot continue. However, I hope this book helps to generate new research and helps to move the ball forward. It is going to take lots of dedicated people to make this happen. I hope it helps investigators learn more about what they might look for in crime scenes, in offenders, and in victims. The research is sparse to say the least, so without speculation, it is important to remain objective, impartial, and committed to resting investigations on facts instead of conjecture.

I have learned something about crime scene staging from every author who has taken the time and care to publish a case review, their anecdotal experience, or their new ideas for dealing with staging. I appreciate each of their contributions to my learning. While the contributions by these authors were not underpinned by empirical research, their work should be embraced as contributions to the literature published by a small group of people who really care about this topic and who are trying to help.

There are specific individuals without whom this book would not have been possible. First and foremost, my friend and colleague, retired former District Attorney Michael D. Parker of Prosecutorial District 20A of North Carolina. I have learned more from Michael Parker about homicide and prosecuting homicides than I have ever learned from anyone else in the world. Michael Parker is the best prosecutor I have ever had the pleasure of working with, and without his contributions to my learning, I would not have the understanding of this vast subject the way I have today. Along with writing the Foreword to this book, Michael has supported my journey to study and research staging from the time I declared I was going to hone in on that area. Without Michael Parker, this book would not have been possible and I would not have become the practitioner I am today.

I knew when I set out to write this book that it would probably be met with possible praise and definite criticism. I have learned in my career to appreciate any praise and embrace the criticism because I learn and grow from both. There has never been a book dedicated to the examination of crime scene staging grounded by the very little empirical research that has been focused on staging specifically. This book aims to help fill this gap. Again, because this book is "the first log on the fire" so to speak, I know that I will learn more from its publication than I could imagine and I am counting on it. As new research is published, some concepts in this book will continue to gain momentum, while other concepts will wane or become obsolete. That is the beauty of empirical inquiry.

One of the goals of book is inspiration. I am excited about the opportunity for the growth of this topic because this book might not even be a snapshot of the whole staging phenomenon as we know it so far; as we set on the tip of the iceberg, I hope it gets people talking about moving forward in an empirical manner. I hope this book inspires others to pursue research on this topic. To think that not only has it been reported that approximately 185,000 homicides have gone cold since 1990 in the United States, but those are also the ones we know about. What about all the homicides staged as interrupted robberies, home invasions, burglaries, suicides, accidents, drowning, car accidents, household falls, and other types of incidents resulting in victims' deaths that were ruled suicide, accident, natural, or otherwise that were really murders? The red flags of staging were missed and victims were not served justice. So the number of homicides reported by Hargrove in 2010 could actually be much higher because the staged murders that are ruled legitimate deaths in the United States are not included. They are homicides staged as legitimate deaths so offenders can get away with murder. As the vice president of the American Investigative Society of Cold Cases, I am committed to working to reverse this trend by publishing useful and credible research on crime scene staging.

Working homicide has changed me. Once I am engulfed in forensic criminology in relation to crime scene staging, studying it, uncovering it, predicting it, measuring it, and solving it as I proceed in my journey—thinking about murdered victims and staging offenders is always on my mind. There is so much to do in the world to solve the problem staging creates, my wheels never stop turning. It is not uncommon to realize a key point about the case that could change the trajectory of the investigation and sitting straight up in bed in the middle of the night, jumping up, getting to the computer while simultaneously texting a colleague the crux of a revelation.

Investigators need forensic criminologists and forensic criminologists need investigators. Of the two general groups who publish on staging, primarily police and criminologists, neither has all the answers. As a former district attorney's investigator, currently appointed deputy coroner by retainer, and forensic criminologist, I have learned to appreciate the best seat in the house. Training is important. Field experience is important. Education is important. But not one is more important than the other in this plight.

In light of unity, another hope for this book is that it helps to inspire the concept of embracing diversity. Investigators and criminologists are best to work together toward justice for victims. Without diversity, we would spin our wheels in only one direction. As everyone does not ever agree with anyone else 100%, diversity sends us in different directions in pursuit of the same goal. We get further that way picking up more knowledge about stagers and their victims. My hope is that this book has highlighted that investigators and criminologists should be working as a team in this plight and instead of disregarding the value of diversity, look across the table and embrace what each unique practitioner brings to the table toward thwarting the staging offender. Working staged cases is very, very difficult. Like cold cases, working staged cases is not for the faint hearted. I have seen investigators just give up because they did not know where to go and they felt the case had reached a dead end because no physical evidence overwhelmingly pointed to one specific manner of death. There is always somewhere to go, something new to try, and something that can be reinvestigated, reviewed, or reexamined. Never give up.

Another hope for this book is that people will disagree with what I have said and want to build something better, more systematic, more empirical, more applicable, and more analytical that contributes to the literature of staging, helping us all learn and move forward. The ideas of Hans Gross 100 years ago pursuant to staged suicides being mostly hangings might not be supported in 2014 by the few studies we have on staging today, but his contributions to the concept of crime scene staging are unmatched. This has been a journey. A journey I welcomed and was one of the best of my life. Writing this book was one of the most challenging things I have ever done, but it was well worth it if it helps other people. If every reader takes away at least one small thing from this book, we have moved forward.

I could not have done this without the support of my family. My incredible father is one of the most brilliant people I know. He would constantly call me to ask "what page are you on now?" His encouragement and support have spanned my entire life that I could never repay in one million lifetimes, so this book would not have been possible without him.

My aunt and uncle, Drs. Florence and Alvin Segelman, are two of the greatest scientists in the world inspiring me as a young child to pursue science and helping me learn by dissecting everything I could find. My mother sacrifices many a phone conversation to allow me to concentrate on my research. Without her support and encouragement, I could not have accomplished this goal. No one has sacrificed more than my husband Kevin. He has "carried our house" twice now: once when I wrote my dissertation on staging and again when I wrote this book. It seems that staging is always affecting his life. He is an extremely tolerant individual, and without his unwavering commitment to my mission to move the ball forward, this book would not have been possible. My daughter Alexis supported me through my dissertation when conducting research on staging and always contributing her ideas and observations, and without whom this book would not have been possible.

I cannot express my gratitude enough to Drs. Charles Tiffin, Duane Dobbert, James McCabe, and Ayn Embar-Seddon for supporting me through the dissertation process that resulted in one of the only empirical studies on staging in the world. The university was not too keen at the time about me wanting to do my dissertation on staging, but Dr. Tiffin made it happen. These scholars should be commended for supporting this effort in this way because it was an uphill battle. Without their knowledge, experience, and input, one of the few empirical studies on staging might not exist today. They are tremendously important when acknowledging those who directly and indirectly contributed to this book.

And to my partner, colleague, and friend, Detective Kenneth L. Mains, who I chase the dream of one day establishing the American Investigative Society of Cold Cases Institute and with whom I have created a tremendous outreach toward addressing the American Cold Case Epidemic through AISOCC's mission. Another hope for this book is that it directly impacts those charged with investigating cold cases and something contained herein might spark something new that helps bring justice to a victim. Nothing could be better. Again, we never give up.

So from here we forge onward and upward. We focus on publishing research on staging with sound empirical research design that helps move the ball forward. We aspire to inspire. Additionally, special recognition must be given to forensic criminologist Dr. Claire Ferguson, my colleague with whom I share a passion for the pursuit of knowledge about staging. Dr. Ferguson owns the title of the most published author in the world on crime scene staging to date. Without Claire Ferguson, this book would not have been possible.

Additionally, I give special recognition to the following individuals (in no particular order), who contributed to my learning in my life and in my career, thus helping in a diversity of ways to make this book possible:

Retired Former North Carolina
  District Attorney Michael D. Parker

Former Sheriff Rick Burris

Cpt. Kelly Williams

Former Det. Scott Williams

Chief Scott Waters

Det. Gary Carter

Ret. Chief Ronnie Michaels

Chief Deputy Coroner Karla
  Knight-Deese

Coroner Sabrina Gast

Coroner Mike Morris

Deputy Coroner Marie Broome

Coroner Rae Wooten

Deputy Coroner Tony Broome

Deputy Coroner Glen Crawford

April J. Isaacs

Alexis Q. Pettler

Special Agent Kevin
  M. Kimbrough

Assistant Attorney General Tim
  Rodgers

Former Chief John Haywood

Lt. Tommy Lytle

Lt. Det. Billy Scoggins

Sheriff Chris Francis

Former Sheriff Jack Conner

Lt. Det. Kelly Aldridge

Det. Leon Godlock

Det. Mike Benfield

Dr. Luciano Garafano

Dr. Paolo Frantini

Dr. Suzanna Gamba

Silvia Alvarez, Esq.

Retired Sheriff Tommy Allen

Anita Zannin

Herbert Leon MacDonell

Assistant District Attorney Alex
  Bass

ME'S Chief Investigator Harold
  "Rus" Ruslander

Lt. Koren Colbert

King Brown

Dawn Watkins

Jan Johnson

Chief Joe Lowder

Dr. Galen Collins

Former Det., Officer Jody Cook

Det. John Valentine (dec.)

Lt. Jason Crayton

Sheriff George Burris

Cpt. Ricky Crisp

Sheriff Dudley Green

Det. Dan Shook

Former District Attorney Brad
  Greenway

Chief Bill Halliburton

Brad Brown

Pat Sneddon

Lesley Hammer

Brian Hanson

Haria Haught

Former Judge Wayne Heasley, Esq.

Former NC Senator Eddie Goodall

Claudia Soto, Esq.

Stuart James

T. Paulette Sutton

Lt. Joe Kenda

Dr. Werner Spitz

Former Det., Officer Misty Mabry

Donnell Christian

Det. Kenneth Mains

Dr. Jim McCabe

Dr. Duane Dobbert

Dr. Ayn Embar-Seddon

Dr. Charles Tiffin

Dr. Marian Mosser

Former Det. Craig Moore

Charly Osteen

Deputy Kaitlin Robillard

Dave Pauly

Donald H. Pettler

Dr. Bari Lateef

Dr. Florence Segelman

Dr. Alvin Segelman

Paul Pettler

William St. Lawrence

Adelaide St. Lawrence

Jason Pettler

Brandon Edge

Mary Davis

Jim Davis

Mary Ardeth Davis Molello

Minter Molello

Michael Molello

Charlotte Cannon

Jillian Butela

Tommy Robinson

Lou Naccarato

Richard O'Bryan

Jennifer Arnold Hale

Jack Arnold

Melinda Buch Fair

Ashley Halsac Mitko

Carla Chambers Hickman

Maria Sabino Palmer

Allison Landis

Ryan Greene

Ryan Lampkin

Bob Ruckert

Sandi Hinman Trussell

Monica Eubanks

Micah Eubanks

R. Travis Marshall

Shane Robillard

Frankee Benner

Lonnie Bulger

Barry Watson

Joe Stinnett

Eric Morris

Jillian Butela

Sherry Cantrell

Barbara Libby

Molly Vickerman Tubbs

LaVarr McBride

Gemma Lynch

Theresa Blue

Andreas Schweizer

Luigi Saravo

NCSHP Officer Anthony Barnes

Ken Taylor, CSI

Norman Tiller

Jerry Cole

Robyn Singletary, Esq.

Ret. NCSHP Sgt. Sam Smith

Trey Smith, Esq.

Fred Rench, Esq.

NY Supreme Court Judge Richard McNally

Christa Book, Esq.

Retired Cpt. Bob Steele

Heather Vranich Brantley

Dick Warrington

Ret. Det. Gordon Jackson

John Kwosnoski

Assistant Chief Det. Andrew Gall

Don Wilbanks

Dr. Anna Barbaro

Danna Newell

Bill Newell

Author

Laura Pettler, PhD, is a forensic criminologist, author, educator, and inventor. She is a crusader for justice for victims in homicide cases. She is dedicated to using her life to make a difference. She holds a BSc in preprofessional psychology; an MSc in criminal justice, where she focused on death investigation, forensic psychology, and aspects of forensic science; and a PhD in public safety, specializing in criminal justice, where she focused on forensic criminology and specifically on the study of intimate partner violence and crime scene staging behaviors. Pettler is an International Association for Identification (IAI) Certified Senior Crime Scene analyst and is currently the chairwoman of the IAI's Bloodstain Pattern Analysis Subcommittee.

Pettler was inducted into the American Investigative Society of Cold Cases (AISOCC) and served one year on its honorary review board while simultaneously serving as AISOCC's director of development before being promoted to vice president in 2014. She dedicates a tremendous amount of time and resources toward furthering AISOCC's mission in support of cold case victims and their families in the pursuit of justice and serves on AISOCC's professional journal committee as well.

Pettler is a private consultant in homicide cases as the owner and founder of North Carolina–based company Carolina Forensics. She is the inventor of the Kaleidoscope System, which is a field-based laser trajectory system for reconstructing bloodstain distributions and bullet paths carried by 18 distributors and sold in nearly 30 countries worldwide. She focuses her research on homicide studies and crime scene staging, and in 2011 launched www.crimescenestaging.com, which houses the Crime Scene Staging Awareness Initiative. She is an international speaker and law enforcement continuing education instructor having presented in the United States, Costa Rica, France, and Italy. She has also built academic programs related to criminal justice and forensic science and has taught in academic through the graduate levels online and on the ground in crime analysis and intimate partner violence. She is currently an appointed deputy coroner in Lancaster, South Carolina, retained on a case by case basis to specifically work on staged cases and intimate partner homicides.

Pettler is a former district attorney's investigator and is the cofounder and former director of Prosecutorial District 20A's Crime Scene Reconstruction and Behavioral Analysis Program, a program instituted by retired former

District Attorney Michael D. Parker. Under the umbrella of the Crime Scene Reconstruction and Behavioral Analysis Program, she was the cofounder and director of the district's Cold Case Task Force, the former Richmond Community College International Forensic Institute, and was a founder of the Forensic Association of the Carolinas and the district's Forensic Science International Forensic Science Internship Program. She was also an integral member of building additional community initiatives designed to help communities learn and grow and was involved in pushing legislative efforts on behalf of Michael Parker's office that focused on domestic violence law and allocation of resources in the prosecutorial branch of the North Carolina government.

Contributor

Denise R. Womer, PhD, received her master's degree in criminal justice from Hodges University (2003) and her doctorate degree, with a specialization in criminal justice, from Capella University (2012). She was a deputy sheriff in South Carolina and Florida for 17 years. She has 14 years of experience in higher education at various universities and is currently a professor at Kaplan University, teaching in the School of Social and Behavioral Sciences.

Introduction to Staging

I

Any deliberate effort made by an offender before police arrive to alter the pristine condition of a crime scene to purposely thwart the investigation and frustrate the overall criminal justice process is the essence of crime scene staging. Crime scene staging could be increasing due to public fascination with crime scene–related media, enhanced awareness of forensic science applications, and/or offenders' belief in their understanding of how crime scenes should look. This book is designed to heighten awareness of crime scene staging and for crime scene investigators, detectives, crime laboratory analysts, and other forensic professionals involved in crime scene examination related work. This book explores what is known about crime scene staging and offers ideas for how to use a new methodology for the early detection and analysis of potentially staged crime scenes.

History of Crime Scene Staging* 1

Lady Macbeth: Go get some water,
    And wash this filthy witness from your hand.
    Why did you bring these daggers from the place?
    They must lie there: go carry them; and smear
    The sleepy grooms with blood.
Macbeth: I'll go no more:
    I am afraid to think what I have done;
    Look on't again I dare not.
Lady Macbeth: Infirm of purpose!
    Give me the daggers: the sleeping and the dead
    Are but as pictures: 'tis the eye of childhood
    That fears a painted devil. If he do bleed,
    I'll gild the faces of the grooms withal;
    For it must seem their guilt.

The Tragedy of Macbeth is one of William Shakespeare's (1892) most haunting plays. Written in the early 1600s, it is the story of how Scottish General Macbeth and his pushy wife, Lady Macbeth, planned and executed the murder of Scotland's King Duncan so the overly ambitious Macbeth could be King of Scotland. Consumed by the desire for power, Macbeth stabbed the sleeping King to death with daggers, but fearing someone heard the King's screams, Macbeth took the daggers back to the couple's sleeping quarters enraging his selfish wife. Furiously, Lady Macbeth demanded that Macbeth return the daggers to lie with the King's dead body and then smear the blood of their dead King on the cloaks of the sleeping guards.

To deceive or not to deceive, for that is the question. And the answer to that question is a resounding *yes* when it comes to murderers who want to kill and cover-up to protect their identities. In the aforementioned story, Macbeth and Lady Macbeth tried to hide their involvement in the murder of King Duncan and point the finger at the sleeping guards so they could get what they want in the end. Murder is a very messy situation and those who commit murder, but who do not want to take responsibility for their behavior, sometimes chose to change things around in the crime scene just like Lady Macbeth urged her husband to do to make it look like something else actually happened.

…this is the essence of crime scene staging.

* Background research and articles for inclusion in Chapter 1 identified by Denise Womer.

Early Historical References to Crime Scene Staging

In order to understand crime scene staging and why there is so little known about such a common phenomenon, a review of both the empirical and anecdotal literature is the place to start. Gaining perspective of just how short the list of literary reference to crime scene staging is throughout the course of history is a foundational building block for one's knowledge of this subject. This is not to say that it is necessary to be proficient in reciting the historical review, but what is important is gaining proficiency in knowing the difference between what has been empirically found about crime scene staging versus what is anecdotal, subjective, or speculative in nature.

Crime scene staging is the physical manifestation of a person's imagination for how things should appear when trying to turn a murder scene into a legitimate death scene, such as an accident of some kind, a suicide, or even a natural death. As seen in the example earlier, Shakespeare wrote about crime scene staging and had actors acting out the scenes in live performance in the seventeenth century. Dating back even further to ancient times, there are those who simply refused to take responsibility for their actions and chose to put themselves before all others. In the book of Genesis, Jacob had several children. However, Jacob favored Joseph more than the other children and to show his favoritism, Jacob had a robe made of many fine, brightly colored fabrics sewn for Joseph. Two of Jacob's other sons were jealous of Joseph because Jacob loved Joseph so much and one brother said to the other, "And Judah said unto his brethren, what profit is it if we slay our brother and conceal his blood?" (Genesis 37:26). Here the brothers conspired to kill Joseph and then acted on their plan by taking Joseph into the woods, imprisoning him down in a pit, and then selling him into slavery. The brothers needed to cover-up their crime in order to gain the love of their father Jacob so the brothers "took Joseph's coat and killed a kid of the goats and dipped the coat in the blood; and they sent the coat of many colors and they brought it to their father; and said, this have we found: know now whether it be thy son's coat or no?" (Genesis 37:31–32). Jacob believed his two sons because he immediately recognized the beautiful robe he had sewn for his beloved son Joseph. Jacob believed Joseph was dead and went into mourning; he could not be comforted by any of his children including Joseph's two conniving brothers. The brothers' crime did not earn them the payoff they expected and Jacob never loved them the way he loved Joseph. Today, the story of Joseph and his robe is theatrical production called *Joseph and the Amazing Technicolor Dreamcoat*; and with that, the story of Joseph's *dreamcoat* is the earliest reference of crime scene staging in the world.

According to MacDonell (1992), around 100 AD in ancient Rome, a blind son was born to a caring mother and father. The mother died and the father remarried, but regardless, the father made his blind son his heir and gave him a bedroom in the far corner of their house. The next morning, the father was found dead in his bed impaled with his blind son's sword. Bloody handprints covered the wall leading from the father's bedroom toward the blind son's bedroom in the far corner of the house. The blind son was arrested for the murder of his dear father. Quintilian, a well-known orator and Roman lawyer, was hired to defend the blind son. Quintilian argued to the court that the bloody handprints found on the wall near the body could not have been made by the murderer because the murderer would have been gripping the sword so tightly therefore making it impossible to have gotten blood on his or her hands in the first place. Second, Quintilian argued that if the bloody handprints were made after the murder, the blood would have started to fade as the prints moved along the wall. Quintilian also pointed out that the amount of blood remained the same in all of the bloody prints, and then he accused the father's second wife of staging the scene to cover-up the fact that she murdered her new husband out of rage that she was not made his heir. Quintilian argued that the wicked stepmother tried to make it look like the blind son stabbed his father to death with his own sword and then groped the wall with bloody hands feeling his way back to his room. Unfortunately, no verdict was recorded in this case.

1514 The Story of Richard Hunne

According to Forbes (1985), in 1514, Richard Hunne was known to be a good Catholic and of sound character but was brought before Dr. Horsey, the Chancellor of the Bishop of London to answer to heresy charges. Hunne was remanded to jail in the custody of the bell ringer John Spalding. Hunne was found hanged the next morning and charged with self-murder in addition to 13 other charges after his death. There was a public hearing on all 18 charges and Hunne was convicted posthumously. The coroner acted quickly to retrieve Hunne's body and clothes before Hunne's body was burned as the law allowed. The coroner held his inquest over the next 2 days in the bell tower of the jail where Hunne was found. By examining the scene, the coroner found that Hunne's hands were bound before he was hanged in his cell. The others working with the coroner also discovered that Hunne's neck was broken before he was hanged as well because two flow patterns of blood streamed in an opposing direction from where Hunne was hanged. The coroner determined that the coroner's inquest resulted in Hunne being acquitted of the charge of self-murder.

1841 The Story of Mister

In 1911, C. Ainsworth Mitchell discussed how murderers remove bloodstains from their clothing (Mitchell, 1911). Mitchell illustrated his suggestions with a case from 1841 about a man named "Mister" who used a solvent to remove bloodstains from his clothing when he was charged with a murder. Although Mister was successful in removing the blood from his clothing, he was convicted of the crime when the solvent bottle was found in his room.

1859 The Budge Case

According to Dr. John Swineburne (1862), the 1859 case of the murder of Mrs. Budge provides another historical reference to crime scene staging. Mrs. Budge was found in her bed with her throat slashed and a razor blade near her hand. The coroner came to Mrs. Budge's bedroom to investigate her death and wrote, "Her throat was cut completely across and very deep severing both carotid arteries and only stopped when it reached the vertebrae" (p. 94). The coroner noted that there was no evidence of bleeding consistent with injuries of this nature in the bed, but he ruled her suicide, put her back together, and sewed her back up. Songwriter Caleb Lyon did not agree with the coroner and wrote a song about Mrs. Budge's husband, Reverend Budge, and musically accused him of murdering his wife. Budge filed a lawsuit against Lyon for slander and all the attention on the matter resulted in Mrs. Budge being exhumed. Mrs. Budge's second autopsy resulted in a murder indictment against Rev. Budge. The jury appeared politically motivated ignoring the lack of bloodstain evidence and acquitted him anyway. Lyon lost the lawsuit and was ordered to pay $100.00.

1882 Bloodstains on the Doorjamb

According to MacDonell (1992), Juan Vucetuch was an Argentinian police official who was the first to identify an individual using a bloody fingerprint. A woman accused her neighbor of attacking her and slitting the throats of her two sons killing them. The woman argued that the neighbor left his bloody fingerprints on the doorjamb of the house as he fled. Although the neighbor was a highly respected individual in the community, he was arrested and held on suspicion of killing the children and attacking the woman. The bloodstain evidence revealed that the woman cut her own neck, and Vucetuch identified the woman as the person who left the bloody fingerprints on the doorjamb. The neighbor was released and the woman was imprisoned.

1882 Dr. Carl Liman and Staged Weapons

"Absence of evidence is not evidence of absence" (MacDonell, 1996, p. 160). In light of MacDonell's quote, Dr. Carl Liman (1882) argued, "The accused will deny all. He'll say that he has never seen the knife, or that he could not have used it since there are no blood stains on the knife, or he admits that the stains could be blood stains, but that they came from an animal, etc."

Liman focused on the importance of investigating weapons that might not seem like they are involved but with close examination can be determined if they were actually involved in a crime.

1887 Dr. Eduard R. von Hofman Murder Staged as Suicide

Dr. Eduard R. von Hofman (1887) wrote about a case where a staged crime scene went undetected even though a suicide victim had a bloody left hand-print on the back of his left hand. In reviewing this synopsis, Strassman (1985) supported von Hofman's claim in that "Blood can be spread after the fact, and accidentally by unaware persons, or can be spread on purpose to mislead…A dead person lying on his back had a blood print on his left hand showing a left hand print. It cannot be a print of his own left hand" (p. 341). Further, von Hofman (1887) wrote, "Blood spatter will be able to tell if the victim was transported there…" (p. 423). Von Hofman discussed two other cases related to crime scene staging and how crime scene stagers protect themselves by either removing all of their clothing before the murder or clothing themselves with additional clothing before the murder.

1892 Lizzie Borden

In 1892, Lizzie Borden was acquitted of the brutal ax murders of her parents. However, according to Brown (1991), the crime scene was staged and Lizzie Borden got away with murdering Andrew and Abby Borden (p. 382). During the trial, prosecutors argued that Lizzie Borden planned the murders of her parents because her father was preparing to write her out of his will (interesting when compared to the case of the blind son). Prosecutors further argued that Lizzie Borden's behavior was consistent with having murdered parents claiming that Lizzie had motive and was predisposed to wanting them dead. In light of these findings, Brown described the bloodstains found on the wall behind Andrew Borden in such tremendous detail and, thus, wanted to exhume the victims' bodies to use new technology that could finally resolve the mystery of these horrifying murders in quiet Fall River, Massachusetts.

1902 Glaister

According to Dr. John Glaister (1902), "in the first place, caution and carefulness must be exercised throughout the whole inquiry, for, if possible, and an opportunity offers a guilty person will attempt to wash away the evidences of his guilt" (p. 238). Dr. Glaister recognized the critical nature of approaching a potentially staged crime scene with extra care because critical evidence can be lost early in the investigation possibly ruining any chance at justice.

In this particular instance, Glaister recognized the likelihood that crime scene stagers will attempt to wash or clean up crime scenes for various reasons but primary to absolve themselves of suspicion.

1924 Hans Gross

Hans Gross is the most influential historical voice in the field of forensic criminology. His words, some written more than a century ago, still ring true today as they will for centuries to come. Gross had an uncanny way about him that allowed him to keenly express his observations and predictions about how offenders behave in crime scenes. From the forensic criminological perspective in relation to the study of crime scene staging, the importance of Hans Gross' contributions to the literature cannot be understated. According to MacDonell (1992), in 1899, Hans Gross argued, "if one is suspicious that bloodstains have been removed, one should administer Kleesalz or sulfuric acid and soda, respectively. If the results are positive one had discovered almost as much as if the blood itself had been in evidence" (Gross, 1924, p. 264). Gross recognized the potential of the crime scene stager to clean up the crime scene and his ability to conceal evidence by cleaning up blood specifically. Further, Gross (1924) echoed Glaister's suggestions and "argued that offenders fail to stage the crime scenes properly in most cases, thus making some staging efforts obvious to law enforcement professionals" (Pettler, 2011, p. 51). To note, Hans Gross offered a tremendous amount of valid points on crime scene staging in addition to the discussion points here (see Ferguson, 2011). The history of crime scene staging, while sparse, is demonstrative that scholars and practitioners have recognized the importance of scientific criminal investigation toward thwarting the efforts of crime scene stagers since at least circa 100 AD.

1936 O'Connell and Soderman

O'Connell and Soderman (1936) stressed the importance of crime scene reconstruction in distinguishing homicide cases from suicide cases. O'Connell and Soderman focused much of their discussion on the importance of wound pattern analysis, which can aid in the understanding of a victim's injuries pursuant to consistencies and inconsistencies, locations, sizes, and so on. O'Connell and Soderman also stressed the importance of studying each type of death and their related weapons independently, such as suicides apart from homicides, deaths by hanging, death by lacerations, death by gunshot wounds, ligatures, incised and puncture wounds, poisoning, and vehicle-related accidents (Ferguson, 2011). In cases of asphyxiation, for example, O'Connell and Soderman argued that crime scene reconstruction could help determine if a victim was hanged or was strangled with a rope ligature. Thus, O'Connell and Soderman discussed the *Goddefroy method* or the examination of rope ligatures in cases of asphyxiation death, which they recommended for determining if a victim hanged himself or herself or had been hanged by someone else. The major premise of the Goddefroy method is that the fibers of a rope used to hang someone would be directed downward since a body slides in a downward direction, likewise, compared to a rope used to strangle someone where the fibers would be pointed upward on that portion of the rope where the offender pulled upward. Goddefroy's method is one of the earliest crime scene staging methodologies grounded by marked physical evidence parameters (Ferguson, 2011).

1962 Soderman and O'Connell

Soderman and O'Connell (1962) contributed to the literature on crime scene staging again as the first to discuss the *falsification* of crime scenes from an investigative standpoint in modern literature. It was clear by this reference that their study and experience had spanned more nearly 30 years, but what even was more significant was that even after almost three decades, they were still discussing staging and how to investigate it. The works of Hans Gross (1924), Soderman and O'Connell's (1936), and O'Connell and Soderman (1962) all support the early identification and detection of staged behaviors using red flags left by offenders while setting the stage for future research on the topic. (For an in-depth look at O'Connell and Soderman's work, see Ferguson, 2014.)

1972 O'Hara and Osterberg

O'Hara and Osterberg first published their book, *Introduction to Criminalistics: An Application of the Physical Sciences to the Detection of Crime,* in 1949, and then the book was reprinted in 1972. O'Hara and Osterberg (1972) focused their discussion on how crime scene stagers are a threat to the criminal justice process because innocent people can be convicted of crimes they did not commit. O'Hara and Osterberg were two of the first authors to discuss the behavior of lying and crime scene stagers' propensity toward lying about the crime, about the individuals involved in the crime, and so on toward starting trouble for those not responsible for it at all. O'Hara and Osterberg were the first to specifically address homicides being staged as something else by way of the offender manipulating the physical evidence. They too argue that scientific investigation is the way to go and suggest that most evidence should be tested in a crime laboratory. What is also fascinating about their work is that they mention the emotional component of murder, which will be discussed later in this book, and how emotionality plays a role in crime scene staging behaviors during the actual alteration of the scene. On the heels of this interesting notion is the fact that these authors also make mention of something else that is of great importance today, which is that most crime scene stagers have little experience with criminal activity and, therefore, have no idea how a murder scene should differ from a suicide scene from a interrupted robbery scene or otherwise. Because of this, O'Hara and Osterberg suggested that many of the blunders criminals make when trying to make a murder look like a suicide, accident, or something else are detectable because the offender is essentially "flying blind" for how to stage a scene.

1974 Svensson and Wendel

On the heels of O'Hara and Osterberg (1972), Svensson and Wendel (1974) argued that homicide investigation must be scientific and systematic and that forensic scientists, detectives, and others would be wise to verify each case as being a true homicide before casting final judgment as to whether the death was a suicide or accident. Although they did not recommend a specific methodology per se, Svensson and Wendel advocated for physical evidence to be compared by analytical evaluation toward determining if the death was a homicide, suicide, or accident and note the important aspects of the stager as follows (p. 292).

Even when the murderer has carefully planned the crime and taken all imaginable precautions to avoid leaving traces, they are still found. As a rule, the murderer comes to a sudden realization of the terrible results of his deed after the killing. He may then lose his head completely and try to obliterate the evidence of his act, but his confused state of mind only works against himself by leaving new clues.

Again support for the emotional component of murder and how emotionality can influence an offender during the time when he or she is trying to get away with murder is highlighted here.

Contemporary References to Crime Scene Staging

Even though the literature pool on crime scene staging is very shallow, there are two primary communities or groups that work very hard to publish on this underresearched topic: scholars and law enforcement professionals. Over the past few decades, only a few law enforcement professionals have discussed crime scene staging within the context of their works, but those contributions and their suggestions for how to investigate staged crime scenes are largely based on their professional experience and are not accompanied by research that supports their ideas. Suggestions for investigation are mostly nonscientific, which, as can be seen in the early historical references to crime scene staging, even criminalists, doctors, and law enforcement professionals argued that scientific investigation was the only way to unravel a murder disguised as a legitimate death. The greater problem with this is that because the published literature on crime scene staging overall is so sparse, investigators in search of credible information have been left with only case studies written in narrative form and a few checklists based on what some think might be helpful to look for in crime scenes. In contrast, while the hard work of the scholars who have taken the time to build research designs, form hypotheses, conduct testing, and report results even in the most simplistic of statistical ways are tremendously important because when it comes down to what the world can *take to the bank* about crime scene staging, it is the empirical data that hold water rather than the experience-based observations. However, many scholars in general who conduct empirical research and who are tremendously important to helping move the ball forward in crime scene staging research might have very little field experience, have never worked as an investigator of any kind, and do not possess the understanding one acquires by working a staged murder from its onset. Then there are those who are in the middle of the road like the author. The author was an investigator in charge of investigating and reconstructing many staged murder cases and who currently works in the field with law enforcement both as a deputy coroner in one South Carolina county and in the private sector. However, the author is also a scholar who studies and conducts crime scene staging research. So the author, being a scholar–practitioner, has a unique perspective because having been an investigator herself, she embraces the law enforcement, anecdotal case studies published by investigators, and, in being a scholar, the empirical research published by other scholars. Regardless, the bottom line is that at this point in the literature, every contribution should be embraced, and those who care enough to focus their time and energy on this virtually unchartered territory should be applauded because both correct and incorrect information helps to move the ball forward. However, from the perspective of this scholar–practitioner, it is very important to recognize that one can find himself or herself in trouble when adopting experience-based information as fact because the American criminal justice system standard of admissibility relies solely on scientific, empirically supported evidence, testimony, and research. In other words, an investigator might be hard-pressed to sell the notion to a judge that he or she *thinks, feels,* and *believes* a crime scene is staged based on his or her experience or based on the experience of another investigator who might have published about having a similar experience. What is likely to be accepted, however, is the investigator who argues that he or she has based his or her findings about a crime scene having been staged on the empirical data published on the topic to date (Eke, 2007; Ferguson, 2011, 2014, 2015; Geberth, 2010; Hazelwood & Napier, 2004; Keppel & Weis, 2004; Pettler, 2011; Schlesinger, Gardenier, Jarvis, & Sheehan-Cook, 2012; Turvey, 2000).

In support of the discussion earlier, what happened in the case of *Washington v. Kunze, 1999*, drives this point home. Kunze was a defendant who was originally convicted of bludgeoning someone to death in Kunze's Clark County, Washington, state home. Kunze appealed his conviction, and the court of appeals held that the prosecution had not satisfied the requirement that the latent ear print testimony presented during the trial was generally accepted in the scientific community as all scientific methodologies pursuant to legal proceedings are required for admissibility under *Frye v. United States*, 1923. However, the appeals court let stand the testimony by two investigators, one of whom was a criminal profiler from the Federal Bureau of Investigation that the crime scene *could possibly have been staged*, based on their review of the crime scene case file and their experience in crime scene investigation. Herein lies the dire need for empirical research to support investigators in the judicial system in rendering their opinions and handing down their judgments on admissibility in a criminal proceeding where someone has lost his or her life potentially at the hand of a murderer.

1984 Puschel, Holtz, Hildebrand, Naeve, and Brinkman

Puschel, Holtz, Hildebrand, Naeve, and Brinkman (1984) studied a sample of six cases where the deaths of each victim presented like suicide but were eventually determined to be homicides. In four cases, the victims were strangled to death, with or without head injuries, and then suspended by some type of rope. In the sample, investigators solved five of the six cases fairly easily because two offenders confessed to the police, one offender killed himself after the staged murder by hanging, and two cases contained injuries on the victim's head inconsistent with a hanging death. Puschel et al. argued that murder is difficult to accomplish unless the other person is somehow incapacitated first and the crime scene might look like a suicide at first glance when it is really a homicide. Further, Puschel et al. advocated for investigators to analyze every detail of the scene toward eventual scientific reconstruction of the victim's position before, during, and after suspension coupled with the extensive examination of the rope or material used to hang the victim, knots in the material or rope, and, as discussed pursuant to Goddefroy's method discussed in Svensson and Wendel's (1974) publication, the direction of the fibers on the rope because they may lead investigators to realize the victim was hung by someone else.

1989 Ueno, Fukanaga, Nakagawa, Imabayashi, Fukiwara, Adachi, and Mizoi

Ueno, Fukanaga, Nakagawa, Imabayashi, Fukiwara, Adachi, and Mizoi (1989) conducted a case study on the case of a 38-year-old woman who was found lying dead beside a bed in a hotel guest room. She was found with a cotton cord tied around her neck and then tied to a bedpost making it appear as though she hanged herself in the lying down position. Investigators determined that a man had been staying with the woman in the hotel room but fled when she died. Upon closer examination of the cotton cord, investigators determined that the woman's jewelry and hair were intertwined with the rope. The forensic pathologist found conjunctiva, petechial hemorrhages, and congestion in the face and upper neck along with a very dry, light brown in color ligature mark measuring approximately one centimeter in width. The forensic pathologist found that the ligature mark crossed the front of the neck and had been tightened from the back. Additionally, the forensic pathologist found another similar-looking ligature mark on the victim's posterior neck. The forensic pathologist's findings were consistent with the first ligature mark having been there before the second ligature mark was formed on top of it. Therefore, the victim had been strangled and then hanged to make it appear to look like a suicide. The woman's husband confessed to murdering his wife a week later.

1992 Douglas and Munn

Douglas and Munn (1992) published an article, "Violent Crime Scene Analysis: Modus Operandi, Signature, and Staging," in the February 1992 *FBI Law Enforcement Bulletin*. Douglas and Munn argued that the analytical skill level of the investigator determines the outcome of a murder case because all savvy investigators have the ability to understand and tell the story from beginning to end in the proper terms. In other words, the investigators' ability to understand the dynamics of human behavior ultimately determines whether or not the case will come to fruition. Douglas and Munn argued, "speech patterns, writing styles, verbal and nonverbal gestures, and other traits and patterns give shape to human behavior" (p. 1). Further, these authors argued, "These individual characteristics work in concern to cause each person to act, react, and function or perform in an unique an specific way" (p. 1). Douglas and Munn suggested that investigators should look for behavioral clues left by the offender when investigating crime scenes and that crime scene stagers most often make mistakes when staging crime scenes because they try to stage scenes based on what they think they should look like but are under so much stress at the time that they typically do not assemble the pieces together in the right way. Douglas and Munn argued that if investigators recognize these red flags early in the process, it could prevent them from being misguided. The authors recommended investigators examine all points of entry and exit, inventory for missing valuables, interactions between the victim and offender, assess the body position of the victim, and assess the offender's risk level.

Douglas and Munn also published a chapter on crime scene staging in Burgess, Burgess, Douglas, and Ressler's (1992) *Crime Classification Manual: A Standard System for Investigating and Classifying Crimes*. From the motivational perspective, Douglas and Munn defined crime scene staging as

> Staging is when someone purposefully alters the crime scene prior to the arrival of the police. There are two reasons why someone employs staging: to redirect the investigation away from the most logical suspect or to protect the victim or the victim's family. (p. 251)

The latter portion of this definition has not been endorsed anywhere else in crime scene staging literature. Douglas and Munn also created a checklist of questions for investigators to use to detect staged crime scenes and provided case study examples to support their claims from a generalized standpoint. As in their previous article, Douglas and Munn recommended investigators to ask questions to determine if the entry by the offender makes sense with the layout of the crime scene. Also, investigators must determine if any items were taken from the crime scene and assess how much risk was posed to the offender to commit the crime. Douglas and Munn further recommended demonstrating caution when the male spouse or intimate partner is the sole survivor of a fatal intruder attack on his wife or the only individual left at a crime scene is the one who posed the most physical threat to an intruder. Further, Douglas and Munn and Douglas and Douglas recommended that law enforcement professionals always look for behavioral clues left by an offender when approaching a crime scene, again confirming what is known empirically so far about crime scene staging to date. It is arguable that crime scene investigation is complicated enough without adding the component of potentially staged evidence to the situation.

1996 Geberth

Geberth (1996) published an article where he reviewed case studies, identified and discussed crime scene staging behavior throughout, and then rendered his professional opinion based on his 40+ years as a homicide investigator on the strengths and weaknesses of each investigation, fact pattern, and so on, toward alerting investigators to behavioral patterns exhibited by crime scene stagers toward misdirecting investigations. Geberth recommended equivocal death investigations for all cases because the question existed as to the manner of death in each case.

1996–2006 Geberth

Homicide investigation has become a focal point for many law enforcement agencies with the increase of crime scene–related television (Geberth, 1996a, 2006). Lieutenant Commander Vernon Geberth is a retired homicide detective from the New York City Police Department's Bronx Homicide Task Force who has dedicated his life to public service (Geberth, 1996a, 2006). Geberth has also authored numerous articles and numerous books on specific topics related to homicide investigation during his career toward helping others (Geberth, 2006). In one of his articles entitled "The Staged Crime Scene," Geberth (1996b) argued that staging is a deliberate, purposeful act by the offender and that there are red flags that "alert investigators to the phenomena of the staged crime scene" for those who can learn to recognize them (p. 45). Further, Geberth argued that throughout his experience, he observed three types of staged crime scenes most often, which are as follows: (1) the offender makes the scene look like an accident, (2) suicide, or (3) a sex-related homicide has occurred. Geberth also offered an explanation for why he believes there could be a rise in the number of staged cases in the United Stated today: "crime scene staging is positively correlated with increased public access to homicide investigation through the news, true crime books, television, and movies" (p. 37). In light of his experience with crime scene staging, Geberth (1996a) offered a 10-item checklist for crime scene detection as well (p. 37):

1. Assess the victimology of the deceased.
2. Evaluate the type of injuries and wounds of the victim in connection with the type of weapon employed.
3. Conduct the necessary forensic examinations to establish and ascertain the facts of the case.
4. Conduct an examination of the weapon(s) for latent evidence as well as ballistics and testing of firearms.
5. Evaluate the behavior(s) of the victim and suspects.
6. Establish a profile of the victim through interviews of friends and relatives.
7. Reconstruct and evaluate the event.
8. Compare investigative findings with the medicolegal autopsy and confer with the medical examiner.
9. Corroborate statements with evidential facts.
10. Conduct and process all death investigations as if they were homicide cases.

As mentioned earlier, Geberth (1996, 1996a, 2006) has published four editions of his book *Practical Homicide Investigation: Tactics, Procedures, and Forensic Techniques*; however, information about the first and second editions could not be located. Geberth is a well-established leading homicide investigation policing expert in the field of homicide investigation. Additionally, Geberth has acknowledged the existence of crime scene staging and the importance of learning how offenders stage crime scenes in homicide cases. Further still, Geberth also described crime scene staging as a *phenomenon* based on his examination of several cases that involved homicide staging to look like suicide. Interestingly, in his books, Geberth (1996a, 2006) cautioned and reported that upon first glance, all of the crime scenes appeared to look like suicides. However, upon more discerning examination, Geberth discovered that the scenes were staged. Additionally, Geberth argued that he believes homicides staged to look like suicides are the most commonly staged crime scenes; however, this is not supported by Ferguson's (2011) findings, which were that accidents are the most commonly staged scenes in that sample. Also, he posited that in his experience, homicides staged to appear like sex-related homicides were also quite common. Geberth further argued that offenders might set fire to a crime scene to conceal the truth. Setting fire is a behavior opined by some experts as a *precautionary* crime, while other experts include fire setting in their operational definition of crime scene staging (Ferguson, 2011; Pettler, 2011). Although Geberth's (2006) book contains decades of noteworthy and very valuable experience he shared toward helping others, it is important to recognize that no individual's personal/professional experience is an empirical study. Regardless, however, Geberth writes in such detail that the value of his work is a tremendous contribution to the literature.

1996 Leth and Vesterby

Leth and Vesterby (1996) published a case review on a homicide that was staged as a hanging suicide. The victim was a 61-year-old man killed in his home and then hung up to mimic a hanging suicide. The forensic pathologist found that the blunt force trauma injuries to his head were inconsistent with having died by asphyxiation and ruled the death a homicide. Further, the forensic pathologist found that the victim was not dead at the time of the hanging but was unconscious instead. The forensic pathologist was able to determine a range for time of death, which puts one person there with the victim during that time. The person responsible for the death of the victim was convicted of manslaughter.

Generally speaking, the literature on homicidal hanging was virtually nonexistent in 1996, thus even though Leth and Vesterby's study is only a study on one case, it was still very important to the development of information on homicidal staging of a hanging suicide. To note, this was a case where the victim knew the offender, supporting the victim–offender relationship as it relates to crime scene staging to be discussed later in this book.

Leth and Vesterby (1996) went further to suggest that resistance by the victim toward the offender was a possible explanation for homicide staging of a hanging suicide. However, it is important to remember that resistance by a victim is often observed in intimate partner violence; thus, Leth and Vesterby suggested that studying crime scene staging is important to the law enforcement community as it relates in that direction. A drawback of Leth and Vesterby's case study was that it did not follow a traditional qualitative research design for studying one case; instead, the researchers reviewed the case within the framework of their own unproven model. So because their sample consisted of only one single case, it is important to note that their results are inapplicable to the general population.

1998 Yamamoto, Hayase, Matsumoto, and Yamamoto

Yamamoto, Hayase, Matsumoto, and Yamamoto (1998) studied what is known as the Kobue case. This was a notable Japanese case about the issues surrounding the cause of death of a 45-year-old woman named Kobue Hiramatsu. In late June 1926, the decomposed bodies of Hiramatsu and three young girls were found dead in Hiramatsu's house. Hiramatsu was found hanging; a waistband tied to a wooden beam that spanned the top of a doorway (i.e., a lintel) and it appeared that the three young girls had been strangled. The way Hiramatsu was hanged was interesting in that the noose has been wrapped around the lintel several times and her neck was in the noose under her chin, but her feet were touching the straw mat that covered the floor lain across the doorway (i.e., a tatami mat). Also peculiar were a cutting board and charcoal-colored brazier at her feet. Hiramatsu had two abrasions on the front of her neck, but they were not parallel. The first abrasion was created antemortem under her chin, but the second was about two centimeters below the first and had an accompanying bruise and was created postmortem. An expert in the case argued that the first abrasion was created when Hiramatsu was strangled and the second was created when someone hanged Hiramatsu after she was dead. An investigation ensued and investigators arrested a former employee who denied killing the foursome. During the trial, the critical issue was the mechanism by which the lower abrasion was created, and after expert testimony, the defendant was acquitted. Experts argued that both marks were created by hanging when asphyxiation caused Hiramatsu to convulse during the hanging, but experts could not agree on the effect Hiramatsu's body weight impacted her neck or the position of her body while she was allegedly convulsing.

1998 Mallach and Pollak

Like Puschel et al. (1984), Ueno et al. (1989), Yamamoto et al. (1998), Leth and Vesterby (1996), and Mallach and Pollak (1998) studied homicides staged and hanging suicides. Even though they believed staged suicides were rare, these authors suppose that many occurrences were reported in the German literature. The case Mallach and Pollak reviewed was that of a 23-year-old man who killed his 58-year-old father by strangling him with an electric cable until the son thought his father was dead. Then the son created a hanging noose, tied it to the staircase handrail, and hanged his father from there. Upon autopsy, the medical examiner's findings disputed the cause of death by hanging idea because the congestion in the victim's face along with head injuries were inconsistent with death by hanging. The victim had both a horizontal ligature mark and a noose mark and blood was found at the scene as well in a location inconsistent with a hanging death. Mallach and Pollak stressed the importance of intricate medical examination when a body is recovered by what appears to be death by hanging.

1999 Adair and Dobersen

Additionally, Adair and Dobersen (1999) argued that investigators rarely encounter a homicide staged as suicide but that most homicides if staged as suicide involve a firearm (p. 1307). Interestingly, the second part of their opinion is supported by Ferguson's (2011) findings that firearms are the most utilized weapons in staged suicide. Like Puschel et al. (1984), Ueno et al. (1989), Yamamoto et al. (1998), Leth and Vesterby (1996), and Mallach and Pollak (1998), Adair and Dobersen also studied death by hanging. However, their study was unique and is interesting to include herein because the victim in their case review staged his own suicide to look like death by homicidal hanging. In relation to crime scene staging by offenders trying to self-preserve, Adair and Dobersen's contribution is important to note because just as a crime scene might contain evidence of murder staged as suicide, for a victim's personal reasons, upon discrete examination, these scenes can also be the result of the victim him or herself staging his or her own suicide as a homicide for insurance money purposes, to spare familial grief, or even to gain infamy. Like many of the contributors earlier, Adair and Dobersen also recommended very careful crime scene investigation to rule out both murder by staged suicide and the rare occurrence of the suicide being staged as a homicide by the victim.

1999–2011 Turvey

Turvey's (1999, 2002, 2008, 2011) book, *Criminal Profiling: An Introduction to Behavioral Evidence Analysis*, included information about crime scene staging. One of the interesting points Turvey (2002) made pertained to offender actions during and after committing a crime. Turvey (1999, 2002) argued that the quality of the evidence left behind is based on the *during and after* and that some offenders take *precautionary* measures to confuse or hamper investigators' work in the crime scene. Turvey (1999) defined staging as a specific group of precautionary actions made by the offender to detract suspect concentration from him or her. Further, Turvey (1999) argued that staging involves the creation or removal of evidence from a crime scene in order to make it appear as though there was a different motive for the crime than actually what the offender's motive was.

In the fourth edition of *Criminal Profiling: An Introduction to Behavioral Evidence Analysis*, Turvey (2011) expanded his ideas about crime scene staging to include a lengthy discussion about how investigators cannot use the usual generic crime scene indicators, such as ransacking, forced entry, missing personal property, or even a life insurance policy, which might raise suspicion that a death scene could be a murder staged as a legitimate death, but that by focusing on offender fumbles made during the crime scene staging process when using a scientific reconstructive method can allude to the truth of the matter as substantiated by the scientific evidence. Turvey also advocated for a full examination of every crime scene via scientific inquiry because staging could be a possibility in every death scene that investigators encounter. Turvey cautioned those who jump to conclusions too quickly and that doing so is a narrow, slippery slope that can cause an enormous amount of trouble on the back end.

2000 Turvey

Turvey (2000) conducted a descriptive study on crime scene staging by selecting 25 staged homicide cases from a national database. In order to study the ways in which the scenes in this sample were studied, Turvey defined crime scene staging as "the alteration of simulation of physical evidence at a location where a crime has occurred, or where a crime is alleged to have occurred, in order to mislead authorities and/or redirect their investigation by attempting to simulate an offense, or event, that did not actually take place" (Turvey, 2002, p. 265). Turvey's sample contained 25 cases, with 33 offenders, 25 of whom were male with eight of whom were female along with 31 victims, 17 of whom were female and 14 of whom were male. Turvey found that a prior relationship existed before the death of the victims in all 33 cases. Eke (2007), Ferguson (2011), and Pettler's (2011) combined victim–offender relationship findings support Turvey's findings from the victim–offender relationship perspective in that males are most often the offenders and that females are most often the victims in staged cases.

In further analysis of this sample, Turvey (2000) found that 21 murders occurred either inside or outside of the victim's home (p. 265), again consistent with Ferguson (2011) and Pettler's (2011) findings. However, six cases had multiple victims and four cases had multiple offenders; 13 were staged as burglaries and four as suicides. Yet again consistent with the findings of other experts, of the cases that occurred inside a residence, 17 cases occurred in a bedroom, two occurred in a living room, one occurred outside of a residence, and one occurred in a swimming pool (Ferguson, 2011; Pettler 2011). Interestingly, this sample revealed four cases where the location of the staged scene was a vehicle on the side of a road. Again consistent with Ferguson (2011) and Pettler's (2011) findings, Turvey found that firearms were the most commonly utilized weapons in that 12 offenders used handguns; four offenders used rifles, while three offenders used knives (p. 265). Further, still in addition to Ferguson (2011) and Pettler's (2011) findings, Turvey found that 18 offenders discovered the victims, 6 offenders arranged or positioned the weapon, and 2 offenders transported the victims' bodies to other locations. However, one of the most interesting findings in this sample was that five of the offenders were law enforcement professionals, which demonstrated the need for more research to be conducted in this area.

2001 Meloy

Meloy (2001) argued that there is no empirical research on crime scene staging and that only single case study reviews imply that it exists. Toward contributing to the literature, Meloy published a case study of a 63-year-old husband who murdered his wife and staged the crime scene and dump site before turning himself into police 2 days later. The behavioral evidence suggested that the murder was the result of a narcissistic rage, which generated enough momentum for the husband to bludgeon his wife to death with an iron, paint can, and a rock. The husband drove the body of his deceased wife to a dump site 87.3 miles away from their residence where he positioned her body in a sexually revealing pose exposing her breasts and under garments (Meloy, 2001, p. 395). Meloy argued that the husband's attempt to stage the crime scene and pose the body in a sexual position was a deliberate attempt to misdirect the investigation (Douglas, Burgess, Burgess, & Ressler, 2006; Geberth, 1996a, 1996b; Walton, 2006). Meloy's (2001) findings are supported by Turvey's (2011) argument that disposal location is purposefully chosen by the offender specifically to misdirect the investigation and Pettler's (2011) findings that some crime scene stagers will transport the victim to a disposal site that meets the offenders needs in some way with the purpose of sending the investigation off track.

2002 Adair

Adair (2002) published a case review about an alcoholic woman who staged a rape in her home in order to elicit sympathy from her employer and others. The woman had several unauthorized absences from work and her employer told her if she missed work one more time that she would be fired. The woman missed several days prior to the day when she called the Sheriff's Office to report that an intruder had sexually assaulted her with a steak knife in her home but that there was no penile penetration or ejaculation during the attack. Investigators processed the crime scene and found bloodstains on the bed and floor adjacent to the bed along with bloodstains on a few items in the crime scene. Upon examination, several crime scene indicators began to alert investigators that the scene did not add up. The garbage cans in the house were either full or half full and some contained bloodied paper towels. The house mop was bloodied and bathtub drain contained coagulated blood and hair. The victim reported to investigators that she stayed in bed for 2 days after the attack and could not bring herself to clean up all the blood. Upon physical examination at the hospital, the victim's injuries were found to be consistent with blunt force trauma instead of sharp force trauma. In addition, investigators at the hospital overheard the woman telling hospital personnel that the attack happened while she was out walking her dog; however, no evidence that a dog lived with the woman in her home was found by investigators. These findings support Pettler's (2011) findings that crime scene stagers will not only create evidence but will lie to family, friends, investigators, and others toward bolstering their staged actions in the crime scene. Adair also advocated for a thorough investigation of every crime scene because crime scene staging is a real possibility in all cases.

2004 Hazelwood and Napier

Hazelwood and Napier (2004) conducted a survey study entitled *Crime Scene Staging and Its Detection*. Hazelwood and Napier argued that crime scene staging is a recognized phenomenon and that the frequency of crime scene staging is more common than is reported. The purpose of Hazelwood and Napier's study was to define staging, identify the offender motives for staging crime scenes, and identify precipitating factors, which led to the staging behaviors. For the purpose of their study, Hazelwood and Napier defined crime scene staging as "the purposeful alteration of a crime or crime scene in an attempt to mislead investigators and frustrate the criminal justice process" (p. 745). Hazelwood and Napier also argued that crime scene staging was increasing due to crime scene related television programs that saturated the television industry in the United States.

This study conducted by Hazelwood and Napier included 20 law enforcement professionals who had experience with staged crime scenes. Participants of the study reported via telephone interviews that, in their combined experience, greed was the most commonly revealed motive for offenders to stage crime scenes (p. 747). Further, Hazelwood and Napier differentiated between homicidal motive and crime scene staging purpose as the author of this book does as well in a later part of this book. Participants of Hazelwood and Napier's study reported that self-preservation appeared to be the purpose offenders staged crime scenes as well (p. 747). Additionally, Hazelwood and Napier separated results of offenders staging murders from family members altering death scenes toward protecting the dignity of loved ones following a suicide or potentially embarrassing accident (p. 747). Further, Hazelwood and Napier reported that there is no end to how a crime scene might be staged and found in this sample that the most commonly staged crime scenes were (1) homicides staged as suicides, (2) homicides staged as sexual-related homicides, and (3) homicides staged as traffic accidents, which is very similar to what Geberth's (1996, 2006) reported experience was. Additionally, Hazelwood and Napier (2004) offered a list of five suggestions for law enforcement professionals who investigate violent deaths (p. 756):

1. Conduct a comprehensive and thorough review of the documented scene, giving little thought to the time involved.
2. Study and take account of the victim (i.e., victimology).
3. Identify and document all indicators of staging.
4. Identify and document possible motives for the original act and for the staging of the crime.
5. Determine who would have benefitted from the original act and the staging of the scene; keeping in mind that the responsible person may be the victim, even in death-related scenes.

Hazelwood and Napier also mentioned the concept of likelihood of verbal staging or lying whereas offenders will kill and dispose of a victim's body and then call law enforcement to report the victim missing; however, these authors also noted that verbal staging is not limited to the example earlier and can extend into other areas of the crime as well. Sometimes, Hazelwood and Napier's study provided foundational information for future research on crime scene staging. Qualitatively speaking, the sample of investigators while small represented a combined 560 years of crime scene related experience. The validity of their answers was assumed to be accurate at the time of data collection. Thus, the efficacy of the study might be increased when applied to the broader population and when attached to an empirical study of similar design.

2004 Keppel and Weis

Keppel and Weis (2004) conducted a study on a sample drawn from the Washington State Attorney General Homicide Investigation Tracking System during the years spanning 1981–2000, which rendered a sample containing 5224 victims of homicide. Keppel and Weis were interested in studying the frequency of staged crime scene occurrence coupled with studying body positioning in staged scenes. Keppel and Weis' findings indicated that discovering a body posed in an unusual position by the offender is rare. However, Keppel and Weis did not support this idea by way of statistical analysis making it impossible to know for sure, but plausible just the same using descriptive analysis in this case. Keppel and Weis focused their study on examining each case for similar characteristics shared by victims who were posed and whose crime scenes staged. Keppel and Weis determined that 0.1% or approximately 522 victims were posed and/or staged in the 5224 cases they reviewed. Keppel and Weis' study supports the victimology component in death investigation. However, this study was very limited in scope because it focused on studying posed victims rather than focusing on the other potentially staged evidence itself.

2006 Douglas and Douglas

Douglas et al. (2006) published the second edition of their *Crime Classification Manual: A Standard System for Investigating and Classifying Crimes* that included a chapter on crime scene staging by Douglas and Douglas (2006). Douglas and Douglas suggested that offenders do not usually happen upon a victim or randomly decide to stage the scene; rather, crime scene stagers usually have a relationship or an association to the victim (Eke, 2007; Ferguson, 2011; Pettler, 2011). Further, Douglas and Douglas argued that because crime scene staging behaviors are most often exhibited by offenders who have a relationship with the victim or whom are associated with the victim, crime scene stagers attempt to make the crime appear to have been committed by someone other than the most logical suspect. For this reason and in addition to others, law enforcement professionals need reliable information about crime scene staging in order to conduct well-organized homicide investigations. Douglas and Douglas's suggestions support the necessity of conducting victimology in death investigation as will be discussed later in this book.

Douglas and Douglas (2006) suggested that paying close attention to minute details is the first step in the process of the assessment of a homicide crime scene and discussed how crime scene behavior mirrors the personality of the offender. Second, these authors suggested that personation, which is the insertion of personal agendas or fantasies into the crime scene (i.e., posing the body, mutilation), is an unusual behavior exhibited by an offender and in turn is unnecessary to commit a crime but plays a significant role for the offender toward satisfying his needs. They stressed that it is important to recognize that scenes staged by family members to protect the dignity of the deceased victim are not to be categorized as staged for criminal purposes. It is important to note that Douglas and Ressler are retired from the Federal

Bureau of Investigation's National Center for the Analysis of Violent Crime where they studied homicide cases worldwide. It is also important to note that the work of Burgess et al. and Douglas et al. has had an enormous effect on the development of theoretical models of criminal profiling, but because the information contained in both their publications was not supported by empirical research or referenced with attached data, their crime classification system continues to be widely controversial.

2007 Eke

Until Angela Eke (2007) published the first truly empirical study on crime scene staging entitled "Staging in Cases of Homicide: Offender, Victim, and Offence Characteristics," the preceding articles and mention of staging were the only literary publications related to crime scene staging known to date. While this literature review is by far not exhaustive herein, the author would argue it is extensive and though every quote and/or detail mentioned by every contributor is not included, the literature review contained in this book could be the most comprehensive literature review on crime scene staging to date.

Eke (2007) conducted two studies using a mixed methods research design. The first study was a descriptive study where Eke rank-ordered identified crime scene staging behaviors coupled with offender characteristics in staged homicide cases. Eke's second study was a comparison of only intimate partner homicides with and without staging. Eke found that intimate partner homicides are staged more often than homicides involving individuals who are unknown to each other. Eke noted that it appeared that staging may be a function of the level of association between the victim and the offender (2007, p. 92). Eke's findings appear to be valid based on what is known about crime scene stagers' behaviors to date, and was also the springboard for Pettler's (2011) study on crime scene staging. Eke and Pettler's findings run concurrent along with Ferguson's (2011) findings in support of each other from the standpoint that staged cases most often involved victims and offenders who have a prior association or relationship. Further, Eke's study provided an empirical basis for further scientific inquiry about crime scene staging, victim–offender relationship in crime scene staging, and intimate partner violence as it relates to crime scene staging.

Eke (2007) argued that a continuum or a model of crime scene staging behaviors would work toward helping to solve the problem law enforcement professionals experience in their plight to conduct thorough and effective homicide investigations where staged crime scenes are included. However, no model or empirical system existed to assist law enforcement professionals in detecting staged crime scenes early in the homicide investigation process. It is also important to note that from the research methodology perspective, in order for descriptive studies to be considered sophisticated in general, studies must be conducted at the *ratio* level of measurement. However, in this case, Eke's purpose for conducting a basic descriptive study first was to generate data for the secondary highly sophisticated and scientific qualitative portion of the study. From that standpoint, Eke's development of and choice of methodology was sound and proved to be viable. As mentioned earlier, it is important to note the fact that only one empirical study on crime scene staging existed until the publication of Eke's 2007 study and does not discount the importance, validity, or efficacy of the scholar–practitioners, law enforcement professionals, and expert contributors who have published homicide investigation and crime scene staging literature or who conduct various types of research on crime scene staging. Expert experience grows new opportunities to learn from experienced scholars, practitioners, and law enforcement professionals who have forged the new ground for modern homicide investigation today. Eke's findings support Ferguson (2011) and Pettler's (2011) findings and the suggestions made by Turvey (2000, 2002) and Walton (2006) in that some of the most commonly observable patterns of crime scene staging behaviors are (1) lying or misguiding an investigation, (2) providing false assistance, (3) manipulating the physical evidence, or (4) disposing of the body, challenging investigators, and making an already complicated situation even more complex (Eke, 2007, p. 4).

2007, 2011 Chisum and Turvey

Chisum and Turvey (2007, 2011) published the first and second editions of their book entitled *Crime Reconstruction*, which included a chapter entitled "Staged Crime Scenes" (pp. 211–243). In this chapter of their book, Chisum and Turvey begin by citing Svensson and Wendel's (1974) work that mentions not only how a clever murderer will stage a crime scene but the fact that in order to catch these offenders, the investigation must be scientific, systematic, and accurate toward revealing the killer's real intent. Similar to Turvey's (1999, 2002, 2008, 2011) mention or discussion full or in part about how crime scenes might appear to have been staged and/or in light of the fact that specific indicators, such as ransacking and/or forced entry might raise suspicion, but do not independently indicate that the crime scene is staged, Chisum and Turvey (2007, 2011) discuss these same elements again as they relate to scientific, systematic, and accurate crime reconstruction. Chisum and Turvey discuss points of entry and exit, weaponry including firearms, gunpowder deposits, clothing, bloodstains, hair, and movement of the body in relation to staged scenes along with a discussion of Turvey's (2000) 25 case studies as discussed earlier. Part of their work is carried over into the empirical research conducted by Ferguson (2011) and in Pettler (2011).

2009 Cobin

An article authored by Cobin (2009) published by the Center for Homicide Research discussed crime scene staging in relation to a case study about a lesbian couple who were gunned down by a cave dweller in 988 while camping on the Appalachian Trail. One victim died at the scene, but one victim survived. When questioned, the cave-dwelling man said that the shootings were an accident. However, the survivor told a different story and that the cave dweller shot she and her intimate partner eight times because he came upon them engaged in intimate activity. Cobin (2009) defined crime scene staging as "the practice of altering a crime scene to mislead investigators or conceal the true nature of the crime" and noted, "it remains one of the least studied aspects of crime scene analysis" (p. 1). Cobin argues that what are claimed to be hunting accidents require the same level of intricate investigation as do unexpected deaths caused by other mechanisms. Cobin argued that the problem lies with the public in that they regard most hunting-related shooting deaths as accidental regardless of whether the deceased was shot mistakenly for game or while firing on a rapidly moving target. Cobin further argued that hunting-related staged crime scenes are extremely difficult to detect because these types of stagers could plan well in advance to kill the victim, but by studying the victim–offender relationship, sometimes they can be detected. Further, Cobin argued that the easiest staged hunting-related murders to detect are those that occur in open fields claiming it was accidental. Furthermore, Cobin recommended a set of questions to investigators charged with the duty of investigating hunting-related deaths as follows (pp. 2, 3):

1. Were the injuries consistent with the hunting mishap?
2. Were the circumstances surrounding the shooting consistent with the shooting mishap?
3. Was the shooter's reported behavior before and after the shooting consistent with an actual mishap?
4. Was the forensic evidence consistent with the shooter's story?
5. Were there motives for a homicide?

As many others before him, Cobin advocated for a thorough investigation of all hunting-related deaths in order to determine if the death was a staged murder or a legitimate accident.

2010 Geberth

Geberth (2010) conducted a survey study of 43 highly trained homicide investigators about the frequency of crime scene staging and characteristics of offenders who sexually pose the body of the victim in homicide cases.

The 43 investigators responded to the survey, who collectively had been involved in a total of 44,541 homicide cases averaging 1,035 homicide cases per investigator, respectively. Survey results revealed that offenders posed the victim's body in a sexual position in less than one percent (1%) or approximately 445 of those cases. Additional results indicated that manual and ligature strangulation was the most common modality of death in 71% or approximately 316 of the cases (p. 1). Additionally, the most prevalent motive for posing the body was fantasy (71%), then anger/retaliation (22%), and sexual posing to misdirect the investigation (7%) of the cases in this sample (Geberth, 2010, pp. 8–10).

2011 Ferguson

Ferguson (2011) conducted the first international empirical study on crime scene staging with the goal of identifying the red flags that indicate a crime scene is staged, which brought forth phenomenal results. Ferguson analyzed the behaviors and behavioral patterns of crime scene stagers using a purposive sample of 141 known staged homicide cases from Australia, the United States, Canada, and the United Kingdom. Ferguson categorized the cases by type, such as suicides, burglaries, sexual homicides, accidents, car accidents, and self-defense homicides. Ferguson aimed to identify characteristics of the offenders, victims, the crime itself, and the motives behind the offenders' behaviors and built a typology toward further categorizing her results. Ferguson utilized sophisticated descriptive analysis coupled with multidimensional scaling to identify behavioral patterns in the data. Ferguson found that the most common characteristics in this sample were as follows:

1. Offenders had multiple victims.
2. The cause of death was strangulation or blunt force trauma.
3. The victims had a previous relationship with the offenders.
4. Offenders most often discovered the victim at the murder scene location, which was most often the victim's home.
5. Personal property might have been disrupted at the crime scene, but was not removed from the crime scene.
6. The body was positioned or the weapon was positioned in the crime scene.
7. Offenders opted to clean up and/or destroy physical evidence.
8. Offenders did not have an alibi previously established before the murder.

One of the most interesting findings Ferguson discovered was that each type of scene presented differently from the others depending on what kind of scene the offender attempted to stage depending on if the offender was trying to stage a legitimate death or an illegitimate death. Second, while Ferguson argued that a typology of some kind could be useful going forward, Ferguson found that her results did not support the use of the crime scene staging typology she designed for this study and instead proposed a different typology that could be tried in future research. Ferguson argued, "However, before this new typology is addressed, it is important to also examine why the original typology was not supported by the quantitative data, and what this means in light of the previous research" (p. 184).

Additionally, as mentioned earlier, Ferguson's results confirmed the existence of the victim–offender relationship as significant in relation to crime scene staging and found that the most common offenders were the ex-spouses of the victims, followed by friends, acquaintances, domestic relationships, and nondomestic relationship partners (p. 162). Ferguson also found that firearms are the most commonly used weapons in murders where crime scene staging is involved followed by blunt force trauma injuries sustained by victims and that most murders occurred after or during an argument/conflict between the victim and the offender. Ferguson's findings were a tremendous contribution to the empirical literature and were relevant to various types of practitioners, such as forensic pathologists and medical examiners, coroners, law enforcement professionals, and attorneys because her findings empirically confirm that staging behaviors do exist among crime scene staging offenders. However, another interesting point about Ferguson's findings was that they contradicted some of the previous literature published on crime scene staging related to offender characteristics. One of the most impressive things in addition to Ferguson's findings was the literature review included in this study. Ferguson's literature review was an outstanding compilation of gathered works by some of the most influential theorists, scholars, and practitioners in the world. Ferguson's study was a tremendous contribution to the empirical literature on crime scene staging from both the domestic and international standpoints. Ferguson's additional findings and suggestions are embedded throughout the remainder of this book. Ferguson's 2011 study is by far the most impressive and the most comprehensive empirical study on crime scene staging known to date.

2011 Pettler

Pettler (2011) conducted a qualitative study of 18 known staged homicide cases. The author used *content analysis* for data analysis because there was currently no proven method commonly used to study crime scene staging at this time (and there still is not). Pettler's study aimed to answer the question: What are the most common behaviors utilized by crime scene stagers? The sample contained 27 offenders and 19 victims from North Carolina. Like Ferguson (2011), Pettler also developed taxonomies or themes or typologies of behavioral patterns: *the cleaner, the concealer, the creator, the fabricator, the inflictor,* and *the planner.* Pettler analyzed the entire case files using a qualitative research method called content analysis to study crime scene behavior in this sample. Pettler noted that the collection of criminal records and historical backgrounds of the offenders and victims, so victimologies and suspectologies could be completed for each, would have made the data analysis and results more meaningful in this study.

Although descriptive research is useful for identifying crime scene staging behaviors, qualitative research has also proven to be useful for generating a substantial amount of empirical data that describe crime scene staging behaviors, thus contributing to the dearth in the overall knowledge of crime scene staging behavior in general. Pettler empirically identified 62 new crime scene behaviors of crime scene stagers that were condensed into similar behavioral sets and then categorized into the typologies or theoretical themes that were appropriate:

1. Eighteen homicide case files and 24 offenders containing information consistent with concealing behaviors were categorized under the Concealer.
2. Eighteen homicide case files and 24 offenders containing information consistent with creating false evidence were categorized under the Creator.
3. Eighteen offenders and 25 offenders containing information consistent with fabricating false statements were categorized under the Fabricator.
4. Ten homicide case files and 11 offenders containing information consistent with cleaning behaviors were categorized under the Cleaner.
5. Ten homicide case files and 18 offenders containing information consistent with planning behaviors were categorized under the Planner.
6. No homicide case files or offenders were categorized under the Inflictor.

The discovery of these 62 behaviors within this sample of 18 homicide case files implies that what Pettler discovered is marginal in comparison to what might be discovered in a study with a sample size of 100 of more cases (Ferguson, 2011). While the transferability of any qualitative study is relative to the reader's ability to apply it to a broader population, the results of Pettler's study suggest that crime scene stagers clearly exhibit crime scene behaviors consistent with intending to avoid apprehension (Geberth, 1996a; Hazelwood & Napier, 2004).

Again, like Ferguson's (2011) findings regarding typologies or categorizing crime scene staging behaviors by behavioral pattern, Pettler's results suggested several important implications about crime scene staging, one of which was that typologies are *not helpful* for field use due to the sheer overlap seen in staged crime scenes overall.

Rather, Pettler argued that this study yielded results where at least 19 of 27 offenders could be categorized under at least three theoretical themes, while three offenders could be categorized under as many as four theoretical themes. The value of identifying crime scene behaviors of crime scene stagers cannot be understated and thematic analysis appears to be theoretically promising to the criminal justice field (p. 199).

Second, Pettler found that the victim–offender relationship was significant in the cases analyzed in this sample because 16 of the cases revealed that the victims had relationships of some kind with the offenders. Third, Pettler not only wrote the first criminological theory of crime scene staging derived from empirical findings, but the author is the first to suggest that not only is crime scene staging a function of the victim–offender relationship and emotionality of the offender but that crime scene staging also appeared to be a function of personality, emotion, and culture and recommended future research toward building a taxonomic hierarchal arrangement of crime scene staging behaviors recommending all crime scenes by systematically analyzed scientifically using proven methodology for early detection.

In addition, the results of Pettler's (2011) study suggested that an empirical method toward the early detection of staged crime scenes might be able to be developed with additional research because this study demonstrated that by triangulating as the author did in this study various pieces of the events and the evidence, crime scene staging behaviors could be validated and verified. In a broad sense, Pettler opined that law enforcement professionals might benefit from a new strategy for approaching homicide cases when the verbal statements and the physical evidence do not add up by combining traditional investigatory methods with a modified version of qualitative triangulation and other scientific applications, thereby creating an interdisciplinary, scientific, systematic hybrid approach to death investigation for potentially staged crime scenes (for another example, see Ferguson, 2015).

2012 Schlesinger, Gardenier, Jarvis, and Sheehan-Cook

Schlesinger, Gardenier, Jarvis, and Sheehan-Cook's (2012) empirical study of 946 homicide cases, of which 79 cases were found to include staged crime scenes. Schlesinger et al. aimed to study the prevalence, types, levels, and motives of intimate partner homicides, nonserial sexual homicides, serial sexual, and felony murders. Consistent with the literature, Schlesinger et al. argued that the ways in which crime scene stagers can manipulate crime scenes are virtually endless and limited only by the victim's body characteristics, such as size, shape, condition, and maneuverability, in relation to the offender's physical attributes coupled with the offender's levels of creativity and motivation (Ferguson, 2011; Pettler, 2011). In studying this sample, Schlesinger et al. found that arson was the most common staging behavior as observed in 25% of sample and was more commonly seen in nondomestic or intimate partner homicide cases than in domestic or intimate partner homicide cases. Second, Schlesinger et al. found that 22% of offenders lied, where in contrast to arson, lying or verbal staging was more often involved in domestic or intimate partner homicides rather than nondomestic or intimate partner homicides. Schlesinger et al. also found burglaries, home invasions, or robbery-related staging behaviors in 18% of the cases, accident-related staging behaviors in 14%, suicide-type staging behaviors in 8%, and homicide–suicide-related staging behaviors in 5% of this 79 case samples. The findings in this study were consistent with previous literature and anecdotal discussion published on victim–offender relationship in that 77% of the victims and/or offenders were intimate partners or family members and that the level of effort can range from very simplistic to elaborate (Eke, 2007; Ferguson, 2011; Pettler, 2011; Turvey, 2000).

2014 Chancellor and Graham

Chancellor and Graham (2014) proposed a set of motivational typologies for staged crime scenes. Chancellor and Graham (2014) defined *primary staging* or the intentional misdirecting of a criminal investigation by way of manipulating physical or verbal evidence and *secondary staging* or anything an offender does to manipulate the crime scene or victim devoid of the intention to misdirect an investigation as the two types of staging that exist. These authors proposed that there are two types of primary staging: *ad hoc staging* or when an individual tampers with a crime scene for the purpose of misdirecting an investigation as the result of postcrime impulsivity and *premeditated staging* or when the offender plans to stage the crime scene before the crime takes place. These authors illustrated their proposed typologies with examples from five case reviews and categorized scene behaviors by an individual other than an offender in attempt to preserve a victim's dignity as *tertiary scene alterations*.

According to Ferguson (2015), investigatory suggestions based solely on personal experience or the expertise of others "run the risk of being at best inaccurate, and at worst misleading and detrimental to serious criminal investigations" (p. 92). The absence of an empirical literature review on crime scene staging in this article only partially explains the scope of Chancellor and Graham's proposal notwithstanding the empirical studies that found that typology-related behavioral patterns are not mutually exclusive, thus possibly reducing their practical use for effective field application (Ferguson, 2011, 2015; Pettler, 2011).

2014 Ferguson

Ferguson published two significant additions to the dearth of crime scene staging literature in 2014. Included in Petherick's (2015) book entitled *Applied Crime Analysis: A Social Science Approach to Understanding Crime, Criminals, and Victims*, Ferguson (2015) published a chapter entitled "Detecting Staged Crime Scenes: An Empirically Derived 'How-To.'" Ferguson highlighted the significant early and contemporary crime scene staging literature from Hans Gross (1924) through Pettler (2011). Ferguson discussed death investigation as it relates to potentially staged death scenes and argued that systematic, scientific equivocal death investigation based on empirical findings within a collaborative effort is required rather than reliance upon expertise of oneself or others because both are at high risk of being inaccurate and/or misleading, which can cause serious damage to the successful prosecution of a staged murder case (Ferguson, 2015, p. 92). Ferguson went on to discuss the most prudent findings and implications of her 2011 doctoral dissertation as discussed earlier (see Ferguson, 2011). There is not much literature published on how to determine the presence of staging based on empirical data; however, many authors have made suggestions based on any combination of descriptive studies and personal experience for what to look for (Douglas & Douglas, 2006; Douglas & Munn, 1992; Geberth, 1996, 2010; Hazelwood & Napier, 2004). Toward the empirical detection of a staged crime scene, Ferguson discussed and agreed with previous authors that crime reconstruction was an extremely effective method for determining the presence of staging in that crime reconstruction is objective and scientific, therefore limiting subjectivity and chance (Chisum & Turvey, 2007, 2011; Pettler, 2011). In addition to the use of crime reconstruction and based on the empirical findings of her doctoral dissertation, Ferguson (2015) developed a preliminary checklist for determining the presence of staging in various types of cases that could be used alone or in tandem with the recommendations made by Chisum and Turvey (2007) in relation to how the following elements of a crime scene present to investigators (adapted from Petherick, 2015, pp. 94–95):

1. Points of entry and exit in the scene
2. Weapons at or removed from the scene
3. Firearms at the scene
4. Gunpowder deposits
5. Movement of the body
6. Hair of the victim
7. Clothing of the victim
8. Shoes of the victim
9. Bloodstains in the crime scene

Ferguson (2015) emphasized that her theoretical checklist should be used to help investigators determine the next logical step in the investigatory process along with identifying elements of a crime scene that warrant further inquiry. First, Ferguson recommended assessing the situation for confrontation, that is, evidence of verbal or physical confrontation between the victim and offender and if confrontation evidence is found that the physical evidence at the crime scene is consistent with the specific type of confrontation revealed. Second, Ferguson points out the importance of who discovers the victim's body in relation to if the discovering individual was going about legitimate business at the time of the discovery in comparison to those who might have been expected to discover the victim's body, but whom did not. Upon these two preliminary inquiries, Ferguson suggested asking a series of questions related to the following four types of potentially staged crime scenes (adapted from Petherick, 2015, pp. 97–101):

1. *Staged burglary/homicides*—To point of entry/exit, valuables, cleanup, injuries, and alibis
2. *Staged suicides*—To weapons, injuries, cleanup, body movement and positioning, and valuables
3. *Staged accidents*—To weapons, body movement and positioning, and cleanup
4. *Staged car accidents*—To the vehicle, body movement and positioning, injuries, fire, and cleanup

As will be discussed later in this book, Ferguson's (2015) theoretical checklist can be utilized in compilation with additional methods, including Chisum and Turvey's (2007) checklist for identifying the earmarks of staged crime scenes. For more information, see Ferguson (2015).

In her second article of 2014 entitled "Staged Homicides: An Examination of Common Features of Faked Burglaries, Suicides, Accidents and Car Accidents," Ferguson (2014) examined 115 cases that were originally part of her 2011 doctoral dissertation in much greater detail. The cases were known staged cases that occurred between 1973 and 2007 in the United States and contained 188 offenders and 138 victims. Ferguson aimed to identify commonalities, such as victim and offender characteristics, and types of staged crime scenes, such as staged suicides, accidents, or other types of legitimate or illegitimate deaths. Ferguson studied this sample in relation to the most common façade that the offender is most likely to create in a staged homicide crime scene, what evidence is most often manipulated to send the investigation offtrack toward addressing both Schlesinger et al.'s (2012) findings and Hazelwood and Napier's (2004) and Geberth's (2006) predictions that crime scene staging was on the rise.

Ferguson (2014) found that only one offender was involved in staging the scenes in all 115 cases (61.7%), but in 37.4%, the number of offenders ranged from two to five with two offenders (20%) being most common and 79.1% being males. Based on Turvey's (2000) findings that 5 of 25 offenders in his sample had law enforcement experience, Ferguson found that seven cases involved offenders with previous law enforcement, though yielding to the fact that law enforcement experience was unknown in 43% of the cases. Additional significant findings in Ferguson's study related to the victim in that in 84.3% of the cases, there was only one victim involved and victims were most often female (51.3%), ranging in age between 19 and 29 years old (16.5%) or 30 and 44 years old (14.8%). As Ferguson found in her 2011 doctoral dissertation, staged cases increased by 104% between 1973 and 2007 based on this sample. Again, the most common type of staging that Ferguson found when analyzing this sample was burglaries (40.9%), followed by suicides (13.9%), and then staged accidental deaths and car accidents, respectively, each at 13.9%. Ferguson found that staged self-defense or self-wounding cases presented much more infrequently supporting Pettler's (2011) similar findings. Interestingly, Ferguson (2014) found that missing persons cases were never staged in this same way. This is in contrast to Pettler's (2011) findings and in conjunction with Hazelwood and Napier's (2004) and Schlesinger et al.'s (2012) argument that verbal staging is implemented by stagers to stage missing persons cases and in turn their accompanying scenes. Further, Ferguson (2014) found that firearms (37.4%) were the most common weapon used in staged homicide cases followed by multiple weapons (20%), blunt force trauma (13%), strangulation (14%), and then sharp force injury (7%) to the victim. Interestingly, 26.1% of these cases involved a confrontation between the victim and offender prior to the murder but was undetermined in 37% of the cases. Weapons were most often brought to the scene by the offender and rarely by the victim in this sample and again in support of several other authors to date, Ferguson found that in 98.3% of these cases, the victim and offender had a prior relationship in that 72.2% were intimate partners and/or cohabiting family members of the victims with 26.1% being friends or work-related associates of the victims supporting Schlesinger et al.'s (2012) assertion that offenders stage because they believe they are a likely suspect based on their involvement with the victim. In only two cases were the victims and offenders strangers. Ferguson noted that nowhere in the literature to date has it been addressed that nondomestic staged crime scenes are most often staged in relation to profit, but these findings along with Pettler's (2011) findings support that nondomestic staged homicide cases are most often connected to profit (Turvey, 2000).

Ferguson and Petherick (2014) published *Getting Away With Murder: An Examination of Detected Homicides Staged as Suicides* that reported their results of having studied 16 U.S.-based homicides staged as suicide cases.

The current sample was selected from the larger sample of the 115 cases examined in Ferguson's 2014 study, *Staged Homicides: An Examination of Common Features of Faked Burglaries, Suicides, Accidents and Car Accidents.* Ferguson and Petherick aimed to identify and examine behaviors and their details exhibited by offenders who stage suicides. These authors intended to address three research questions (adapted from Ferguson & Petherick, 2014, p. 6):

1. Of the crime scenes where staging was detected, what evidence was manipulated and were these behaviors premeditated?
2. What was the nature of the victim–offender relationship prior to the murder?
3. Are staged suicides on the rise?

Using descriptive analysis, Ferguson and Petherick found that males (93.8%) were the most common offenders and firearms (56.3%) were the most common weapons used in this sample. Interesting however and in contrast to other recent findings, males were predominantly the victims in nine cases of this sample and in only 50% of the cases did the offender discover the victim. Fake suicide notes were not present in most of the cases (75%), but offenders did position the bodies of most victims in this sample (68.8%). The victim and offender were cohabiting spouses 43.8% of the time and cohabiting partners 6.3% of the time, but were nondomestic family members or friends in 50% of the cases in this sample. These findings, while still in support of the victim–offender relationship connection to crime scene staging, are in contrast to other studies that found that the victim–offender relationship is more often an intimate relationship than an associate or friend relationship (Ferguson, 2011; Schlesinger et al., 2012; Turvey, 2000). These authors found that crime scene staging increased over time across this sample, which included 1 case from the 1970s, 1 case from the 1980s, 4 cases from the 1990s, and 10 cases between 2000 and 2007. Pursuant to conflict or confrontation between the victim and offender prior to the murder, the authors found that 7 of 16 homicides (43.8%) occurred during the course of a conflict or argument, 5 cases (31.3%) were unclear as to what precipitated the murder, and in 4 cases, no conflict preceded the murder (25%). Further, in 14 cases (87.5%), the victim's personal valuables were disrupted by the offender, but not removed from the scene, and 8 offenders (50%) cleaned up the crime scene, where 7 offenders (43.8%) did not clean up the crime scene, and cleanup was unknown in 1 case of this sample. In other findings, no points of entry or exit were found to be staged, no phone service tampered with, and in all the crime scenes examined, all outdoor lighting was intact. Further, no scene was found ransacked, bloodstains were not tampered with, nor did any offender self-injure in this sample. While this sample contained only 16 cases, it is yet again a tremendous contribution to the literature on crime scene staging.

2015 Pettler

In an in press descriptive study conducted by the author, several of Eke's (2007), Ferguson's (2011, 2014), Ferguson and Petherick's (2014), Hazelwood and Napier's (2004), Pettler's (2011), Schlesinger et al.'s (2012), and Turvey's (2000) findings along with observations and interpretations suggested by numerous authors as cited throughout the historical references of crime scene staging literature (Douglas & Douglas, 2006; Douglas & Munn, 1992; Geberth, 1996, 2000) were supported. A summary of the study is as follows:

Statement of the problem: This study was undertaken as an outcrop of the author's 2011 doctoral dissertation. In light of findings in recent studies and the many implications brought forth by the results of the author's 2011 study, further inquiry is warranted. Implications regarding the victim–offender relationship, a preceding conflict, the discovery of the victim's body, verbal staging, and murder scene location were deemed to be some of the most important topics for continued research. For the purpose of this study, crime scene staging is operationalized as the behavior, physical and verbal, exhibited by an offender in the physical crime scene or in the discourse designed to specifically misdirect a homicide investigation by concealing the identity of the offender pursuant to self-preservation. Therefore, the problems this study aims to address are the frequency of the aforementioned variables and how the results of this study relate to findings in recent studies of similar research design.

Research questions: Ferguson (2015) suggested an empirically derived *how-to* checklist for identifying red flags in staged burglaries–homicides, staged suicides, staged accidents, and staged car accidents. Ferguson also found that relevant information regarding preceding victim–offender confrontation (i.e., conflict) and the discovery of the victim's body underpinned these checklists. Ferguson recommended determining if there was any evidence that the victim and offender were engaged in either a verbal or physical confrontation prior to the murder of the victim in relation to how the crime scene presents. Second, Ferguson recommended determining who discovered the victim's body and was the individual who discovered the victim's body justified by the nature of what business was being carried out at the time of the discovery and was there anyone who should have discovered the victim's body, but did not, and if so, why did this individual not discover the victim's body.

Hazelwood and Napier (2004) suggested that offenders verbally stage in many different ways toward misdirecting the investigatory process. Douglas and Munn (1992) suggested that the drives that influence everyday conduct are the same drives that influence the offender during the acts of murder and rape, which implies that those who lie during the course of a murder investigation are most likely liars outside the scope of the murder investigation in their daily lives as well (p. 249). Schlesinger et al. (2012) found that verbal staging was prevalent in 17 of the 79 staged homicides they studied and that verbal staging was the most common form of staging in domestic cases.

Ferguson (2011) found that firearms were the most commonly used weapons in staged cases, that most staging offenders were male, and that most victims were female. Eke (2011), Ferguson (2011), and Schlesinger et al. (2012) found that victim–offender relationship played a role in crime scene staging in that most victims and offenders has some association prior to the murder of the victim. Therefore, the discussion of these findings will address the following research questions:

1. What is the frequency of victim–offender conflict preceding the murder of the victim?
2. What is the frequency of the offender having been the last person to see the victim alive?
3. What is the frequency of the offender having been the first person to discover the victim's body or report the victim missing?
4. What is the frequency of offender-to-law enforcement verbal staging?
5. What is the frequency of offender-to-friends/family verbal staging?
6. What is the frequency of victims killed with firearms compared to other weapons?
7. What is the frequency of the murder scene being familiar to the victim, offender, or both?
8. Do the results of this study support findings in studies of similar research design?

Data collection: The 18 cases in this purposive sample, which contained 27 offenders and 19 victims was drawn from a pool of adjudicated cases from North Carolina having occurred between 1987 and 2009 as an outcrop of the author's 2011 doctoral dissertation. This study aimed to contribute to the knowledge of offender characteristics, victim characteristics, and specifically regarding preceding conflict between the victim and offender, the last known individual to see the victim alive, the discovery of the victim's body, evidence of injury, and specifically verbal staging as part of the overall staged scene.

Method: According to Leedy and Ormrod (2005), descriptive quantitative research "involves either identifying the characteristics of an observed phenomenon or exploring possible correlations among two or more phenomena" (p. 179). Descriptive studies are nonexperimental studies that do not alter or modify any aspect of the data nor do descriptive studies determine cause and effect relationships. Descriptive studies can be conducted using a survey, by observation, using correlative research, or by developmental design. The data gleaned from these designs can be quantitatively analyzed using statistical analysis. Descriptive research is most often seen in society in polls and online surveys and used by government agencies and others to collect vast amounts of information that can be quickly analyzed and reported.

The purpose of research is to respond to a problem or, rather, answer a research question (Leedy & Ormrod, 2005). The entire process is systematic beginning to end, although levels of sophistication vary between research designs and methodologies significantly. Descriptive research is a type of research categorized as quantitative research that can be measured using one of four scales of measurement: *nominal, ordinal, interval,* and *ratio* (Leedy & Ormrod, 2005, p. 25). The nominal level of measurement differentiates one thing from another, but the nominal level of measurement is unrefined and restrictive because it places the thing being measured into one, static category, such as *male criminal* or *female criminal*. Thus, a group of individuals can be categorized into male or female criminal types and measured or counted. The positive side of nominal data is that it helps to categorize large amounts of information into clearly defined groups while avoiding crossover or blurred lines between categories. Yet another negative aspect of the use of nominal level of measurement in a descriptive study is that few statistical analyses are applicable. For instance, *mode* is defined as the most frequent number to occur in a set of data. The mode can be useful when analyzing crime-related data because researchers are often interested counting how many crimes, individuals, and so forth, in a specific static category occurred most often toward calculating percentages for comparison and analysis.

Crime scene staging literature is sparse to say the least. Empirical literature on crime scene staging is even less resting on very few empirical studies. However, to date, several authors have utilized descriptive analytical methods for studying crime scene staging because the empirical data are barely scratching the surface as of yet. For example, Turvey (2000) collected 25 cases from Westlaw's database (p. 265). Although Turvey did not state a problem or a research question, applying the nominal level of measurement to his data, Turvey reported his findings from this purposive sample using descriptive statistics (i.e., frequencies). Turvey reported the frequencies or modes for each category and then interpreted results based on numerous other sources of information. Despite the choice of descriptive research design and level of measurement, Turvey's study significantly contributed to the empirical literature on crime scene staging published to date.

In another example, Geberth (2010) conducted a descriptive study to answer the research question: How many crime scene stagers posed victims in sexual positions? Using a survey study design, 46 homicide investigators contributed information about 44,451 homicides of which 428 involved sexual posed victims or less than 1% (Geberth, 2010, p. 8). Despite the fact that survey research is often viewed by the scholarly community as lower-level quantitative research because of its overuse in daily life, it is arguable that Geberth's contribution to the literature on crime scene staging was profound regardless due in part to the large sample size and second because the results directly map back to the statement of the problem, the research question, and the answer to the research question, which provided a baseline to move forward from here.

Ferguson (2011, 2014), Ferguson and Petherick (2014), and Schlesinger et al. (2012) also conducted frequency research using descriptive analysis. Due to the fact that there is still no proven sophisticated research design for which is commonly used to study crime scene staging with proven and replicated success, the author has well analyzed the data in this sample using descriptive analysis toward contributing to the descriptive literature pool about what is known about crime scene stagers.

The author manually analyzed the data in this sample toward establishing broad trends among the variables. The cases were categorized by component derived from the stated research questions and were as follows:

1. Victim–offender relationship
2. Victim–offender conflict
3. Victim last seen alive
4. Discovery of victim's body
5. Verbal staging (i.e., fish tales) to investigators
6. Verbal staging (i.e., prescriptive stories) to friends and family
7. Cause of death
8. Murder scene location

Results: This sample contained 27 offenders and 19 victims: 25 male offenders, 2 female offenders, 8 male victims, and 11 female victims. Male offenders ranged in age between 18 and 59 years old, one female offender was between the ages of 18 and 21 years old, and one female offender was between 42 and 45 years old, and victims ranged between the ages of 18 and 74 years old. Further, 22 offenders were single, 1 offender was divorced, and 4 offenders were married. Table 1.1 summarizes the results of this study in relation to the statement of the problem and in relation to the stated research questions.

Pursuant to victim–offender relationship, 66.7% or 18 offenders in this sample had a previous relationship with the victim in that 22.2% or 6 offenders were the intimate partners of their victims, 11.1% or 3 offenders were the spouses of their victims, 11.1% or 3 offenders were the children of their victims, 11.1% or 3 offenders were acquaintances of their victims, 7.5% or 2 offenders were neighbors of their victims, and 3.7% or 1 offender was the employee of the victim. In contrast, 33.3% or 9 offenders were strangers to their victims. In this sample, the author found that 66.6% or 18 offenders were in conflict with the victim prior to the victim's murder or had some type of confrontation preceding the murder of the victim compared to 9 or 33.4%

Table 1.1 Victim–Offender Relationship, Conflict, Verbal Staging, and Murder Characteristics

	n	%
Victim–offender relationship		
Intimate partner	6	22.2
Spouse	3	11.1
Child	3	11.1
Acquaintance	3	11.1
Employee	1	3.7
Neighbor	2	7.5
Stranger	9	33.3
	27	100
Victim–offender conflict		
Conflict preceding murder	18	66.6
No conflict preceding murder	9	33.4
	27	100
Victim last seen alive		
Victim last seen alive with offender	14	51.8
Victim not last seen alive with offender	13	48.2
	27	100
Discovery of victim's body		
Victim's body discovered by offender	3	11.1
Victim's body not discovered by offender	24	88.9
	27	100
Verbal staging (i.e., fish tales) to investigators		
Lied to investigators; story given was unbelievable	15	55.5
Lied to investigators; story given was believable	12	44.5
	27	100
Verbal staging (i.e., prescriptive stories) to friends and family		
Gave prescriptive stories to friends and family	14	51.8
Did not give prescriptive stories to friends and family	8	29.6
Did not talk to friends or family	5	18.6
	27	100
Victim's cause of death		
Blunt force trauma	4	21
Gunshot wound	14	73.7
Asphyxiation	1	5.3
Stabbing	0	0
	19	100

(Continued)

Table 1.1 (*Continued*)   Victim–Offender Relationship, Conflict, Verbal Staging, and Murder Characteristics

	n	%
Murder scene location		
Victim's environment	3	15.8
Offender's environment	3	15.8
Victim–offender common environment	10	52.6
Neither victim's or offender's environment	3	15.8
	19	100

of the offenders who were not in conflict with their victims prior to the murder of the victim. Obviously, the offender is always the last person to see the victim alive in all murder cases except for possibly those where an offender leaves the victim for dead, but the injured victim survives and is rescued or the like; however, in this sample, the offender was the last person reportedly to have been seen or to have seen the victim alive 51.8% (i.e., 14 offenders) of the time, but 13 offenders or 48.2% were not the last individuals to reportedly have been seen with the victims or to have seen the victims alive prior to their deaths. Pursuant to discovery of the victims' bodies, 3 offenders or 11.1% discovered the bodies of their victims in 2 cases compared to the 24 offenders who did not discover their victims' bodies in the remaining 17 cases in this sample. Further, although all 27 offenders lied or verbally staged in this sample, 55.5% or 15 of the offenders told far-fetched, "fish tales" or far-fetched, unrealistic, hard-to-believe lies about the victim and/or the victim's whereabouts to investigators, while 12 offenders or 44.5% lied to investigators, but did not tell far-fetched, unrealistic, hard-to-believe stories about the victim and/or the victim's whereabouts. Additionally, 14 offenders or 51.7% told "prescriptive stories" or stories grounded by information idiosyncratic to the victim himself or herself specifically designed for friends and family of the victim, offender, or the victim and offender about the whereabouts of the victim compared to 8 offenders or 29.6% who did not tell "prescriptive stories" about the victim to friends and family, while 5 offenders or 18.6% did speak to friends and/or family of the victims at all. Further, 4 victims or 21% died of injuries sustained from blunt force trauma, 14 victims or 73.7% died of injuries sustained from one or more gunshot wounds, 1 victim or 5.3% died of asphyxiation, and no victims were stabbed to death in this sample. Additionally, 3 victims or 15.8% were murdered in their environments, 3 victims or 15.8% were murdered in their offender's environment, however, 10 victims or 52.6% were murdered in the common environment of both the victim and offender compared to 3 victims or 15.8% who were murdered in a location that did not belong to neither the victims or offenders.

Discussion: The results of this study are in support fully or in part of some findings in studies conducted using similar research design, such as in Eke's (2007), Ferguson's (2011, 2014), Ferguson and Petherick's (2014), Pettler's (2011), Schlesinger et al.'s (2012), and Turvey's (2000) descriptive studies. In this sample, 21 offenders (66.7%) were associated to the victim prior to the victim's death. Eke (2007), Ferguson (2011), and Pettler (2011) argued that crime scene staging appears to be influenced or be a function of the victim–offender relationship. Findings in this current study support Eke's, Ferguson's, and the author's previous arguments. Also in relation to the victim–offender relationship, Eke (2007), Ferguson (2011), Pettler (2011), and Schlesinger (2012) found that intimate partners, such as boyfriends, girlfriends, spouses, or ex-spouses, were more likely to stage crime scenes as seen in the results of this study, which revealed that 33.3% or 9 offenders were current or former intimate partners of their victims.

Ferguson (2015) argued that investigators should assess whether or not evidence of confrontation exists in a case and, if so, is the crime scene consistent with the type of confrontation evidenced therein. The results of this study supported Ferguson's argument in that 66.6% or 18 offenders were found to have been in conflict or where evidence of a confrontation either verbal or physical was present prior to the death of the victim. With regard to this sample specifically, the broad definition used to define staging in Pettler's (2011) study yields to the fact that cases included herein contained behaviors defined as precautionary by some other authors in other published literature. Thus, this is to account for the nine or 33.3% of the offenders who were strangers to their victims prior to the murders, six of whom abducted and killed their victims, two of whom killed their victim and set the crime scene on fire, and one who was hired and paid to kill a victim in three cases, respectively, whereas no evidence of prior conflict between these victims and these offenders was found in these cases. Interestingly, 14 offenders or 51.8% either self-reported or were reported to have been the last ones seen with their victims compared to the 13 offenders or 48.2% who were not the last individuals to see the victim alive. Of the 13 offenders who were not the last individuals to see the victims alive, 9 of offenders were strangers to the victims; no one reported seeing the other 4 with the victim prior to the murder of the victim.

Ferguson (2015) argued as well that another preliminary inquiry investigators should assess is that related to discovery of the victim's body. The results of this study revealed that three offenders or 11.1% discovered the bodies of their victims in two cases compared to the 24 offenders who did not discover their victims' bodies in this sample. While these findings might be in contrast to some of the most recent findings about victim-body discovery, it is arguable that it is specifically related again to the types of cases included in the original sample of 18 cases rather than a reflection of the likelihood or the unlikelihood that victim discovery is a key piece of the phenomenon of crime scene staging. Like contrasting results of other recent studies, results of this nature should be taken in light of the sample analyzed and types of cases included in the sample pursuant to the ability of the application of findings of small sample sizes to the broad target population.

Hazelwood and Napier (2004) argued that offenders might verbally stage when having killed a victim and disposed of the victim's body by contacting law enforcement to report the victim missing. Further, Hazelwood and Napier argued that in addition to the type of verbal staging related to missing persons, offenders might verbally stage many other aspects of their crimes as well. All 27 offenders verbally staged their crimes in this sample. Of the 15 offenders or 55.5% who lied to investigators, the author would opine that further inquiry is warranted in a subsequent descriptive study that specifically addresses the types of lies perpetrated by these offenders. Second, in relation to the what the author calls "fish tales" and "prescriptive stories," 13 offenders told both fish tales and prescriptive stories to both investigators and friends/family of the victim, offender, or both the victim and offender in this sample. However, of the nine offenders who were strangers to their victims prior to the murders, none of them lied to family and friends about their general whereabouts at the time of the victim's murder, six of them did not give information about their whereabouts at the time of the victims' murders, and one of them did not give any information to anyone about his whereabouts or the whereabouts of the victim at the time of the victim's murder.

Ferguson (2011, 2014) and Ferguson and Petherick (2014) found that firearms were the most commonly used weapons in staged homicide cases. The results of this study supported these authors' finding in that 73.7% of the victims in this study died from injuries sustained from at least one or more gunshot wounds. Second, according to Spitz, "Blunt force is probably the single most common type of trauma" (p. 460). Thus, analysis of this sample revealed that 21% died of injuries sustained from blunt force trauma indicative that blunt force injuries are the second most common injuries sustained by victims in staged homicide cases. The results of this study (e.g., asphyxiation death of one victim) also rendered modest support for findings in Ferguson's (2014) study in 14% died of strangulation (i.e., asphyxiation), but this study's results of no victims having been stabbed to death were in contrast to Ferguson's findings where 7.0% of the victims in her 115 case sample died of sharp force injuries.

With regard to murder scene location, the results of this study indicate that further inquiry is necessary because like findings in recent studies, results of this study demonstrated that victims are most often killed in an environment that is familiar to either the victim, offender, or victim and offender as seen in 16% or 84.2% of these 18 cases. The 3 victims or 15.8% who were murdered in locations unfamiliar to the offenders were abducted and driven to rural, wooded, deserted locations where they were shot and killed by the offenders in these two cases.

Conclusions: The results of this study imply that further research is necessary with regard to verbal staging and murder scene location specifically. The results of this study supported in full or in part several of the findings in recent studies on crime scene staging when using similar research design. Although descriptive analysis is limited in scope to only separating information in static categories, the significance of these findings even in its smallest measure is relevant to the study of crime scene staging in relation to the current research being undertaking by the criminal justice community.

Summary of Crime Scene Staging Literature

Today, the literature on crime scene staging is sparse. Not much has been published on crime scene staging other than the occasional anecdotal case study in nearly the past two decades. Although Hans Gross (1899, 1924) recognized staged crime scenes more than a century ago, not many resources have been dedicated its empirical research. Known to the author to date at this point, eight studies exist on crime scene staging (Ferguson, 2014, 2015; Geberth, 2010; Hazelwood & Napier, 2004; Keppel & Weis, 2004; Pettler, 2015 *in press*; Schlesinger et al., 2012; Turvey, 2000) along with three doctoral dissertations (Eke, 2007; Ferguson, 2011; Pettler, 2011) with several descriptive studies, case studies, and discussions about crime scene staging scattered throughout its history. If nothing else, scholars, scholar–practitioners, and practitioners agree on one thing: the frequency of investigators encountering staged crime scenes is on the rise due to the CSI effect and possibly other learned-behavior-related factors. Thus, based on this extensive, but not exhaustive, summation of key points contained in the crime scene staging literature today, the need for resources to be dedicated to the empirical study of crime scene staging cannot be understated (Chisum & Turvey, 2011; Eke, 2007; Ferguson, 2011, 2014, 2015; Ferguson & Petherick, 2014; Pettler, 2011; Schlesinger et al., 2012; Turvey, 2002).

References

Adair, T. W. (2002). The reconstruction of a staged sexual assault. *Journal of Forensic Identification, 52*(2), 137–142.

Adair, T. W., & Dobersen, M. J. (1999). A case of suicidal hanging staged as homicide. *Journal of Forensic Sciences, 44*(6), 1307–1309.

Barker, B. (1995). *The NIV study Bible.* Grand Rapids, MI: The Zondervian Corporation.

Brown, A. (1991). *Lizzie Borden: The legend, the truth, the final chapter.* Nashville, TN: Rutledge Hill Press.

Burgess, A. W., Burgess, A. G., Douglas, J. E., & Ressler, R. K. (1992). *Crime classification manual: A standard system for investigating and classifying crimes.* Lexington, MA: Lexington Books.

Chancellor, A. S., & Graham, G. D. (2014, January). Staged crime scenes: Crime scene clues to suspect misdirection of the investigation. *Investigative Science Journal, 6*(1), 19–35.

Chisum, J., & Turvey, B. (2007). *Crime reconstruction*. London, UK: Academic Press.

Chisum, J., & Turvey, B. (2011). *Crime reconstruction*. London, UK: Academic Press.

Cobin, S. B. (2009). Staged Hunting Mishaps and Criminal Homicide. Minneapolis, MN: Center for Homicide Research.

Douglas, J. E., Burgess, A. W., Burgess, A. G., & Ressler, R. K. (2006). *Crime classification manual: A standard system for investigating and classifying crimes* (2nd ed.). San Francisco, CA: John Wiley & Sons.

Douglas, J. E., & Douglas, L. (2006). The detection of staging, undoing and personation at the crime scene. In J. Douglas, A. Burgess, A. Burgess, & R. Ressler (Eds.), *Crime classification manual* (2nd ed.). San Francisco, CA: Jossey-Bass.

Douglas, J. E., & Munn, C. (1992). The detection of staging and personation at the crime scene. In A. Burgess, A. Burgess, J. Douglas, & R. Ressler (Eds.), *Crime classification manual*. San Francisco, CA: Jossey-Bass.

Eke, A. W. (2007). *Staging in cases of homicide: Offender, victim, and offence characteristics* (Doctoral dissertation). Retrieved from ProQuest (1390310091).

Ferguson, C. (2011). *The defects of the situation: A typology of staged crime scenes* (Unpublished doctoral thesis). Bond University, Gold Coast, Queensland, Australia.

Ferguson, C. (2014, July). Staged homicides: An examination of common features of faked burglaries, suicides, accidents and car accidents. *Journal Police Criminal Psychology*, Springer Publishing. doi: 10.1007/s11896-014-9154-1

Ferguson, C. (2015). Detecting staged crime scenes: An empirically derived "How-To." In W. Petherick (Ed.), *Applied crime analysis: A social science approach to understanding crime, criminals, and victims*. Waltham, MA: Elsevier.

Ferguson, C., & Petherick, W. (2014, October 13). Getting away with murder: An examination of detected homicides staged as suicides. *Homicide Studies*, doi: 10.1177/1088767914553099

Forbes, T. R. (1985). Surgeons at the Bailey—English forensic medicine to 1878 (pp. 75–82). New Haven, CT: Yale University Press. In H. L. MacDonell's (1992) *Segments of history: The literature of bloodstain pattern interpretation: Segment 00: Literature through the 1900s*. Corning, NY: Author.

Frye v. United States, 293 F. 1013, 1014 (D.C. Cir. 1923).

Geberth, V. J. (1996). *Practical homicide investigation: Tactics, procedures, and forensic techniques* (3rd ed.). Boca Raton, FL: CRC Press/Taylor & Francis Group.

Geberth, V. J. (1996a). The staged crime scene. *Law and Order Magazine, 44*(2), 45–49.

Geberth, V. J. (2006). *Practical homicide investigation: Tactics, procedures, and forensic techniques* (4th ed.). Boca Raton, FL: CRC Press/Taylor & Francis Group.

Geberth, V. J. (2010). Crime scene staging: An exploratory study of the frequency and characteristics of sexual posing in homicides. *Investigative Sciences Journal, 2*(2), 1–19.

Glaister, J. (1902). A text-book of medical jurisprudence: Toxicology and Public Health. Ediinburgh: E&S Livingstone. In H. L. MacDonell (Ed.), *Segments of history: The literature of bloodstain pattern interpretation: Segment 00: Literature through the 1900s*. Corning, NY: Laboratory of Forensic Science.

Gross, H. (1899). Comments, archive. fur kriminal-anthropologie und krimininalistik (p. 264). Leipzig: Von F.C. Vogel. In H. L. MacDonell (1992), *Segments of history: The literature of bloodstain pattern interpretation: Segment 00: Literature through the 1900s*. Corning, NY: Laboratory of Forensic Science.

Gross, H. (1924). *Criminal Investigation*. London, UK: Sweet & Maxwell.

Hazelwood, R. R., & Napier, M. R. (2004). Crime scene staging and its detection. *International Journal of Offender Therapy and Comparative Criminology, 48*(6), 744–759. doi: 10.1177/0306624X04268298

Keppel, R. D., & Weis, J. G. (2004). The rarity of unusual dispositions of victim bodies: Staging and posing. *Journal of Forensic Science, 49*(6), 1–5.

Leedy, P. D., & Ormrod, J. E. (2005). *Practical research: Planning and design* (8th ed.). Upper Saddle River, NJ: Pearson.

Leth, P., & Vesterby, A. (1996). Homicidal hanging masquerading as suicide. *Forensic Science International, 85*, 65–71. doi: 10.1016/S0379-0738(96)02082-8

Liman, C. (1882). Zweifelhafte blutflecke auf werkzeugen und stoffen, gerochtlichen medicin. Berlin, Germany: Hirschwald.

MacDonell, H. L. (1992). *Segments of history: The literature of bloodstain pattern interpretation: Segments 00*. Corning, NY: Author.

MacDonell, H. L. (1996). Absence of evidence is not evidence of absence. *Journal of Forensic Identification, 46*(4), 160–164.

Mallach, H. J., & Pollak, S. (1998, July–August). Simulated suicide by hanging after homicidal strangulation. *Arch Kriminol, 202*, 1–2, 17–28.

Meloy, J. R. (2001). Spousal homicide and the subsequent staging of a sexual homicide at a distant location. *Journal of Forensic Sciences, 47*(2), 395–398.

Mitchell, C. A. (1911). *Science and the criminal.* Boston, MA: Little, Brown, and Company.

O'Connell, J., & Soderman, H. (1936). *Modern criminal investigation.* New York: Funk & Wagnalls.

O'Hara, C., & Osterburg, J. (1972). *An introduction to criminalistics.* Bloomington, IN: University Press.

Pettler, L. G. (2011). *Crime scene behaviors of crime scene stagers* (Doctoral dissertation). Retrieved from ProQuest (2251577601).

Puschel, K., Holtz, W., Hildebrand, E., Naeve, W., & Brinkman, B. (1984, November–December). Hanging: Suicide or homicide? *Arch Kriminol, 174*(5–6), 141–153.

Schlesinger, L. B., Gardenier, A., Jarvis, J., & Sheehan-Cook, J. (2012, April). Crime scene staging in homicide. *Journal of Police and Criminal Psychology, 29*(1), 44–51.

Shakespeare, W. (1892). *The tragedy of Macbeth.* New York: Harper.

Soderman, H., & O'Connell, J. (1962). *Modern criminal investigation.* New York: Funk & Wagnalls.

Spitz W. U. (2006). *Medicolegal investigation of death guidelines for the application of forensic pathology to crime scene investigation* (4th ed.). Springfield, IL: Charles C Thomas.

Strassman, F. (1985). Blood examinations (pp. 341–342). Stuttgart, Germany: Ferdinand Enke. In H. L. MacDonell's (1992), *Segments of history: The literature of bloodstain pattern interpretation: Segment 00: Literature through the 1900s.* Corning, NY: Author.

Svensson, A., & Wendel, O. (1974). *Techniques of crime scene investigation* (2nd ed.). New York: American Elsevier.

Swineburne, J. (1862). A review of the case: The people against reverend henry budge (p. 94). Albany, NY: C. Van Benthuysen. In H. L. MacDonell (1992), *Segments of history: The literature of bloodstain pattern interpretation: Segment 00: Literature through the 1900s.* Corning, NY: Laboratory of Forensic Science.

Turvey, B. E. (1999). *Criminal profiling: An introduction to behavioral evidence analysis* (1st ed.). London, UK: Academic Press.

Turvey, B. E. (2000, December). Staged crime scenes: A preliminary study of 25 cases. *Journal of Behavioral Profiling, 1*(3). Online journal.

Turvey, B. E. (2002). *Criminal profiling: An introduction to behavioral evidence analysis* (2nd ed.). London, UK: Academic Press.

Turvey, B. E. (2008). *Criminal profiling: An introduction to behavioral evidence analysis* (3rd ed.). London, UK: Academic Press.

Turvey, B. E. (2011). *Criminal profiling: An introduction to behavioral evidence analysis* (4th ed.). London, UK: Academic Press.

Ueno, Y., Fukanaga, T., Nakagawa, K., Imabayashi, T., Fukiwara, S., Adachi, J., Mizoi, Y. (1989, February). A homicidal strangulation by ligature, disguised as a suicide. *Nihon Hoigaku Zasshi, 42*(1), 46–51.

von Hofman, E. R. (1887). *Gerichtlichen medicin*. Wien und Leipzig: Urban & Schwarzenberg. pp. 423–428.

Vucetuch, J. (1882). Dactiloscopia comparada (pp. 54, 106). La Plata, Argentina: Peuser. In H. L. MacDonell (1992) *Segments of history: The literature of bloodstain pattern interpretation: Segment 00: Literature through the 1900s*. Corning, NY: Laboratory of Forensic Science.

Walton, R. H. (2006). *Cold case homicides: Practical investigative techniques*. Boca Raton, FL: CRC Press/Taylor & Francis Group.

Yamamoto, K., Hayase, T., Matsumoto, H., & Yamamoto, Y. (1998, March–April). Suicidal hanging or simulated suicide? Once again a case of Kobue: A spectacular case in the history of Japanese legal medicine. *Arch Kriminol, 201*(3–4), 97–102.

Introduction to Crime Scene Staging

2

Introduction

The story of Jacob and Joseph from Genesis 37 demonstrates that people have been trying to get away with wrongdoing since ancient times. However, although Chapter 1 of this book containing many of the empirical and anecdotal historical references made in regard to crime scene staging might appear lengthy, this number of entries pales in comparison to other areas of crime scene investigation (CSI) and forensic science. Until the past two decades at best, the phenomenon of crime scene staging has received relatively no attention by the criminological or law enforcement community. While some notable authors have mentioned staging or written about staging within the body of their works, the phenomenon of crime scene staging has gone profoundly underresearched. In addition, with the exception of the few studies presented in the previous chapter, empirical examination of staged crime scenes is virtually unchartered territory.

Many types of crimes can be staged, such as financial crimes, larcenies, and the like; however, this book focuses on staging behaviors as they relate to homicide or murder cases staged as accidents, suicides, or in other ways that point the investigation away from the true perpetrator specifically. Homicide and murder are not interchangeable terms in the medical community, but the author uses these terms interchangeably for discussion purposes throughout this book. Further, for the purpose of this discussion, staging behaviors are purposeful acts exhibited by an offender who intends to misdirect an investigation by manipulating physical or verbal evidence to make it appear that his or her victim died legitimately in an attempt to conceal the evidence that might prove the victim was actually murdered by the offender. Staging is a mind game; a mind game played by the offender. The ways in which an offender can stage a crime scene are endless and are only limited by his or her imagination, creativity, and physical abilities in relation to the physical stature and condition of the victim (Schlesinger, Gardenier, Jarvis, & Sheehan-Cook, 2012). Some staged crime scenes are *monothematic* or simplistically staged. In contrast, some staged crime scenes are *polythematic* or elaborately staged by the offender. As far as terminology goes, those who write and talk about staging might refer to it as *staging* or *crime scene staging*; regardless of the usage of the term or phrase, everyone is talking about the same thing—deception.

Physical evidence might be the first thing many individuals might think of when thinking about crime scene staging, and while the American criminal justice system is firmly seated on physical evidence often being what tips the scale in the courtroom during murder trials, physical evidence is not always present in every case. The CSI effect has created the myth that there are fingerprints and DNA in every case in modern criminal investigation, which is just simply not true. There is really nothing more incorrect than that statement actually. The importance of detecting and identifying staged physical evidence cannot be understated, but Hazelwood and Napier (2004) argued that verbal staging, or the purposeful acts exhibited by the offender to contact authorities regarding the victim's whereabouts and well-being when the offender has already murdered the victim and disposed of his or her body, and the type of lies related to covering up the murder of the victim in general are also very important to investigate and bring forth. Just as an offender can physically stage a crime scene, an offender can easily verbally stage a scene as well. Verbal staging often supports the offender's work in the crime scene, but it has been the author's experience that at some point, the lies overwhelm some offenders, and they cannot remember what they did, what they did not do, what they need to say, what they should not say, and so on, sometimes all within the same conversation with investigators. This is why it is so important to be ready, willing, and able to capture that information. It is arguable that innocent individuals behave totally differently from guilty ones, and the more one learns about the dynamics of human behavior, the better one will be at identifying staging behavior (Douglas & Munn, 1992).

Crime scene staging is not mindless and random work on the part of the offender. As mentioned earlier, scenes can be simplistically or elaborately staged, but the mind of the offender is what drives the process from beginning to end. Staging behaviors are purposeful and deliberate, specifically enacted by the offender in an attempt to misguide investigators' efforts toward apprehension. Sometimes in cases where offenders are asked why they did it (why they staged the scene), replies range from *I don't know* to *I just panicked and didn't know what to do...* and then run the gamut from there. Staged crime scenes are perplexing. They are illusions. They are reflections of the impressions an offender has of what some type of accident, suicide, other type of murder, or some other legitimate death scene is supposed to look like. What is so interesting about that idea is that once investigators study the victim and the suspect and they learn everything they can about them, it becomes very clear as to why the offender thought the crime scene should look a certain way toward simulating something else.

Recent empirical findings allude to the fact that due to the CSI effect, crime scene staging is on the rise (Eke, 2007; Ferguson, 2011; Geberth, 1996b; Schlesinger et al., 2012). And the best predictor of future behavior tends to be past, relevant behavior, but unless dealing with a serial killer, offenders have no experience with staging crime scenes, no experience with what a suicide should look like, no experience with what a botched home invasion, interrupted robbery, sexual homicide, serial homicide with signature, or any other type of crime scene looks like except for what they see in the media. Regardless, even though many citizens with no training, education, or experience in forensic science, CSI, or the like, think they know forensic science and CSI from watching television, they are unfortunately incorrect in that assumption. The same goes for offenders. Just because offenders watch crime-related television does not mean they know how any of the previously referenced crime scenes actually look in real life. This limitation greatly impedes their attempt at successful deception and increases their likelihood of getting caught when investigators understand this concept and apply it liberally through empirically derived deception detection methods.

Staging versus Scene Alteration

Within any definition of crime scene staging, the element of criminal intent to misdirect must be embedded soundly within its construct reflective of the desire to achieve successful deception by sending a death investigation off course. Definitions devoid of the mention of intent to misdirect tend to be ambiguous; thus, they can be confusing and detrimental overall to those trying to understand crime scene staging and its phenomenon. However, crime scene staging is in stark contrast to *death scene alteration*. According to Douglas et al. (2006) scene alteration is defined as "when a person purposely alters a crime scene to protect the victim or victim's family" (p. 34). While friends and family might alter crime scenes to protect the dignity of a loved one, sometimes they also alter scenes because they cannot *look* at the victim. Sometimes friends and family might cover the victim with a towel, blanket, or something else, close the victim's eyes, and so on. All of these behaviors are not for the purpose of misdirecting an investigation at all; instead these behaviors are purely out of care for the victim and arguably the trauma experienced by those observing their loved one in a death scene situation. Death scene alteration does not always mean crime scenes either. Death scene alteration might be observed in rape–murder cases, suicides, or autoerotic deaths. If it is a crime scene or a suspicious death investigation, investigators need to ask friends and family to identify any alterations they made so those changes can be documented appropriately. Whether the reasons are to protect the victim, family, financial, or religious, the investigator needs to closely examine the scene behavior and evidence. Of course the hope is that if it is a crime scene, it is untouched, but sometimes that is not the case, so due diligence is necessary, which means having to ask tough questions to make sure the foundation of the CSI is built on solid ground.

Staging versus Precautionary Acts

There are several types of crime scene behavior. Precautionary acts are one type of crime scene behavior and staging behaviors are specific types of precautionary acts (Ferguson & Petherick, 2014). For example, a man and his wife separated and she moved on with another man. The estranged husband returned to the marital residence and bludgeoned his estranged wife and her new boyfriend to death with his fists. Then the husband doused both bodies with bleach and cleaners and fled the residence. In this example, the husband is trying to cover-up evidence that might be on the bodies from him hitting them. In contrast, if the husband bludgeons the victims to death and then sets the house on fire in an attempt to make it look like both victims died as a result of injuries sustained from the fire and not from the injuries they sustained from the beatings, then that is an act of staging.

Because staging behaviors and precautionary acts are similar, the boundary for where staging leaves off and precautionary acts starts can be a bit confusing. Staging in most cases means that an offender tries to make the scene look a certain way so that investigators do not think a victim died by the hand of the offender, while precautionary act means that an offender takes precautions before, during, and after the crime by choosing his or her behaviors wisely, such as wearing gloves so he or she does not leave fingerprints, wearing a mask so no one knows who he or she is, and wearing protective clothing so that he or she does not leave trace evidence (Turvey, 2011).

Deception

Of their hands and of their mouths the illusion comes to fruition.

Hollywood has a wonderful way of embellishing everything in one way or another including how the truth arises in precarious situations. "If you've seen one, you've seen them" is arguable when it comes to spy movies and shows where *good guys* and *bad guys* are routinely held and injected with *truth serum* to keep them from being deceptive to their captors. While this discussion will not debate the viability of truth serum, polygraphs, voice stress analysis tests, or any other truth-related idea, the point of this jovial example is that people have focused on overriding others' commitment to deceive in many unique ways.

When an investigator brings a suspect in a death investigation in for an interview, the investigator normally approaches such situations with great skepticism; or so they should. Being the skeptical one on the team is a positive thing when it comes to crime scene staging because just when crime scene investigators at the scene are reporting back to the department that the crime scene has given them pause, the investigator receiving the call or text is sitting across from a suspect listening to a story that does not make sense, seems far-fetched, and simultaneously has undercurrents that seem to echo what is being preliminarily reported by CSI about the look of the crime scene. If the suspect staged the scene in this hypothetical example, it appears that the CSIs were alert to identify and detect things that were not adding up early on. Second, the investigator now knows what is going on at the crime scene and what they are finding in real time, which can spin the interview in many different ways, but one thing is for sure, less a confession, the suspect is going to hold tight to his or her physical staging efforts because most often it has been the experience of the author that offenders believe that if they do not waiver they will walk out of the interview, and sometimes they do. Regardless, the suspect aims to deceive the investigator so his or her behavior is going to be illustrious of that goal. The suspect also aims to deceive the crime scene investigators specifically, so his or her behavior pursuant to staging physical evidence is going to be illustrious of that goal as well. Thus, the more investigators learn about deception, the better they will be at detecting deception in discourse and in the crime scene.

The aforementioned hypothetical example shows how offenders do not always stop at just manipulating the physical evidence, and empirical research has shown that it is common for offenders who stage physical evidence in the crime scene to support their efforts with corresponding lies or verbal staging toward highlighting and lending credence to their work. And while it might be true that people in general lie for lots of reasons, crime scene stagers lie to protect themselves specifically. Their endgame is clear: muddy the waters, obliterate the truth, and send the investigation flying in the wrong direction. The sheer desire to deceive is at the heart of this issue.

Scholars have studied deception for centuries, and there is no doubt after reviewing the history of crime scene staging that people's desire to deceive has survived every turn of events throughout history and is still alive and well today. Hans Gross (1924) recognized more than 100 years ago that staged crime scenes are the culmination of the offender's efforts to be thorough and meticulous in order to simulate a suicide, for example, when the victim was actually murdered. Thus, to deceive is to trick someone. It does not necessarily mean that the person being tricked knows he or she is being tricked or lied to. However, the skeptic cannot be lied to. The skeptic is the one who believes everything that comes from the mouth of the suspect or offender is a lie, a trick, deceptive, or anything else. The only thing that the skeptic believes is true is that the offender is probably lying.

Crime Scene Staging Statistics and No Repository

No one knows how many crime scenes have been staged in the United States to date. No one knows how many crime scenes are staged per year. Nor does anyone know how many deaths ruled suicide, accidental, natural, undetermined, or even unclassified were actually murders where offender deception was successful. There is no clearinghouse that records staged cases, and until recently, there have been no statistics that might be applicable with a broad brush, but crime scene staging is on the rise (Ferguson, 2011, 2014; Ferguson & Petherick, 2014). Geberth (1996a) argued, "These events seem to be on the increase as people learn more about the process of death investigation through the media, true crime books, television mystery shows, and movies" (p. 37). In light of Geberth's argument, again, Douglas and Munn (1992) also argued, "An offender who stages a crime scene unusually makes mistakes because he stages it to look the way he thinks a crime scene should look" (p. 251). Again, no agency in the United States maintains a repository of the number of forensically determined staged crime scenes located per year (e.g., Center for Disease Control Morbidity Studies, Regional Organized Crime Information Center, Violent Criminal Apprehension Program, the Federal Bureau of Investigation Behavioral Analysis Unit, or the National Center for the Analysis of Violent Crime) (Geberth, 2010, p. 5). However, Hazelwood and Napier (2004) estimated that as much as 3% of the total number of crime scenes per year might be staged (p. 746). Hazelwood and Napier calculated this estimation based on the number of staged crime scenes a sample of 20 crime scene experts claimed they had worked throughout their careers. Additionally, Keppel and Weis (2004) estimated that approximately 0.1% of crime scenes might be staged (p. 1308). However, Keppel and Weis' statistic was derived using a narrow definition of crime scene staging (i.e., body positioning only) and a small sample (i.e., Washington State Attorney General's Homicide Investigation and Tracking System's Database, 1981–2000). It was not until 2012, when Schlesinger et al. conducted their study of 946 homicides and estimated the prevalence of crime scene staging at 8%. Thus, Schlesinger et al.'s findings are the most applicable to the broader population known to date.

Crime Scene Staging Is a Problem

Crime scene staging is a problem. Crime scene staging threatens public safety. Crime scene stagers are a danger to their families and to others. Law enforcement professionals are trained to protect and serve citizens and communities. They are charged with duties most individuals could not perform under the best of circumstances (Gardner, 2005). The profession of law enforcement is challenging, though competent and well-trained individuals who know the law and know how to apply the law build prosecutable cases. For inexperienced or young investigators, a homicide case where crime scene staging might be present creates a unique set of challenges to overcome. But if those circumstances yield results consistent with the offender's successful deception of the truth, then he or she remains in society with an opportunity to reoffend, and some do. In addition, some community members, such as previous victims of violent crime might not feel safe and might be fearful until an arrest is made in a case. Again, crime scene staging is a problem.

Crime scene staging causes agencies to waste resources. Take, for example, the case of Susan Smith, the woman who on October 10, 1991, claimed that she had been car jacked with her two young boys in the back seat of the car. A massive investigation ensued, but eventually the boys' bodies were found in the car submerged in a nearby body of water. Smith was charged in their deaths and is serving her sentence in a South Carolina State Prison. The preceding example exemplified the stager who verbally stages a crime and sends the investigation careening off the right track. A tremendous allocation of resources was dedicated to the manhunt in search for the two missing children in the Smith case only to discover that their own mother killed them before she reported the carjacking and that they were actually never missing at all (e.g., Hazelwood and Napier's 2004 argument precisely). Wasteful depletion of valuable financial and human resources is an enormous problem for law enforcement agencies, especially state and local agencies because most often these resources are in short supply in the first place. Following false leads provided by offenders sometimes goes on for extended periods of time before investigators realize, even if they do, that the offender lied to send them off course.

Another problem crime scene staging creates for law enforcement relates to the crime lab. Due to backlog, some crime labs might be in a position where they cannot process physical evidence when there is no suspect in the case. Even though television portrays the crime lab as the entity that often establishes the suspect, this is not always true in theory or practice. Some agencies might require suspect samples in order to proceed with evidence testing purely because their focus must remain on cases that are more developed than cases lacking a suspect or even a person of interest. This is not the situation with all crime labs throughout the United States, but could be the situation with some.

In relation to the preceding, crime scene staging in homicide cases is a problem for victims and families for obvious reasons, because victims' families depend on law enforcement to conduct thorough and thoughtful CSI toward making an arrest in the case. The more tools law enforcement professionals have in their arsenals, the more thorough and thoughtful their investigations can be. If staging efforts have prevented a suspect from being developed and physical evidence cannot be submitted to a lab for testing, investigators are at a disadvantage right off the bat. Thorough and thoughtful investigations are crucial to the apprehension of suspects and to the proper adjudication of cases, but crime scene staging can inhibit that process. Additionally, families often get very angry when no arrest is made in a case in a timely manner most often because they compare real cases to those depicted on crime-related media. Families feel cheated by the system, and the author has met with families who will not be consoled; will not be turned away; will not take yes, no, or maybe for an answer; and do not understand that there are many reasons why arrests are not made in murder cases in regard to legal procedure and what constitutes proof. Because staging behaviors are often part of this mix and investigators cannot disclose what they might think about a case, some families are left without closure regardless of investigators' reassurance that they are doing everything possible to resolve each case.

Further, Eke (2007) argued that crime scene staging is also a problem for expert witnesses who are called to testify on potentially staged evidence because they have very little empirical evidence to substantiate their opinions. At the direction of the prosecutors, experts would testify on staged crime scenes to illustrate for a jury the deceptive nature of a defendant. Without substantial proof or empirical research to support an expert's opinion as to the staged nature of a crime scene, defense counsel has a sturdy platform to argue that expert opinions are unfounded and are based purely on speculation. To reiterate, in the murder case of *Washington v. Kunze* (1999), two law enforcement professionals testified based on their training and experience that the crime scene might have been staged (Turvey, 2002, p. 251). The Washington State Court of Appeals upheld the trial court's discretion in allowing the law enforcement professionals to testify on aspects of a crime scene that might have been, rather than on forensically determined and empirically supported evidentiary facts. The opinion of the law enforcement professionals, while it might have been justified by other evidence within the fact pattern of the case in chief, the appellate decision does not negate the fact that evidence with sound empirical methodology that is generally accepted in the scientific community is necessary per *Frye v. United States* (1923).

To illustrate how crime scene staging is a problem during a criminal proceeding, consider the facts of the *Estate of Sam Sheppard v. State of Ohio* (Holmes, 1966). According to Holmes (1966), Gregg O. McCrary was hired to testify that the crime scene was staged in the murder of Marilynn Sheppard. Dr. Sheppard and his wife Marilynn were home on a July night 1954. Dr. Sheppard claimed an intruder broke into their home and murdered Mrs. Sheppard on the second floor while he and his son were sleeping on the first floor. It was determined that the offender had attempted to sexually assault Mrs. Sheppard during the attack. Investigators thought this discovery was interesting because the level of difficulty of committing a sexual assault while her husband and son were sleeping in the residence would have been very risky for the offender. Further, Mrs. Sheppard's timepiece (i.e., wristwatch) was recovered on a table on the first floor of the residence. If the motive had been robbery, after removing the timepiece from Mrs. Sheppard's arm, the killer would have made sure he or she kept it in during the escape. McCrary testified that in assessing crime scene evidence, he found investigators did not err in their determination that the scene was staged. However, the judge opined that McCrary's findings were unreliable and instructed that any discussion on staging be limited to general terms rather than expert opinion concerning the Sheppard case.

References

Douglas, J. E., Burgess, A. W., Burgess, A. G., & Ressler, R. K. (2006). *Crime classification manual: A standard system for investigating and classifying crimes* (2nd ed.). San Francisco, CA: John Wiley & Sons.

Douglas, J. E., & Munn, C. (1992, February). Violent crime scene analysis: Modus operandi, signature, and staging. *FBI Law Enforcement Bulletin, 61*(2), 1–10.

Eke, A. W. (2007). *Staging in cases of homicide: Offender, victim, and offence characteristics* (Doctoral dissertation). Retrieved from Proquest (1390310091).

Ferguson, C. (2011). *The defects of the situation: A typology of staged crime scenes* (Unpublished doctoral thesis). Bond University, Gold Coast, Queensland, Australia.

Ferguson, C. (2014, July). Staged homicides: An examination of common features of faked burglaries, suicides, accidents and car accidents. *Journal Police Criminal Psychology*. Springer Publishing. doi: 10.1007/s11896-014-9154-1

Ferguson, C., & Petherick, W. (2014, October 13). Getting away with murder: An examination of detected homicides staged as suicides. *Homicide Studies*. doi: 10.1177/1088767914553099

Frye v. United States, 293 F. 1013, 1014 (D.C. Cir. 1923).

Gardner, R. M. (2005). *Practical crime scene processing and investigation*. Boca Raton, FL: CRC Press/Taylor & Francis Group.

Geberth, V. J. (1996a). The staged crime scene. *Law and Order Magazine, 44*(2), 45–49.

Geberth, V. J. (1996b). *Practical homicide investigation: Tactics, procedures, and forensic techniques* (3rd ed.). Boca Raton, FL: CRC Press/Taylor & Francis Group.

Gross, H. (1924). *Criminal Investigation*. London, UK: Sweet & Maxwell.

Hazelwood, R. R., & Napier, M. R. (2004). Crime scene staging and its detection. *International Journal of Offender Therapy and Comparative Criminology, 48*(6), 744–759. doi: 10.1177/0306624X04268298

Keppel, R. D., & Weis, J. G. (2004). The rarity of unusual dispositions of victim bodies: Staging and posing. *Journal of Forensic Science, 49*(6), 1–5.

Schlesinger, L. B., Gardenier, A., Jarvis, J., & Sheehan-Cook, J. (2012, April). Crime scene staging in homicide. *Journal of Police and Criminal Psychology, 29*(1), 44–51.

Turvey, B. E. (2002). *Criminal profiling: An introduction to behavioral evidence analysis* (2nd ed.). London, UK: Academic Press.

Turvey, B. E. (2011). *Criminal profiling: An introduction to behavioral evidence analysis* (4th ed.). London, UK: Academic Press.

Crime Scene Dynamics

3

Dynamics are *patterns of activity*. Crime scene dynamics are therefore the patterns of activity exhibited by the victim and offender that might vary in force or intensity before, during, and after a crime. Crime scene dynamics are a reflection of the personality, behavior, emotions, ways of thinking, and the totality of how an offender experiences his or her environment, how he or she experiences society, and how he or she experiences his or her culture. In a two-person, victim–offender crime, crime scene dynamics can fluctuate from passive to intense, an even 50%–50% split to any other percentage for each along the continuum. Traditional homicide investigation has primarily focused on the suspect, and in doing so, the most critical information about the victim has been widely neglected. The paradigm shift today places more focus on the victim, how the individual becomes a victim, why the individual became a victim, and thus, how did the patterns of activities (dynamics) play out between the victim and offender in a crime scene in relation to their presence, force, and intensity. The study of crime scene dynamics is very important to the study of staging behaviors specifically because it is arguable that to identify what is abnormal, one must first learn to recognize what are normal dynamics in human behavior first.

Heart of It All: Ethics

Death scene investigation is an overarching term that describes the investigatory nature of exploring why someone died. Crime scene investigation in homicide cases is part of that process. There is a gap between the medical and law enforcement communities when it comes to death investigation and homicide investigation. This book is an attempt to help bridge that gap in that death investigation for these purposes not only includes the medical examination of the deceased victim, but also encapsulates all aspects of the investigation in relation to how the victim died in totality. So for all intents and purposes here, death investigation and homicide investigation are the same, but it is important to remember that generally speaking not all death scenes are crime scenes and not all crime scenes are death scenes, just like not all homicides are murders in the field of forensic pathology. However, the author would argue that any suspicious death should be thoroughly investigated as if it were a murder in the event it turns out that it is a murder.

When someone is reported or found dead, no one knows immediately how to proceed because no one knows what to expect. Typically, first responders arrive first and usually offer very basic information based on the very basic first glance of the victim and scene. In some cases, when first responders arrive on scene, they have to back right back out because after cursory assessment, they believe they know they will need a search warrant to proceed. Then after investigators get their feet on the ground, their education, training, and experience help guide this exploratory process. The quality of the death investigation and crime scene processing is a reflection of the education, training, and experience of the death investigators and/or crime scene investigators. Many other factors influence the investigatory process as well, such as suspect statements, victim statements, witness statements, interviews with family and friends, neighborhood canvasses, the autopsy of the victim, physical evidence recovered at the scene, forensic testing, and a host of additional resources. Death scene characteristics related to the manner of death are determined from the medical standpoint by the forensic pathologist, coroner, and so on, such as the following:

- Does the victim appear to have died of natural causes?
- Does the victim appear to have died as the result of an accident?
- Does the victim appear to have died as the result of a self-inflicted injury?
- Does the victim appear to have died as the result of a violent attack?
- Is there no way to figure out how the victim died based on what can be observed in the death scene?

In addition, investigators overlap in this area pursuant to crime scene staging because they too are using a culmination of the evidence to try to arrive at how they believe the victim died as well. Regardless, any death scene investigation under the advisement of any type of practitioner should be grounded in ethics and guided by law.

"Every crime scene every time" might be a mantra that could describe the professional standards of death investigation in general and homicide investigation specifically, which yield to the notion that investigators should be objective and impartial at all times because they are not judges nor juries but rather investigators are information-gathering professionals whose job is to gather as much information about an individual's death as possible without jumping to conclusions, attributing value to any particular piece of evidence independently, all while guarding against investigator bias. For instance, investigators working the death of a poor, homeless, homosexual prostitute found dead in a seedy hotel room handcuffed to the headboard with drug paraphernalia on the nightstand should investigate his death the same way as they should investigate the death of the wealthy, socialite, author, world traveler, speaks four languages, medical doctor, lawyer, or professor found dead in her home handcuffed to a headboard with drug paraphernalia on her nightstand. But sometimes, investigators do not approach these very different yet the same death scenes the same way because the rich socialite is perceived as a *sympathetic victim* and the homosexual prostitute is often perceived as an *unsympathetic victim.* Death scenes that involve sympathetic victims or educated, middle- to upper-class, and attractive females are sometimes handled differently by some practitioners than death scenes that involved the poor, minority individual with no social status to speak of. They should not be of course, but politics, social structure, the media, and other factors can play a role into how these types of death scenes are handled from onset. Also, it is true that law enforcement professionals *live in glass houses.* That means that anything and everything they do both in their professional and private lives can come under scrutiny at any time for any reason. Some elected officials want to avoid such scrutiny, and some believe that no one will care if not much investigative attention is paid to the poor, homosexual prostitute because "he put himself in that position and deserved it." Criminal justice professionals both government and private sector, which includes law enforcement professionals of every kind, should live by a very high standard of integrity of which should spill over to underpin the foundation of everything they do to avoid undermining the core principles of homicide investigation as a profession.

Death Scene Characteristics Indicative of Homicide

When a death investigation points to homicide being the most likely manner of death, the investigation shifts to focus on the method, means, and mode of the killing of one human being by another human being. That means investigators want to find out what method or the way the killer killed victim: Did the offender shoot, stab, strangle, and so on, the victim? What means did the offender use to kill the victim: a gun, knife, screwdriver, rope, his hands, and so on? And what mode or particular pattern of behavior did the offender use to kill the victim? Identifying these characteristics in a death scene will help point the investigation in the right direction. No two homicide death scenes are alike, and while each might have similar features in relation to the nature of victim injuries, biological evidence, impression evidence, trace evidence, and so on, each homicide death scene is unique. However, the key to everything is for investigators to gather as much information and evidence as they can in order to later piece everything together. A simple example of this cause-and-effect relationship might be blood is related to bleeding, and bleeding is related to a bloodletting injury, and the injury is related to a force, and the force is related to a weapon, and the weapon is related to an activity (dynamic), and the activity is related to a behavior, which is related to a thought, which tracks back to the origin of it all…the totality of offender. Gathering all the right pieces and putting them into a rank-ordered thread, then weaving all of those uniquely colored threads together makes up the robust mosaic, that is, homicide investigation.

Anatomy of a Homicide

There are several types of evidence, such as direct evidence and circumstantial evidence. An example of direct evidence might be when a witness testifies he or she saw or heard the accused kill or not kill the victim. This witness is offering direct evidence that the accused is in truth guilty or innocent of killing the victim. In contrast, many people do not consider physical evidence to be "circumstantial" in nature because in some cases physical evidence overwhelmingly supports the guilt or innocence of a suspect. However, while physical evidence can infer the guilt or innocence of a suspect alone, it does not always. There is no perfect science. Every scientific test has a margin of error, even for forensic applications related to fingerprints, DNA, ballistics, or by way of other physical evidence presented in court by experts. One item of direct, circumstantial, or physical evidence alone might not be enough to overwhelmingly infer guilt or innocence, but several interrelated threads of evidence can be woven into a tight fabric that can point to guilt or innocence in some cases.

As mentioned in the previous chapter, crime scene–related television has taught America that there are fingerprints and DNA in virtually every case from bike larcenies to homicides. So sometimes, what happens is when a case only has testimonial evidence presented in court, jurors might think the investigation was incompetent, the witness is lying because no physical evidence supports it, or they arrive at some other conclusion and ask "Sure, right, but where's the DNA?" It is highly unlikely and unreasonable that DNA tests are going to be conducted in a bike larceny, for example, but that is what is on TV, so that is what the general public thinks anyway.

Like focus on the suspect, traditional homicide investigation has, again, been focused largely on testimonial evidence. But with the advancement of technology combined with the CSI effect, testimonial evidence is just not enough anymore in most homicide cases. The phrase, "Show me the DNA…" illustrates the pressure some feel toward presenting a convincing murder case. Just like not all death scenes are crime scenes and not all crime scenes are death scenes, not all crime scenes that are homicide death scenes contain physical evidence. However, studying crime scene dynamics in homicide cases serves as one component of the base for understanding crime scene staging dynamics in homicide cases.

Physical Evidence

Physical evidence is identified by its class and individual characteristics. Class characteristics are general attributes that indicate a piece of physical evidence is part of a particular group and individual characteristics are the item's specific attributes that make it a unique member of that group. Forensic scientists use various methods to identify the class characteristics and individual characteristics of evidence of many kinds toward explaining the evidence and its interpretive value.

The types of physical evidence that can be found are overwhelming to think about, so focusing on some of the kinds most commonly found in homicide crime scenes is most relevant for this discussion. The following is not an exhaustive list and does not contain exhaustive explanations of each type of evidence, rather the purpose of this list is to identify and describe some of the most common types of physical evidence recovered in homicide crime scenes.

Biological evidence: Biological or serological evidence includes saliva, semen, sweat, blood, bodily organs, and their physiological fluids. Evidence of this nature might be subjected to biochemical, toxicological, or serological testing, such as DNA testing in attempt to identify their origins, the presence of drugs or alcohol, levels of concentration all toward establishing ownership, and influence in a crime.

Bloodstain pattern analysis: Bloodstain pattern analysis "focuses on the analysis of the size, shape, and distribution of bloodstains resulting from bloodshed events as a means of determining the types of activities and mechanisms that produced them" (James, Kish, & Sutton, 2005, p. 1). The aim of bloodstain pattern analysis is to identify the individualistic characteristics of human blood in relation to how they interrelate in size and shape and in other ways to the distribution of the whole. Bloodstain evidence and bloodstain pattern analysis will be discussed at length in Section III of this book.

Impression evidence: The number of impressions that could be made by any number of objects on or in any number of items is endless. Generally speaking, impression evidence might easily be observable in an object at a crime scene or might have to be enhanced in a crime lab to identify and classify its characteristics. Impression evidence can include the following:

- Fingerprints
- Tire tracks
- Footprints
- Shoe prints
- Tool marks

Trace evidence: Trace evidence is "microscopic material recovered as evidence that is used to help solve criminal cases" (Houck, 2004, p. 1). Trace evidence cannot be discussed without the mention of Edmund Locard of Lyons, France and what is known today as Locard's exchange principle. The major idea of Locard's exchange principle is whenever two objects collide, like in a car accident, the material from each of the two objects is transferred between them. Trace evidence recovered at homicide crime scenes might include the following:

- Organic or synthetic fibers
- Human or animal hair

- Paint
- Soil
- Glass
- Plant material

Firearms and ammunition: Due to the vast number of firearms-related homicides in the United States, firearms and ammunition are commonly found in homicide crime scenes. Firearms examiners focus on examining firearms, fired and unfired ammunition, and all of their related parts. Firearms examination plays an integral role in shooting trajectories in relation to wound tracks identified and examined by the medical examiner.

Drugs: Illegal drugs are often found in homicide crime scenes. Drugs ranging from street drugs to illegally obtained prescription-like drugs, such as Vicodin, are illegal if not being used or if were distributed to anyone in an unlawful manner. Drugs are analyzed in order to determined their type and possibly related characteristics relevant to an investigation.

Other weapons: Other weapons that might be recovered in a homicide crime scene are anything used in the assault and murder of a victim. Like impression evidence, almost anything can be a weapon. From a lamp to a piece of wood to an offender's fists to knives, rope, belts, axes, and shovels, murder weapons are virtually anything used in the unlawful killing of another human being.

Behavioral Evidence

Behavioral evidence is another type of evidence commonly found at crime scenes. As mentioned in the previous chapter in relation to the simplicity versus complexity of crime scene staging behaviors, behavioral evidence can be *monothematic* or *polythematic*. In music, monothematic means to continue with one dominant theme throughout multiple movements; in homicide and crime scene investigation, monothematic means continuing with one dominant theme throughout the murder. An example of monothematic behavioral evidence would be that of an offender who walks up to the victim, points, and shoots once killing the victim and who then walks away without any other involvement with the victim or crime scene. This example of a one-theme, single behavioral pattern (i.e., walk in, shoot, and walk out) illustrates the dynamic 50%–50% interactional split between how an offender and victim interrelate in a crime scene and in that the offender provided 50% of the interaction and the victim provided 50% of the interaction. In stark contrast, polythematic behavioral evidence in a crime scene means that more than one observable theme is present, such as the victim was shot, stabbed, beaten, and strangled. In relation to the subject of this book and its conjoined concepts, *crime scene staging dynamics in homicide cases,* the behavioral evidence in staged crimes and/or staged crime scenes is either monothematic or polythematic as it pertains to the method, means, and mode of killing and the cover-up before, during, and after the murder in the way it connects to the patterns of activity demonstrated by the victim and offender in both force and intensity presented in the evidence toward the identification, examination, analysis, synthesis, and evaluation of the totality of circumstances. Therefore, the study of crime scene staging is not simply about a *mono*concept of physical evidence in a crime scene. As discussed earlier, physical evidence and its analysis is considered circumstantial or inferential of guilt or innocence based on sophisticated statistical analysis. In cases where crimes and crime scenes are staged, because physical evidence does not stage itself, rather the behaviors of the offender create the staged evidence, the study of human behavior and how important it is to homicide and crime scene investigators cannot be overstated.

Circumstantial Evidence

It is understandable that a homicide or crime scene investigator wants to cut through the diatribe and get down the heart of what is staged in the crime scene and might feel that learning about the empirical nature and theory of crime scene staging is a waste of time because the time and resources are always in short supply in the first place; consider this: *What* is quantitative; it only identifies the measurable attributes of a piece of physical evidence, such as the size, shape, weight, amount…really anything that can be *quantified.* Answering the quantitative questions is a fantastic place to start, but far too often, the crime scene investigation stops there. The hyperfocus on the crime scene's quantitative features often overshadows the existence and the intrinsic value of the behavioral evidence, which can be largely circumstantial, but regardless created the *what. How* was the evidence created and *why* was the evidence created put the *what* in context of the following:

- The crime scene before, during, and after the murder
- The murder itself before, during, and after the murder
- The personality and motives of the offender

To quote Herbert Leon MacDonell directly, "The absence of evidence is not evidence of absence" (MacDonell, 1996, p. 160). Just because a physical crime scene-related explanation for a piece of physical evidence recovered in a crime scene does not immediately jump out at investigators does not mean there is no explanation for that piece particular item of physical evidence; rather, it means further inquiry into identifying the interrelationships between the item of evidence and all the rest of the evidence, direct and circumstantial (i.e., physical and behavioral), is necessary.

Body as Evidence

Another key component of the anatomy of a homicide is the concept of the evidence, the autopsy might reveal. Autopsies are aimed at concluding the cause, mechanism, and manner of death. A forensic autopsy is the internal examination of a body and identification, documentation, collection, and preservation of evidence found in, on, or even around the body in some cases. Forensic pathologists attempt to hone in on a reasonable range for estimating time of death using the rate of decomposition, for example, in addition to working toward identifying various types of human remains. Autopsy reports generally contain several sections including the results of the external examination, evidence of injury, results of the internal examination, any microscopic examination results, toxicology results, and the forensic pathologist's opinion including what can be ruled out. Forensic pathologists focus on violent deaths, suspicious deaths, unexpected deaths, and deaths while in custody of a law enforcement agency (DiMiao & Dana, 2007).

Victims are murdered in so many different ways. It is important to recognize some of the most common assault dynamics seen in murder cases today, such as blunt force trauma, stabbing, gunshot wounds, and strangulation. According to DiMiao and Dana (2007), blunt force trauma is "an injury produced by a blunt object striking the body or impact of the body against a blunt object or surface (p. 63)." The nature, amount of body surface, force, and intensity, along with the timing and region of the body that was impacted, help in determining the severity, extent, and appearance of the injury. Blunt force trauma injuries or any combination thereof commonly identified by forensic pathologists at autopsy are abrasions, contusions or bruising, lacerations, and bone fractures. A killer's fists or anything else, such as a baseball bat can create injuries consistent with blunt force trauma. In addition, sharp-force injuries created by knives or screwdrivers for example can create stab wounds or "wounds produced by a pointed instrument in which the depth of the penetration into the body is greater than the length of the wound on the skin (p. 107)." The words "laceration" and "stab wound" are not interchangeable and should never used to refer to the absence of tissue bridging because sharp objects tend to cut all the way through. Further, special consideration is given to victims with gunshot wounds in relation to type of firearm used to shoot the victim, its caliber, and the type of ammunition used. Forensic pathologists determine the severity of the injury caused by the gunshot wound based on how the bullet and tissue interrelate in combination with the effects the temporary cavity (i.e., the space created in tissue as the bullet passes through) had on the tissue. The distance of how close the firearm was to the victim when it was fired is determined by the appearance of the wound in relation to the presence of burned (i.e., carbon or soot) or nonburned grains of gunpowder along with the bullet's vaporized metal, the cartridge case, and primer (p. 132). The forensic pathologist then identifies this spatial range as contact (muzzle against skin), near contact (muzzle held short distance from the skin), intermediate (held away from the skin, but close enough for the wound to contain powder tattooing), or distant (muzzle held outside the range for the possibility of power tattooing) (pp. 132–140).

The information identified by the forensic pathologist and how it helps investigators narrow the scope of a homicide investigation is very important to the study of crime scene staging because again, in order to recognize staging and crime scene staging behavior in cases of homicides staged as suicides, accidents, interrupted robberies, fire-related deaths, asphyxiation deaths, or otherwise, it is arguable that learning to identify how things should look in any given case precedes understanding of how they should not look as well.

Staged Scenes versus Other Types of Scenes

Crime scene staging dynamics in homicide cases are the patterns of activities that offenders use to hide their identities so they can escape being held responsible for their murderous actions. Research has shown that staging is most often seen in cases where the victim and offender had some prior relationship (Eke, 2007; Ferguson, 2011; Pettler, 2011). It is best to use this book as an introductory starting point to embark on the study of staging and crime scene–related dynamics, investigation, analysis, synthesis, and evaluation while recognizing that as new empirical research is conducted and published, some of the concepts in this book will continue to gain momentum while others will wane in validity because new research will point us in one direction or the other. That is ok. That is the beauty of research. As a "first log on the fire" type of book, the goal is to spark interest, drive, and commitment toward making the empirical study and scientific application of crime scene staging investigation methodology.

Staging is not always seen in every type of murder case. According to Douglas, Burgess, Burgess, and Ressler (2006), staging is generally absent from several types of murder they call (pp. 105–187) as follows:

- *Gang-related murder* is a killing of someone by a gang member(s) normally in public place within gang territory in the form of drive-by shootings characterized by no offender concern for the victim's body or injury to innocent bystanders.
- *Criminal competition* or when someone is killed because of conflict between two organized crime groups over territory.
- *Kidnap murder* is when someone is kidnapped and held for ransom then killed regardless of whether or not the ransom is paid or not.
- *Drug murder* is when someone is killed to facilitate the operation of a drug business.

- *Personal cause homicide* is when someone is killed by an offender motivated by an emotional drive to kill.
- *Argument/conflict murder* is the result of a dispute between two unrelated individuals or individuals who live together.
- *Authority murder* is the killing of an either real or symbolic figure of authority who is perceived by the offender as having wronged him or her.
- *Extremist murder* is the killing of someone for political, religious, or other reasons.

It is easy to see that some of these types of murder are similar and some are extremely different, but these are examples of crime scenes characterized by dynamics that are unlike the staged crime and crime scene even though some of the underlying motives might be similar. One similar motive might be that of the murder between two intimate partners over a dispute where the killer panics and tries to cover-up his or her crime. Overall, the remainder of this book will provide introductory knowledge of some of the things known about *crime scene staging dynamics in homicide cases.*

References

DiMiao, V. J. M., & Dana, S. E. (2007). *Handbook of forensic pathology* (2nd ed.). Boca Raton, FL: CRC Press/Taylor & Francis Group.

Douglas, J. E., Burgess, A. W., Burgess, A. G., & Ressler, R. K. (2006). *Crime classification manual: A standard system for investigating and classifying crimes* (2nd ed.). San Francisco, CA: John Wiley & Sons.

Eke, A. W. (2007). *Staging in cases of homicide: Offender, victim, and offence characteristics* (Doctoral dissertation). Retrieved from ProQuest (1390310091).

Ferguson, C. (2011). *The defects of the situation: A typology of staged crime scenes* (Unpublished doctoral thesis). Bond University, Gold Coast, Queensland, Australia.

Houck, M. M. (2004). *Trace evidence analysis: More cases in mute witnesses.* Burlington, MA: Elsevier

James. S., Kish, P., & Sutton, T. P. (2005). *Principles of bloodstain pattern analysis: Theory and practice.* Boca Raton, FL: CRC Press/Taylor & Francis Group.

MacDonell, H. L. (1996). Absence of evidence is not evidence of absence. *Journal of Forensic Identification, 46*(4), 160–164.

Pettler, L. G. (2011). *Crime scene behaviors of crime scene stagers* (Doctoral dissertation). Retrieved from ProQuest (2251577601).

Offenders and Victims

II

Offender Characteristics and Behaviors

4

Introduction

Most often characteristics or traits are things about an individual, group of individuals, or thing that differentiates one from another. In other words, characteristics and traits are special qualities that make something unique (*Merriam-Webster*, 2014, para. 1). When exploring crime scene staging dynamics in homicide cases, it is very important to consider the characteristics or traits of the offender. Although a few empirical studies have identified information about the offender through scientific research on numerous staging behaviors, additional research is desperately needed in this area toward filling the gaps in some of the grayer areas toward really understanding *who is the offender?*

Offender Characteristics

A tremendous amount of financial and human resources are necessary in order to study crime scene staging in a scientific environment. Without the dedication of such resources, developing an empirical model of the offender is impossible. However, even though this deficit in the literature reveals gaping holes in what is known about crime scene staging in general, an exploration of offender characteristics based on studies in homicide, psychology, crime scene staging, and other topics is helpful in identifying some of the most common behaviors of the offender (Eke, 2007; Ferguson, 2011; Geberth, 2010; Pettler, 2011).

Offenders Are Most Often Male

There are currently eight studies and three dissertations on crime scene staging known to the author including the author's *yet-to-be-published study* at the time that this book was written: Eke (2007), Ferguson (2011, 2014), Ferguson and Petherick (2014), Geberth (2010), Hazelwood and Napier (2004), Keppel and Weis (2004), Pettler (2011), Schlesinger et al. (2012), and Turvey (2000), have all generated descriptive characteristics of the offender in staged cases in some form. A total of 340 offenders were studied when combining the offender sample sizes from Eke's (2011), Ferguson's (2011), Pettler's (2011), Schlesinger et al.'s (2012), and Turvey's (2000) studies. Of the 340 offenders studied by these researchers, respectively, 268 offenders or 78.8% were male. Additionally, Hazelwood and Napier (2004) studied approximately 411 fatality-related staged cases by using data collected from 20 investigators and found all 20 investigators unanimously agreed that the offenders in these cases were male. Further, Keppel and Weis (2004) studied 5224 cases and found, of the staged cases in that sample, which was less than 1%, that all of the offenders in that sample were male as well. Thus, the most current research comprehensively indicates that male offenders are more likely to stage homicide crime scenes more than female offenders.

Some studies have delved deep into the demographics of offenders, while other studies have not. Ferguson (2011) and Turvey (2000) both reported that some offenders have a prior background in law enforcement as seven offenders in Ferguson's sample and five offenders in Turvey's sample were found to have background in law enforcement. Additionally, Pettler (2011) found that of the 27 offenders in her sample, 17 offenders were unemployed, 1 offender was self-employed, 4 offenders were unskilled workers, and 5 offenders were semiskilled workers. Eke (2011) found that 2 offenders were students, 5 offenders were retired, 7 offenders were unskilled or semiskilled laborers, 5 offenders worked in lower management, six offenders worked as managers or in a professional capacity, nine offenders were on disability or social assistance, 2 offenders were reported to work *other* jobs, and six offenders' occupational data were missing in Eke's 53-offender sample.

In relation to substance abuse and the staging offender, Pettler (2011) found that 7 offenders were under the influence of alcohol at the time of the murder, 11 offenders were under the influence of drugs at the time of the murder, 16 offenders were known alcoholics generally speaking, and 18 offenders regularly used drugs generally speaking. Eke (2011) also studied offenders in relation to substance abuse and found that 1 offender never used alcohol compared to 11 offenders who never used drugs of Eke's 53-offender sample. Additionally, Eke found that 17 offenders reportedly had no problems with alcohol abuse, 14 reportedly had some problems with alcohol abuse, alcohol reportedly interfered in the lives of 7 offenders, and 14 offenders' information related to alcohol abuse was unavailable. Likewise, Eke found that 10 offenders reportedly had no problems with drug abuse, 5 offenders reportedly had some problems with drug abuse, drug abuse reportedly interfered with 12 offenders' lives, and information on drug-related problems was unavailable for 15 offenders in the sample.

It goes without saying that additional descriptive research is quite necessary when it comes to offenders who stage crime scenes.

Personality

Personality might be defined as how an individual behaves, what emotions an individual expresses, and how an individual thinks about everything in his or her life. To summarize, personality can be encapsulated by identifying behaviors, emotions, and thought or *cognition*. It is arguable that no two people are exactly alike; therefore, that although we can identify behaviors, emotions, and cognition of offenders, no two offenders' personalities are exactly identical either.

Personality theory can be broken into several categories: biological, behavioral, psychodynamic, humanist, and trait theories. One of the most famous biological personality theorists is Hans Eysenck who focused his theory on cortical arousal (Eysenck, 1947). Eysenck (1947) argued that introverts and extroverts experienced very different levels of cortical arousal. That is, that the cortical arousal levels of introverts was very high, so they did not need to seek out external stimulation, while on the other hand, extroverts were quite the opposite experiencing very low levels of cortical arousal and therefore constantly seeking external stimulation. Although Eysenck remains a very controversial psychologist in the history of personality theory development, he is also regarded as one of the most cited and noted personality theorists of all time.

Interestingly, behavioral personality theorists, such as B.F. Skinner, differ tremendously from other categories of personality theorists in several ways. First, Skinner rejected that any internal emotions or cognitions (i.e., thoughts) influence personality, and rather, personality was shaped solely by an individual's interaction with his or her environment (Nye, 1996). Skinner developed what he called *behaviorism* and argued that behavior is determined not by what reinforcement occurs before the stimulus but instead what reinforcement occurs after the stimulus, a process that he called *operant conditioning*. Although behaviorism is not considered a dominant school of thought today in the field of psychology, Skinner's research on operant conditioning is evident in many areas of application.

Sigmund Freud is one of the most recognizable names in the history of psychology and personality development. Freud developed personality theory that included three pieces, the id, the ego, and the superego (Nye, 1996). Freud argued that the id was the unconscious drives that are responsible for identifying an individual's needs and urges that influence the ego and superego. The ego, Freud argued, was the mediator between the id and the superego, while the superego is responsible for an individual's morality and belief system (Nye, 1996). Freud's contributions to personality theory development are some of the most significant in the world. Though many of his ideas are not at the forefront in psychological theory today, his research and dedication to the field cannot be understated.

On the humanistic psychology side, Abraham Maslow was one of the most influential theorists of his time (Nye, 1996). Maslow is known for developing his *hierarchy of needs*, in which he argued that every individual has an innate need to achieve self-actualization, which fosters positive personality development. One of the most notable and unique aspects of Maslow's work was that during a time when most theorists were focused primarily on abnormal behaviors, Maslow chose to focus on positive behaviors. Today, Maslow is still regarded as a prominent figure in the positive psychology movement.

Trait theory is probably one of the most intriguing categories of personality psychology related to crime scene staging. Trait theorists argue that there are five domains or broad traits of personality known collectively as the *Big Five*: extroversion, agreeableness, openness, conscientiousness, and neuroticism (McCrae & Costa, 1987). These five traits, or the *five-factor model*, serve as the fundamental building blocks of personality for trait theorists. Additionally, when it comes to crime scene staging, there is evidence that suggests using the five-factor model as a framework for beginning to flesh out the most commonly observed core personality traits of the offender could be promising (Ferguson, 2011; Pettler, 2011). Again, as with all other areas of crime scene staging research, abundant resources are required to move toward developing a viable, applicable model of the offender.

Criminal justice professionals of all kinds definitely benefit from understanding the psychology behind various types of offenders. When speaking with seasoned law enforcement professionals, it is often they demonstrate inductive thinking by beginning to identify patterns of behavior, emotion, and cognition over time. A specific area that has a plethora of research abound is the area of causality of homicide offenders. It is well known throughout the law enforcement community that many offenders were victimized as children sexually, physically, emotionally, or in other ways, which is believed to have shaped them as individuals resulting in them becoming adult offenders. Additionally, there is a common belief that homicide and substance abuse go hand in hand in many cases, thus the abundance of research which is dedicated to this specific subset of criminality. Being socially isolated is another characteristic often generally associated with some homicide offenders because apprehended offenders are found to be loners and the like.

While some of these premises have been supported by scientific research, it is important to recognize that human judgment is imperfect; thus, it is critical that the accuracy of one's findings on which the research is relied upon for determining which behaviors, emotions, and cognitions are actually present in offenders are combined with criminal justice professionals' education, training, and experience.

Behavior

> Without behavior, there is no event. Without an event, there is no evidence. Without evidence, there is no proof. Without proof, there is no crime. Without a crime, there is no justice for the victim of the offender.

The efforts of the offender to cover-up his or her crime are unique when compared to other types of homicide offenders. For example, a homicide offender who kills via a gang-related drive-by shooting does not normally have any interest in covering up his or her crime. Instead, the gang-related drive-by shooter often kills in an open area, many times a public place that is located within the boundaries of the gang's territory (Douglas, Burgess, Burgess, & Ressler, 2006). Gang-related shootings of this nature differ tremendously from that of the offender in not only location but also in how the crime is executed. While the behavior of the offender is purposeful, directed inward toward self-preservation and frustrating the criminal justice process, the behavior of drive-by shooters is more outwardly reckless demonstrating a complete disregard for public safety while focusing only on their target.

Generally speaking, the behavior of homicide offenders has been scientifically linked to abuse, social isolation, and substance abuse, and likewise in a limited number of studies related to crime scene staging (Eke, 2011; Pettler, 2011). Unlike other types of homicide, the offender in cases where crime scene staging is involved knows no boundaries when it comes to self-interest. The overarching theme, which is observable in every crime scene staging behavior is deception. It appears that some offenders take pride in their work for the most part. That is, they are very keen to ensure they have covered every detail that they can think of before the police are called, before anyone else knows what happened, and before anyone knows what is going on. However, Douglas and Munn (1992) argued that offenders most often make mistakes during the process and that investigators must be aware of the forensic red flags left by the staging offender. Going forward, it is possible that empirical research on offenders could link them to development factors, such as impulsivity and intelligence quotients, but for now, the research rests on simply identifying offender characteristics, victim characteristics, crime scene staging behaviors, and patterns of behavior exhibited by offenders.

Emotionality

It is arguable that murder is highly emotional act and that murder could be one of the most highly emotional experiences an individual might experience in life. There is an enormous amount of tremendously complex emotionality or *affect* involved in committing murder, and it is arguable that anger is the most common negative emotion experienced by an offender during a violent attack. For nearly 20 years, researchers have allocated numerous resources toward the study of emotionality and its factors (Howells & Stacey, 2006). In particular, the focus has centered on specific traits of homicide offenders and how those traits might influence their emotionality, such as anger, during the commission of a homicide. Although anger is not a necessary component in order to commit murder, it is important to recognize the emotion of anger and the role that it plays during the heat of the moment in some cases. In the case of the offender, it has been the experience of the author that the crime scene is reflective of the personality of the offender (Douglas & Douglas, 2006). That means that the offender's personality traits, which drive his emotionality, are evident in the crime scene, even if it is staged. For example, it is arguable that a victim with multiple stab wounds, who is pummeled and beaten to the point that he or she cannot be visually identified, has experienced an extremely powerful and angry attack. This type of attack differs tremendously from the single gunshot coming from 20 yards away because there is no hand-to-hand contact between the offender and the victim in that situation, and second, one gunshot wound to any part of the body differs greatly in nature from multiple stab wounds and multiple blunt force trauma impacts to the victim. Even though the offender might experience a tremendous amount of anger during the assault in hand-to-hand contact or from a distance, while the victim might have taken the brunt of the offender's anger, the offender manipulates the crime scene from what looks like a frenzied attack in its pristine condition completely reflective of anger into a more organized-looking environment maybe by cleaning up or disposing of evidence, for example. Offenders intend to deceive, so once the offender's anger is sated, the offender could experience a euphoric, calm feeling that enables the offender to appear concerned, brokenhearted, or sobbing for the benefit of law enforcement's perception. So, while anger could play a key role in the behavior and emotional response of the offender, the extinguishment of that anger is necessary as well as not to reveal that the offender had anything to do whatsoever with the murder under investigation.

Human beings get angry. At one time or another, everyone experiences anger from time to time. Certain triggers can make certain people very angry, while others do not anger easily at all. Therefore, it is reasonable to explore in this segment what might trigger an offender based on what is known to date from the empirical research to become violent. In addition to anger as discussed earlier, there are several other life-related factors that might trigger an individual to become violent, which could lead to murder leaving the offender panicked over the event that just took place and how to self-preserve. As will be discussed in a later chapter, it is important to mention here that the victim–offender relationship is arguably one of the primary contributors of what triggers the would-be offender and the ebbs and flows that are associated with victim–offender relationship especially when it comes to changes in intimate relationships. Things like intimate partner love triangles, physical abuse, substance abuse, and the like could all be contributing factors to triggering the homicide offender who becomes the offender without any warning. Along with beginning to explore what events are antecedents or precipitators for violent attacks, homicide, and crime scene staging, research has shown that anger varies not only by frequency, that is, how often a homicide offender becomes angry and what triggers precipitate such anger, but also along the lines of anger intensity or to what degree the individual's anger reaches during a triggering event that either leads to a violent assault or escalates all the way to becoming a homicide (Davey, Day, & Howells, 2005).

Cognition

Researchers have demonstrated that some homicide offenders exhibit profound deficits in their cognitive ability (Howells & Stacey, 2006). Howells and Stacey (2006) argued that such deficits might affect the way in which homicide offenders process information and self-regulate. Revisiting trait theory, Barkley (1997) argued that impulsivity, one of the Big Five of trait theory, could play a role on the neurophysiological side of an offender's cognitive skills. Overall, research has demonstrated that self-regulation and cognitive deficiencies contribute to the innate abilities of the homicide offender in the areas of problem solving, information processing, and how the individual perceives his or her environment.

Mental disorders and the offender: Eke (2011) found that 36 of 53 offenders in her sample had a criminal history prior to the murders of the victims in cases analyzed in Eke's study. Of the 36 offenders with prior criminal records, 20 offenders had convictions for violent offenses, 32 offenders had convictions for nonviolent offenses, 4 offenders had convictions for sexual offenses, and 10 offenders had been convicted of domestic violence-related offenses. In relation to these findings, Eke found that 9 offenders had a known mental illness and 7 offenders had been previously diagnosed with having a personality disorder. As with most topics related to crime scene staging, ample financial and human resources are needed to research the vast array of crime scene staging subtopics, such as mental disorders and crime scene staging.

The study of mental disorders and psychiatric illnesses of homicide offenders has long been a controversial subject among researchers (Howells & Stacey, 2006). However, even so, some very clear observable and measurable mental disorders have been diagnosed and documented within incarcerated offender populations (Howells & Stacey, 2006). For example, the new *Diagnostic and Statistical Manual of Mental Disorders,* Fifth Edition (DSM-V) of the American Psychiatric Association is a newly organized manual for diagnosing mental illnesses. The DSM-IV as with previous versions were organized by axis, or a group of similar disorders classified by similar characteristics under one broad heading. The new DSM-V, however, has moved to a nonaxial diagnostic system that combined axes I, II, and III, while recognizing the importance of delineated areas for medical conditions (i.e., cancer), psychosocial, mental deficiency, and the contextual elements of mental disease found in axes II and III (WebMD, LLC, 2014). Axis I, for example, which previously included anxiety, depressive, and schizophrenic disorders, is now integrated with axis II's personality disorders, such as borderline personality disorder and antisocial personality disorder. This new approach is thought to provide a more suitable foundation for treatment providers to develop more highly effective treatment plans overall. There was a high occurrence of homicide offenders who were diagnosed using the DSM-IV's axis system before the new nonaxial system in the DSM-V was released. These homicide offenders were commonly diagnosed with axis I and axis II disorders, such as schizophrenia and personality disorders alike (Howells & Stacey, 2006). In particular, more than half of the population analyzed met the criteria for antisocial personality disorder, an axis II disorder, which was the most commonly diagnosed personality disorder of this spectrum, citing historical factors in offenders' histories, such as conduct disorder, failure to take responsibility for one's actions, lying, lawbreaking, and inability to show remorse (Howells & Stacey, 2006, p. 79).

Again, it is unknown at this time whether the majority of offenders or even some would fall on the formerly known axis II diagnostic continuum of the DSM-IV, but based on Eke's (2011) findings combined with the author's education, training, and experience, it is arguable that they might. Another interesting aspect of this type of research is the work of Robert Hare (1991). Hare (1991) explored the psychological realm of psychopathy, which over time became very important in the field of psychology toward understanding homicidal offenders. The first reason Hare's (1991) work has been brought to the forefront by scholar–practitioners is because Hare developed a quantitative checklist system to measure psychopathy called the Psychopathy Checklist–Revised (PCL-R) (Howells & Stacey, 2006). Because of the overall success of Hare's (1991) PCL-R, it is widely used toward assessing inmates in correctional facilities and used as a basis for predicting recidivism or the unknown variable of will an offender reoffend upon release (Howells & Stacey, 2006). The author would argue that a fascinating study on crime scene staging might include applying Hare's (1991) PCL-R to a purposive sample of incarcerated offenders coupled with a longitudinal qualitative piece designed to track each known stager's behaviors during incarceration and postrelease.

Envirosocioculturalism

During the course of the author's experience, education, training, and research in homicide studies, forensic psychology, forensic science, crime reconstruction, and crime scene staging, it became apparent that the crime scene stager is a unique and fascinating type of homicide offender. The author would argue that in order to begin to understand the complexity that is the crime scene stager, one must delve deep in the numerous aspects that generally influence any individual's personality, cognition, emotionality, and behavior as it relates to an individual's cumulative environment, social group, and culture (Figure 4.1).

Thus, the author created the concept of *envirosocioculturalism*, which is the aggregate of environmental, social, and cultural conditions that influence the life of an individual combined with the circumstances by which one is surrounded as part of a community distinguishable by particular ways of living within the social construct and its unique identity as seen in its beliefs, customs, religion, lifestyle, professions, interpersonal relationships, and routine activities.

Environment: Environment is the foundation and framework of envirosocioculturalism. It might be helpful to think of one's environment as the skeleton of life. Everything an individual experiences are products of environment in one way or another. Shelter, food, safety, and other physiological resources are all drawn from various sources and locations within an environment. Abraham Maslow (1943) argued in his article "Theory of Human Motivation" that individuals develop along a hierarchy of needs that begins with physiological needs and moves through several other categories, such as safety, love and belonging, esteem, and finally to self-actualization. Maslow (1943) argued further that achievement of each step of the hierarchy is necessary in order to eventually achieve the goal of self-actualization.

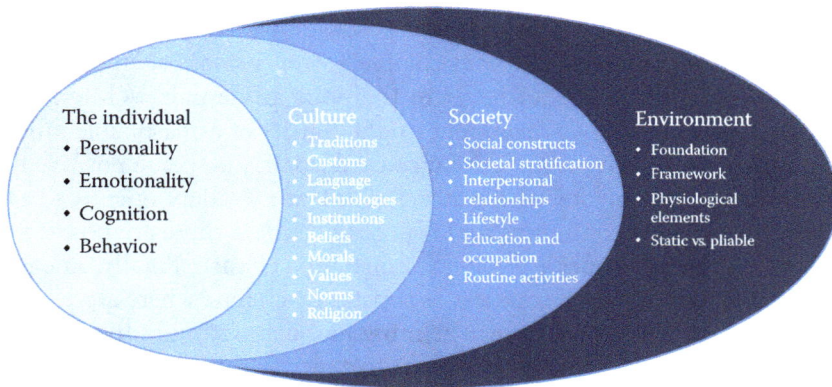

Figure 4.1 Envirosocioculturalism

Environmental psychology can be defined as the study of the interrelationships between environments and the affect, behavior, and cognition of human beings. Numerous researchers have studied affect, behavior, and cognition in relation to environment over the years and theorized that environmental factors play a role in how human beings function (DeYoung, 2013). It is important to recognize when discussing environment that environments are both organic and man-made constructs that fall on a continuum ranging from static, to pliable, to fluid based on the amount of change of their environmental patterns. A static environment might be defined as an environment where no environmental conditions or factors, such as physiological needs like shelter, food, water, and safety, change in pattern at any time. That is, an environment where all necessary components remain stable and constant over time. A pliable environment might be defined as an environment that experiences a reasonable amount of change in conditions and factors resulting in a normal amount of an environmental pattern shift over time. In other words, a pliable environment might be one where change is managed and expected. However, a fluid environment might be defined as an environment that is constantly changing. A fluid environment might be one where no environmental pattern remains consistent over time and one where conditions and factors change constantly.

When considering these hypothetical types of environments and their conditions, it is easy to understand that static, pliable, and fluid environments could also fall on a continuum of positive or negative. Everything that surrounds an individual are constructs of his or her environment that each individual might experience positively, negatively, or both. In a positive static environment, individuals understand exactly what to expect, when, where, what, why, and how. There are no surprises, no last-minute changes, and no reason to alter any response to any environmental factor. In contrast, a negative static environment containing negative factors and conditions, such as a lack of resources of all kinds, oppresses individuals to where most cannot find their way out. Additionally, a positive pliable environment might include environmental factors that change within reason, such as shifts in resources and structures, but never to the point of despair. While in contrast, a negative pliable environment might consist of a reasonable amount of change negatively to resources that cause despair. Further, a positive fluid environment might be one where individuals learn to adapt quickly to ever-changing fast-paced conditions and factors and where there are no expectations except that resources are going to constantly change. Finally, a negative fluid environment might be one that is constantly chaotic where all resources ebb and flow to the point of overwhelming and distracting individuals who never know what is coming next or what to expect.

Environment in relation to offenders is a topic that is yet to be formally and extensively researched using empirical research design specific to offenders as a special population at a sophisticated level. Regardless, in conjunction with the belief that there is credence to Maslow's hierarchy of needs and environmental factors, such as food, water, shelter, and safety in relation to affect, behavior, and cognition, the authors would be remiss to negate the importance the implied influence environment might have on the offender and how he or she stages a crime scene.

Society: Society is the second piece of envirosocioculturalism. Societies are built within environments. Society might be defined as the totality of social constructs of a given environment. Generally speaking, societies share the same geographic location and are maintained within a specific territory. *Societal stratification* is the way in which a society is divided into subgroups based on some common or differential factor, such as resources and roles within the society, for example. Historically speaking, since ancient times, societies were built within newly discovered environments. As groups of people began to traverse planet earth, societies, such as hunting and gathering, pastoral, agrarian, and horticultural, were formed based on what resources were available in the environment. Hunting and gathering societies maintained themselves by gathering food and hunting wild animals, while pastoral societies relied almost entirely on herded life stock for survival. Agrarian societies focused on cultivating the land by growing crops for sustainment, but horticultural societies established in jungle-like environments grew plants in containers to feed the people.

It is arguable that offenders are influenced by societal factors found within their environments. Take, for example, the individual who grows up in an urban environment in the lower socioeconomic status of society. This hypothetical individual's environment could be positively or negatively static, pliable, or fluid in relation to resources, such as shelter, food, water, and safety, because societally speaking, this individual has little to rely on toward securing adequate amounts of each. This individual might be passed by for employment, friendships, scholastic opportunities, or other societal constructs that the authors would argue are necessary components for normal human development simply because he or she is *poor*. It is a well-known debate among scholar–practitioners of various types and even in some groups of the general public that poverty causes crime, but to date, research has only demonstrated a correlation between poverty and crime rather than poverty being identified as a primary causal factor of crime. So why is it then that it is important to recognize society as a piece of the puzzle in relation to understanding characteristics of the offender? It is because of the major premises argued in the philosophical debate of *nature versus nurture*.

The nature versus nurture debate is one of the oldest psychological debates in the history of psychology and is almost timeless at this point. The basic idea of this debate is the amount of influence an individual's genetic code or heredity has versus the amount of influence an individual's environment has on his or her ability to advance within a society. Proponents for nature might argue that all individuals are genetically predispositioned toward societal advancement, while opponents might argue that an individual's environment is the key factor for societal advancement. Regardless of which side of the argument one might sit on, the fact is that the debate exists due to the extreme importance of both heredity and physiological needs combined with how the environment might point an individual toward societal advancement.

Interpersonal relationships: Interpersonal relationships might be defined as the ongoing social interactions one individual has with another individual or group of individuals within a societal structure. Interpersonal relationships might vary in intensity, intimacy, and purpose in relation to why two individuals or more are related based on societal constructs, such as lifestyle and profession. The study of interpersonal relationships is one of the most important areas of focus in relation to crime scene staging. Eke (2007), Ferguson, (2011), and Pettler (2011) found that more crime scenes were staged where there was an intimate interpersonal relationship versus scenes were there was no relationship between the victim and offender. More about interpersonal relationships will be discussed in Chapter 6.

Lifestyle: Psychologist Alfred Adler studied lifestyle in relation to personality development (Powers & Griffith, 1987). Lifestyle might be defined as a sociological construct that involves how an individual lives on a daily basis. It is all the rage in today's media that living a healthy lifestyle includes healthy food and exercise for starters. Proponents of healthy living advocate for a variety of lifestyle choices that arguably promote happiness and prosperity.

But what about lifestyles that breed the risk of becoming a victim of violent crime? Though victimology and suspectology will be discussed in Chapters 5 and 10, within the discussion of lifestyle, it is important to recognize that certain lifestyles put individuals at a greater risk for becoming a victim of violent crime than others. For example, an individual who is well educated, maintains stable employment, is married with children, and lives in a suburb of a metropolitan area is at much less risk of becoming a victim of violent crime than, for instance, an unmarried and without children, high school dropout substance abuser living on the streets of an urban area and prostitutes him or herself for food and temporary shelter. Lifestyles that involve substance abuse (e.g., alcohol and drugs), homelessness, drug dealing, prostitution, and the like are considered high risk by the authors because of the environmental, societal, and cultural issues surrounding those types of lifestyles. Further, low-risk lifestyle examples might include individuals who are educated with steady jobs and who are nonsubstance abusers.

It is true that offenders come from all *walks of life*. That means just because someone is a substance abuser living on the streets does not mean he or she could become a murderer just as someone living in suburbia might not become a murderer either. What is interesting in relation to the discussion of lifestyle and crime scene staging is that preliminary research has generally implied that like affect, personality, behavior, cognition, environment, and society, lifestyle plays a role in how and why an offender decides to stage a crime scene. As empirical research has confirmed, it is the experience of the author that far less street crimes are staged than are intimate partner relationships throughout all socioeconomic strata (Eke, 2011; Ferguson, 2011; Pettler, 2011). So, it is critical to consider what it is about intimate partner crime scene staging that might be related to lifestyle.

The author would argue that domestic violence or intimate partner violence, while it is criminal, unethical, and inhumane for starters, can affect one's lifestyle in many negative ways. Intimate partner violence is an encompassing term that describes patterns of behavior an individual exhibits to gain power and control over another individual. Intimate partner violence can affect a victim's lifestyle because the battered victim might not be psychologically, emotionally, and/or physiologically well enough to maintain healthy living habits. Additionally, engaging in a violent relationship arguably increases the chances of becoming a victim of violent crime. Aside from the obvious damage physical abuse would cause short term or long term on any battered victim male or female; domestic violence, the victim–offender relational connection, and lifestyle are intrinsically related when it comes to crime scene staging.

Education and occupation: Although no empirical research exists that correlates profession to offender in relation to crime scene staging, anecdotally speaking, the way in which offenders stage crime scenes may be related to the offender's education and occupation. Again, Douglas and Munn (1992) argued that the drives that influence daily behavior influence criminal behavior as well. Additionally, Petherick and Ferguson (2009) argued that offenders demonstrate behavioral consistency, that is, that their behavior runs concurrent in both their criminal and noncriminal acts. Thus, it is arguable that offenders stage crime scenes based on what they know, what is familiar, what is available, what is convenient, and what they believe is going to be believable to law enforcement. For example, in 2013, former medical doctor Martin MacNeill was found guilty of first-degree murder for killing his wife Michele MacNeill (Cable News Network, 2013). According to a Cable News Network (2013) article recapping the trial, former Dr. MacNeill staged the crime scene to appear as though Michele MacNeill died as the result of an accidental drowning in their home. Husband Martin MacNeill was having an affair with the couple's nanny and wanted to marry her, so he convinced his wife Michele that she needed to undergo face-lift surgery. Subsequently, witnesses testified during the trial that MacNeill overmedicated his wife in the early stages of her recovery leaving her in a semiconscious state. After drugging his wife and as she took a bath, prosecutors argued that MacNeill offered to assist his wife in getting out of the bathtub but instead held her head under water until she drowned. Prosecutor Chad Grunander argued to the jury in the following closing arguments:

> Martin MacNeill murdered his wife Michele. Her death was not the result of an accident, and it certainly was not the result of a heart condition...The defendant carried out a cold and calculated plan to murder his wife. He relied on his knowledge and experience as a doctor and also as a lawyer to accomplish this. (para. 5)

It is arguable that in the MacNeill case, profession and education played a key role in how this offender chose to kill his wife and stage the scene to look like an accident. For comparison, would the drug user living in a motel with his live-in on-again off-again girlfriend chose the same method of staging? Arguably he would not. It is important to recognize in the MacNeill case that this offender stayed on course with what he knew in relation to his profession and education; therefore, this is a case where victimology and suspectology are so critically important so that the fine details of what outweighs why this case is a staged homicide and not an unfortunate accident are revealed. The MacNeill case is a great example of the integration of behavioral and physical evidence toward building a robust and substantial case that ultimately convicted this offender.

Routine activities: Related to lifestyle, profession, socioeconomic status, education, and related ideas is the concept of criminality being connected to an individual's routine activities. Routine activities can be just about anything: drinking and substance abuse, prostitution, drug dealing, sports, recreation, scholastic, religious, work, and all other types of activities of which an individual might engage. For the purpose of this discussion, routine activities could be defined as the normal, regular, and frequent activities engaged in by a victim and/or a homicide offender either individually or collectively. Again, embedded in the foundational principles of victimology and suspectology, routine activities are important in understanding who the victim and the suspect are. It is critical to all death scene investigations that just because the surviving party called 911 claiming that their intimate partner just committed suicide does not mean that is the truth! The intricate analysis of the crime scene and physical evidence matched up to the behavioral evidence often revealed throughout the investigation and in victimology and suspectology is the way to decipher if the scene is staged as a suicide versus being an actual murder. It is the opinion of the author that routine activities play a large role in the staging of homicide crime scenes because, generally speaking, offenders, although experiencing the extreme emotionality that is homicide, *stick to what they know* and do not stray too far outside the scope of what is familiar, regular, and comfortable.

Cohen and Felson (1979) proposed a *routine activities theory*, which was grounded by the following three major premises:

1. An individual's lifestyle contributes to the amount of contact an individual has with potential criminal offenders.
2. Would-be offenders typically evaluate their potential victims for how vulnerable they are toward becoming a victim. That is, do potential victims have individuals who will protect them or are they more isolated and responsible for self-protection?
3. Potential victims' lifestyles or routine activities are correlated with becoming a victim.

Therefore, it is arguable based on Cohen and Felson's (1979) routine activities theory that not only do routine activities influence how individuals could become victims of crime, but in turn offenders as well not only size up their potential victims' degree of isolation, but the routine activities (i.e., lifestyle) of the offender are correlated to how and why they stage crime scenes the specific ways they do.

For example, as discussed earlier, the now convicted former Dr. Martin MacNeill's routine activities as a physician were genuinely reflected in how he chose to stage his crime scene as a substance-induced accident or the result of an unknown medical condition. In contrast, it is unlikely that an individual without medical training would have chosen to stage his or her crime scene in the same manner because the knowledge used by MacNeill was innately embedded in the culmination of his profession, education, training, and experience. Routine activities are integral parts of any individual's lifestyle. Familiarity is often connected to feeling safe and secure, thus activities that are normal and regular are often reflected in staged crime scenes as well.

Culture: Culture is the third piece of the theoretical concept, envirosocioculturalism. For the purpose of this discussion, culture could be defined as the traditions, customs, language, beliefs, morals, values, norms, technologies, institutions, religion, and forces by which individuals construct their daily lives. There are many different types of cultures. Take, for example, one small city of 10,000 people. The entire 10,000 people make up one society of course, but dissecting the group further requires examination of culture. Popular trends related to culture might identify various subcultures that are specifically related to routine activities and lifestyle, such as drinking alcoholic beverages, illicit drug use, drinking coffee, art, music, sports, games, entertainment of all sorts, food, profession, and many more. So it is arguable that even within a society of 10,000 people, there can be shared and differential cultural aspects embedded within each social group maintained simultaneously with each subculture's aspects as well. Even though it is true that some cultural elements might overlap, such as elements of the drinking culture with the entertainment culture, it is vital to recognize as well how distinctive each culture is from one another.

Because emotionality, behavior, and cognition are interrelated among themselves, it is also the case that they play an integral role in an individual's culture. As discussed throughout this chapter, it is arguable that offenders are influenced by a variety of factors encompassed in the concept of envirosocioculturalism. Though it is speculative at best, it has been the experience of the author that culture plays a role for the offender when it comes to determining what is most likely the most believable when staging a crime scene. Regardless of the type of scene staged, homicide was made to look like an accident or suicide, for example, the offender stages the crime scene based on a combination of weighed factors that the author would argue are influenced by innate factors, such as personality, emotionality, cognition, and behavior, in relation to envirosocioculturalistic factors like environment, society, and culture. Culturally speaking, it is arguable that the offender from Montana holds different envirosociocultural values than the offender from Miami Beach, Florida. Therefore, these could be two very differently staged crime scenes. The crime scene from Miami Beach might involve routine activities, lifestyle, and profession or education influences while the same can be said for the Montana crime scene, but the two scenes are staged totally differently. Though research is yet to be conducted on variables related to culture and how it might influence or predict crime scene staging behaviors, the implication that crime scene staging is influence by envirosocioculturalistic factors is certainly observable and notable even in this early stage.

Subcultures of violence: Subculture of violence theory stems from subculture theory in general, which was developed by the Chicago School of Professional Psychology. The overarching idea of subculture of violence theory is that within a culture, certain subcultures can develop that accept violence as a means to an end. That is, violence is an acceptable method for settling arguments, gaining power and control, and maintaining respect from an individual or group of individuals under all circumstances. A subculture accepts violence as part of their lifestyle, and therefore the cultural norms, beliefs, and values of the subculture revolve around violence. But when examining and breaking down the subculture of violence idea even further, it is arguable that even families comprised of merely two intimate partners can develop their own subculture of violence that transcends into lifestyle adaptations in acceptance of violence as the way of life. A lonely woman, for example, who recently was divorced from a cheating husband who did not love her moves in with a new boyfriend.

The new boyfriend might never have displayed any type of aggression or violence toward the woman prior to her moving into his house. However, the new boyfriend now has power and control over the woman once she is settled in his house, and he blames her for making him so angry all the time. Extremely, emotionality leads to negative thinking, and negative thinking eventually leads to violence against the woman while he convinces her his violent outbursts is just the way things are there. Having moved into the subculture of his particular environment, the woman accepts violence as just being part of their lifestyle and continues being abused; until 1 day, he strangles her to death and stages it as a suicide. Suicide is common in this subculture, so this offender weighs the factors, and based on everything he knows about his envirosocioculturalism, he thinks suicide is believable. Even in this hypothetical example, it is observable how a subculture can capture and hold someone within its invisible walls until it is too late to escape, risk escape, or seek refuge. More about intimate partner violence in relation to crime scene staging is discussed in Chapter 6.

Culture in relation to violence is an age-old debate; and a hot topic of recent years has been centered on a related debate between the sports culture in relation to how it responds to violence against persons. One of the pivotal cases that brought this debate to the forefront was the case of former Pennsylvania State University football coach Jerry Sandusky. Over the span of several years, it was alleged that Sandusky sexually assaulted male children he met through a community organization. Further, it is currently alleged that the first reported instances of abuse went without repercussion, but later when Sandusky was arrested on the heels of subsequent reports, Pennsylvania State University responded in a much different manner. One of the key points discussed by individuals of all kinds was the issue of the *football culture* at Pennsylvania State University. Supporters argued that the situation was handled appropriately generally speaking. Opponents argued that Pennsylvania State's interests in its football program trumped the interest of children who claimed to have been abused by Sandusky. Sandusky was eventually convicted of abusing male children, and in turn, this case brought forth numerous issues surrounding Pennsylvania State's football culture and its reaction to alleged violence within itself.

Another example of how culture might influence a response to violence against persons is that of law enforcement itself. It is arguable that law enforcement is a very close-knit, closed culture. This means it is very difficult to be allowed into the group in the first place; then one must demonstrate adherence to specific norms in order to gain acceptance and further to remain as an accepted member of this social group. The law enforcement culture in some ways is similar to the cliché "Don't ask, don't tell" often heard in the military regarding homosexuality. Using domestic abuse as an example, it is arguable that victims might not report for a variety of reasons. One reason might be that victims do not think anyone will believe them.

Crime Scene Staging Behavior

At this point, it is important to have a brief discussion about *epistemology*. Epistemology simplistically speaking might be defined as *the study of knowledge*. First, it is important to define terms. For the purpose of this discussion, there are three types of knowledge, which include:

1. Knowledge of what something is.
2. Knowledge of why something is.
3. Knowledge of how to do something.

Quantitative knowledge is the knowledge of what something is. Quantitative knowledge is numerically measurable. So, for example, quantitative characteristics of a car would be its size, shape, and weight. When applying this concept to crime scene staging, empirical research can confirm quantitative aspects of what crime scene staging is, such as the manipulation of both physical and verbal evidence toward misdirecting an investigation in simple terms. The knowledge of why something is, is *qualitative knowledge*. Qualitative knowledge about a car might be its color, texture, or its smell. When applying this concept to crime scene staging, researchers have hypothesized that offenders stage crime scenes ultimately to avoid apprehension. Third, while the author would argue that it is important to know what something is (i.e., the quantitative data), it is equally as important to know why something is (i.e., the qualitative data), but knowledge does not stop there. The third type of knowledge of how to do something is just as important as knowing the *what* and the *why*. Knowing how to do something is very different than knowing what or why something is because knowing how involved behavior. One might know what a cup of coffee is and further knows why people like to drink coffee in general, but knowing how to create, produce, or make a cup of coffee depends on the education, training, and experience of the individual. Clearly, this portion of a discussion on knowledge alone could go on and on, but the focus is centered on understanding that there are different types of knowledge in relation to anything in the world including crime scene staging.

Next, it is important to differentiate between belief and truth. A belief might be defined as something one trusts or something for which one has faith. For example, an individual climbs into a boat believing that it is safe, but when the boat sinks, it is obvious that the individual was wrong and the boat was not safe. Second, simply speaking the truth might be defined as having proof of a belief. Although that might sound strange, consider the murder trial, *North Carolina v. Alan Tessnear*, of which the author was a part. In this case, the defendant asserted that he was simply attempting to retrieve a firearm from beneath a living room end table when as he waved it through the air, it went off accidently shooting his wife dead. The defendant claimed that he was not near his wife at the time and the firearm discharged at some distance away. Upon investigation, investigators believed that Alan Tessnear was lying. Instead, investigators believed that the defendant pointed the firearm at his wife at very close range and deliberately shot her in the head. Based on investigators' education, training, and experience, the aforementioned assertion is what they *believed*. But a belief is not the truth in an American court of law, rather a belief could be contrived as even a mere thought or feeling. The thing that tips the scale and makes investigators' beliefs turn into truths is not personal knowledge, but empirical testing. In the Tessnear case, investigators chose to test the firearm and measure the diameter of the gunshot residue left on targets at 1 in., 2 in., 3 in., and so on. In consultation with the medical examiner in this case, investigators were able to substantiate or turn their belief into truth by demonstrating to the court that the diameter of gunshot residue left on the victim's head was similar in diameter to the gunshot residue left on the 2 in. target. This demonstration helps explain to the jury that what the defendant claimed in this case was scientifically untrue. The defendant was convicted of his wife's murder, sentenced to life in prison, and his appeal was denied.

So when examining the evidence left by offenders, it is imperative to not only answer and identify the *what*, but it is also important to identify the *why*, as well as it is critical to identify the *how*, therefore ending up with what the offender did, why the offender did it, and how the offender did it. Is the *why* necessary for successful prosecution? Not necessarily, but motive can be very helpful to prosecutors when arguing during opening and closing statements about why this victim in particular is dead. This concept is discussed more in Chapters 5 through 7.

Categorizing Crime Scene Staging Behaviors

Resting on the discussion of epistemology earlier, few studies have confirmed the existence of crime scene staging and identified various types of staging and related behavioral patterns, but it does exist. For the purpose of this discussion, empirical means scientific information, that is, having gained knowledge through a research design with the stated objectives to observe and/or to experiment, which are then analyzed quantitatively, qualitatively, or both. This definition begs the question: Is personal experience empirical? Pardeck (1996) argued, "empirical knowledge is grounded in traditional scientific inquiry, whereas personal knowledge is based on one's objective interpretation of personal experience" (p. 14). In theory, it is typical and appropriate for investigators to use a combination of empirically based knowledge and their own personal/professional experience-based knowledge to do their jobs. However, it is arguable that drawing from one individual's knowledge base of personal/professional experience only is a slippery slope. As illustrated in Chapter 1, crime scene staging has a long way to go before many of the beliefs about crime scene staging are converted to truths or mistruths. In the meantime, it is important therefore to remain ultraconservative, as to not overreach or state beyond the scope of what is empirically known to date about crime scene staging, offenders, and their victims.

Crime Scene Staging, Research, and Typologies

Some might argue that crime scene staging is an admission of guilt because if the offender believed he had done nothing wrong, then there would be no reason to stage the scene. While that could be true in some cases, in the author's opinion, research is still necessary in order to continue identifying offender characteristics and victim characteristics that is useful and effective for crime scene fieldwork (Ferguson, 2011; Pettler, 2011).

At this point in the discussion, it is important to lay a foundation that explains a bit about research in order to understand the crime scene staging behaviors and patterns identified in Pettler's (2011) study, "Crime Scene Behaviors of Offenders." As discussed in Chapter 1, Pettler's (2011) qualitative study examined the case files of 18 individual homicide victims and 27 offenders. Each of the 18 cases was adjudicated, and offender crime scene staging was evident in each case. Pettler developed six theoretical categories or typologies in order to classify the more than 100 crime scene staging behaviors confirmed to exist in her study. Pettler called these hypothetical categories (1) the cleaner, (2) the concealer, (3) the creator, (4) the fabricator, (5) the inflictor, and (6) the planner. In order to develop these speculative six *typologies* in the first place, based on her education, training, the published literature, and her experience working staged homicide cases, Pettler placed 31 crime scene behaviors known to her between the six categories. For example, Pettler placed the crime scene behavior of cleaning up blood in *the cleaner* category. During the data analysis portion of her study, Pettler identified 62 new crime scene staging behaviors. Because some crime scene staging behaviors generously overlapped with other similar behaviors, Pettler merged similar behaviors into one behavior, for example, the behavior *cleaned-up crime scene* and *cleaned-up house* were combined into *cleaned-up crime scene*. Definitions and descriptions of each of the six crime scene staging categories or *typologies* along with their associated crime scene behaviors and behavioral patterns are as follows.

The Cleaner

The cleaner's whole mission as an offender is to clean up the mess created by the homicide. Maybe there was a struggle and household items were broken or maybe blood was spattered throughout the inside of a car. Regardless of the location of the crime scene or the type of evidence that needs to be cleaned, the cleaner attempts to strip the scene of all evidence of the crime. Interestingly, the cleaner uses either household cleaners he or she has readily available or goes out before or after the crime to purchase such items. The cleaner attempts to remove every trace of blood or other biological evidence using bleach, air fresheners, powder cleaners, fans, air conditioners, and various types of fabrics. Another interesting behavior of the cleaner is that he or she might wash his or her clothes or even sometimes wash the victim's clothes after the commission of the crime. Some cleaners clean other items affected by the crime like knives, tools, weapons, furniture, and just about anything that might contain evidence of the crime. It is important to recognize the significance of a car involved in the homicide, and the cleaner wastes no time cleaning and scouring his or her vehicle even in inclement weather, in the middle of the night, or any other time of day normally immediately following the homicide. There are several behaviors associated with the cleaner as found in Pettler's (2011, pp. 161–162) study:

1. Offender cleaned areas of the crime scene.
   a. Offender cleaned the residence.
   b. Offender cleaned the vehicle.
   c. Offender bathed the victim.
   d. Offender bathed him- or herself.
2. Offender used cleaning products to clean areas of crime scene.
   a. Offender used bleach.
   b. Offender used other cleaning products.
   c. Offender used air freshener and/or carpet deodorizer.
3. Offender used fans and/or air conditioner to clean the air of crime scene.

Pettler's (2011) analysis of the cleaner crime scene staging data revealed that 10 offenders attempted to clean the crime scene, cleaned their cars, cleaned the victims, or cleaned themselves.

The Concealer

The concealer is even more about secrets than the cleaner. The primary objective of the concealer is to hide anything related to the crime that he or she thinks might reveal his guilt. The concealer hides weapons, the victim's body, or other crime scene evidence attempting to conceal his or her involvement in the crime. One of the more interesting behaviors of the concealer is the way he or she destroys evidence in order to conceal it. Most often, Pettler (2011) found that the concealer destroyed evidence using fire, water, or both. Further, it is critical to note that running parallel with the act of concealing, the concealer was also found to flee the crime scene and he or she might or might not report the victim missing. According to Pettler (2011), crime scene staging behaviors and behavioral patterns associated with the concealer are (pp. 162–164) as follows:

1. Offender wore gloves/mask or covered his or her hands.
2. Offender redressed victim in fresh clothes.
3. Offender removed the evidence from the scene.
   a. Removed victim's clothes from the victim and the crime scene.
   b. Removed bedding from the crime scene.
   c. Removed the carpet from a house or vehicle.
   d. Removed the clothes from the person or was naked during the crime(s).
4. Offender changed his or her own clothes before and/or after committing the crime(s).
5. Offender discarded the evidence in a field.
6. Offender discarded the evidence along a road.
7. Offender hid the weapon or disposed of the weapon.
   a. Discarded the weapon in the water (e.g., river, pond, lake).
   b. Discarded the weapon in the water from the middle of a bridge.
   c. Put the weapon in a box and discarded with garbage.
8. Offender wrapped the victim's body in bedding and/or plastic.
9. Offender placed towels and/or plastic around the victim's head.
10. Offender fled the crime scene where the victim's body would be found.
11. Offender asked a friend for a ride from the crime scene or near the crime scene.
12. Offender transported the victim's body for disposal.
13. Offender drove the evidence to different state or distant location.
14. Offender disguised the evidence (e.g., painted evidence, remodeled).
15. Offender burned the evidence.
16. Offender did not report that the victim was missing.

Pettler's (2011) analysis of the concealer crime scene data revealed that all 27 offenders hid crime scene evidence before or after the murders.

The Creator

The creator is an interesting offender. The creator adds to the crime scene instead of taking from the crime scene like the cleaner and concealer. The creator moves the victim, moves the weapon, or any relevant item in order to make the crime scene appear as though something else besides what actually happened took place. This is the type of offender that builds the crime scene to make it look like an accident, suicide, or sexual assault homicide (Geberth, 1996a, 2006). Some offenders in this category might even take blood and put it in the crime scene in places that do not make sense to seasoned investigators or that do not make sense in accordance with the rest of the crime scene.

One of the other ways these offenders stage their scenes is by making the crime scene into a home invasion–type crime scene. They attempt to stage a break-in by breaking windows, marking up doors or windows with tool marks, or making obvious attempts at forced entry into the location. The creator contains the following behaviors and behavioral patterns (Pettler, 2011, pp. 164–165):

1. Offender approached the victim for assistance.
2. Offender offered gift to the victim or victim's relative.
3. Offender lured the victim with something the victim wanted.
4. Offender created the evidence in the scene.
   a. Staged as a home invasion/robbery/murder.
   b. Staged stranger abduction/sexual assault/murder.
   c. Staged as suicide.
   d. Staged as accident.
   e. Staged as other.
5. Offender moved the live victim in the crime scene one time.
6. Offender moved the live victim in the crime scene multiple times.
7. Offender moved the victim's body in the crime scene once.
8. Offender moved the victim's body in the crime scene multiple times.
9. Offender moved the weapon in the crime scene.
10. Offender positioned or posed the victim's body at the crime scene or a dump site.
11. Offender planted the evidence at another location.

Pettler's (2011) analysis of "the creator" crime scene data revealed that all 27 offenders created crime scene evidence before or after the murders.

The Fabricator

The fabricator might not be as into cleaning up, destroying evidence, or making a crime scene appear to be a break-in, but instead, this type of offender relies heavily on his or her persuasive ability by lying to investigators about what happened. The fabricator concocts sometimes very elaborate, far-fetched stories about victims and their whereabouts, such as (Pettler, 2011, p. 165) the following:

1. The victim ran away from his or her children, family, friends, and life.
2. The victim committed suicide.
3. The victim was killed in an accident (e.g., drowning).
4. The victim attacked the offender.
5. The victim ran away with an individual of whom he or she was having an extramarital affair.
6. The victim attempted to rob the offender (e.g., pulling a weapon such as a knife or gun).

Another fascinating aspect of the fabricator is that he or she might also concoct specific lies especially made for only friends and family about the victim and his or her whereabouts and/or even about the offender and his or her whereabouts. It is important to note that this informational exchange most often occurs before the victim is reported missing either by the offender or by someone else. It is not uncommon that the offender continues the charade with friends and family during the investigation as well. The fabricator might (Pettler, 2011, pp. 165–166) do the following:

1. Offender contacted the police.
2. Offender gave statement(s) to the police.
3. Offender lied to the police.
4. Offender gave false name to the police.
5. Offender claimed it was an accident.
6. Offender claimed it was suicide.
7. Offender claimed that the victim ran off.
8. Offender claimed to see the victim leave.
9. Offender claimed to not see the victim leave.
10. Offender robbed the victim.
11. Offender lied to family, friends, and acquaintances, as to the victim's location.
12. Offender sold the victim's resources, claimed the victim loaned resources to the offender, or purchased the resources.

Pettler's (2011) analysis of "the fabricator" crime scene data revealed that all 27 offenders lied before or after the murders.

The Inflictor

The inflictor is a simple yet determined offender. So determined that the inflictor actually creates wounds on him- or herself in order to stage evidence of an attack that didn't happen during the event. Normally, the inflictor claims he or she too was attacked either by the victim or by an attacker who attacked both the offender and the victim. The inflictor might (Pettler, 2011, p. 167) do the following:

1. Self-inflict wounds
2. Claim self-defense

Pettler's (2011) analysis of "the inflictor" crime scene data revealed that none of the offenders inflicted injuries on themselves before or after the murders.

The Planner

The planner is cunning and calculated. This offender spends a lot of time preparing for the murder. He or she organizes every little thing and plans the murder down to the smallest foreseeable detail. One of the most important things to recognize about the planner is that he or she is strongly associated with borrowing things or buying things prior to or immediately following the murder. Things a planner might borrow from friends, neighbors, and family are weapons, shovels, vehicles, documents, or other necessary tools before actually approaching the victim (Pettler, 2011, p. 168). In addition, a planner will bring the weapon to the crime scene even if it is only his or her hands. Planners who are partnered with another offender might utilize that second party as a lookout during the approach and murder of the victim. Another use of the second party is as a driver for a getaway vehicle near the crime scene to make sure they can make a clean escape. Another behavioral pattern seen in planners is that they might plan the kidnapping of the victim at the primary crime scene instead of murdering the victim during the initial criminal trespass. Planners might also restrain a live victim or their kidnapped victims then transport them somewhere else where the murder and disposal of the body will actually occur. Behavioral evidence of the planner are as follows (Pettler, 2011, p. 168):

1. Offender brought the weapon to the crime scene.
2. Offender used a lookout.
3. Offender kidnapped and/or restrained the victim.
4. Offender tried to or transported the victim to another location for murder.
5. Offender staged getaway driver/vehicle near the crime scene.
6. Offender borrowed weapon or other items to commit murder.
7. Offender used a shovel.
8. Offender staged an alternate location to commit the murder.

In Pettler's (2011) study, 16 offenders "appeared to have planned the primary crime scene, possibly a secondary crime scene, and the murder" (p. 168). Further, in summary, Pettler's (2011) findings can be generally stated as follows in relation to categorizing crime scene behaviors identified through data analysis and in identifying the number of offenders who exhibited these behaviors overall:

1. Only 9 offenders could be categorized as planners.
2. Only 10 offenders could be categorized as cleaners.
3. But every offender in the study could be categorized as a concealer/creator/fabricator.

Evaluating Typologies

The synthesis of Pettler's crime scene staging categories revealed that it is impossible to exclusively categorize crime scene staging behaviors revealed in the data analysis of this study using these six typologies when applied to this sample. Accurate typology development requires extremely large sample sizes. Because Pettler's (2011) study contained only 27 offenders, the application of these typologies was rendered ineffective for practical application. In conjunction with Ferguson's (2011) findings, both studies confirmed that crime scene typologies are not mutually exclusive therefore reducing their application for practical use. In other words, sample sizes need to be expanded, and a better typological system is required toward establishing the relevance crime scene staging typologies that might have been in field application. Thus, it is arguable that typology proposal at this point is premature and overreaching based on the empirical findings (e.g., eight studies and three dissertations) to date and would be solely based on belief instead of truth, speculation instead of research, and experience instead of science. The analysis conducted by both Ferguson (2011) and Pettler (2011) confirmed that crime scene staging behaviors can be categorized by behavioral theme, but the questions remain about (1) how to categorize them, (2) using what types of categories, and (3) based on how many staged homicide cases in the sample.

Building Theories about Crime Scene Staging

Pettler's (2011) qualitative study was designed to discover new behaviors, patterns, and themes of offenders. The study was successful and the results revealed useful information about offenders that helped to explain why and how offenders might stage crime scenes. It is important to realize that explanations for violent crime and specifically homicide have been published for decades, but like some of the personality theories have experienced, explanations that are loosely based on science or simply mere opinion are most often discarded eventually because they cannot substantiate the major premises of the explanation's idea (Douglas et al., 2006; Geberth, 1996a, 2006; Gross, 1924; Hazelwood & Burgess, 2009; Hazelwood & Napier, 2004; Turvey, 1999, 2002). Even though unsubstantiated explanations of crime scene staging, staging categories or typologies, behavioral pattern models, and so on, have been published and might be useful in conversation in general terms, building an actual theory derived by empirical data that is underpinned with experience along with published literature that can be verified expands the explanation and theoretical basis of crime scene staging of how and why individuals stage crime scenes. It is also important to recognize that theories are meant to be tested, so by building a reasonable theory about crime scene staging, it is arguable that researchers who read the theory might choose to test it in attempt to move the field forward and in attempt to prove it true or false. Interestingly, researchers show respect to each other by applying critical thinking to published ideas, expanding on each other's research, and testing each others' theories, which in turn builds an eclectic foundation of lots of ideas for future research to rest upon. "The more the merrier" as the old adage goes, but building a good theory is much more challenging than it might appear.

Development of a Substantiated Theory on Crime Scene Staging

It is true that behavioral theories attempting to explain criminal behavior, abnormal behavior, or the like, and even published in reputable places can fall into very broad multiple categories including *good* and *bad* or even *strong* or *weak* theories. Generally speaking, a good theory or strong theory contains five key components (Strauss, 2002). Recognizing these five key components of a good theory is paramount not only to the success of the theory but also for the reader's broad understanding of the theory's topic. The first key component of a good theory is that the theory predicts observable behavior (Strauss, 2002). The second key component of a good theory is that it identifies a problem (Strauss, 2002). Third, a good theory will attempt to explain within the theory why the issue is a problem for society (Strauss, 2002). Fourth, good theories identify possible solutions, and fifth, a good theory will identify both the strengths and weaknesses of the theory itself as they apply toward rectifying each weakness going forward (Strauss, 2002).

Pettler's 2011 Theory of Crime Scene Staging

Pettler's (2011) crime scene staging theory is the first crime scene staging theory in the world developed based on empirical research. Though Eke (2007) and other scholars, practitioners, experts, and so on have offered definitions, no definition to date has included the five key components of theory Strauss (2002) identified and discussed earlier. As a pioneer in research dedicated exclusively to crime scene staging and its related concepts, the author used her research to springboard and expand the empirical findings of her initial study, the published literature, and her own professional experience toward developing a very broad, theoretical continuum of offenders' behavioral patterns based on the original broad typologies used in her study.

Like Ferguson (2011) the results of the author's (2011) study revealed that crime scene staging behaviors could be categorized into broad patterns, but how applicable those patterns will be in practical application is yet to be seen. However, the most common, observable, and predicable behaviors of offenders revealed in Pettler's study were categorized into a pattern of behavior called *the fabricator*. Second, the next most common, observable, and predictable crime scene staging behaviors were categorized into a pattern called *the concealer*. Third, observable behaviors that could be predicted were categorized under the pattern name *the creator*. Fourth, the pattern name *the cleaner* housed, common, observable, predicable behaviors most commonly seen in staged crime scenes. *The planner* pattern of crime scene staging behaviors ranked fifth along a continuum-like apparatus. And even though the *inflictors'* pattern was developed to categorize crime scene staging behaviors involving self-inflicted wounds, no behaviors revealed in Pettler's (2011) study were placed in this category.

Therefore, Pettler built the first theory of crime scene staging of *predictable and observable crime scene staging behavior* that (1) addressed the problem of crime scene staging, (2) presented the beginnings of an overarching solution to crime scene staging, and (3) recognized the appropriate value the proposed solution should have based on (4) the limited empirical results of Pettler's (2011) study, (5) the published literature on crime scene staging at that time, and (6) Pettler's education, training, and experience. Pettler then in 2011 proposed the first empirically based theory of crime scene staging, crime scene staging behaviors, their patterns, and the victims of offenders:

> Crime scene staging is a problem because it depletes valuable resources by misdirecting investigations, hindering the pursuit of justice, and allowing violent offenders to threaten public safety by remaining in society with the opportunity to reoffend. Empirical research determined that a common set of behavioral patterns exists among offenders and they are most likely to verbally fabricate or falsify evidence first, conceal or destroy evidence second, create evidence third, clean up evidence fourth, or preplan a murder well in advance towards the ultimate goal of avoiding apprehension. A potential solution to this problem might be to develop a conceptual model of offenders (e.g., taxonomic hierarchal arrangement) coupled with developing an early detection hybrid-methodology to work in tandem to be used by law enforcement professionals and scholar–practitioners that could enable them to utilize resources more efficiently and to remove dangerous offenders from society more quickly. (Pettler, 2011, pp. 185–186)

Breaking Down the Theory: The Problem of Crime Scene Staging

When building good crime scene staging theory, a good place to start is by identifying the overall problem. Until 2011, it was unknown if there were patterns of behaviors commonly utilized by offenders in homicide cases. Pettler's (2011) study confirmed that behavioral patterns of offenders do actually exist, but that was as far as Pettler's study could go. Today, it is still unknown how far and wide confirmed patterns of crime scene staging behaviors can be applied and without tremendous resources dedicated to studying the behaviors alone would be allocated for broad research. Therefore, an ultraconservative approach toward placing strict parameters on definitively identifying patterns of crime scene staging behaviors, building typologies of patterns of crime scene staging behaviors, or otherwise is strongly recommended. In order to build typologies or categories of anything, whether it is crime scene staging or something else, very large sample sizes are required. Thus, suggesting typologies based on experience is not helpful. By large sample sizes, it is implied several hundred to many thousands of staged crime scenes would have to be analyzed.

Breaking Down the Theory: The Problem for Society

As mentioned in Chapter 2, crime scene staging is a problem for society in many ways. First, crime scene staging is a complex problem for law enforcement professionals because staged scenes can point investigations in the wrong direction while absorbing countless financial resources and man power that most agencies are short on to begin with. Staged scenes are a problem for law enforcement professionals because false leads can literally lead nowhere, to dead ends, to a lot of wasted time, and toward people who had nothing to do with the crime being investigated. In addition, crime scene staging creates a public safety problem for society because staged scenes that go undetected leave an offender free to roam throughout communities, therefore posing a threat to the safety and security of would-be victims. In other words, when an offender is not apprehended in relation to the homicide of which he or she staged the scene, that offender remains in society having new opportunities to reoffend. It is important to note that Eke (2007) and Ferguson (2011) found that the most commonly staged scenes are revealed in the empirical research so far as domestic violence–related or *intimate partner homicides*. In a later chapter, victim–offender relationship will be discussed in detail, but it is critical to point out here that because it does appear that staged scenes are most often scene in intimate partner homicide cases, the new partners of undetected offenders could be most at risk for victimization.

Breaking Down the Theory: Identifying Solutions

So far, the research compiled to date on crime scene staging has not identified an overarching solution to the problem of crime scene staging that would completely eliminate crime scene staging from society entirely. As discussed in Chapter 1, staged crime scenes are referenced in published literature dating back to the first book of the Bible. To identify a solution that would eradicate crime scene staging completely would require additional research on offenders, their behaviors, behavioral patterns, and especially their victims, but it is important to mention that published empirical research thus far has proved promising toward the beginnings of a conceptual model that would help law enforcement professionals and those charged with investigating crime scenes that are identified as staged (Eke, 2007; Pettler, 2011).

A development of Pettler's (2011) study revealed information that led the author to develop a conceptual crime scene staging early detection methodology that could be used by law enforcement professionals and scholar-practitioners. The long-term idea is to combine such a methodology with a conceptual model of offenders that could be applied in tandem alerting those charged with homicide investigations that the scene they're standing in is potentially staged. Identifying that a scene is staged at the beginning of an investigation as opposed to any time after the beginning is very important to the overall success of the investigation toward prosecution of the offender. Additionally, one of the most noticeable benefits of such an application would be in the accounting departments of law enforcement agencies in that valuable financial resources would be pointed in the right direction from the onset instead of wasted on what some might call *a wild goose chase*.

Breaking Down the Theory: Strengths and Weaknesses

It is very important to recognize one of the primary limitations of qualitative research. That is, that qualitative research is not predictive in nature nor is it applicable to the broad target population in most cases; therefore, the information revealed in a qualitative study of any kind cannot be used to independently predict behavior. Hazelwood and Napier (2004) argued that offenders ultimately stage crime scenes to avoid apprehension (p. 745). Clearly, it is reasonable and arguable based on the results of Pettler's qualitative study or any other crime scene staging study that the primary purpose for staging a crime scene could be to avoid apprehension, but it would be completely inappropriate and misleading to independently make that suggestion based on qualitative data alone. Further, it is arguable that some law enforcement professionals or scholar–practitioners might suggest that it is appropriate to predict that all homicide offenders will attempt to avoid apprehension somehow regardless of the type of research used to study homicide (e.g., intimate partner, street crime, etc.). However, this is not always the case even in intimate partner homicide. This idea can be illustrated in the case of an offender who was convicted of shooting his wife causing her death after a domestic dispute. The offender then phoned 911 to report the incident after shooting his wife 14 times with a six-shot revolver, which he reloaded three times during the incident with ammunition from at least two locations at their marital residence. After the fateful

911 call, the offender phoned his son and asked him to come home right away. When first responders and his son arrived, the offender told them that he shot his wife and that she was in the bedroom of their home. The offender never tried to avoid apprehension after shooting his wife.

One of the strengths of the author's crime scene staging theory is that it is primarily derived from empirical data coupled with having been partially based on her practical field experience as an investigator, which helped her analyze the data with a more application-based approach. Based on the author's education, training, and experience, she developed the six typologies that were synthesized with the empirical findings of her theory: (1) the cleaner, (2) the concealer, (3) the creator, (4) the fabricator, (5) the inflictor, and (6) the planner, regardless if the typologies were useful or not.

Another strength of this theory is that it is the first empirically based theory of crime scene staging known to date. Even though there are not very many empirical studies in the published literature on crime scene staging itself, the author used theoretical constructs and traditional investigatory methodologies as the foundational pieces of her theory. Further, this theory is strengthened by the historical account of crime scene staging presented in Chapter 1 of this book. As discussed before, crime scene staging dynamics in homicide cases can be observed going as far back as biblical times.

One of the weaknesses of the author's theory is that there is currently no place in the United States that houses all the data known about every staged crime scene throughout the country (e.g., Center for Disease Control Morbidity Studies, Regional Organized Crime Information Center, Violent Criminal Apprehension Program, Federal Bureau of Investigation Behavioral Analysis Unit, or National Center for the Analysis of Violent Crime) (Geberth, 2010, p. 5; Hazelwood & Napier, 2004). Because there is no repository for crime scene staging data, researchers are left to recruit participants, find cases, and the like for any study on crime scene staging as opposed to being able to search a clearing house of sorts for such information. Another limitation or weakness of the author's study overall was the inability to accurately attribute value to any potential or suggested solution to the problem of crime scene staging. Unfortunately, there is no theoretical standard of comparison of any kind known to date, so again, the scope of the validity of the theoretical solution was not applicable. In relation, yet another weakness of the author's theory is due to the sample size of her sample. Again, qualitative studies cannot predict behavior independently, so the author's theory, while empirically derived, is greatly limited because her study contained only a small number of staged homicide cases.

Behavioral pattern overlap: As discussed throughout this chapter, probably the most important weakness of Pettler's research and theory to point out came in the form of the overlap in crime scene staging behavioral patterns of offenders. This is the primary reason it is strongly recommended to refrain from defining typologies of crime scene staging scenes, staging behaviors, patterns, and so on too narrowly until further empirical research is conducted. As a scholar–practitioner, the author recognized the problem that this extreme limitation is presented but met the challenge head on. Quantitative research is designed to predict. So, in order to accurately develop serial homicide offender, crime scene staging, or other types of typologies, it is arguable that more than a few hundred participants are needed for accurate data analysis.

References

Barkley, R. A. (1997). *ADHA and the nature of self control*. New York: Guilford Press.

Cable News Network, Inc. (2013). Former Utah doctor convicted of wife's murder. Retrieved from http://www.hlntv.com/article/2013/11/08/martin-macneill-murder-trial-verdict- guilty

Cohen, L., & Felson, M. (1979). Social change and crime rate trends: A routine activity approach. *American Sociological Review, 44*, 588–608.

Davey, L., Day, A., & Howells, K. (2005). Anger, overcontrol, and violent offending. *Aggression and Violent Behavior, 7*, 477–497.

De Young, R. (2013). Environmental psychology overview. In S. R. Klein and A. H. Huffman (Eds.), *Green organizations: Driving change with IO psychology* (pp. 17–33). New York: Routledge. See more at: http://www-personal.umich.edu/~rdeyoung/envtpsych. html#sthash.HJw9AGtJ.dpuf

Douglas, J. E., Burgess, A. W., Burgess, A. G., & Ressler, R. K. (2006). *Crime classification manual: A standard system for investigating and classifying crimes* (2nd ed.). San Francisco, CA: John Wiley & Sons.

Douglas, J. E., & Douglas, L. (2006). The detection of staging, undoing and personation at the crime scene. In J. Douglas, A. Burgess, A. Burgess, & R. Ressler (Eds.), *Crime classification manual* (2nd ed.). San Francisco, CA: Jossey-Bass.

Douglas, J. E., & Munn, C. (1992). The detection of staging and personation at the crime scene. In A. Burgess, A. Burgess, J. Douglas, & R. Ressler (Eds.), *Crime classification manual*. San Francisco, CA: Jossey-Bass.

Eke, A. W. (2007). *Staging in cases of homicide: Offender, victim, and offence characteristics* (Doctoral dissertation). Retrieved from ProQuest (1390310091).

Eysenck, H. J. (1947). *The structure of human personality*. New York: John Wiley & Sons, Inc.

Ferguson, C. (2011). *The defects of the situation: A typology of staged crime scenes* (Unpublished doctoral thesis). Bond University, Gold Coast, Queensland, Australia.

Ferguson, C. (2014, July). Staged homicides: An examination of common features of faked burglaries, suicides, accidents and car accidents. *Journal Police Criminal Psychology*, Springer Publishing. doi: 10.1007/s11896-014-9154-1

Ferguson, C., & Petherick, W. (2014, October 13). Getting away with murder: An examination of detected homicides staged as suicides. *Homicide Studies*. doi: 10.1177/1088767914553099

Geberth, V. J. (1996). *Practical homicide investigation: Tactics, procedures, and forensic techniques* (3rd ed.). Boca Raton, FL: CRC Press/Taylor & Francis Group.

Geberth, V. J. (1996a). The staged crime scene. *Law and Order Magazine, 44*(2), 45–49.

Geberth, V. J. (2006). *Practical homicide investigation: Tactics, procedures, and forensic techniques* (4th ed.). Boca Raton, FL: CRC Press/Taylor & Francis Group.

Geberth, V. J. (2010). Crime scene staging: An exploratory study of the frequency and characteristics of sexual posing in homicides. *Investigative Sciences Journal, 2*(2), 1–19.

Gross, H. (1924). *Criminal Investigation*. London, UK: Sweet & Maxwell.

Hare, R. D. (1991). *The Hare Psychopathy Checklist—Revised*. In D. J. Cooke & C. Michie, (1997). An item response theory analysis of the Psychopathy Checklist—Revised. *Psychological Assessment*, 9(1), 3–14.

Hazelwood, R. R., & Burgess, A. W. (Eds.). (2009). *Practical aspects of rape investigation: A multidisciplinary approach* (4th ed.). Boca Raton, FL: CRC Press/Taylor & Francis Group.

Hazelwood, R. R., & Napier, M. R. (2004). Crime scene staging and its detection. *International Journal of Offender Therapy and Comparative Criminology, 48*(6), 744–759. doi: 10.1177/0306624X04268298

Howells, K., & Stacey, J. (2006) Psychological characteristics of offenders. In M. R. Kebbell & G. M. Davies (Eds.), *Practical psychology for forensic investigators and prosecutors*. West Sussex, UK: Wiley & Sons, Ltd.

Keppel, R. D., & Weis, J. G. (2004). The rarity of unusual dispositions of victim bodies: Staging and posing. *Journal of Forensic Science, 49*(6), 1–5.

Maslow, A. H. (1943). A theory of human motivation. *Psychological Review, 50,* 360–396.

McCrae, R. R., & Costa, P. T. (1987). Validation of the five-factor model of personality across instruments and observers. *Journal of Personality and Social Psychology, 52,* 81–90.

Nye, D. R. (1996). *Three psychologies: Perspectives from Freud, Skinner, and Rogers*. New Paltz, NY: International Thomson Publishing Company.

Petherick, W., & Ferguson, C. (2009). Behavioral consistency, the homology assumption, and the problems of induction. In W. Petherick (Ed.), *Serial crime: Theoretical and practical issues in behavioral profiling* (2nd ed.). London, UK: Academic Press.

Pettler, L. G. (2011). *Crime scene behaviors of offenders* (Doctoral dissertation). Retrieved from ProQuest (2251577601).

Powers, R. L., & Griffith, J. (1987). *Understanding life-style: The psycho-clarity process*. Chicago, IL: Americas Institute of Adlerian Studies.

Pardeck, J. T. (1996). *Social work practice: An ecological approach*. Westport, CT: Greenwood Publishing Group.

Schlesinger, L. B., Gardenier, A., Jarvis, J., & Sheehan-Cook, J. (2012, April). Crime scene staging in homicide. *Journal of Police and Criminal Psychology, 29*(1), 44–51.

Straus, R. (2002). *Using sociology: An introduction from the applied and clinical perspectives* (3rd ed.). Lanham, MA: Rowman & Littlefield.

Trait. (2014). *Merriam-Webster* (11th Edition Online). Retrieved from http://www.merriam-webster.com/dictionary/trait

Turvey, B. E. (1999). *Criminal profiling: An introduction to behavioral evidence analysis* (1st ed.). London, UK: Academic Press.

Turvey, B. E. (2000, December). Staged crime scenes: A preliminary study of 25 cases. *Journal of Behavioral Profiling, 1*(3).

Turvey, B. E. (2002). *Criminal profiling: An introduction to behavioral evidence analysis* (2nd ed.). London, UK: Academic Press.

WebMD, LLC. (2014). A guide to DSM-5. Retrieved from http://www.medscape.com/viewarticle/803884

Victimology

5

Introduction

Hazelwood and Napier (2004) argued that when it comes to staged crime scenes, investigators have to rely the study of the victim and the study of the scene to help move the investigation forward. The more focus placed on studying the victim in any homicide case, the more that can be discovered about the crime and the offender. Research has shown that most victims of staged scenes are female murdered by male offenders. Traditional homicide investigation has primarily focused on the suspect so much that no one knows who the victim was. That is not to say that suspectology is not important or working toward developing a suspect based on the totality of evidence, but focusing solely on the suspect or closing any case "by arrest" is a misstep that is often made with grave consequences. More recently, the paradigm shift toward viewing homicide investigation as a system and analyzing the role the victim plays within that system is where this aspect of criminology is focused today (Wilcox, 2010). The breadth and depth of victimology is quite vast and could not possibly be thoroughly discussed in one chapter alone, but for the purpose of introducing the concept of victimology toward beginning to gain insight into crime scene staging in relation to offenders and their victims, how victims become victims, and why victims become victims, an overview of victimology is appropriate and required.

Defining Victimology

Simply stated, victimology is the analytical scientific study of victims (Turvey, 1999). Victimology focuses on analyzing everything about a victim, such as lifestyle, personality, behavior, and many other important aspects of every victim. The definition of victimology can be expanded to include a how groups of individuals become victims or are victimized, such as in the case of women being sexually abused in groups or individuals who become victims in their places of employment for example. The definition of victimology can even expand into gaining insight about the relationship between a victim and an offender. No matter what definition one might choose to adopt or how broadly or narrowly one chooses to define victimology as a whole, it is arguable that a victim and his or her characteristics could make up at least half of a homicide investigation and for that, even that reason alone, the importance of analytical, synthesized, evaluative victimology cannot be understated.

Part of the reason for this paradigm shift is because researchers have identified gaps of recurrent crime-information-gathering studies when it comes to victims, such as the in Uniform Crime Report (Wilcox, 2010). The Uniform Crime Report is generated based on only reported crimes. It is arguable that because not every victim reports every crime that occurs throughout the United States that the Uniform Crime Report is limited by data collected and by the nature of reported crimes only. Further, the National Crime Victimization Report started during the 1970s collects information about crimes through the eyes of the victim. Clearly, the National Crime Victimization Report is a critical resource of cumulative information for criminologists and psychologists for learning more about crime victims, their characteristics, and their victimization overall.

Dating back to ancient cultures and civilizations, the concept of *victim* has been defined many ways. For example, the Hebrews defined a victim as scapegoat; one of which was sacrificed to a deity or hierarchy to satisfy the people's obligation (Friedmann, 2011). Over the centuries, victim has come to mean other things as well, for example, during the twentieth century, Hans von Hentig, Benjamin Mendelsohn, and Marvin Wolfgang suggested that victims precipitate their own victimization (Friedmann, 2011). Today, it is arguable that when speaking about having been a victim, being a victim, or becoming a victim, the general consensus is that victims experience harm or loss of some important factor, whether it be financial, emotional, sexual, or even their lives.

Victimology Theory

Many criminologists have studied the victim's role in relation to criminal investigations. According to Tobolowsky (2000), from the 1930s to the 1950s, "fathers of victimology" von Hentig and Mendelsohn studied victims in relation to how victim characteristics influenced the commission of a criminal offense or even how they precipitated it. As their research developed, Mendelsohn built six typologies of victims to describe their role in the commission of criminal acts. Later, von Hentig studied additional homicide cases and suggested that the victim causes the crime and based on that suggestion developed six victim typologies expanding on Mendelsohn's work, which served as a sturdy foundation for the future development of what is known as *victim-precipitation theory* today (Ressler, Burgess, & Douglas, 1988, p. 7). Further, Wolfgang (1957), another of the first criminologists to study and discuss the victim's role in criminal homicide, springboarded from the work of von Hentig and Mendelsohn by developing Wolfgang's theory of *victim-precipitated criminal homicide*. Wolfgang did not accuse the victim of causing his or her own death in his theory, but rather, Wolfgang theorized based on his extensive research that the victim–offender relationship or interaction actively or passively manifests certain circumstances that intentionally or unintentionally precipitate the victim's death. One of the best examples that illustrates Wolfgang's victim-precipitated theory is via Douglas, Burgess, Burgess, and Ressler's (2006) concept of *argument/conflict murder*. Douglas et al. defined argument/conflict murder as "a death that results from a dispute between individuals, excluding family or household members" (p. 169). Characteristic of this type of murder is the young adult, male, unemployed, or blue-collar worker, with minimal education, who is known for his use of violence to settle disputes (Douglas et al., 2006, p. 169). This victim impulsively responds to trivial issues in his environment and in turn, because of his impulsive, violent outbursts, he puts himself in a position to become a victim of violent crime.

Case Example

Several years ago, a young, adult, unemployed male named Tony knocked on the door of a man named John. Tony was accompanied by two friends and John knowing the trio, opened the door and let them into his singlewide trailer. The four sat in John's living room drinking beer without incident until Tony told John that John owed Tony money for cocaine. John explained to Tony that he did not have the money to pay John for the cocaine, then Tony asked John to go the bank to withdraw the money. John did not have any money in the bank, which made Tony very angry. Tony and his two friends attacked John, dragged him to his bedroom, gagged him with a green washcloth, and beat him with brass knuckles until there was unexpected knock on the door. John's friend Mark and Mark's girlfriend stopped by to see John and walked in on what was going on. Mark was much bigger than Tony or his two friends, but Mark sat on the couch patiently waiting after Tony told Mark that they were discussing business with John in the bedroom. After a period of time, Mark got the feeling Tony was not telling Mark the truth, so Mark made his way back to the bedroom. When Mark discovered John gagged in the back bedroom with Tony holding a screwdriver to John's throat demanding money, Mark attacked Tony and his two friends. A very violent, yet brief fistfight ensued, then after being struck repeatedly by Mark, both of Tony's friends retreated and fled with Mark chasing them. Tony had been pushed to the kitchen floor and as he rose up, John came down the hallway with a firearm and said something to the effect of, "It ain't happenin' Tony." Tony, in a rage and wielding the screwdriver, charged John and John fired the gun hitting Tony in the chest. Tony fell to the kitchen floor, looked up, and, according to John, blasted John with his final obscenities and died. John was applying pressure to the gunshot wound and was on the phone with 911 within seconds of the incident. The screwdriver was recovered beneath Tony's body. Mark ended his pursuit of Tony's friends and paramedics observed two individuals running furiously down the nearest road as the paramedics traveled to the crime scene. Police picked up Tony's friends and John continued rendering aid to Tony until the paramedics arrived.

Tony and John's case is an example of Wolfgang's (1957) victim-precipitation theory. Proponents for Tony's side of the story advocated for him by arguing that John shot Tony because he did not want to pay Tony. Proponents for John's side of the story argued that John's behavior as supported by uninvolved witness friend Mark demonstrated that John acted in self-defense. John was originally charged with murder, but pleaded guilty to a lesser, but related charge during the trial because the state conceded that they could not prove their murder case against John.

In addition to Wolfgang's (1957) theory, several other theorists have attempted to explain the role the victim plays in the homicide system. Hindelang, Gottfredson, and Garafolo (1978) argued that victimization is a function of lifestyle (Wilcox, 2010). Hindelang et al. (1978) examined survey data collected from victims and found that specific groups of individuals were more likely to become victims than were other groups (Wilcox, 2010). For example, young Americans and African-Americans were more often victims of crime when compared to older Americans and Whites (Wilcox, 2010, para. 6). Essentially, Hindelang et al.'s lifestyle-exposure theory posits that exposure to certain lifestyles increases an individual's propensity toward victimization via exposure to criminal offenses, while other types of lifestyles could reduce the risk of becoming a victim. For example, under this theory, a young male whose associates are involved in criminal activity is more likely to become a victim than would be even a young male who is not affiliated with criminal associates. Another example might be the notion that elderly individuals tend to be more cautious and/or fearful of becoming victims of any crime, violent or property, so their behaviors might be more consistent with taking extra precautions. Maybe, elderly individuals concerned about victimization choose not to travel alone or go out at night and instead choose to always have caretakers accompany them on all outings. Another group who might be more vulnerable to becoming victims of crime are women. Women, because they are more cautious, might be less likely victims because they are cognizant of risk factors, such as traveling alone at night or the like. Overall, the key feature of this theory is that the choice that lifestyle plays a role in the likelihood of becoming a victim.

Chapter 4 of this book in part discussed Cohen and Felson's (1979) *routine activities theory*. Cohen and Felson argued that the commission of a crime requires three components (Wilcox, 2010, para. 8):

1. Offender motivation
2. A potential target
3. Lack of effective protection

These three components were thought to create the perfect storm for crime to occur. Arguably, a victim must come into contact with a potential offender of any kind in a location or during a period of time where no one is there to help rescue the potential victim or prevent the commission of the crime. This concept can be illustrated using the example of an individual carrying his or her belongings by bicycle down an otherwise deserted or rural road. If a would-be offender observes that the individual is alone and that no one is around to protect the potential victim, someone looking to rob this innocent victim could maximize the opportunity and commit a crime. The author would argue that routine activities are critically important to understand crime scene stagers and their victims. According to Douglas et al. (2006), the same drives and motivations that propel individuals through regular daily life are the same drives that in fact propel an individual throughout the commission of a rape or murder. With that said, it is interesting to consider then the idea that if drives could be correlated to the participation in daily activities, and the same drives propel one throughout the duration of committing rape and/or murder, and then routine activities might also be directly correlated to crime scene staging as opposed to being driven to behave in a manner completely inconsistent with motivations normally driven by commonality and familiarity.

Victimology and Politics

The American criminal justice system has long been grounded in punishment confirming it as an offender-centered criminal justice system. Even though the system functions along a punishment–rehabilitation continuum, liberal criminology has been focused on protecting offenders' interests thereby oftentimes forgetting the victim altogether and repeatedly risking public safety as a result. In turn, nothing has been more neglected that the victim in the American criminal justice system (Holmes and Holmes, 2002). Along with the paradigm shift in homicide investigation moving from a suspect-centered investigation to a victim-centered investigation, the scientific study of victims that is known as victimology has created a platform that does not allow the victim to be forgotten. An example of this shift can be illustrated by the story of a habitually violent offender convicted of physically and sexually assaulting two elderly women on different occasions and in different locations who came up for parole. This habitual felon had been convicted not only of the latter crimes but also of several other assaultive crimes as a juvenile, which were sealed and not considered when sentencing the habitual felon later. Additionally, this individual was suspected of killing a man in an unsolved case that to date has not been resolved. Upon learning of her rapist's pending release on parole, one of this offender's elderly victims approached the elected district attorney for assistance because the concept of this convicted rapist reentering society was abominable to her and was causing her severe health issues. In turn, a current judge, then the prosecutor who prosecuted her case, stepped up to assist making the claim that the habitual felon was by far the most dangerous individual, the then-prosecutor now-judge ever prosecuted in his career. The former and retired chief of police of the city at the time of the assaults also stood up for the victim in this case attesting to the dangerous nature of this habitual felon. Further, upon review of prison records, the individual had 38 infractions over a period of time, but had remained infraction-free for 90+ days making him eligible for parole. Numerous individuals implored legislators for support in attempt to influence the parole board to therefore put the interest of public safety first and the victim's fear of the offender forefront. One particular legislator was an elderly female and when asked if she would stand for the victims in this case, she made mention of the lack of programming for the offender as a child. The habitual felon was released regardless of all the pleas to keep him incarcerated. As expected by all of those who knew the individual and knew that he was of high risk to reoffend, the habitual felon reoffended very soon after, which resulted in his parole being revoked and he was sent back to prison.

It is very important for criminologists to be intimately involved in the formation of law. Though it is true that criminology might be defined very simply as the scientific study of crime, aspects like society and crime, victims and crime, and societal responses to crime are critically important for policy makers to understand toward valid and reliable ways to shape laws to enhance public safety.

Importance of Victimology

To date, no study on crime scene staging has included a victimological study. Pettler (2011) argued that conducting victimology and suspectology in her study would have enhanced the results. The importance of victimology cannot be understated. Victimology is essential for understanding the victim from the inside out or outside in, whichever way one prefers to look at it. Turvey (1999) argued that victimology is essential because it provides the necessary context in which to understand the victim, whether the victim was chosen at random or was a calculated target, how the victim was interconnected throughout the victim's life, and through all of this investigative direction can take shape. Consider the following example.

Case Example

A construction-type worker found a body dumped on the side of the road. Upon recovery, it was clear that the victim was female, but the ethnicity and race of the victim was unclear. During the course of the crime scene investigation, a neighboring law enforcement agency suggested that the victim was indeed a missing person from their jurisdiction, so the investigation proceeded under that premise. Unfortunately, upon completion of the autopsy, the next day, the neighboring agency reluctantly announced that their missing person was found alive and that the deceased victim found in the rural area was not their missing person. To complicate things further, the female victim was not carrying identification. The case went cold for several months until the discovery of another victim in a nearby location when the two cases were generally linked. An arrest was made in the second case, but investigators in the first victim's case reanalyzed the file and arrest information of the suspect in attempt to determine if the two cases could be specifically linked to the same suspect. Although the analysis revealed the two cases were not linked, through a myriad of strategic maneuvering on the part of the investigators, the Jane Doe was finally identified and a suspect was developed. The next day, it was suggested by the author that because the case had been cold for approximately 1 year, the case dynamics were much more complex, and a complete full-blown victimology on the victim and a complete suspectology on the newly identified suspect in the case were both critical to the integrity of the investigative structure and strategic in nature for investigating cold cases. Instead of learning everything they could about the victim and the suspect before approaching the suspect, investigators chose instead to approach the suspect within 24 hours of identifying the victim without knowledge of the suspect beyond what was revealed during a criminal record check. Investigators' attempt at interviewing the suspect failed and the case was stifled again. A period of time later, a search warrant was executed on the location thought to have been the potential primary crime scene, but a lack of understanding of who the victim was and who the suspect was limited their understanding of (1) what they were searching for and (2) what they were looking at and in turn yielded extremely limited results coupled with forensic evidence in the scene being repeatedly missed due to the lack of understanding of staged crime scenes. Although a narrow scope of circumstantial evidence was recovered, no resolution has been made in this case to date.

In the aforementioned example, no one asked the question, "Who was in conflict with the victim?" or "Why did the victim have to die?" or "Was the victim somehow an obstacle for the suspect?" Because neither the victim nor the suspect in this case were analytically studied before the approach, the investigation did not go well and no arrest was ever made in this case. It is fair to say that it is not possible in every case to not to have any contact with a suspect when the suspect is a family member or the like. But the hard questions should be reserved for when everyone is ready to get down to business. There's an old British Army adage that goes like this: *Proper Planning and Preparation Prevents Poor Performance.* The author adopted this adage as a foundational piece of her personal investigative strategy for homicide investigation and it has served her well. Essentially, failure to prepare and plan means failure to build the foundation of the case, thus resulting most often in weak cases that can frustrate the criminal justice process and thwart successful prosecution.

One of the very first questions that should be asked when investigating a homicide case is, "Who benefits from the death of this victim?" Sometimes, the answer is *no one*, but sometimes, the answer can be found in victimology. One of the following questions the authors' recommend asking during the course of an investigation is "How did this individual become a victim of homicide?" as in the determination if the victim was targeted or happened to become a victim based on circumstance (Petherick, 2014a). Additional attention should focus on answering questions revolving around how the victim most likely would have responded to an attack (Petherick, 2014a), that is, would the victim have acquiesced, attempted to escape, fought back, and so on. Further, assessing the risk the offender took in order to carry out the crime must be established. Did the offender act covertly in his or her approach at night or was the crime committed in context of an open, public, highly traveled area with plenty of witnesses who observed the crime? These are the types of critical questions that underpin the beginnings of building a solid foundation for any homicide investigation when staging is involved.

Research-Based Forensic Victimology: A Suggested Approach

Analyzing all available information about a victim during the course of an investigation is critical to investigatory success. The author's concept of research-based forensic victimology essentially implies the two fundamental cornerstones of empirical research; validity and reliability should anchor victimological study. From a research perspective, *validity* generally means that the system design or method of which research is conducted is sound. On the other hand, *reliability*, from a research perspective, generally means that the systematic design or instrument used to measure the variable produces consistent results applicable beyond the study's sample to a broad population. The concepts of validity and reliability are by far a broader topic, but for the purpose of this discussion about research-based forensic victimology, *validity is the structural soundness of the information gathering system* and *reliability is the applicable soundness of the information in part and as a whole.* Because resources are scare in American law enforcement today, it is fair to say that it is most always impossible to validate every piece of information gathered during the course of victimology. Recognizing this obstacle as real and reasonable is imperative to determining the allocation of resources toward identifying the most useful and verifiable information. It is arguable that information gathered during this course might be divided into one of three or more categories, such as follows:

1. Empirical (can be validated and is reliable)
2. Quasi-empirical (can be partially validated or is partially reliable)
3. Nonempirical (cannot be validated and/or is not reliable)

Empirical information or knowledge is information that can be validated and that is reliable. Therefore, empirical knowledge gained about the victim must come via observation or experimentation. One way investigators might empirically validate a piece of evidence is by way of a research method called triangulation. Just like measuring physical evidence in a crime scene, the method of research-based triangulation works much in the same way. Triangulating information using victim-centered modified triangulation is seen in Figure 5.1.

Victim-centered modified triangulation means that information will be confirmed using three pieces of corresponding evidence or information. A simple example might be investigators get an anonymous tip that the victim was running a tab by credit card and drinking vodka shots with friends at a local bar hours before his or her death. Investigators might attempt to validate that the victim was drinking vodka, the victim's reportedly preferred drink hours before his or her death by triangulating it, such as follows:

1. Asking the bartender what he or she served the victim
2. Checking the victim's credit card receipt
3. Asking at least one friend what the victim was drinking prior to his or her death

If the bartender, credit card receipt, and at least one friend objectively and independently confirm the victim was drinking vodka shots on the night of

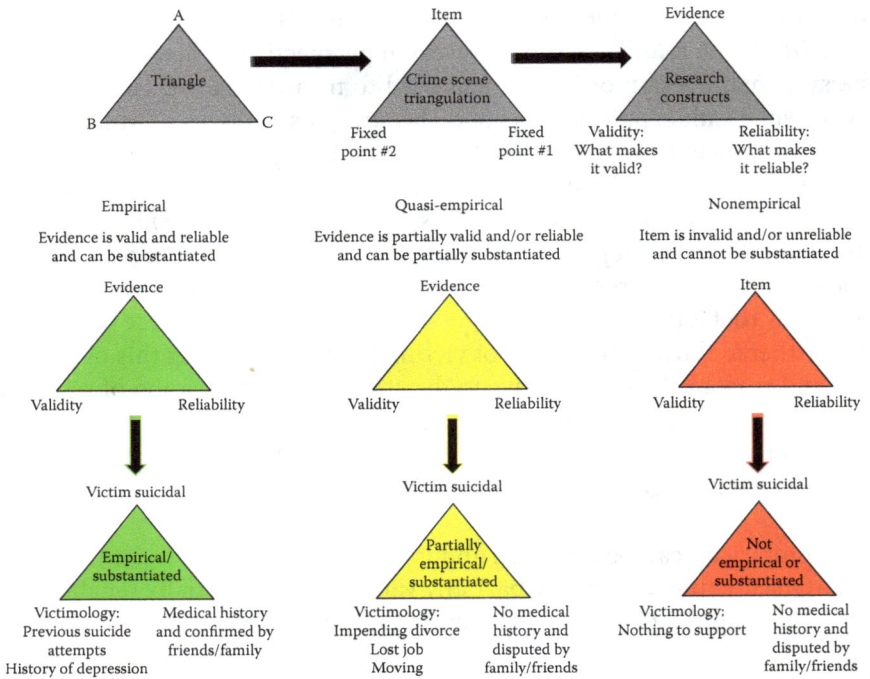

Figure 5.1 Victim-Centered Modified Triangulation

his or her murder, then the anonymous tip is empirically validated through modified research-based triangulation (i.e., empirical observation).

Second, quasi-empirical knowledge or information might be victimo- logical information that could be partially true or seemingly true, but can- not be confirmed via modified triangulation completely. Using the same example, if the bartender does not remember serving the victim and there is no credit card receipt because the victim paid with cash, but at least one friend confirms that he or she actually simultaneously drank vodka shots with the victim at the bar, then the information that the victim was drinking vodka before his or her death is allegedly true as partially veri- fied by the friend only. Further, nonempirical knowledge is victimological information that cannot be validated and that is not reliable at all, that is, information that is brought forth during the course of a victimological investigation, but nothing can be found or used to either support or refute the information one way or the other. The best type of information to build a solid foundation of victimology upon is empirical information. It is fair to say that any sound foundation of victimological information will con- tain shades of grayer quasi-empirical and even nonempirical pieces embed- ded throughout the finished product, while it is completely arguable that based on this concept, victimology built on nonempirical information and otherwise hearsay, and so on, is a slippery slope and one that is not good for the victim, offender, investigation, or for the pursuit of justice in any case.

Taxonomic Hierarchal Arrangement of Victimological Components

Abraham Maslow (1943) developed a theory he called Maslow's hierarchy of needs. Maslow argued all individuals traverse through five stages of growth: physiological, safety, loving and belonging, esteem, and self-actualization. Human beings in the physiological stage need to be able to breathe and find food and water, for example, while the safety stage was centered on feeling secure as an individual, as a family, or in one's job. Further, the loving and belonging stage included friendship and family, for example, while the esteem stage focused on confidence and achievement, therefore working toward the last stage of human development, that is, self-actualization or one's morality and belief system. What is so interesting about Maslow's hierarchy of needs in relation to victimology is that it is arguable that a structurally sound, valid, empirical research-based victimological design can be systematically arranged in a similar taxonomy. Taxonomy is nothing more than a structure of interrelated components or variables where one builds upon the underlying level or levels. For example, kindergarten comes first and the information learned in kindergarten is used and applied in the first grade. Then the information learned in kindergarten and first grade is used in second grade and so forth. The scholastic structure is a good example of a taxonomic hierarchal arrangement of interrelated components that depend on the foundational level toward maintaining the structural soundness and actual achievement of the rest of the components. Therefore, when it comes to victimology, expanding on current victimological research and the seminal research in developmental psychology, victimology components could be arranged into a systematic order, so that each category underpins the next category. Using Maslow's hierarchy of needs as scaffolding or as a conceptual framework to support such a hypothetical model of an analytical victimological study in a homicide case, it is arguable that understanding any victim from the nature of his or her mere existence as a biomechanical human being to the pinnacle of who he or she is as an individual at the time of death could be instrumental in gaining deeper insight into the victim as a whole. When applying the study of victimology to Maslow's hierarchy of needs, the following categories could be relevant toward the development of a conceptual model of this nature:

1. *Physiological*—Victim's physical demographics and attributes
2. *Safety*—Victim in relation to personal, familial, financial, and occupational safety

    3. *Love and Belonging*—Victim in relation to relationships
    4. *Esteem*—Victim in relation to personality, cognition, emotionality, behavior, and achievements
    5. *Self-Actualization*—Victim in relation to relative adoption of worldly concepts

Conceptual Model of Research-Based Forensic Victimology

Considering that information gathered during the course of victimology could be categorized as empirical, quasi-empirical, or nonempirical via an empirical research-based victimological approach, the following list, while not an exhaustive list of informational categories, contains categories that are critical to understanding the victim analytically toward the synthesis of the totality of evidence and the determination of strategic planning moving forward in a homicide investigation. It is very important to note that an empirical study aimed at identifying through observation and/or experimentation each informational category and determining its rank order within the theoretical framework of Maslow's hierarchy of needs could prove to assist in adding, deleting, and revising this proposed conceptual model. See Appendix A.

    1. *Physiological*: Victim's Physical Demographics and Attributes
      a. Demographics
      b. Home
      c. Transportation
      d. Health and medical
    2. *Safety*: Victim in Relation to Personal, Familial, Financial, and Occupational Safety
      a. Personal safety
      b. Family safety
      c. Financial situation and socioeconomic status
      d. Occupational safety
      e. Other resources related to safety
    3. *Love and Belonging*: Victim in Relation to Relationships
      a. Marital status
      b. Intimate partners
      c. Friends
      d. Acquaintances
      e. Strangers
      f. Enemies
      g. Conflict
      h. Media and communication

4. *Esteem*: Victim in Relation to Personality, Cognition, Emotionality, Behavior, and Achievements
   a. Personality traits
   b. Cognition
   c. Emotionality
   d. Behavior
   e. Achievements
5. *Self-Actualization*: Victim in Relation to Relative Adoption of Worldly Concepts
   a. Envirosocioculturalism
      i. Environment
      ii. Society
      iii. Culture
   b. Victim risk
   c. Victim routines and routine activity maps
6. Appendices
   a. Live photos of the victim
   b. Family and friends organizational chart
   c. Timelines and calendars

Implications of Research-Based Forensic Victimology

It is important to recognize that the research-based forensic victimology should be adapted on a case-to-case basis. Maslow (1943) posited that individuals are motivated by the need for self-actualization. Beyond developmental psychology, interestingly, Maslow's hierarchy of needs has been applied in various fields, such as nursing and business, for example. Applying Maslow's hierarchy of needs to nursing suggests that nurses identify the specific needs of each patient and respond to them accordingly within the realm of the five stages; therefore, assisting the patient with moving forward toward the next stage. When applying Maslow's hierarchy of needs to victims, while it might be important in cases where live victims are self-reporting to respond to the intrinsic needs of victims, it is arguable that Maslow's hierarchy might help investigators identify gaps in a victim's life or needs that were not being met for a victim in one place or the other. The reason identification of such strengths and weaknesses might be important is because, for example, if a woman is in an unhappy marriage and seeks passionate encounters to sate the needs she is not getting from her husband, this behavior could result in the woman increasing her likelihood of becoming a victim of a violent crime. Another reason identification is important is because it might help investigators understand how a victim might respond to his or her killer. The author opines that behavior is derived from cognition, and cognition is derived from the culmination of personality, emotionality, esteem, and a myriad of other factors. So identifying strengths and weaknesses in these areas is critical to empirically surmising how an individual would respond: would the victim fight back physically or verbally, try to escape, acquiesce, or respond in another way consistent and related to his or her personality, emotionality, cognition, behavior, envirosocioculturalism, and so on?

Physiological: Victim's Physical Demographics and Attributes

Stage one or the physiological stage of Maslow's (1943) hierarchy of needs in relation to victimology might contain all of the demographic information about a victim, such as name(s), date of birth, date of death, sex, race, height, weight, build, hair color, hair type, hair length, eye color, jewelry, other important demographic information, and physical identifiers (i.e., tattoos) (Posner, 2010; Walton, 2006). Additionally, this stage or category of victimology might include the addresses and information about the victim's past and present physical residences (i.e., homes) and transportation information past and present, such as did the victim use public transportation and/or have his or her own car, plane, boat, and so on. Further, this category might also include health and medical information such as physical and mental health histories, substance abuse, physical and mental handicaps or limitations, and fitness level.

Safety: Victim in Relation to Personal, Familial, Financial, and Occupational Safety

Stage two or the safety stage of Maslow's (1943) hierarchy of needs in relation to victimology might contain information about the victim's perception of personal safety past and present both as an individual and within his or her own environment. It might also include familial information about current, estranged, and former members in relation to the victim. Additionally, this category of victimology might include characteristics of the victim's family, such as the following (Posner, 2010; Walton, 2006):

1. Family was affectionate.
2. Family was hostile and/or indifferent.
3. Family has high mental abilities.
4. Family has poor mental abilities.
5. Family was prosperous during the individual's upbringing.
6. Family lived in poverty during the individual's upbringing.
7. Parents graduated from high school.
8. Parents have low social status.
9. Parents were motivated and gave direction.
10. Parents sat around and failed to instruct.
11. Parents strived for success and achieved success.
12. Parents stagnated and remained in the same place for years.

Further, the safety category might include financial security and socioeconomic status information, such as was the victim wealthy, middle-class, poor, social position, and educational level both past and present. Occupational safety, past and present, or in other words how safe the victim felt in his or her occupation, where he or she worked, and so on, might be included in this category. One of the most important questions to answer in relation to occupational information is how much contact the victim had with strangers. Though statistically victims are more likely victimized by someone they know, identifying how much time the victim spent with strangers is very important when determining a victim's risk level. Often, victims have additional resources related to safety like security systems, firearms, and weapons of other kinds.

Love and Belonging: Victim in Relation to Relationships
Stage three or the love and belonging stage of Maslow's (1943) hierarchy of needs in relation to victimology might contain information about the victim's current marital status in addition to past and estranged or once estranged spouses. Second, this category might contain information about the victim's intimate partners past, present, and estranged and any noticeable or memorable information friends and family recall about them. Next, this category might contain information about the victim's interpersonal relationships and friendships past, present, and estranged. It is usually helpful in many cases to speak with the victim's best friend or closest circle of friends or those whom the victim confided in most, but be mindful, the victim's spouse is not always the closest individual to the victim. Acquaintances both past and present who might be significant from work, the victim's lifestyle, and so forth, would be important to gather information about in this category. Further, strangers whom the victim might have mentioned and why the stranger was noticeable to the victim both past and present along with sexual encounters, stalking, police reports, and so on, dealing with strangers or anything related to stranger encounters that were out of the ordinary for the victim should also be included. If strangers become significant, gather information, such as gender, age, physical description, other demographic information, and the location of the encounter(s). Not always the most important, but certainly worth mentioning are the victim's enemies both past and present. Again, it is critical to recognize that someone they know kills most murder victims. And finally, pursuant to how the victim communicated with all of these individuals, was it in person, via the telephone landline or cellular, over the computer, through social media, and did the victim have an online presence is an additional critical piece of information necessary toward a complete and thorough analysis of the victim. A computer and online presence would also include gathering information on e-mail addresses and e-mails, instant messages, and social media interaction including screen names, log-ins, and passwords. Phone records are often helpful; text messages, voice mail messages, and landline phone messages should also be collected.

Esteem: Victim in Relation to Personality, Cognition, Emotionality, Behavior, and Achievements

Stage four or the esteem stage of Maslow's (1943) hierarchy of needs in relation to victimology might personally contain traits and the victim's likes and dislikes, identifying whether the victim was normally argumentative or apologetic, aggressive, or passive, and other characteristics in context (see end of Appendix A). Another very important subcategory of esteem might be cognition or the process by which an individual perceives the world and how he or she processes it in context to navigating life. Understanding the in-depth way in how a victim thinks is critical to an analysis of the victim because based on assumptions, presumptions, or conceptions, the victim might respond to a violent attack one way or the other in combination with other factors, such as emotionality. Cognition is tied to emotionality, which is tied to behavior and can be illustrated in this example. An individual thinks of losing his or her parent. The individual begins to feel sadness. The individual's behavioral response to thinking about the loss and feeling of sadness is to physically cry.

Emotionality also includes analyzing information the victim might have kept in diaries and journals, notes, or letters the victim might have written to himself or herself or to others, the victim's psychological problems, and/or emotional disturbance not otherwise collected in the physiological category along with other expressions of emotions, such as anger, anxiety or depression, low self-esteem, suicide attempts, and the nature of what, how, why, and so on.

It is also important to establish and analyze the victim's behavior and establish an understanding of normal behavioral patterns, what was reasonable or unreasonable for the victim, how the victim conducted himself or herself under normal circumstances, and so on. Finally, the victim's achievements, such as a good reputation among family, friends, peers, colleagues, and so forth, and knowing whether the victim perceived himself or herself as being attractive, unattractive, successful, or unsuccessful in things like school, work, and life are always critical pieces of information to be analyzed as well.

Self-Actualization: Victim in Relation to Relative Adoption of Worldly Concepts

Stage five or, simply speaking, Maslow's (1943) concept of self-actualization might be summed up with the phrase "find the meaning of life" because self-actualization encompasses everything that an individual becomes having reached such a pinnacle in life. Individuals want to give back, be good stewards, and find the meaning of life! The obstacle for some when reaching self-actualization takes shape in the form of fighting so hard to fulfill needs on the physiological that self-actualization is never achieved. For instance, a musician, with an incredible voice and incredible songwriting ability and plays multiple instruments, works as an auto mechanic, which does not lend opportunity for the musician to use expressed talents. Further, it is interesting to consider the concept of envirossocioculturalism in relation to self-actualization. To reiterate from Chapter 3, *envirosocioculturalism* is the aggregate of environmental, social, and cultural conditions that influence the life of an individual combined with the circumstances by which one is surrounded as part of a community distinguishable by particular ways of living within the social construct and its unique identity as seen in its beliefs, customs, religion, lifestyle, professions, interpersonal relationships, and routine activities. It is important to learn through victimology everything that can be gleaned about the victim's environment, societal interaction, and culture, which includes involvement with social institutions and movements, volunteer work, criminal activity, criminal records, recent court decisions that affected the victim, vigilantism/vengeance, problems and conflicts, and insurance policies and claims. While it is true that victim-precipitation theory is not thought well after by victims and victim advocacy groups generally speaking, this empirical research-based victimology approach is designed to identify, define, examine, analyze, synthesize, and evaluate all information toward establishing everything that can be learned about the victim and, in turn, the offender. Other aspects related to envirosocioculturalism to be considered are victimization, personal protection and awareness, identifying if the victim was paranoid or fearful to violent crime, exposed to violent crime, was security conscious, and took precautions, and what defense mechanisms if any might the victim have employed to thwart an attack.

Educational information related to the victim could play a vital role in that if the victim is school-age, teenage, or young adult age, academic and related information might lead to a deeper understanding of the victim's level of self-esteem, areas of interest, training, experience, and the like. Information should be gathered about the victim's

1. Elementary school and location
2. Middle school and location
3. High school and location
4. College, location, major, minor, degree, and date awarded
5. Graduate school, location, major, track, concentration, internships, thesis/graduate research paper/dissertation, degree, and date awarded
6. Doctoral school (if separate from graduate school), location, major, track, concentration, internships, thesis/graduate research paper/ dissertation, degree, and date awarded

Culture is the third leg of envirosocioculturalism and is interrelated to a victim's routine activities and lifestyle. All information about the victim's clothing style and daily routine established in 24-hour time periods; how the victim traveled to work; what the victim did during morning work, on his or her lunch break, and as an afternoon routine; the victim's after-work travel; what the victim ate for a pre-evening meal, evening meal, and post-evening meal; and the victim's nighttime and bedtime routines, in addition to notable changes in any part of the victim's routine or lifestyle, places the victim stopped going to, and the victim's interests, hobbies (i.e., music, books, television programs, movies, and gaming), extracurricular activities, clubs, and sports engagements, are all critically important lifestyle-related pieces of information to collect and analyze about the victim.

Appendices
Several appendices should accompany or be embedded within the construct of a thorough, analytical victimological study, such as (see Appendix A)

1. Live photos of the victim
2. Family and friends organizational chart
3. Timelines and routines
   a. 24-hour—timeline by the hour 0000–1159
   b. 48-hour—timeline by the hour 0000–1159
   c. 72-hour—timeline by the hour 0000–1159
   d. Week—timeline by the day
   e. Month—timeline by the day
   f. Year—timeline by the month (calendars are helpful to use here)

Victim–Offender Relationship

Victim–offender relationship information is contained in Section III Love and Belonging. It has been discussed in the previous chapters that research has shown that crime scene staging appears to be a function of the victim–offender relationship and/or their level of association both in the empirical data and in anecdotal accounts. Thus, crime scene staging is an indication that the offender has some prior relationship to the victim (Napier & Baker, 2005). There are many ways a victim and an offender might be related, such as by biological connection, spouses, intimate partners, friends, colleagues, neighbors, strangers, and enemies (Turvey, 2012). (See Chapters 1 and 4 for more information.) It is arguable that crime scene stagers manipulate homicide crime scenes because they believe they will be named as suspects simply because of how they knew the victim. As many investigators and researchers have suggested in the historical literature on staging discussed in Chapter 1, it is not surprising to observe that most often that the victim and offender are at a minimum familiar with one another in cases where crime scene staging is evident (Douglas & Munn, 1992).

Importance of Victim–Offender Relationship Examination

There are approximately 200,000 cold cases in this country (Hargrove, 2010). It is arguable that the general public presumes all law enforcement officers, forensics professionals, or laboratory analysts automatically know how to properly investigate death scenes based on their occupational titles. Just like medical doctors who specialize in one area of human anatomy or another, the title investigator, analyst, detective, rank titles, or the like do not translate to death scene expert, homicide expert, DNA expert, trace evidence, or firearms expert to name a few. While there are countless excellent officers, detectives, and other types of criminal justice professionals who are superb death scene experts based on their combined education, training, and experience, many are not due to reasons beyond their control. Again, crime scene investigation is a reflection of the education, training, and expereince of the crime scene investigator, the more eduaction, training, and expereince coupled with an open mind and willingness to work on a team of people who posessess various skill sets, the better a scene will be processed. Consider for a moment the homicide clearance rates in the United States. According to the U.S. Federal Bureau of Investigation (2011a,b), approximately 64.8% of 14,612 homicides were cleared "by arrest or exceptional means" in 2011 (2011a, para. 8; 2011b, para. 7). That means 9,468 murders were solved or resolved leaving approximately 5,144 murders unsolved, cold, or otherwise. It is unknown how many of these cases might involve staged crime scenes.

There are many reasons why this number is so high. Some jurisdictions simply do not deal with homicide and especially staged crime scenes often enough to really know what to do when tragedy does strike. They might not ever heard of the victim–offender relationship and do not know how to complete victimology. There are jurisdictional roadblocks where some agencies do not want to work with other agencies. Some investigators have argued, "Whose crime scene is this anyway?" Answer: It is the victim's crime scene. It was the victim's life, it is the victim's death, and it most certainly is the victim's justice. Justice belongs to the victim. Investigators seek justice for victims, not for themselves. Justice belongs to the victim, and, therefore, so does the crime scene. There are professional roadblocks related to some criminal justice professionals not wanting to ask for help among a plethora of other reasons. Maybe, there is no forensic evidence in the case. Maybe, investigators know who committed the murder, but do not have enough evidence to make an arrest. Maybe, there is backlog in the state laboratory and an arrest depends on test results. Maybe, it is due to the sheer volume some agencies deal with in homicide per year. There are countless reasons for why murder cases are unresolved, but one thing is for sure, education, training, and experience is necessary toward the prevention of adding more cold cases to the pool.

Regardless, the most crippling thing anyone can do when charged with the duty of investigating a death scene is to fail to consider alternatives. A murder arguably could fall anywhere along an interactional continuum of 50% victim and 50% offender plus or minus. Therefore, failing to consider the significant dynamics between the victim and offender, choosing not to complete victimology, rushing to judgment, assuming the pristine condition of the crime scene, and accepting at-the-scene witness statements as fact or "empirical evidence" devoid of any type of substantiation whatsoever can create monumental-sized problems for the case in the future that sometimes cannot be undone. Justice is not served in such cases and what is worse in unsolved murder cases or cases where an arrest cannot be made allows violent offenders to remain in society with the opportunity to reoffend…and they do. Consider the case of *Illinois v. Drew Peterson*. Former police officer, Drew Peterson, was convicted of killing his third wife, Kathleen Savio, and staging her death to look like an accident (Kotb, 2007). According to Kotb (2007), Kathleen Savio's body was recovered in a dry bathtub in her home in 2004, and her death was ruled accidental citing drowning as a cause of death. Questions were always raised about the dry bathtub and how Savio could have drowned in a dry bathtub. Accurate and complete victimology in this case would have identified things about the victim and the victim in relation to the offender paramount in resolving the case in 2004, but that was not done. In 2008, the case was reviewed and the manner of death was changed to homicide. Then, in 2007, Drew Peterson reported that his fourth wife, Stacy Peterson, was missing. Peterson claimed that Stacy Peterson had run off with another man to flee from life's obligations. Peterson was the only individual ever suspected of killing Kathleen Savio and continues as the only suspect in the disappearance of Stacy Peterson. The victimology was very important in the Savio case. Savio wrote letters to the District Attorney's Office claiming that Peterson was going to kill her and that no one would do anything to protect her because Peterson was a law enforcement officer. Failure of investigators to recognize the staged crime scene in this case allowed a violent offender, Drew Peterson, to remain in society so that he could acquire yet another victim, this time a younger woman, who appears to potentially have met a similar fate as Kathleen Savio. Peterson was no stranger to these women; he was their intimate partner, spouse, father of their children, and so on. The Peterson case is illustrious of the importance of victimology and in studying the victim–offender relationship.

Importance of Victim–Offender Relationship: Circumstantial Evidence

For the purpose of this discussion, circumstantial evidence might be defined as evidence that when interrelated and in totality helps to prove that the victim's death is a homicide rather than accident, suicide, or otherwise. Some staged cases do not contain physical evidence that could tip the scale in the courtroom for the jury as to the guilt or innocence of a defendant. In these cases, the evaluation of the circumstantial evidence in relation to how it might be linked to build a substantial circumstantial case against a defendant is warranted. Offenders just do not all of the sudden change their lifestyles and do something differently on the day of the murder that they have done another way for the past 30 years for example. As discussed earlier, breaks or changes in routine are earmarks of staged crime scenes that should help raise the question, immediately within an investigation, "Is the scene staged?" Take, for example, the couple that has been married for 30 years. They have a daily regimen that includes getting up together in the morning, the husband goes running, they eat breakfast and watch the news, then they spend the day working in their yard, they eat dinner together while watching television in the evening, and then retiring to bed in separate bedrooms. They do not go out at night. The husband only runs in the morning. The husband is not friendly, so they do not have a large social circle with whom they visit often. But on the day of his wife's disappearance, the husband uncharacteristically waved to neighbors as he left the marital residence after dark driving his wife's vehicle. Another neighbor returning from an evening shift at the hospital saw the husband jogging within a few miles of the marital residence after the neighbors saw him leave in his wife's car.

During a conversation the next day while the husband was cleaning the garage, a neighbor asked where his wife was and the husband replied that she did not want to help clean the garage. The husband asks the neighbor if he would like to go out to eat, and the two make their way to a local cafe for a midday lunch. While at lunch, the husband excuses himself from the table, goes to his car, retrieves a bag, then walks to the dumpster behind the café and then back to the table without the bag claiming that he just remembered he had spoiled dairy products in the car he forgot to discard. Then later that evening, the husband leaves the marital residence after dark again this time, but driving his car and waves to neighbors sitting on their front porches as he drives past. The next day, sirens awaken the neighborhood and when neighbors convene at the couple's residence, the husband tells them his wife was not there when he arrived home last night from running errands and still this morning when he awoke she was not home so he reported her missing.

Investigators interview the husband who claims the couple has maintained their very regimented routine over the past few days and he cannot imagine where his wife went. Neighbors give a different story. They too confirm the couple follows a very strict routine, but they have noticed changes in the husband's behavior and have not seen the wife at all. Over the course of the next week, investigators search for the missing woman. The husband makes public pleas for her return and volunteers canvas neighboring areas. Investigators complete a thorough and accurate victimological study on the victim and can find no reason why the wife would leave her marriage, her home, and so on. The wife was not depressed and did not have a mental health history. Investigators find no evidence of an extramarital affair for either the husband or wife and have only foul play to suspect in her disappearance.

Two weeks after the wife goes missing, the husband packs up her clothing and drives to a donation drop-off 100 miles away where he discards her clothing. He closes her bank and credit card accounts and remarks to the creditors that his wife is deceased. He speaks of her always in the past tense to neighbors inquiring about the case and, after the first week, makes no effort to find her. Being computer illiterate, the elderly husband has never even sent an e-mail, but he buys a computer and sets up a social media account. Before long, a new woman is seen frequenting the house and not soon after she moves in. The new couple is seen by neighbors coming in and out of the house at all hours of the day and night, they are seen at nightclubs and social functions, and the husband has returned to being unfriendly to neighbors. The skeletal remains of the wife are found 18 months later off the side of a back road 3 miles from the marital residence and her vehicle was recovered in a nearby swamp. Autopsy determined she had been bludgeoned to death.

The author would argue that victim–offender relationship is one of the primary reasons offenders stage crime scenes. Mize and Shackelford (2008) found that the severity of injury to the victim was related to the closeness of the relationship between the offender and the victim. Therefore, bludgeoning would fall right in line with their finding in this hypothetical case example. Moving bodies is not easy, so offenders do not move bodies that they do not believe have to be moved in order to avoid detection. This is not to say that every domestic violence homicide offender removes his or her victim's body from his or her environment. There are many offenders who do not discard the victim's body and instead of making the missing person claim, make the claim of suicide, accident, intruder, natural, and so forth, still detracting attention from the offender and the connection between him, her, and the victim. In this hypothetical case, the suspected offender, the husband, felt that he had to move the body out of his environment to avoid being connected with the wife's disappearance and death. The husband believed that he would be suspected of bludgeoning his wife to death if he did not remove her body and her vehicle from their common environment. Instead, his claim was that she left one evening and never came back and he had no idea what happened to her. The husband completely changed his lifestyle after his wife went missing and there is no physical evidence tying him to the crime scene. However, this is a case where there is circumstantial evidence that that in totality helps to prove that the victim's death is a homicide rather than accident, suicide, or natural. Ultimately, it would be up to a state attorney to decide if charges could be brought and possibly a jury to decide if the husband was guilty of homicide, but the point of this example is to illustrate that the dynamics of the intimate connection between the victim and the offender, the changes in the husband's routine immediately following his wife's disappearance, is so overwhelmingly significant that it cannot be ignored.

Facilitation, Precipitation, and Victim Risk

The concepts of victim facilitation and precipitation are controversial in nature. Victim facilitation and precipitation are not concepts accepted by victims or victim advocacy groups because some victims feel they insinuate that victims cause their own victimization (Friedmann, 2011). One of the first things very important to recognize about the concepts of victim facilitation and precipitation in relation to victim–offender relationship and crime scene staging dynamics in homicide cases is that at no time are the authors inferring, implying, or suggesting that the victims in any staged homicide case caused their deaths. Further, it is important to define causality in order to lay the foundation for comparison going forward. Therefore, for the purpose of this discussion, causality or causation is defined as a cause and effect relationship where the cause elicits the effect as a direct and measurable consequence of the cause. Another important aspect to recognize in building the foundation for this discussion is that victim facilitation and precipitation is not reflective of offender motive, and excuse for murder, a viable defense, and is included herein pursuant to investigatory purposes only.

Facilitation could be defined as anything that might increase the likelihood of becoming a victim of violent crime. It is true that certain occupations and/or lifestyle choices definitely expose individuals to situations that create an amount of risk to one's life. For example, it might be said that being a hospital administrator is less dangerous than being a prostitute meeting strangers for intimate encounters. Second, it is also true that an older, suburban family, with two working parents and two young children and who frequent locations, such as the local family gym, their church, the kids' school, and extracurricular sports complexes, is at a much less risk for becoming victims of violent crime than say a drug dealer who carries a gun for personal protection, who has no permanent address, no spouse, and no education and is a habitual felon out on parole. When comparing the coal miner to the intrinsic occupational hazards of the hospital administrator to the prostitute and the lifestyle choices of the suburban family compared to the habitual felon drug dealer, it is easy to see that occupational and lifestyle choices could facilitate or increase the likelihood of becoming a victim of violent crime. Embedded within the construct of scientific victimology is the idea that high-risk activities, such as prostitution or drug dealing, could reasonably contribute to being in the wrong place at the wrong time with individuals with a propensity toward violence.

Case Example 1

While working two separate murder cases, the author interviewed the same witness in both cases. Neither of the two murders happened in the same location or at the same time, but this particular witness was present for both. The interesting thing about this witness was his ability to recognize the danger he himself was in by hanging around with individuals who were being murdered on a regular basis. The witness was a drug dealer and the two murder victims were drug dealers as well. Both had been shot and killed in blitz attack style shootings. The witness knew he could be next, but claimed he could not stop selling drugs because he had too many children to take care of and that a job at a fast-food restaurant would not pay the bills. The witness continued his high-risk lifestyle of being a drug dealer because he needed money regardless of the risk dealing drugs brought to his life.

Victim-precipitation theorists, such as von Hentig, Mendelsohn, and Wolfgang (1978), were proponents of examining the victim for how he or she facilitated and/or precipitated their own victimization (Friedmann, 2011). Precipitation could be defined as the active or passive behaviors of the victim that coincide with circumstances of becoming a victim. Conflict is something else that could arguably heighten the likelihood of becoming a victim very quickly and unexpectedly in some cases. Road rage killings are good examples of how two strangers end up angry with one another over driving decisions where one stranger ends up killing the other stranger out of essentially an argument. Understanding who, why, what, and where any conflicts existed for a victim can help sometimes identify a pool of suspects to examine further. It does not mean that these victims facilitated or precipitated their own deaths; it only means that there were people who possibly harbored reason to want a victim dead for one reason or another. This is often the case in jealousy-motivated homicides between two family members, intimate partners, or even former friends. Jealousy is a powerful catalyst for homicide that sometimes compels individuals to do things they might not otherwise do given different circumstances.

Case Example 2

Two Hispanic immigrant brothers settle in the United States. One brother is married with children. The other brother is single with no children. The first brother's wife has an affair with her brother-in-law, subsequently divorces her husband, marries her former brother-in-law, and has his baby. The trio fights and feuds constantly and are in and out of domestic violence court on a regular basis. After one particular court appearance involving protective orders from abuse for all three parties, where the divorced brother was granted a protective order from his brother and ex-wife and the newly married couple were granted protective orders from the estranged brother, the three exit the courthouse arguing outside the building and leave in separate vehicles. Upon arriving home, the wife and her new husband walk around the back of their house where the wife's ex-husband (the new husband's brother) is lying in wait. The estranged brother/ex-husband shoots and kills his brother and flees the scene.

In this case, the brother from whom the wife divorced was jealous over her affair and new relationship with his brother. He chose to respond to his emotionality in this case through a violent attack. This scenario happens frequently in some shape or form in many love triangles. Proponents for classic victim-precipitation theory might argue that this victim precipitated his own death by stealing his brother's wife, while opponents of victim-precipitation theory might posit that victim's actions did not precipitate or facilitate his death. Regardless, exposure to violent situations on all sides in this case appear to have actively played a role both inside and outside the courtroom.

An example of a passive precipitant factor might be a wealthy man who gets lost on his way to an out of town appointment and drives his expensive car into a gas station to buy gas. A group of individuals standing nearby notice the man and they decide to rob him. He is oblivious as they approach acting as they are going to ask the man for directions. A fight between him and them ensue as they try to steal his car, so one of the robbers pulls a gun and shoots the man dead at the gas pump. The victim did not actively precipitate his death, but became a victim because robbers who saw a way to make fast cash targeted him.

Assessing Risk Level

Assessing risk level for becoming a victim is paramount to successful completion of victimology. In essence, level of risk, or an individual's propensity toward becoming a victim, can be divided into three categories: low, medium, and high risk (Petherick, 2014b). In relation to the victim's envirossocioculturalism, it is also important to identify any high-risk situations, for example,

1. Is the victim in a domestic violence relationship?
2. Is the victim involved in gang activity?
3. Is the victim involved in selling illegal drugs or substance abuse?
4. Is the victim a prostitute?
5. Does the victim gamble?

These situations are often connected to various types of homicide cases including staged homicide cases where the victim–offender relationship is significant enough to warrant staging the scene. While the mention of these situations do not infer that every domestic violence victim, every individual involved in gang activity, every drug dealer, every drug addict, every prostitute, or every gambler will become a homicide victim because of his or her involvement in activities related to these situations, it is well established in the critical literature, the Federal Bureau of Investigation's Uniform Crime Reporting system, and within the law enforcement community that individuals who engage in these types of situations are more often the victims of violent crime than are those who do not engage in these types of activities.

Interestingly, an individual's personality, cognition, behavior, emotionality, and envirosocioculturalism can arguably also play a role in victim risk. Individuals who are aggressive and demonstrate extreme emotionality like emotional outburst, fits of rage, or similar outbursts are at a higher risk of becoming a victim than those who do not. Overall, pursuant to forensic victimology, the significance of the victim–offender relationship and the role it plays in crime scene staging, exposure to violence, criminal activity, and other high-risk situations should be fully examined during the course of all victimological studies.

References

Cohen, L., & Felson, M. (1979). Social change and crime rate trends: A routine activity approach. *American Sociological Review, 44*, 588–608.

Douglas, J. E., Burgess, A. W., Burgess, A. G., & Ressler, R. K. (2006). *Crime classification manual: A standard system for investigating and classifying violent crimes* (2nd ed.). San Francisco, CA: John Wiley & Sons, Inc.

Douglas, J. E., & Munn, C. (1992, February). Violent crime scene analysis: Modus operandi, signature, and staging. *FBI Law Enforcement Bulletin, 61*(2), 1–10.

Federal Bureau of Investigation. (2011a). *Uniform crime reports: Clearance rates.* Retrieved from http://www.fbi.gov/about-us/cjis/ucr/crime-in-the-u.s/2011/crime-in-the-u.s.-2011/clearances

Federal Bureau of Investigation. (2011b). *Uniform crime reports: Murder.* Retrieved from http://www.fbi.gov/about-us/cjis/ucr/crime-in-the-u.s/2011/crime-in-the-u.s.-2011/violent-crime/murder

Friedmann, M. (2011). *Victimology theory.* Retrieved from http://www.thebenjaminfoundation.us/18789/19010.html

Hargrove, T. (2010, March 23). *Unsolved homicide analysis: A look at what kinds of murders get solved.* New York: Scripps Howard News Service.

Hazelwood, R. R., & Napier, M. R. (2004). Crime scene staging and its detection. *International Journal of Offender Therapy and Comparative Criminology, 48*(6), 744–759. doi: 10.1177/0306624X04268298

Hindelang, M. J., Gottfredson, M. R., & Garofalo, J. (1978). *Victims of personal crime: An empirical foundation for a theory of personal victimization.* Cambridge, MA: Ballinger.

Holmes, R. M., & Homes, S. T. (2002). *Profiling violent crimes: An investigative tool* (3rd ed.). Thousand Oaks, CA: Sage.

Kotb, H. (2007, December 21). *Deadly suspicion.* Retrieved from http://www.msnbc.msn.com/id/22316689//

Maslow, A. H. (1943). A theory of human motivation. *Psychological Review, 50*, 360–396.

Mize, K., & Shackelford, T. (2008). Intimate partner homicide methods in heterosexual, gay, and lesbian relationships. *Violence and Victims, 23*(1), 98–114.

Napier, M. R., & Baker, K. P. (2005). Criminal personality profiling. In S. H. James & J. J. Nordby (Eds.), *Forensic science: An introduction to scientific and investigative techniques* (2nd ed.). Boca Raton, FL: CRC Press/Taylor & Francis Group.

Pettler, L. G. (2011). *Crime scene behaviors of crime scene stagers* (Doctoral dissertation). Available from ProQuest (2251577601).

Petherick, W. (2014a). *Victimology: The study of victims in criminal investigations.* Retrieved from http://www.crimelibrary.com/criminal_mind/profiling/victimology/1.html

Petherick, W. (2014b). *Victimology: The study of victims in criminal investigations.* Retrieved from http://www.crimelibrary.com/criminal_mind/profiling/victimology/5.html

Posner, R. (2010). *The miraculous phenomenon of life response* (1st ed.). California: Author.

Ressler, R. K., Burgess, A. W., & Douglas, J. E. (1988). *Sexual homicide: Patterns and motives.* New York: The Free Press.

Turvey, B. E. (1999). *Criminal profiling: An introduction to behavioral evidence analysis* (1st ed.). London, UK: Academic Press.

Turvey, B. E. (2012). *Criminal profiling: An introduction to behavioral evidence analysis* (4th ed.). London, UK: Academic Press.

Tobolowsky, P. (2000). *Understanding victimology.* Cincinnati, OH: Anderson

Walton, R. (2006). *Cold case homicides: Practical investigative techniques.* Boca Raton, FL: CRC Press/Taylor & Francis Group.

Wilcox, P. (2010). Victimization, theories of. In B. Fisher & S. Lab (Eds.), *Encyclopedia of victimization and crime prevention* (pp. 978–986). Thousand Oaks, CA: Sage Publications, Inc. doi: 10/4135/9781412979993.n334

Wolfgang, M. E. (1957). Victim-precipitated criminal homicide. In J. E. Jacoby, T. A. Severance, & A. S. Bruce (Eds.), *Classics of criminology* (4th ed.). Long Grove, IL: Waveland Press.

Purposes and Motives

6

Introduction

Crime scene staging is a deliberate, purposeful act by an offender to manipulate elements of the crime and its scene to misdirect the investigation with criminal intent in reflection of what the offender thinks, feels, and believes will be the most believable to investigators, family members, friends, and so on, based arguably on the crime scene offender's personality, cognition, behavior, emotionality, and envirosocioculturalism. Hans Gross (1924) argued that practitioners should study personality characteristics of murderers. Douglas, Burgess, Burgess, and Ressler (2006) argued that the crime scene is a reflection of the personality of the offender. Though some have defined crime scene staging limited in scope to physical evidence only, the act of staging at any level in and of itself is a behavior observable often in the form of both physical and verbal evidence. Physical evidence does not stage itself. It does not position itself, clean itself, destroy itself, and so forth. Rather, the physical behaviors of the offender are the acts that stage physical evidence on purpose. The answer to every question one could ask about the why and how of an offender's actions are twofold: (1) The answer to the "why" is always the same, which is, "Because it met the needs of the offender." (2) The answer to the "how" part is always specific to the case itself, namely, the offender, victim, specific type of conflict if present, and a myriad of other factors. Take, for example, the homicide staged as a suicide in a firearm-related death. Firearms do not put themselves into the hands of murdered victims. Offenders put them there. Human beings do not have to think about breathing in order to breathe nor do they have to think about blinking in order to blink, but human beings have to think consciously or unconsciously about most other acts in order for the body to physically move. For the purpose of this discussion, the point is that it is important to recognize that generally speaking thinking precedes behavior. An offender thinks something then does it, and in the aforementioned example, the offender thinks the firearm has to be in the hand of the victim in order for it to look like a suicide, so then the offender physically places the firearm into the hand of the victim to make that happen. Most offenders have no idea what real suicides look like, and Douglas and Munn (1992) argued that it is for this very reason that many offenders make mistakes in this area.

It is the responsibility of the homicide investigator, crime scene investigator, or others charged with the duty of investigating death scenes to educate themselves on what is known about deception in both the physical and behavioral senses. An investigator once said to the author that he was not going "to put all his eggs in that basket" referring to behavioral evidence. The author would argue that like footwear impression evidence, for example, behavioral evidence is one of the most overlooked types of evidence in crime scenes that the author has seen in her 15-year career. So, going back to the example previously mentioned, the offender physically places the firearm into the hand of the victim and arguably positions the firearm the way the offender *believes* it should look as if the victim shot him- or herself. This is the very essence of crime scene staging. Douglas et al. (2006) argued that the drives that influence everyday life influence behavior the very same way during the acts of murder and rape. Thus, the offender's personality, cognition, behavior, emotionality, and envirosocioculturalism arguably influence how he or she perceives, then thinks, then feels, then acts (maybe not in that exact order): the who, what, when, where, why, and how the crime scene should look, the way it should feel, what needs to be added, what needs to be removed, and so on, are all toward meeting the needs of the offender and accomplishing his or her objectives. Everything observable in the crime scene meets the needs of the offender. The location meets the needs of the offender. The timing meets the needs of the offender. The type of weapon used all the way to how and who finds the victim's body meets the needs of the offender. When working in the field oftentimes, questions are posed during the course of crime scene investigation, such as "Wonder why the body is on the floor next to the wall?" The answer is, because it meets the needs of the offender. The tricky part is *why* and *how* does it meet the needs of the offender. In order to figure that out, one must identify what the needs of the offender are in the first place.

The phrase "crime scene staging" implies that there has been a crime, that there is a scene or location where the crime occurred, and that the scene of the crime has been manipulated or tampered with. Empirical research suggests that offenders do stage crime scenes and that the crime scene staging behaviors of crime scene stagers are deliberate. The ways offenders can stage scenes are endless, limited by only their imagination, creativity, and the physical constraints of the offender in relation to the victim (Schlesinger et al., 2012). Research has identified patterns of behavior, such as cleaning, concealing or hiding, creating or building, destroying, lying, and planning, on the part of offenders who manipulate any of the preceding toward misdirecting an investigation. Numerous authors have written about why offenders stage. Arguably, some offenders do not want to admit their guilt, take responsibility for what they have done, or pay the consequences for their behavior; thus, the overarching purposes of crime scene staging are within the realms of

1. Disconnecting the victim–offender relationship
2. Deception
3. Misdirect investigations
4. Self-preservation
5. Avoid apprehension

Disconnecting the Victim–Offender Relationship

Once an offender murders a victim, especially when there is a prior association, intimate relationship, or the like between them, the offender really wants to disconnect from the victim. This means that the offender wants to put distance between him- or herself and the victim at all costs. Therefore, because the offender's personality is mirrored in the crime scene, his reflection is thus embedded in the physical evidence. Hazelwood and Napier (2004) argued that when it comes to the staged crime scene, all investigators are left with the victim and the scene. This is true. As discussed in the previous chapter, the importance of victimology cannot be understated. The anchor of any investigation is the crime scene of course, and successful prosecution definitely begins with the crime scene itself; however, victimology is the baseline for which everything including the crime scene evidence is compared to. The more one learns about the victim, the more one knows about the crime, its scene, and in turn the reflection of the offender within the construct of the physical evidence in the crime scene begins to take shape. The best predictor of future behavior is past, relevant behavior, so for instance, the female victim reported to having killed herself by shooting herself in the chest, but who has never been known to have any association to any firearm anytime in her life, by the boyfriend who is known to carry a gun, threaten others with a gun, and view his firearm as an extension of his power symbolic of the control he maintains over his environment and those who live within its boundaries, is a prime example of the offender who murders his victim with the very weapon that means something to him, not her. This is the offender who stages the crime scene as a suicide, home invasion, interrupted robbery, or even claims to have found the victim in this condition after arriving home from work. The offender is trying to disconnect from the victim. The offender is trying to put time and distance between them so he is not viewed as a likely suspect. Thus, the victim–offender relationship is paramount to the study of staging behaviors exhibited by offenders because it alludes to the offender's personality and his or her criminal and noncriminal behavioral consistencies as seen during the act of murder and the offender's behavior otherwise. Offenders need to disconnect from their victims because they recognize that their association to the victim increases the likelihood that they will be named suspects, so again, if an offender feels compelled to stage a scene, recognize this compulsion as an admission to having an association to the victim prior to the victim's death. Even though the most commonly staged scenes are staged by offenders who are current or former intimate partners of some kind of the victim, other types of victim–offender relationships, such as employer–employee and neighbors, compel offenders to stage murder scenes as well. For example, two acquaintances that know each other from a commonality, such as a grocery store clerk and a customer, might casually interact on a regular basis. Their conversations might be along the lines of small talk, the weather, and so forth. But when one becomes a victim at the hand of the other, the dynamics significantly change. Acquaintances *know* each other, but do not know each other intimately. So when one becomes the victim of the other, the knowledge and experience gleaned from the store-based interaction might end up playing a role in cases where an offender is trying to stage the scene based on what he knows about the victim in combination with his or her own personality, cognition, behavior, emotionality, or envirosocioculturalism. The next chapter will analyze intimate partner homicide in relation to crime scene staging at length, but to note, individuals who are friends, related, intimately involved, or the like know a lot more about each other than do strangers or acquaintances. Therefore, it is arguable that the victim–offender relationship in those cases might influence the way in which the stager chooses to stage the scene versus ways in which he or she chooses not to stage the scene simply based on what the stager knows about the victim coupled with his own personality, cognition, behavior, emotionality, or envirosocioculturalism.

Deception

Geberth (2006) stated, "Homicide investigation is a highly professional and specialized undertaking, which requires years of practical experience coupled with a process of continual education and training" (p. 1). Therefore, keeping up with what is new in the world of homicide studies is a must for investigators so they are aware of what is being studied, tested, and discovered within the construct of empirical research design. Investigators want to solve crimes, but those who dismiss the value of empirical research toward helping investigators solve their crimes are remiss to say the least. As mentioned before, this is not to say that investigators should be able to recite verbatim the historical references of crime scene staging. This is to say, however, that investigators should make every effort to verify that who they are learning from, reading, and following is teaching based on empirical knowledge and not by their experience alone, speculation, or what they *think, feel, and believe* about crime scene staging. One of the most impressive things about Vernon Geberth as a homicide investigator is that he did not stop at surmising that based on his experience crime scenes are staged in three primary ways and that offenders often stage victims' bodies in cases of staged sexual homicide because the victims' bodies were posed in 109 of Geberth's cases during his career (Geberth, 2010). Geberth *empirically tested* what he *thought* or *believed* based on *his experience* and found that in actuality, what he thought and observed in his experience was incorrect when compared to the experience of 46 other homicide investigators who investigated nearly 45,000 cases collectively. This is impressive. And take note that not only is Geberth's work remarkable for the obvious reasons in his tremendous contributions to the homicide literature, but the fact that as a homicide investigator Geberth knew he needed to empirically test what he thought in order to substantiate what he observed based on his experience is one of the greatest examples of his commitment to disseminating only what he knows to be correct information. Therefore, based on the incredible example of Vernon Geberth, homicide investigators need to continue their educations so they learn new ways to recognize deceptive behaviors generally speaking and how the art and science of deception relates to the staged homicide crime scene, but choose to learn from those who have *tested what they teach and practice what they preach.*

Deception is "the act of deceiving or trickery" and is arguably the most logical and obvious purpose of crime scene staging (Deception, n.d., para. 1). The easiest way for an offender to try to deceive investigators is to verbally lie to them. Empirical research has found that offenders show signs of deception verbally and nonverbally during homicide investigations (Hazelwood & Napier, 2004). Some offenders might even try to help or insert themselves into the investigations appearing like they are trying to assist investigators with the case. But one of the key points to remember about verbal and nonverbal deception is that both will be reflected in the staged crime scene. When investigators begin summing up everything they have in an investigation at any given point, the savvy investigator, well trained to recognize both behavioral and physical signs of deception, will recognize aspects of the crime scene do not add up.

Offenders lie often and lie a lot about where they were at the time of a victim's death. "Why?" Because it meets the needs of the offender. Toward accomplishing the goal to deceive, it has been the experience of the author that some offenders, when prompted or unprompted, will offer up an explanation of where he or she was during the commission of the crime. Pay attention to the unsolicited information offenders volunteer because what they are offering meets their needs somehow, some way. Geberth (2006) argued that not only will offenders lie about where they were during a murder, but they will also lie about where the victim is at the time of questioning. There are of course offenders who try to deceive investigators by not talking at all. These are the type of offenders who are attempting to deceive through silence. They might retain lawyers when they have not been named suspects or even named persons of interest. The old adage *silence is golden,* is one they are banking on.

Moving a dead body can be hard work. Sometimes, offenders are successful in moving and disposing of bodies and sometimes they are not. Sometimes, they quit in the middle of trying to move a body because it is just too much. Those who do not move and/or dispose of bodies to disconnect from the victim toward deception might try other means instead. Even though some offender clean up, dispose, hide, destroy, and manipulate evidence in other ways, still some offenders feel compelled to dispose of the bodies. Empirical findings have revealed that in some cases, offenders will dispose of victims' bodies and in some cases they will not. Remember, if the body remains in the crime scene, it is because it meets the needs of the offender, and likewise if the victim's body is not recovered in the crime scene, it is because it also meets the needs of the offender. Everything the offender does is toward meeting his or her needs somehow.

Misdirect Investigations

Generally speaking, offenders stage crime scenes to mislead or change the trajectory of an investigation. In other words, crime scene stagers manipulate or tamper with crime scenes to send investigators off course. The overall goal of the crime scene stagers is to do enough to point investigators in the wrong direction, while not going overboard making their efforts obvious. There is a fine balance for an offender between how and what he or she does to force the investigation off track and overdoing the main components of the staged scene making it so blatantly obvious to investigators that the scene has been manipulated with criminal intent. Overall, misguiding a homicide investigation is top priority for the crime scene staging homicide offender because it meets his or her needs.

Self-Preservation

At this point, it is important to remember that crime scene staging is different than *death scene alteration*. Death scene alteration or the intentional alteration of materials, the victim, or other related evidence in a death scene without criminal intent toward preserving the victim's dignity is not crime scene staging. Sometimes, when a family member finds a deceased loved one who has passed away from autoerotic asphyxiation, for example, to save the victim and even sometimes the family from embarrassment, those who discover the victim will cover the victim and move the victim or items in the death scene toward overall *self-preservation*. However, there are also cases where family members alter a death scene that is actually a homicide death scene because the victim is found in a way that the discovering individual feels is degrading to the victim. It has been the experience of the authors that in these cases, the family member or discovering party often ends up telling investigators that he or she moved the body, picked up the body, held the body, covered the body, or admits to whatever alteration he or she made to the scene in order to make sure investigators can account for those changes in their investigations.

Hazelwood and Napier (2004) argued that offenders stage to protect themselves (i.e., self-preservation). Self-preservation in the human behavioral sense is thought to be instinctual. While it could be that human beings instinctually gravitate away from harm, it is true that many homicide offenders think and behave in ways consistent with moving away from things they perceive as harmful to them. They do not want to lose their life and lifestyle as they know it. Offenders typically do not care that fiscal resources have been wasted or that the family is in anguish not knowing what happened to their loved one or where their loved one is; rather, offenders are in it all for themselves demonstrating complete disregard for the victim and society as a whole.

Avoid Apprehension

Exposure is the greatest fear of the crime scene stager. Ultimately, the purpose of crime scene staging is to avoid apprehension (Douglas & Munn, 1992; Geberth, 1996; Hazelwood & Napier, 2004, p. 745). No matter what they do or how they do it, the overarching goal of the crime scene stager is not to get caught (Douglas et al., 2006). At the heart of the entire issue is that of avoiding apprehension. No matter what the crime scene stager says he did and did not do or even if the offender never admits to his crime ever postconviction, the fact remains that the number one purpose of crime scene staging is to avoid accountability.

Motives for Murder

The purpose for staging does not mean it is the motive for murder. Purposes of crime scene staging are the reasons why offenders stage crime scenes. In contrast, motives for murder are the reasons why offenders kill victims. Offenders stage crime scenes to avoid getting caught, while offenders murder victims most often toward resolving some sort of conflict. Research has shown that some sort of conflict and/or confrontation precedes the murder in most staged cases (Ferguson, 2011; Pettler, 2011). There are countless motives for murder, such as greed, power, control, political reasons, conflicts in social class, and too many to list here. As mentioned in Chapter 2, the mere fact that an offender feels compelled to stage a crime scene demonstrates ill intent and reveals that the offender most likely has a connection to the victim at a minimum or has had a relationship with the victim at some level (Napier & Baker, 2005). But this premise does not explain motive. Even though prosecutors do not have to prove motive, motive is very important for investigatory purposes. When investigators embark on a homicide investigation, it is very important not to assume the integrity of the crime scene, but rather, to approach a scene with an open mind toward comparing what is known to what might be present in a crime scene. Inconsistencies in the offender's story of what happened might be evident to the trained investigator with a keen eye for drawing parallels between behavioral and physical evidence can indicate a staged crime scene, but such parallels can also be illustrious of motive. When it comes to motive and crime scene staging, though they go hand in hand, but they are vastly different at the core. The following cases exemplify a few of the motives identified in homicide cases where crime scene staging was evident.

Motive 1: Argument/Conflict/Confrontation

Again, research has found that arguments/conflict/confrontations precede the murder of most staged cases that have been analyzed to date (Ferguson, 2011; Pettler, 2011). Arguments are a leading reason individuals end up in physical altercations that sometimes end with the death of at least one of the participants. Because arguments and conflicts can be spontaneous and unplanned, if someone ends up dead as a result, the offender can be left with the dilemma of what to do next.

Case Example: The female victim in this case example is 25 years old. The male offenders in this case are 24 and 25 years old. The victim left her place of employment with the offenders to go hang out at their house where she ended up bludgeoned to death by the 25-year-old offender. The victim was reported missing by her family 10 days after they last saw her. Due to the victim's previous history (victimology) of using drugs and disappearing for periods of time, investigators approached the case like a missing person case and began a search of the area and interviewing friends, intimate partners, associates, coworkers, and family. Two hunters walking along a mountain ridge in the area found the victim's skeletal remains 5 months later. The crime scene was very large, a scene that spanned approximately 50–60 feet. Several items were collected, such as skeletal remains, clothing, a shoe, a towel, and a sheet.

The autopsy revealed the victim died from injuries sustained from being struck in the head with a blunt, heavy object. Originally thinking jealousy was the motive for her death, investigators developed four suspects in the case: an acquaintance, an intimate partner, the former spouse, and an associate of the former spouse. But consequently, the investigation revealed that the victim was also very persistent about a family member who went missing before she did. Investigators thought the two cases might be connected and that the victim might have disappeared due to her persistence about her missing family member. The case would go cold for 15 years, until one of the offenders' lives changed and he came forward with information about the victim in this case.

The offender who came forward explained that he and the victim were engaged in a sexual encounter in the bedroom of the offenders' home when his friend, the 25-year-old offender came into the room and asked to have sex with the victim. The 25-year-old offender was very offended when the victim said she did not want to have sex with him and an argument ensued. When the offender who was having sex with the victim tried to protect her, the 25-year-old offender struck his friend in the head practically knocking him unconscious. He then turned the heavy, blunt object onto the victim and beat the victim to death. The bludgeoning offender was charged with first-degree murder and was sentenced to life in prison. His friend, the second offender, was charged with second-degree murder and accessory after the fact to murder, but from testifying against his friend, was convicted of the lesser charge and sentenced to probation.

There were several observable crime scene staging behaviors and patterns in this case. Both offenders working together concealed the murder by wrapping the victim's body in bedding from their house, removing the body from their environment (i.e., house), transporting, and then disposing of her body. Both offenders also worked together to clean their home, they showered, discarded their clothing, and so on. The offender convicted of murder hid the murder weapon, which was never found. Meanwhile, the offender who was put on probation took the victim's purse and staged it in a convenience store trying to make people believe she was alive and had recently been to that store and left her bag.

Motive 2: Property Gain

Case Example: The victim and offender in this case example had an employer–employee relationship only. The offender worked for the victim at the victim's place business. The victim was a white male aged 72, and the offender was a white male aged 45. An off-duty deputy whose wife grew concerned when she saw taillights glowing at the business across their street from their house found the victim, slumped over in his small truck, with a gunshot wound to the right temporal area of his head. Investigators took 10 instant photographs of the scene. Investigators ruled the death as suicide at the scene, but the persistence of the family eventually led to successfully having the investigation changed to a suspicious death. Interviews with friends and family revealed that the victim was last seen with his employee about 6:00 P.M. at the victim's office. When the employee was interviewed, he reported having last seen the victim about 6:30 P.M. at the victim's office.

The victim was sitting in his small, blue truck; the driver's side window partially rolled down, and the victim's head was slumped toward the driver's side window. The victim was fully clothed, had his jacket on, shoes on, and did not appear disheveled. None of the neighbors reported hearing a gunshot, but the victim's feet were depressing the brake pedal. Another unusual aspect of this was that the barrel of the firearm recovered was found on the floor of the truck, but it was tucked beneath a 2 × 4 × 12 in. plank of wood. This was peculiar because the victim's right hand was in his lap as well. The medical examiner said the victim could not have made purposeful movement after the shot. Soon, investigators agreed the victim's position and the position of the firearm were inconsistent with suicide. In addition, there were two distinct flow patterns of blood on the victim's right cheek. Additional autopsy results also prompted investigators to take another look because the medical examiner found the wound track to be inconsistent with a self-inflicted gunshot wound. Investigators did not develop any suspects or a motive for why this victim would have been murdered, and the case went cold for 14 years. Investigators collected the firearm, the vehicle, and a gunshot residue kit from the scene and retained them as evidence. The vehicle was released to the family at some point.

Fourteen years after the death of the victim, someone came forward with information about the case. A woman whose son was murdered with no arrest in that case decided to tell what she knew about the 14-year-old murder of one of the area's most prominent businessmen. The woman said her ex-husband was the best friend of the former employee who was last seen with the victim the night of the victim's death. On the night of the victim's death, the woman said her then husband left the house after getting a call from his best friend to pick him up in a nearby county behind a grocery store. The woman said her husband told her he picked up his best friend after watching him crawl out of a dumpster parked behind the grocery store one county over. On the way home, the men discarded the best friend's clothing over the side of three bridges. She said her husband gave his best friend new clothes to wear and dropped him off at home. Investigators paid a visit to the woman's ex-husband who confirmed her story. He added to the story that the grocery store where he picked up his best friend about 9:45 P.M. on December 31, 1991, was three blocks from where the victim's body was found in his truck. He said his best friend had blood on him when he got into his truck, and they threw all of his clothes in nearby waterways. Quickly, the 14-year-old suspicious death cold case turned into a murder investigation. The former employee was charged with first-degree murder and first-degree kidnapping, but he was nowhere to be found. Several years after the victim's death, the former employee was charged with sex crimes against children, and to evade capture, he faked his own death by leaving his shoes on the concrete, car door open, and vehicle running on a nearby bridge spanning a large river. He fled the area where he became a drug runner but was caught and fingerprinted during a traffic stop. A comparison of fingerprints revealed his true identity, not the alias he gave to authorities during the stop, and he was convicted of federal drug trafficking offenses. After serving a federal time, the former employee suspect in this staged suicide stood trial twice for the victim's murder. The first jury hung, but the second jury found the former employee guilty on all charges, and he was sentenced to life in prison where he died a short time later.

It was determined that the motive for murder was property gain. The victim had agreed to sell to his employee his business for over $100,000, but the employee did not have the money to pay. Investigators postulated that the offender held the victim at gunpoint in his office during the meeting, forced the victim to sign over the business to the offender before the offender abducted and murdered the victim. Investigators believed the offender drove the victim's body in the victim's truck to the location where the victim was found because, interestingly, the offender had spread rumors before the murder that the victim was having an affair with the off-duty deputy's wife who found the body, and the offender spread rumors after the murder that the victim killed himself in front of her house because he was upset over the affair.

The former best friend of the offender reported to the investigators that he and the offender destroyed as much evidence as they could. They threw blood-soaked clothing and other items into the water from the sides of bridges on the night of the murder and from two other bridges on later dates. Also, the best friend told police that the offender did not want to throw his leather jacket in the river, so he tried to have the blood cleaned from the jacket. It could not be cleaned, so his friend destroyed the jacket by throwing it into a river. The former best friend reported he supplied the offender with a change of clothes and the offender left his bloody clothes with his best friend, who destroyed them too. The offender lied to his ex-wife when he got home by telling her that he spilled beer on his clothes, so his best friend gave him other clothes to wear and that the offender took his dirty clothes and jacket to be cleaned.

Motive 3: Robbery

Case Example: The offenders in this case developed a plan to rob and murder the victim in order to buy drugs. The victim was a 39-year-old white female murdered in her home. The offenders were teenage brothers aged 14 and 17 years. On that night, the victim's husband came home to find his wife dead in the living room of their house. The husband ran to a neighbor's house and asked the neighbor to call 911. Once investigators arrived, they discovered the victim's naked body lying on her back between the couch and coffee table in the living room of her house with several gunshots to her body. The victim was partially covered with a blanket. The victim's small dog was lying dead beside her. The house was in complete disarray. The victim's fish tank was knocked over, drawers were pulled out in her bedroom, and lots of miscellaneous items were thrown throughout the house. Investigators thought the victim was murdered during a sexual assault/robbery/homicide. Her husband was very helpful to investigators and identified everything that was missing in the house. Specifically, a 12-gauge shotgun, a pack of cigarettes, and the victim's money were not recovered in the scene. Investigators collected items, such as beer bottles, a video game cartridge, three spent cartridge casings, blankets, a pillow and pillow cases, clothing, a telephone, cigarette butts, trace evidence tapings, a sample of the dog's hair, a strand of hair, a soda bottle, carpet, a sample of the fabric of the couch, beddings, glass fragments, cigarettes, a lighter, and a speaker phone.

Investigators canvassed the neighborhood and interviewed friends, coworkers, and family. Several family members and friends said the married couple had their share of disagreements, but that the husband did not have motive to kill his wife. Eventually, two teenage neighbors were developed as suspects based on interviews with the teens' friends.

In this case, the offenders made a concoction of household chemicals to throw at the victim in order to subdue her. They exhibited precautionary behaviors in that they wore socks over their hands and put on ski masks then walked to the victim's house. One teen offender knocked on the door, the victim opened the door, and one offender asked the victim if she had seen their mother. The other teen offender doused the victim with the concoction and both teens forced their way past her into her house. The victim was beaten, stripped naked, and placed on her couch. The offenders found the victim's shotgun; shot her dog; shot the victim; wrapped the victim in bedding; put her in between the couch and coffee table; stole her money, cigarettes, and shotgun; ransacked the house; and then fled the scene. The younger of the two brothers was convicted of first-degree murder, first-degree burglary, and robbery with a dangerous weapon and was sentenced to 34 years and 9 months in prison. The older brother was found guilty of first-degree murder, first-degree burglary, robbery with a dangerous weapon, accessory after the fact to murder and was sentenced to 7–10 years in prison.

Investigators determined that the offenders planned, executed, and staged the homicide to simulate a rape–homicide so they could buy drugs. They admitted they murdered her to prevent her from identifying them as her neighbors. The medical examiner determined the victim was not sexually assaulted. The offenders blitzed the victim when she opened the door. After forcing their way in, they beat her, removed her clothes, and forced her to lie down on the couch to stage a sexual assault. After shooting the victim, the offenders took all firearm-related evidence from the shotgun with them. When they arrived home, they changed their clothes and hid their bloody clothes in the air ducts of their house. The older brother cut a hole in his mattress where he hid the firearm inside his bed. Both brothers lied extensively about their whereabouts when asked where they were at the time of the murder.

Case Example: In this homicide case, the offender was a 32-year-old white male and was the son of the 72-year-old white female victim. The son murdered his mother in the spring of 1987 in the house they shared. The victim was reported missing after failing to respond to other family members. An investigator responding to the missing person's report visited the victim's home and found her buried in a shallow grave in the backyard that contained loose dirt and appeared fairly fresh. During the crime scene search, the victim was recovered fully clothed, lying on her back with her arms down to her sides in the hole, then covered with dirt and brush. She was lying face up with her arms down to her sides. There was nothing unusual about the grave other than it was very shallow and the victim was not covered with dirt very well. The victim's house was found in good condition, very neat, orderly, and clean. The only mess was in the kitchen and it looked like someone made a meal, but didn't clean up the mess. During the crime scene search, investigators collected a gunshot residue kit, a firearm, ammunition, a rape kit, clothing, and a kitchen rug.

Investigators surmised the victim was murdered due to a domestic dispute and autopsy results showed the victim died from a gunshot wound to the chest. The victim's son, who was arrested and charged with her murder had a long mental health history and was found incompetent to proceed on the murder charge. He eventually pleaded guilty to manslaughter and served 12–18 months in prison. The offender recently was released from mental health and went back to live with his mother. He and the victim had several arguments over the victim not giving the offender money. It was eventually determined that offender murdered his mother to steal her social security checks and spend her money. He was angry that his mother purchased a post office box so he could not take her social security checks. After he killed the victim, he then concealed her body in the freezer with her shoes and her coat before burying her and the firearm in the backyard. The son lied about where his mother was when asked by neighbors and family members. He cleaned the house, removed all traces of blood from the kitchen where he shot her in the chest, and lied to investigators when they came to the house asking where his mother was.

Motive 4: Sexual Assault

Offenders might attempt to alter a crime scene by cleaning it using bleach, by vacuuming, or by straightening in attempt to make it appear that no struggle occurred (Walton, 2006). Further, offenders might also alter a crime scene to stage a home invasion/murder. Self-inflicted injury, damaging clothing, setting fire, and false accusations of sexual assault might also be methods of deception utilized by offenders (Hazelwood & Napier, 2004).

Case Example: The victim, a 12-year-old boy in this case, was reported missing by his family one evening after he did not return home from a bike ride. Investigators and the family thought the victim might have run away or became an endangered youth. Investigators quickly located the victim's bike in the front yard of a nearby house in the neighborhood. When questioning the 30-year-old owner of the house, the man told investigators that he saw the victim get into a red car with two African-American men and the trio drove away (e.g., misdirecting the investigation). For the next 3 days, police searched for the red car and two African-American males who were thought to be driving around the area in the car. The missing person's investigation turned into a homicide investigation 3 days later when the body of the 12-year-old victim was discovered in a cornfield. Thinking the murder had something to do with the red car and its occupants, investigators continued to canvass the neighborhood asking for information about any sightings of the car on the night the victim went missing. Eventually, investigators located the two men and the red car and determined that they had nothing to do with the 12-year-old boy's disappearance. Once they ruled out the red car theory, they again returned to the house where the boy's bike was found in the front yard. When the man who owned the house opened the door, he invited investigators inside to talk. That is when investigators noticed the distinct odor of decomposition in the man's house. They arrested the man for the murder of the boy and took him into custody.

Investigators processed the 30-year-old man's house as the primary crime scene and noticed that the man had spent an exorbitant amount of time cleaning the house recently. The house was thoroughly cleaned including the removal of a carpet and bedding from the man's bedroom. The medical examiner could not determine a cause of death, but several areas of the man's bedroom tested positive for blood in, around, and beneath the man's bed. Investigators believed the murder was secondary to the sexual assault of the boy. There were two crime scenes in this case: the man's house and the cornfield where he dumped the victim's body. The intermediate scene was the man's car, which he used to transport the victim's body to the cornfield. Investigative interviews revealed that the man lured the boy into his house to sexually assault him. After the assault, the man murdered the boy and hid his body under the bed in the man's bedroom and then 3 days later, wrapped the body in bedding, drove the body to the cornfield, and dumped the body there. The offender was convicted of first-degree murder and sentenced to life in prison.

First, the offender concealed and destroyed evidence. He cleaned his residence thoroughly and used carpet deodorizer to try to mask the decomposition smell. He also used fans and air freshener profusely. After dumping the body, the offender thoroughly cleaned his truck and disposed of the bed liner of his truck. The offender also removed and concealed the carpet in the attic of his residence. The offender gave investigators a false name during the first and second interviews and was later discovered that he was wanted for other sex crimes against children in another state.

Case Example: Like the last case example, this case involved a 15-year-old boy who was a known runaway. He was last seen riding his bike in the community where he lived until he did not return home and his family grew concerned. His family notified the police who agreed it was possible the boy ran away again. The police, however, initiated a missing person's search for the boy believing he was in danger regardless. Investigators canvassed the community talking to many people who saw the boy riding his bike the day he went missing. In speaking with one neighbor, a man who lived in a shack on the side of nearby mountain, he claimed he had not seen the boy riding his bike on the day the boy disappeared. Police expanded their search and talked to store owners on the main street of town who reported the boy was at their store and was seen leaving while riding his bike alongside an adult white male. One piece of information led to the other during the interview process, and 2 weeks later, the police ended up back at the mountainside shack talking to the man who said he had not seen the victim.

During a walk-through search of the land surrounding the man's shack, investigators noticed the smell of decomposition and found the victim's hand protruding from the ground behind the shack's outhouse. Investigators continued their search and located the body of the boy buried behind the outhouse. The primary crime scene in this case was a makeshift shack with no running water and no electricity, with garbage and debris stacked 3–4 feet high throughout the shack. The yard was scattered with debris, had a burn pit and an outhouse. The secondary crime scene was the hole where the victim was recovered wearing his clothing, but with his shirt gathered around his armpits that looked as though it had been used to drag him to the hole. The owner of the shack was arrested for murder, but investigators did not have a motive for why the boy was killed; however, they suspected that the offender lured the boy back to his shack after meeting him at the local store to sexually assault him. Numerous witnesses reported the inappropriate sexual nature of the man and his alleged attraction to young boys. The investigation revealed the boy was held against his will by the offender in the shack, and on the first night, a fight broke out between them during the sexual assault and the man shot and killed the boy. The autopsy revealed that the victim died from injuries sustained from multiple gunshot wounds to the head. The offender in this case was charged with first-degree murder but pleaded guilty to second-degree murder and was sentenced to 20 years and 5 months in prison.

The offender staged this scene several ways:

1. The offender tried to destroy evidence by burning the shell casings he collected from the scene after killing the victim.
2. The offender concealed the firearm by putting the firearm in the trash, which was never recovered.
3. The offender lied to police that he had not seen the victim the day he disappeared, lied as to why the victim's body was recovered on his property claiming he had been out of town and that someone else must have buried him there, and lied about how the victim died claiming the victim attacked the offender during the night, so he reached for a gun, shot the attacker, and when he turned on the light, discovered it was the victim.
4. The offender tried to conceal the victim's bicycle by painting it white (including the wheels and the handlebars). The offender even made a fake receipt claiming he bought the bike from someone in town. However, investigators knew the receipt was fraudulent because the word *bike* was misspelled as "bick" on the receipt.

References

Deception. (n.d.). In *Merriam-Webster* Online Dictionary (11th Ed.). Retrieved from http://www.merriam-webster.com/dictionary/Deception

Douglas, J. E., Burgess, A. W., Burgess, A. G., & Ressler, R. K. (2006). *Crime classification manual: A standard system for investigating and classifying violent crimes* (2nd ed.). San Francisco, CA: John Wiley & Sons, Inc.

Douglas, J. E., & Munn, C. (1992, February). Violent crime scene analysis: Modus operandi, signature, and staging. *FBI Law Enforcement Bulletin, 61*(2), 1–10.

Ferguson, C. (2011). *The defects of the situation: A typology of staged crime scenes* (Unpublished doctoral thesis). Bond University, Gold Coast, Queensland, Australia.

Geberth, V. J. (1996). *Practical homicide investigation: Tactics, procedures, and forensic techniques* (3rd ed.). Boca Raton, FL: CRC Press/Taylor & Francis Group.

Geberth, V. J. (2006). *Practical homicide investigation: Tactics, procedures, and forensic techniques* (4th ed.). Boca Raton, FL: CRC Press/Taylor & Francis Group.

Geberth, V. J. (2010). Crime scene staging: An exploratory study of the frequency and characteristics of sexual posing in homicides. *Investigative Sciences Journal, 2*(2), 1–19.

Gross, H. (1924). *Criminal investigation*. London, UK: Sweet & Maxwell.

Hazelwood, R. R., & Napier, M. R. (2004). Crime scene staging and its detection. *International Journal of Offender Therapy and Comparative Criminology, 48*(6), 744–759. doi: 10.1177/0306624X04268298

Napier, M. R., & Baker, K. P. (2005). Criminal personality profiling. In S. H. James & J. J. Nordby (Eds.), *Forensic science: An introduction to scientific and investigative techniques* (2nd ed.). Boca Raton, FL: CRC Press/Taylor & Francis Group.

Pettler, L. G. (2011). *Crime scene behaviors of crime scene stagers* (Doctoral dissertation). Retrieved from ProQuest (2251577601).

Schlesinger, L. B., Gardenier, A., Jarvis, J. & Sheehan-Cook, J. (2012, April). Crime scene staging in homicide. *Journal of Police and Criminal Psychology, 29*(1), 44–51.

Walton, R. (2006). *Cold case homicides: Practical investigative techniques*. Boca Raton, FL: CRC Press/Taylor & Francis Group.

Intimicide

7

Introduction

Crime scene staging research has demonstrated that most offenders who stage crime scenes are male, most victims of staged crime scenes are female, and the most common victim–offender relationship involving staging is intimate partner relationships, such as spouses, ex-spouses, current and former girlfriends and boyfriends, and other types of intimate relationships (Eke, 2007; Ferguson, 2011; Pettler, 2011). Therefore, in order to understand more about crime scene staging at this point in the research, one must do a deep dive into the world of intimate partner violence (IPV) because IPV and crime scene staging empirically go hand in hand.

Although not all crime scenes are staged by offenders intimately involved with their victims, but of the roughly 340 offenders who have collectively been empirically studied thus far by Eke (2007) (e.g., 53 offenders), Ferguson (2011) (e.g., 141 offenders), Pettler (2011) (e.g., 27 offenders), Schlesinger, Gardenier, Jarvis, & Sheehan-Cook (2012) (e.g., 94 offenders), and Turvey (2000) (e.g., 25 offenders), the majority of these offenders are male and are the current or former intimate partners of their victims. While other studies conducted by Hazelwood and Napier (2004), Keppel and Weis (2004), and Geberth (2010) also studied offenders and their staging behaviors, it was unclear as to the exact number of offenders who were male or how many were intimate partners of their victims. Therefore, when realizing that only 340 have been documented and accounted for specifically and descriptively analyzed by the previously referenced authors, it is abundantly clear that this is simply not enough. Going forward, it is the hope of the author that all authors who publish on crime scene staging will include descriptive information for all offenders toward broadening the pool of what is known about this target population.

Intimate Partner Violence

Generally speaking, intimacy is the feeling of being close to another human being emotionally, physically, sexually, or romantically, any or all of the latter combined. Therefore, an intimate partner relationship or interpersonal relationship most often is a relationship between two people characterized by some form of intimacy as described earlier. Intimate and interpersonal relationships are part of the core of the human experience. As Maslow (1943) identified in his hierarchy of needs Stage 3, Love and Belonging, all human beings need love, relationships, and sexual intimacy.

According to the U.S. Department of Justice (2014), domestic violence or IPV is "a pattern of abusive behavior in any relationship that is used by one partner to gain or maintain power and control over another intimate partner" (para. 2). One verbal argument between two intimate partners does not constitute IPV; instead IPV is *a pattern* or the repetitive behavioral way one partner keeps *power* or the greatest influence that *controls*, or the predominant authority over another intimate partner.

There are many patterns of abuse commonly seen in IPV. Intimate partner offenders willfully intimidate their intimate partner victims. Offenders use physical, emotional, sexual, financial, or other abusive behaviors to dominate their intimate partners. IPV is nonspecific by age, race, gender, religion, how educated any individual might be, the jobs they hold, or how rich or poor they are. IPV affects victims from all *walks of life*. IPV is called *closed-room* violence, which means that often only the offender and the victim know what is going on *behind closed doors*. Because this type of violence often remains hidden for long periods of time, even decades or in some cases for a victim's entire life married to an abusive partner, it is often hard and difficult to understand some of the peculiar behaviors that trouble family and friends who do not know what the victim is experiencing at home.

Intimate Partner Violence and Risk Factors Indicating Lethality

Much of IPV research is centered on developing scales and measures for assessing an intimate partner's level of risk of becoming an intimate partner homicide victim toward establishing prevention and intervention programming throughout the United States and abroad. Victim risk level in relation to IPV can be indicated by the presence of lethality factors in an intimate partner relationship, such as physical abuse, emotional abuse, psychological abuse (mental abuse), sexual abuse, or economical abuse (U.S. Department of Justice, 2014). The greater number of or the greater the intensity of lethality factors in an IPV relationship, the greater the level of risk for the victim of becoming an intimate partner homicide victim.

Case Example

John and Mary (names changed to protect identities) were a married couple involved in an ongoing IPV relationship. Violence occurred against both parties by both parties on a regular basis, and the couple frequented the courthouse to appear on domestic violence–related charges they each filed against each other regularly. Both John and Mary had been involved in previous relationships reported to have been abusive as well, so when they entered into a relationship with each other, the general course of their inter-action was negative and abusive as well. The turbulent relationship continued for a period of time and eventually the couple separated. Mary was living in a house and John was living somewhere else. Then early morning, Mary called 911 to report that she just shot her estranged husband John. Law enforcement arrived at Mary's house to find John dead on the kitchen floor with five gunshot wounds through various parts of his body.

Mary said she heard sounds the night before that scared her and in response she placed a firearm on the kitchen counter. The next morning, Mary said she was standing at her kitchen sink when her estranged husband John entered Mary's house through the front door, came through the living room, entered the kitchen, then pulled out a chair, and sat down. Mary said she wanted John to leave so she picked up the gun and pointed it at him. Mary said that John then rose from the kitchen table chair and faced Mary, and then Mary said she shot John *three or four* times in self-defense. Mary said the victim, John, then turned around and *hung over the chair* as Mary exited the kitchen, went through the living room, and out her front door. Mary said she placed the gun on a table on the front porch and went to a neighbor to call 911.

The investigation revealed a witness who claimed the witness spoke with John on the morning of his death and that John had received a phone call from his estranged wife Mary to tell him that her washing machine was bro-ken and to ask him if he would come to fix it. The witness alleged that John went to Mary's residence that morning at her request intending to fix the washing machine. Evidence at the scene indicated two individuals had been sitting at the kitchen table smoking cigarettes and drinking coffee before the violent event.

The author worked this case and her reconstruction disputed the second part of Mary's story. Instead of exiting the residence after the third shot, as the victim in this case hung over the chair, evidence showed that Mary shot John a fourth time and then a fifth time as the victim fell to the floor or was close to the floor. Mary was convicted of second-degree murder and sen-tenced to 10 years and 2 months in prison.

In this case, the history of violence between Mary and John was indica-tive of lethality in their relationship. What is significant in this case, how-ever, is that since both individuals were alleged to have been abusive toward the other, those familiar with the couple and their lengthy domestic violence history were concern that either one of them becomes a victim of intimate partner homicide. Their extensive history of abusive behaviors within their environment ended up in one of them becoming a homicide victim and one becoming a homicide offender, thus a crime scene stager. Mary did not manipulate physical evidence in this scene. Instead, Mary verbally staged the scene by alleging that she was simply washing dishes when John came into her house uninvited and unannounced and would not leave. Mary did not anticipate that John had spoken to anyone that morning who knew he told that he was simply going to Mary's house to fix her washing machine. Further, Mary did not anticipate that the physical evidence would tell a different story than she told to the investigators.

IPV monopolizes the victim in many ways, such as absorbing all of the victim's time, the victim's affection, attention, peace of mind, presence of mind, and the victim's physical body (Parker & Pettler, 2009). Several types of abuse which are used to monopolize the victim are discussed in the following text.

Physical Abuse

Physical abuse in IPV can be defined as when the physical contact of one partner to another intimate partner causes the victim to feel and experience physical injury, physical pain, physical suffering, or some other type of bodily harm. There are several types of physical abuse reported by IPV victims, such as kicking, hitting, scratching, burning, dragging, hair pulling, punching, slapping, pushing, choking, or beating (Weinbaum et al., 2011). Intimate partner victims of physical abuse might try to conceal their physical injuries using makeup, clothing, and lying to others about how the injuries occurred. They are often embarrassed or ashamed and sometimes feel as though no one would believe them or that there is no one to turn to for help. And of course, these behaviors exhibited by an offender work on a continuum of severity that might range from minor scratching to bruising and all the way to murder. Most often, physical abuse begins with a minor assault during an altercation and over time escalates into more harmful physical abuse, which can eventually lead to murder in some cases.

Physical abuse can extend into physical health areas as well (U.S. Department of Justice, 2014). Denying an intimate partner's health care is a form of physical abuse, just as is throwing objects at a victim, using a weapon against a victim, or damaging physical property belonging to an intimate partner victim (Women Against Abuse, 2014).

Emotional Abuse

Emotional abuse in IPV is how the behavior of one partner negatively impacts the mental health of another intimate partner. According to the Women Against Abuse (2014) advocacy group, emotional abuse can include intimidation, stalking, getting unreasonably angry with a victim over nothing, being very jealous or accusing the victim of cheating, calling the victim names or insulting the victim, humiliating the victim privately and even publicly, being extremely possessive of the victim, and having to know where the victim is at all times. All of the aforementioned behaviors are examples of emotional abuse. There are countless ways an abuser might emotionally abuse a victim, but all in all, emotional abuse ends up leading to the IPV victim feeling depressed or anxious or even experiencing posttraumatic stress disorder. Other forms of emotional abuse include causing problems with relationships intimate partners have with their children, undermining an intimate partner, and constantly criticizing an intimate partner in order to diminish his or her self-esteem or self-worth (U.S. Department of Justice, 2014).

Psychological Abuse (Mental Abuse)

Interestingly, psychological abuse is a bit different from emotional abuse in that psychological abuse in IPV refers to the behaviors a partner exhibits toward another intimate partner that makes the victim feel fear or intimidated, or threatening harm to children, family, and/or animals, for example (U.S. Department of Justice, 2014). Psychological abuse is just as devastating to the victim as is physical or emotional abuse and with long-lasting effects. Psychologically abused victims tend not to think clearly and often create problems with friends and family that would not otherwise be created if the victim was not being abused psychologically. Psychological abuse causes a victim to feel unsafe in his or her own home or place of employment or at school, along with skewing the way a victim perceives the world and/or his or her own immediate environment. Partners who psychologically abuse their intimate partners tend to initiate this type of abuse in a similar fashion as physical abuse, that is, by exhibiting a minor infarction that grows and grows into full-fledged psychological abuse. The adage is true: "You teach someone how to treat you …" in this case because the abuser wants to test the waters so to speak before diving head first into psychologically abusing his or her victim. The offender has to figure out how much the victim is willing to take and how much he can get away with. Coupled with other types of abuse, it is arguable that sometimes victims are already weakened to the point that they cannot defend themselves against their abusers' even minor psychological assaults.

Sexual Abuse

Sexual abuse in IPV is anything a partner does to another intimate partner, such as marital rape or forcing the intimate partner to have sex against his or her will, forcing the intimate partner to have sex with someone outside the intimate relationship against the victim's will, having sex or initiating sexual contact with an intimate partner who is not fully conscious that is afraid to say no or who has not been asked, forcing the intimate partner to have unprotected sex, or causing physical harm to an intimate partner's genitals (Women Against Abuse, 2014). Sexual abuse in IPV relationships can culminate from a verbal argument that escalates into a physical fight that further escalates into a sexual assault. Overall, sexual abuse in intimate partner relationships is any sexual activity initiated by one intimate partner that is unwanted by another intimate partner. Sexual abuse can also extend into a partner forcing another intimate partner to partake in reenacting pornographic sexual acts or even mistreating an intimate partner by demeaning him or her in a sexual nature (U.S. Department of Justice, 2014).

Economic Abuse

Economic abuse in intimate partner homicide is an overarching concept that includes any behavior exhibited by a partner over another intimate partner where the partner controls the financial situation of the other intimate partner. Economic abuse might include various types of behaviors, such as preventing an intimate partner from going to work, forbidding an intimate partner from using familial transportation to get to and from work, ruining work-related equipment, harassing an intimate partner while working, delaying an intimate partner from leaving for work on time, or anything related to suppressing an intimate partner's ability to earn money and/or spend money as he or she chooses (Women Against Abuse, 2014). Ultimately, the goal of economic abuse is to make sure the intimate partner victim is fully dependent on the abuser for financial resources. Further, economic abuse extends into an intimate partner forbidding another intimate partner from attending school toward bettering himself or herself due to the threat of the educated intimate partner leaving the abuser and gaining control over his or her own life.

Consequences of Intimate Partner Violence

IPV is at epidemic proportions today. According to the Centers for Disease Control and Prevention (CDC) (2014a), one out of every two women and one in every five men in the United States will be subjected to a domestic violence situation of some kind at some point in his or her lifetime, and domestic violence in general affects millions of people each year throughout the country. At least half of all female victims and nearly half of all male victims have reported that an intimate partner stalked them before the age of 25 years old (CDC, 2014a). Additionally, 27% of women and 12% of men report having been raped during an intimate partner relationship before they were 25 years old (CDC, 2014a, p. 3).

There are dire consequences of domestic violence. At least 3 million children witness some act of IPV or domestic violence each year in the United States, and children who live under these conditions are 30%–60% more likely to suffer from neglect or abuse themselves (Safe Haven, Inc., 2014, para. 2). Additionally, the cost of IPV to society is astounding. According to CDC (2014b), the cost of IPV to society for women alone topped $5.8 million in 1995, which is approximately $8.7 million today. Victims of IPV account for nearly 8 million days of lost work, paid time off, and missed days of school and approximately 5.6 million lost days of regular productivity per year. Victims of IPV also often suffer from unemployment and health problems; so again, abusive men cost society in health-care and unemployment benefits for their abused victims.

Physical Consequences

Black (2011) found that there are a number of health-related consequences for those who suffer in an intimate partner relationship. Several injury-type health problems were found directly related to IPV in Black's (2011) study, such as skeletal problems (i.e., back pain), broken bones, bruises, and traumatic brain injuries. As would be expected, IPV victims reportedly suffer from gastrointestinal disturbance, immune deficiency because of chronic stress, and cardiopulmonary-related issues as well. Women who suffer from chronic abuse might also experience gynecological disorders, sexual dysfunction, and pregnancy-related problems.

Psychological Consequences

Tjaden and Thoennes (2000) found that physical violence and psychological violence often run concurrent. Victims of IPV often experience anxiety and depression, low self-esteem, sleeplessness, and in some cases posttraumatic stress disorder (Black, 2011). Overall, although physical violence is not always present where emotional and psychological violence is present, it is arguable that either type is psychologically damaging to the victim one way or the other. Victims of IPV might also experience social setbacks while with an abuser or even after leaving the relationship. Abusers often isolate victims making them feel alone and insecure, which can impact their social interactions with others in a broad sense. Further, IPV offenders might be so unstable as to cause the family unrest by being homeless, restricting health-care services, or even straining relationships with health-care providers (CDC, 2014b).

Lifestyle-Related Consequences

Roberts, Auinger, and Klein (2005) found that IPV is associated with numerous negative health-related and lifestyle-related consequences as well. For example, the researchers found that victims of IPV are more likely to abuse drugs and/or alcohol and attempt suicide more often than those not victimized by IPV. Further, victims of IPV are more likely to engage in high-risk behaviors, such as but not limited to promiscuity, unprotected sex, and prostitution, along with unhealthy lifestyle choices, such as overeating, fasting, vomiting, or using diet drugs. All in all, intimate partner homicide and its consequences are detrimental to society, the victims themselves, their families, health-care providers, and so many others. There is no question based on the ample empirical research available on IPV that it needs to be a legislative priority toward developing stiffer laws and heavier penalties for offenders.

Intimate Partner Homicide

The reason all of the previously mentioned factors is so critically important to include in a book about crime scene staging dynamics in homicide cases is because it is often what is found in victimological studies in intimate partner homicide cases. The more investigators know about what IPV is and is not, how it manifests, the consequences, and so forth, the more likely they are to ask the right questions when conducting victimology and the less likely they are to overlook a key piece of the puzzle that could point the investigation in the right direction. Again, Hazelwood and Napier (2004) argued that when investigators encounter a staged crime scene, all they have is the study of the victim and the scene itself. In the study of the victim in relation to crime scene staging and based on empirical findings of victim–offender characteristics, IPV many times is what precedes the eventual death of the victim.

As mentioned in Chapter 2, homicide and murder are not interchangeable terms in the world of forensic pathology. For the purpose of this discussion, homicide is the deliberate and purposeful, unlawful act of one individual who kills another individual and homicide is also most often called *murder*. Generally speaking, homicide is the broad term used to describe the death of one individual at the hand of another, but there are many different types of homicide that can be identified and studied specifically, for example,

- Femicide is the killing of women and should be defined within cultural context.
- Neonaticide is the killing of a baby within the first 24 hours of life.
- Infanticide is the killing of an infant younger than 12 months old.

- Matricide is the killing of one's mother.
- Patricide is the killing of one's father.
- Filicide is the purposeful act by a parent to kill his or her own child.
- Sororicide is the killing of one's sister.
- Fratricide is the killing of one's brother or sister.
- Nepoticide is the killing of one's nephew.
- Familicide is the killing of one's family.
- Mariticide is the killing of a husband by the wife.
- Uxoricide is the killing of a wife by her husband.

All of these types of homicide are very interesting in their own way and many examples of each are highlighted throughout history in several of whose stories are told in books, movies, theatrical plays, and the like. Just as it is important for scholar–practitioners, experts, and others to study homicide in general, it is just as important for them to study the specific types of homicide as well. So for the focus of this discussion, uxoricide (pronounced *uck-soar-i-side*) is of particular interest. The Latin word *uxor* means *wife* and therefore, as mentioned earlier, uxoricide is the killing of a wife by her husband. It is important to recognize that young women under the age of 25 are more likely to be killed by an intimate partner including their husbands than are men, and of all female homicide victims per year in the United States, one in three or one-third of female homicide victims is murdered by an intimate partner (CDC, 2014a). One of the most famous examples of uxoricide in recent American history is the murder of Laci Peterson by her husband Scott Peterson. The couple lived in Modesto, California, and Laci was 8 months pregnant at the time of her disappearance. Scott Peterson did not want children, wanted a new life with another woman, and wanted out of his current situation, so he murdered his wife and disposed of her body in the San Francisco Bay on December 24, 2002. Laci and her unborn son Conner's bodies washed ashore in April of 2003, and subsequently, Scott Peterson was arrested, tried, and convicted of their murders. Scott Peterson is currently on California's Death Row for murdering his wife and unborn son.

Intimicide

Like homicide and murder are interchangeable terms to the general public when talking about the unlawful death of one human being by another human being, intimate partner homicide and domestic violence homicide are typically interchangeable terms generally speaking as well. Some might refer to intimate partner homicides to imply romantic involvement, while others might refer to domestic homicide as a death that occurs between family members. However, within the scope of homicide in general, as mentioned earlier, the type of homicide called *uxoricide* specifically means the killing of a wife by her husband, and the type of homicide called *mariticide* specifically means the killing of a husband by his wife, but neither type of homicide includes unmarried intimate partners killed by their former, current, or temporary intimate partners. Therefore, the author coined the term *intimicide* (pronounced *in-TIM-i-side*) to identify and define the type of homicide that encompasses intimate partner homicide: the killing of a former, current, or temporary intimate partner or a member of the intimate partner's familial or social circle by another former, current, or temporary intimate partner.

Intimicide includes the murders of former or current boyfriends, girlfriends or temporary sexual partners, husbands, wives, same sex domestic partners, and the friends and family of IPV victims because they provided shelter and/or support for IPV victims. Intimicide includes the murders between individuals who just met and became sexually intimate, like two people who met at a bar and left together, and then one partner kills the other partner during the encounter. Intimicide also includes individuals who were dating only briefly at the time of the murder of one by another, or intimate partners who were originally strangers but entered into a regular sex-only intimate relationship or an extramarital affair. The definition of intimicide can also be extended to include intimate partners who solicit or conspire to have their intimate partners murdered, because without the initiation and whatever compensation might be agreed upon, the actual hired hit man most often would never even know the victim, ever target, and especially not murder the victim without prompting by the intimate partner wanting his or her partner dead. However, intimicide is *not*

- The murder of a victim by a serial killer
- The murder of a victim engaged in prostitution killed by a patron
- The murder of a victim by a stranger during the commission of nonconsensual sexual act, such as rape (i.e., sexual homicide/rape–murder)

Serial homicide offenders are individuals who kill more than one person but at different times. Serial homicide offenders differ from mass murder offenders in that mass murders kill more than one person at one time. Further, prostitutes killed by patrons do not fall under the definition of intimicide because they are being compensated for a service regardless of its legality, just as Ressler, Burgess, and Douglas (1988) defined sexual homicide as "the killing of a person in the context of power, sexuality, and brutality," which most often means a stranger-to-stranger homicide that might appear motiveless and are typically very difficult to solve (p. 1).

As mentioned earlier, unlike uxoricide or mariticide, intimicide extends to include family of the IPV victim, like when an estranged husband goes to the home of his wife's parents and kills his estranged wife and then her parents all in the same murderous act. The crux or motive for this type of murder is clearly power and control over the estranged wife, but because her parents offer support and a place to stay, sometimes the enraged offender preys upon additional innocent people attached who defend the victim. Further, close friends of a victim are not immune to becoming ancillary victims of IPV. Friends and even acquaintance-type friends from work or a social setting can be murdered *through* IPV in the workplace and, thus too, become part of the statistics of intimicide. Close friends of IPV victims who in some cases offer shelter or refuge from an abuser are at great risk for injury as well. Take, for instance, the case example that follows:

Tracey and Holly have been friends for about four years and waitressed together at various restaurants around town. The most recent place the two young women worked was a steakhouse when Tracey offered Holly a place to stay because her new husband, Michael, was viciously abusing Holly. Holly accepted Tracey's offer to go stay with Tracey, her husband, and the couple's two young children. Tracey was known by friends and family to be a *giver*. She gravitated toward people in need. It was not surprising to anyone that Tracey made such a generous offer to shelter her longtime friend Holly. Holly called police on a Wednesday who escorted Holly to the motel where she had been staying with Michael. Holly moved her belongings to Tracey's house and stayed for two nights. On Friday night, the young women worked a late shift and arrived back at Tracey's house about 2:00am Saturday morning. Tracey and Holly got out of the car to find Michael hiding behind a tree in the front yard holding a shovel. As Tracey ran to get her husband and call police, Michael hit Tracey in the head with the shovel and she fell to the ground. Michael hit Tracey at least a second time before abducting estranged wife Holly, putting her into a car, and fleeing the scene. At approximately 7:00am, Tracey's husband awoke to find that neither Tracey nor Holly were home. He looked outside and saw a shovel lying behind his car but thought a neighbor put it there. Upon walking outside on the front porch, he found Tracey, dead, beneath the couple's master bedroom window. Some time later, Michael released Holly unharmed in a neighboring town. Holly fled and called 911.

The author worked on this case for preparation for trial. A very graphic piece of information was revealed during the course of this preparation: Holly reported that she knew Michael hit Tracey with the shovel at least twice because even though Holly said she could not see Michael and Tracey in the dark front yard, Holly said she heard the *ring* of the shovel as it impacted its intended target. Based on her skill set, evidence recovered at the scene indicated to the author that it was feasible to surmise that Tracey was actually moving across the front yard toward the master bedroom window when she was struck the second time. In order to avoid the death penalty, Michael pleaded guilty to second-degree murder, second-degree kidnapping, and second-degree robbery with a dangerous weapon and was sentenced to 41 years and 12 months in prison.

Intimicides are some of the most predictable types of homicides because of the preceding lethality factors that exist and therefore should be one of the most preventable. As discussed in the previous text, intimicide is about conflict, power, and control and can be about anger, so the time when an abused victim leaves the abuser is the most dangerous and arguably the most predictable time for an intimate partner homicide to occur. It is important during the course of victimology in these cases for investigators to identify who is in conflict with the victim, was there a confrontation of some kind, who was the last person to see the victim alive, was the victim last seen in relation to an interaction with the soon-to-be estranged or recently separated spouse or intimate partner, and so on. In the aforementioned case illustration, Holly moved out of the marital residence 48 hours before Tracey's death.

Intimicide Characteristics

Characteristics are unique qualities that differentiate something from other things making something unique. Intimicide is very different from many other types of homicide in several ways. First, one of the stark differences between intimicide and nonintimicides is that intimicides are preceded by lethality factors that ebb and flow throughout the course of a violent relationship. Often based on circumstantial evidence that is not physically recovered at the scene, these cases can be very difficult to solve. Intimicides most often occur in a location familiar to the offender and/or the victim, such as their common residence. Thus, physical evidence, such as DNA, for example, might not be helpful in these cases sometimes because both the offender's and victim's DNA are expected to be found in their common living space. Like IPV in general, intimicides are *closed-room* murders meaning that there are normally only two people who know what really happened *behind closed doors*: that is, the victim and the offender. Further, intimicide is normally characterized by a lengthy and in-depth history of IPV inasmuch as between 70% and 80% of intimicides are marked by incidents of IPV prior to the murder where other types of victims and homicide offenders have no interaction of any kind at all (CDC, 2014a). This is important for investigators to recognize when investigating the unexpected, suspicious death of one of the partners. However, it is also important to note that in the minority (i.e., an estimated 20%–30%) of intimicide cases with no pervasive patterned history of IPV, other lethality factors are frequently evident, such as sudden extreme jealousy, substance abuse, threats of suicide, current financial strife, and the offender's violence toward others outside the home. As with most lethality factors, violence escalates in severity or frequency until one day the increase in lethality leads to murder. Even though the offender might not have threatened to kill the victim or have threatened to kill himself or herself throughout the duration of the relationship, it is not so uncommon that many intimicides are characterized by recent, *in the past 30 days*, threats or fantasies of homicide and/or suicide, isolation, sexual abuse, pet abuse, or destruction of the victim's property prior to the intimicide (Parker & Pettler, 2009). Clearly, when these threats are made using a weapon, the likelihood of murder is much greater overall. When considering these factors, it is easy to understand why an offender immediately feels compelled to stage these types of crime scenes in order to try to disconnect from the victim and point the investigation in another direction. The offender knows his history with the victim; thus, his knowledge of the nature of their relationship underpins the very reason he feels to stage in the first place.

Stalking, or the act of harassing an individual by continually giving unwanted attention to him or her and/or obsessing over him or her directly or indirectly for the purpose of unlawful contact between the stalker and the victim many times, also precedes intimicide between two estranged intimate partners. Additionally, becoming enraged with jealousy over a new coworker of an intimate partner or similar is prevalent in intimicide. And other factors that often characterize intimicide are hostage taking and prior instances of strangulation (Parker & Pettler, 2009). Important to remember here is Hazelwood and Napier's (2004) argument that verbal staging can come by way of when an offender kills and disposes of a victim and then calls police to report the victim missing. Keep this in mind when encountering circumstances as described earlier (i.e., Scott Peterson).

Case Example: Ted Anthony Prevatte was sentenced to death in North Carolina for the murder of former intimate partner Cindy McIntyre. An excerpt from the *State of North Carolina v. Ted Anthony Prevatte* (2002), Supreme Court appellate case (pp. 1–2) is as follows:

> Thirty-two-year-old victim (Cindy McIntyre) was married with two children (Michael and Matthew). She and her husband, Mike, were estranged but trying to reconcile. The victim and defendant attended the same church, sang together in the choir, and had been dating for about a year. Defendant lived with his mother across the street from the victim.
>
> On 1 June 1993, when the victim and her husband saw each other, the victim's husband gave her a rose, kissed her, and told her he loved her. Later that same day, the victim and her son Matthew were at home when defendant came in with a present for Matthew. As Matthew was opening the present, his mother said, "Oh my God." Matthew turned around and saw defendant pointing a gun at his mother. Defendant had borrowed a gun from his cousin that afternoon. When Matthew saw defendant with the gun, Matthew jumped up, and defendant pointed the gun at him. Defendant took the victim and Matthew to the bedroom and made them get down on their knees. Defendant then hit and kicked the victim. Defendant pointed the gun at Matthew's head and said if the victim did not shut up, defendant would shoot Matthew. Defendant grabbed Matthew and locked him in a bathroom down the hall

from the bedroom. Defendant briefly left the house but shortly returned and brought the victim out of the house, with her hands bound behind her back. Defendant had his hands on the victim's neck and shoulder area. Defendant forced the victim into a car, pulled the victim back out of the car, and then struck the victim three to four times and slammed the victim's head into the car. The victim's hands remained bound behind her back. Defendant next reached into the car and pulled out a handgun. When the victim tried to run away, defendant held the gun with both hands, aimed, and fired more than once. Defendant left immediately after the last shot. An autopsy of the victim's body revealed she suffered three gunshot wounds. Each bullet passed through the victim's body. One bullet went through the middle of the victim's back and completely destroyed her aorta and heart. Massive bleeding occurred in the chest cavity. These wounds caused the victim's death. Inside the master bedroom of the victim's house, investigators found a nylon rope tied to a bed frame and a roll of duct tape on the floor. The roll of duct tape was consistent with the duct tape used to bind the victim's hands. Prior to the murder, the victim told a witness she was afraid of defendant because he knew she was reuniting with her husband. The victim said she was afraid defendant would hurt her, her children, or her husband. Witnesses also heard defendant say he would kill the victim if he could get away with it and he "[felt] like killing her."

Ted Anthony Prevatte waited until dusk to take Cindy McIntyre from her home. As Prevatte banged Cindy's head off the car, she started to run through the backyard of the residence screaming to her neighbors for help. Moments later, neighbors called police to report that Ted Prevatte just shot their neighbor Cindy McIntyre and that she was lying in the backyard of her residence. The first thing investigators did upon arriving on the scene was to release Cindy's son who was locked in a bathroom inside the house. The investigation revealed a secondary crime scene in a wooded area nearby. The secondary crime scene looked like a shrine to Cindy McIntyre decorated with several of the former couple's interpersonal mementos and locks of the victim's hair. Investigators theorized that Ted Anthony Prevatte was trying to abduct Cindy McIntyre from her home because he planned to bring her back to the shrine in the woods to kill her and bury her there. Investigators collected the following items from both crime scenes, such as a painted board with projectile, bread knife, duct tape, a footboard with rope tied to it, hair, bloodstains, bindings from wrists, fingerprints, clothing, numerous pieces of brown paper, a shovel, a firearm, a sunglasses lens, several locks of hair, numerous pieces of white paper, car keys, and greeting cards.

Based on their investigation, investigators believed Prevatte was distraught over Cindy McIntyre rekindling her relationship with her estranged husband and that extreme jealousy was the primary motive behind her murder. Cindy McIntyre had allegedly been very clear with Prevatte by indicating to him that she did not want to continue a relationship with him. Prevatte fled the scene traveling as far away as Arkansas, so investigators could not find him to ask for an interview. However, investigators interviewed numerous friends, family, associates, and neighbors of Cindy McIntyre who revealed telling information in the case. Ted Anthony Prevatte was charged and convicted of first-degree murder, second-degree kidnapping, and second-degree kidnapping of a minor and was sentenced to death.

Intimicide Dynamics

Dynamics can easily be defined as a *pattern of activity*. Intimicide dynamics are therefore the patterns of activity that fluctuate in force or intensity before, during, and after the murder. Dynamics can be passive or intense. Intimicides can be planned or unplanned. They can be the result of long-term planning by the offender, short-term planning by the offender, or the result of a spontaneous attack on the victim that ends up killing the victim. However, the dynamics of intimicide are illustrious of the personality, behavior, emotionality, cognition, and envirosocioculturalism of the offender, which often in turn reveal motivation for the murder, the method of the murder, and the mode of the murder, all of which is observable in the crime scene details along the force and intensity continuum of power and control and anger, respectively, especially when the crime scene is staged. Keppel and Walter (1999) expanded Hazelwood and Burgess' (1997) four rape typologies—power-assertive, power-reassurance, anger-retaliatory, and anger-excitation—to identify, define, describe, analyze, synthesize, and evaluate the act of rape–murder. The author has expanded the application of Keppel and Walter's (1999) work by synthesizing relevant concepts as they interrelate to intimicide dynamics as well:

Power: The ultimate goal of an intimicide is to have power and control over the victim before, during, and after the murder. Intimicide is grounded in the need for power because IPV is grounded in the need to have power and control over the victim. Therefore, because the crime scene details foreshadow the personality, behavior, emotionality, cognition, and envirosocioculturalism of the offender, it is critical to identify activities in the crime scene related to the offender working to gain, regain, or maintain the power and control over the victim. Some male intimicide offenders might simply use their virility and masculinity to intimidate and overpower their victims by only assertively parading around in an angry, heated state that terrifies the victim without ever laying a hand on the victim but, which therefore, renders the victim unable to escape being murdered out of shear fear. Then along this continuum of force and intensity, one way the intimicide offender dominates the victim is by blitzing the victim, brandishing a weapon toward taking control of the victim, and therefore gaining forced submission. Further along this continuum, intimicide offenders might abduct and bind the hands and/or feet of the victim to gain power and control or tie the victim to an object so the offender can have his way with the victim without the victim's resistance. Overall, the intimicide offender is most interested in power and control; he is direct and he makes his victim know he is in charge under all circumstances.

For the intimicide offender, who is most interested in power and control of the victim, killing the victim can be symbolic of success and the offender is typically satisfied that he eliminated the threat or resolved the conflict. It is interesting to consider that the preceding conflict between a victim and offender could be something as simple as the offender's perception that he is losing power and control over the victim. That instance creates conflict, and for this type of offender, conflict is often resolved through violence. Further, it is not surprising that power and control is the primary objective of intimicide offenders pursuant to intimicide dynamics because especially in cases where the prevalence of a long, sordid, pattern of IPV exists, the essence of that violence has always been driven by the offender's need to have power and control over the victim. So when it finally comes down to the murder of the victim, the prowess exhibited by intimicide offenders is illustrious of his perceived competence as the one in control and ultimately, in its force and intensity, directly relates to the ultimate conquest over the victim before, during, and after the victim's actual death.

Anger: The amount of force or intensity of a planned, unplanned, or spontaneous intimicide can contain variations of anger that run concurrent with power and control. Intimicides that contain the element of anger sometimes, but not always, involve the behavior of overkill or causing injury to the victim not necessary to kill the victim. Theorists have postulated that overkill is the earmark of the need to sate excessive anger. Or is it? Could overkill to the staging offender also be *an act?* It can. It is not unreasonable to consider the idea that a crime scene stager could wound the victim in a manner that looks like overkill to misdirect an investigation toward simulating an angry offender as having killed the victim. On the flip side, because overkill of a victim involves the excessive force the offender exhibits toward the victim that is unnecessary to cause the death of the victim, it can also serve the purpose of anger ventilation and anger satisfaction for the offender of which the injuries to the victim can be symbolic in nature of getting revenge.

Victims might be obviously stabbed hundreds of times, pummeled, decapitated, or dismembered by offenders. The attack by the offender is designed to inflict pain by its very nature through the offender's violent outbursts, but this type of retaliation, while it might resolve the conflict between the victim and offender in the offender's eyes, does not necessarily remove the offender's hatred toward the victim in general. Further, it is arguable that in some cases the offender's anguish is distilled by his or her murderous act and the murder itself has a relieving quality for the offender's sense of internal stressors.

But what about those cases that are reflective of the offender's anger, but do not involve such overviolence or even overkill? Angry offenders also kill their victims by softer methods and modes, such as forceful suffocation with a pillow, carbon monoxide, other types of smothering, and poisoning. In these cases, the savvy investigator must recognize the earmarks of what he or she is looking at in the physical evidence in the crime scene and from the autopsy results in that the offender's anger may be outwardly covert, but it is still very recognizable in his or her rage even though the cause of death might not be immediately obvious. In such cases of poisoning, suffocation, or other lethal measures that result in the death of the victim, but that do not cause overt bodily *harm* to the victim that *screams anger*, the goal is to resolve conflict, whatever that conflict might be and everything that is observed in the crime scene that was manipulated by the offender or otherwise somehow meets his needs.

Power–Anger Conceptual Continuum

Keppel and Walter (1999) categorized rape murderers into two overarching types: power and anger. These authors argued that there were two power types, power-assertive and power-reassurance, and two anger types, anger-retaliatory and anger-excitation. While these typologies might be applicable for rape–murder, the author would argue that intimicide offenders might not fall into such strict categories as these. The core of intimate partner lethality is power and control. Thus, intimicide is ultimately the brute extension of an offender's need for power and control over his victim that finally results in the victim's death. Instead of drawing a line in the sand between the two static categories of power types and anger types for intimicide offenders, the author would argue that all intimicides are power based and that some intimicides contain the element of anger, which ranges along a conceptual continuum in force and intensity. Murder is about conflict resolution for the offender. The conflict to the offender could be anything, such as but not limited to a threat to his power and control over the victim, need to resolve a financial conflict, the desire to move on with another intimate partner while avoiding a costly divorce, and resolving an issue related to children. In these cases, the offender might not necessarily be angry with the victim but just the same needs to have control of the victim so the offender can get what he wants. Then there are the situations where the need for power is definitely there, but on top of that the element of anger is present when, for example, an offender is angry that he has lost power and control over his victim and is jealous that she moved on with someone else. In light of this theoretical concept, the author would opine that it is impossible to remove power from intimicide motivation altogether and that anger motivation could be present as well at various levels.

Case Example: Julie (name changed to protect identity) did not show up for work as she always did and her manager was immediately concerned. After a few hours, her manager called police and asked for someone to go to Julie's house to check on her. When an officer arrived, the house was locked, he could not get anyone to answer the door, and Julie's car was not there. The officer contacted the landlord who came and let the officer in. The officer only entered the kitchen, and before walking through the house, he observed a blood-soaked crime scene and Julie's naked body lying faceup on the bathroom floor. The officer backed out, called detectives, and the investigation began. Upon obtaining a search warrant, the commander and the author entered the residence. Immediately, the strong odor of bleach was overwhelming.

The crime scene was in disarray. The living room was covered with bloodstains. The bloodstain evidence was consistent with impact spatter consistent with a potential beating or stabbing. There were bloody drag marks through the living room and part of the kitchen that led to the bathroom where the victim was found. When examining the body of the victim, it appeared as though she had experienced some type of burns on her body, later determined to have been chemical burns consistent with having bleach poured over her body. Bleach had even pooled in her navel. During the investigation, it was discovered that Julie's car was missing, her wallet was missing, and her boyfriend Mike was missing. Autopsy results revealed that Julie actually died from asphyxiation although she was clearly pummeled during the assault as well.

Law enforcement began to search for Mike, who fled along the East Coast until apprehended a few days later. Mike gave a statement about how he tried to stage the scene, but because he was so high and drunk on methamphetamines and alcohol at the time of the murder, he realized he was in over his head and chose to flee instead. Mike said Julie got home from work and got angry with him for being high and drunk. They got into a physical fight that escalated into murder. He said Julie was still alive when he dragged her to the bathroom, so he pressed the shower curtain rod against her throat until she was dead. Mike said he only beat Julie with his hands, no weapons, although a hawk-billed knife was found in the sink. Mike tried to stage the scene first by removing Julie's clothing, which investigators believe he cut off using the hawk-billed knife found soaking in bleach water in the kitchen sink. Julie's clothing was never recovered. Second, Mike moved Julie while still barely alive from the living room where the couple first got into the physical fight to the bathroom where he stripped her naked. Next, he poured bleach all over Julie's body after killing her with the shower curtain rod in attempt to clean all the evidence off her body. Then Mike used a bucket, mop, and bleach to clean the kitchen floor, laundry room floor, and part of the living room floor, all of which blood was discovered using chemical reagents. Finally, before he fled, Mike bathed, changed his clothes, took evidence with him that he discarded along his travels up and down the East Coast, and fled the scene. Upon realizing Julie's credit cards were no longer working, Mike threw them out of his car window along roadways throughout his travels. Much of the evidence Mike threw away was not recovered. Mike was charged and found guilty of first-degree murder, robbery with a dangerous weapon, and identity fraud and was sentenced to 47 years and 9 months and 15 days in prison.

Several things can be observed in this case example. Mike and Julie were intimate partners. Mike and Julie had a history of IPV and Mike had a history of substance abuse. A conflict arose between the victim and offender when Julie got mad at Mike for being high and drunk when she got home. The conflict escalated from a verbal confrontation to a physical confrontation between the victim and offender where the predominant aggressor, Mike, overpowered Julie and ended up killing her. Julie's murder was unplanned so Mike initially made a marked effort to try to clean up the crime scene, destroy evidence, discard evidence, and so on. At some point, Mike gave up on the staging efforts because it was overwhelming to him and fled the scene instead. Mike's staging efforts were obvious in this scene, but it is still a good example of how anger can play a role in these types of cases.

Intimicide Homicidal Pattern

In relation to intimicide, a pattern of abusive behavior is a repetitive behavioral way one partner behaves toward another intimate partner, and interestingly, these modes are typically observable in the homicidal patterns of intimicide offenders revealed in both the overt and covert details of the murder, the victim's injuries, and the crime scene itself. Like intimicide dynamics, intimicide homicidal patterns generally contain elements of power and anger as well. While it is arguable that viable expansive development beyond the power and anger categories might exist in the future study of intimicide, the goal of resolving conflict or confrontation, maintaining power and control, and/or sating anger remains consistent in today's available information about intimicide and is reflective of the intrinsic nature of the preceding historical context of the IPV-based relationship itself in most cases. Again to expound on Keppel and Walter's (1999) arguments, it is reasonable to accept that the majority of intimicide offenders hold the capacity to choose their behaviors including their staging behaviors based on numerous constructs, such as personality, cognition, emotionality, behavior, and envirosocioculturalism and even determination, which culminate into the foundation of their homicidal patterns specifically in relation to their staging behaviors when coupled with meeting their needs with the parameters of the event before, during, and after the murder.

The author opines that expansion of Walter, Stein, and Adcock's (2011) precrime, crime, and postcrime behavioral matrix is an invaluable investigative tool that has tremendous merit for understanding homicidal dynamics, homicidal patterns, and offender characteristics in homicide cases. Walter et al. (2011) argued that this comprehensive approach helps avoid missing evidence during crime scene processing and homicide investigation (Keppel & Walter, 1999). Though an expanded version of their methodology will be presented and discussed in Chapter 12, it is of noteworthy mention in the discussion of a homicidal pattern as well because the author would argue that a homicidal pattern begins before the murder, continues during the murder, and carries on after the actual death of the victim occurs.

Power

From the power and control standpoint, the homicidal pattern of intimicide offenders is securely seated on the satiation of the offender's emotional need for power and control over the victim by killing him or her. The author again would argue that the intimicide offender decides how to resolve conflict and satisfy this need based on the accumulation of his or her personality, behavior, cognition, emotionality, and envirosocioculturalism. The intimicide offender assesses his or her level of stress in relation to the conflict between him or her and the victim and the potential opportunity to kill the victim based on the culmination of who he is as an individual. In planned intimicides, the offender then determines which type of approach would be most powerful, such as approaching the victim at home, breaking into the victim's home, using a ruse to gain entry into the victim's home, approaching the victim at work, approaching the victim in a social setting (i.e., party) or public place, or approaching the victim at his or her place of shelter or refuge (i.e., parent or friend's home). As discussed earlier, most intimicides are *closed-room* murders that take place in a private location mutually known to the victim and offender (Parker & Pettler, 2009). However, it is interesting to note that generally speaking if a victim is killed in an offender's environment or the offender abducts and then kills a victim, he or she might opt to dispose of the body, but if the victim is killed in the victim's environment, the offender might be more likely to leave the body at the murder scene location (Keppel & Walter, 1999). Empirical research has found that most crime scene stagers do not move their victims' bodies and instead leave them in the murder scene locations (Ferguson, 2011). This could be for many reasons, but one of the reasons could be because empirical research has also found that most offenders stage burglary-related (i.e., home invasions gone awry) homicides and suicides before other types of simulated scenes, which requires the body to remain in the scene in most of those cases.

Weapons can be symbolic to an offender or can be weapons of opportunity. However, Keppel and Walter (1999) suggest that the weapon of choice for the offender seeking power and control is typically one that is part of his or her normal image, like a firearm or a knife, which he or she perceives as an extension of his or her untouchable image. Ferguson (2011) found that most crime scene stagers typically bring weapons to the scene. One of the most important aspects of power-related intimicide concepts is for offenders who kill an intimate partner and get away with it learn to use the experience of that murder to intimidate his or her next victim who might regularly be threatened with something to the effect of "You better_____ or I'm fill you with lead you just like I killed _____." Because power and control is the core of IPV even if an abuser continually threatens his or her new intimate partner with being murdered like his or her former intimate partner, sometimes the new intimate partner will not report his or her abuser's confession for numerous reasons, such as fear, disbelief, false sense of security, and a litany of other reasons. However, interviewing friends and family of the victim might reveal that he or she told them that her intimate partner claimed to have killed a prior intimate partner, or in some cases, when asking friends and family about what they know about an offender's past who has killed their loved one, they might say something to the effect of "Well we knew he was married to some girl named _____, but he never told my sister anything about her and we never knew what happened in there." Meanwhile, the former intimate partner of the offender who has now killed his second victim is also dead under suspicious circumstances, and in such cases, it is not uncommon to discover that these deaths were ruled a suicide or accident at the crime scene based exclusively on offender statements without scientific inquiry. The best predictor of future behavior is past, relevant behavior.

Intimicide and firearms: Ferguson (2011) and Pettler (2011) found that firearms were the most commonly used weapons in staged cases where offenders were male, victims were female, and the victim–offender relationship was some kind of current or former intimate partner. Firearms and IPV are a lethal combination. Victims' lives are in immediate and certain danger when abusers have access to firearms. An access to weapons, specifically firearms, is one of the most poignant factors related to IPV. In the author's experience coupled with her research, firearms are used to murder more often than any other weapon (Pettler, 2011). According to the National Network to End Domestic Violence (NNEDV) (2014), firearms are used three times more often by an intimate partner to murder a woman than are a stranger's firearms, knife, or another weapon (para. 2). Further, three women were murdered each day by their intimate partners in 2010 and 52% of intimate partner homicide victims were killed by their intimate partners with firearms (NNEDV, 2014, para. 2). Interestingly, men choose handguns to murder women in intimate partner homicide more often than they choose rifles or shotguns as supported by a recent study finding that 70% of intimate partner homicide victims by firearm are killed with a handgun (NNEDV, 2014).

In addition, intimate partner homes that contain firearms are three times more likely to have a homicide occur than intimate partner homes that do not contain guns (NNEDV, 2014). And interestingly, these statistics drastically increase eightfold when an abuser is the one who owns the gun in an intimate partner common residence. Further still, the likelihood of an intimate partner homicide occurring in a home increases to 20 times more likely when the male firearm owner and his intimate partner have a previous history of domestic violence (NNEDV, 2014). And the abusers who have access to firearms are 500% more likely to inflict more serious injury upon their intimate partners in violent relationships than are abusers employing other methods of abuse (NNEDV, 2014). So based on these statistics, it is not difficult to understand why Ferguson (2011) and Pettler (2011) both found that firearms were used in staged intimicide cases in both samples exclusively.

Anger: Anger also causes conflict between a victim and offender. Even though all intimicide offenders want power and control over an intimate partner, elements of anger can be interwoven into the offender's behavioral patterns that mirror his or her rage. Intimicides reflective of the element of anger are retaliatory in nature, and because they are influenced by an abuser's personality, behavior, cognition, emotionality, and envirosocioculturalism, they often occur in numerous familiar locations, such as in the victim's home, offender's home, their common residence, or at the victim's workplace based on a conflict that has made the offender angry. Regardless if the murder is planned or not, the offender aims to satisfy his anger, thus resolving the conflict through murder. Clearly, there is sound argument for the fact that spontaneous intimicides are *heat of passion*-type murders, but even in the split second or blink of an eye in the heat of passion, premeditation is still often present. Additionally in intimicide specifically, the angry offender might walk or drive a short distance to get to the victim's home like in the case of *State of North Carolina v. Ted Anthony Prevatte* (2002) who lived down the street from Cindy McIntyre and used a ruse (i.e., bringing a gift for McIntyre's son, Matthew) to gain entry into the home where Prevatte viciously confronted McIntyre, initially trying to satisfy his anger toward her by hitting and kicking her because he was extremely jealous that she ended their relationship and rekindled her relationship with her estranged husband. According to Keppel and Walter (1999), anger-motivated murders last until the offender's anger is satisfied, which is unrelated to the victim being alive or dead at that point in the process. Therefore, it is not uncommon for the murder to continue well past the actual death of the victim because the offender has not yet gained full satisfaction from the death. The crime scenes of anger-motivated intimicides can be very unorganized because they can often involve excessive hitting, stabbing, kicking, biting, beating, and so on. As the offender's anger begins to diminish through this violence, he or she might experience a euphoric feeling and no longer feel anger toward the victim. A suspect once told the author during an interview that the suspect "just felt good" while walking away from the crime scene. Ironically, these same feelings of euphoria could underpin how these types of offenders are able to manufacture pseudo-sentimental feelings for the victim in verbal staging to the extent where the offender actually displays tearful pleas for the return of his or her missing intimate partner all the way to physically searching for a missing loved one himself or herself like in the case of Scott Peterson when interviewed by *ABC News* correspondent Diane Sawyer. According to *ABC News* (2003), Peterson cried during the interview with Sawyer when speaking about his then missing wife Laci Peterson and claimed he came forward to speak because suspicion surrounding his potential involvement in Laci's disappearance was impeding search efforts.

Criminal Profiling and Its Value toward Predicting Risk and Preventing Lethality in Intimicide

Criminal profiling could be defined as the process of identifying and analyzing the personality, cognition, behavior, emotionality, and envirosocioculturalism of an offender and how the facets of each interrelate and synthesize to a victim, a crime, and its crime scenes. And as logical as it might sound to embed such a process deep within the construct of homicide investigation, the principles and practice of criminal profiling have long been controversial among the experts. Some sharply disagree with anyone who supports criminal profiling as a viable option for predicting crime or developing a suspect in any case. However, while it is arguable that a multimodal approach to homicide investigation is comprehensive, thorough, and reasonable, there are still many who focus purely on any physical evidence in a case, thus negating the intrinsic value of how behavior intertwines with physical evidence because behavior is what created or caused the physical evidence to exist in the first place. So overall, it is not best to go by the old cliché "put all your eggs in one basket" (as such focusing too much on the physical evidence or the behavioral evidence), such as "case closed by arrest, suspect confessed" (focusing too much on the testimonial evidence), but instead, approach every case, confession or not, with an open mind that embraces the totality of the evidence via scientific reconstructive inquiry, which includes the analysis, synthesis, and evaluation of physical, testimonial, and behavioral evidence.

Additionally, though the author has seen exemplary work that exceeds even the highest bars set forth in comprehensive homicide investigation, throughout her career, she has seen countless cases where there is no "smoking gun" at the crime scene so investigators "jump to conclusions" and render conclusive opinions on homicide, suicide, accident, natural, and so forth, in the crime scene without a thorough scientific investigation. There is no map for intimicide investigation; every investigation is different and every offender is unique. Investigative scaffolding can remain consistent case to case as will be discussed in Chapter 10, but flexibility within the fluid situation that is homicide investigation is a must. Although individuals charged with investigating homicides as a duty, responsibility to society, and public service toward maintaining public safety and social control deserve utmost respect, to sharply dismiss the critical nature of the behavioral evidence of both the victim and suspect in any death investigation where evidence that tips the scale toward one manner of death or the other and that is not immediately observable in a crime scene alone or has been masked by the crime scene stager is to blatantly dismiss the core purpose of investigatory work itself.

Intimicide Offender Characteristics

Toward keeping a *profile* applicable to the broadest population of offenders, when assembling the general characteristics of the most common American intimicide offender, according to the U.S. Department of Justice (2011), three statistics are important to recognize:

1. Most intimicide offenders are male (70.3%).
2. Most intimicide offenders range between the ages of 18 and 34 years (47%).
3. Most intimicide offenders are white males (54.2%) or black males (43.5%) (pp. 5–12).

What is so interesting about these statistics generated by the U.S. Department of Justice (2011) is that it mirrors the empirical findings about crime scene staging offenders in several empirical studies to date (Eke, 2011; Ferguson, 2011; Pettler, 2011; Schlesinger et al., 2012; Turvey, 2000). This is not surprising when considering how that most offenders who stage crime scenes are the current or former intimate partners of the victims. Even though there is no such thing as a typical intimicide offender, but because intimicide is the result of the offender's predominant need to resolve conflict while gaining, regaining, or maintaining power and control over the victim, coupled with the possibility of anger embedded within the offense, these statistics, recognizing that power is the core of IPV as well, are paramount to understanding how it might translate into a staged murder in accordance with the crime, the victim's injuries, and the crime scene. The best way to understand an overarching nature of the most common types of American intimicide offenders is to understand the major premises of IPV in relation to how the need for power and the need to satisfy anger in some cases lead to the finality of death in relation to conflict and/or confrontations that precede the murder of the victim, but it is also critically important to recognize that IPV is a silent crime one whose abusers are typically very difficult to identify.

Generally speaking, the intimate partner abuser might be very friendly to those outside of his relationship, and the harm he causes to his victim might go unnoticed by outsiders because the physical injuries are not severe enough to warrant medical attention and the emotion, psychological, and sexual abuse is kept private by both parties. Because the best predictor of future behavior is normally past, relevant behavior, like victimology, *suspect-ology,* or the analytical study of suspects, means understanding who the suspect is of equal importance. As mentioned in Chapter 4, traditional homicide investigation has been focused on suspectology so much so that the victim was most often forgotten. A well-balanced multimodal, interdisciplinary scientific death investigation that includes victimology and suspectology is one that will arguably lead to information that will support or refute the facts of the case therefore pointing investigators in the direction of homicide, suicide, accident, natural, or undetermined, especially when investigating the complexities of the staged intimate partner death scene.

The essence of the IPV relationship and the roles the abuser plays in that relationship are the foundations of the general characteristics of the intimicide offender who often is also a crime scene stager. The characteristics that underpin IPV carry over in many ways to intimicide and are often reflected in the injuries to the victim, the crime, and the crime scene along with the way in which the offender tries to avoid apprehension. Intimate partner abusers wish to maintain power and control over their intimate partners and do so through physical, emotional, sexual, psychological, economic, or other types of abuse that can escalate into the final event of intimicide. In conjunction, abusers who are motivated by anger toward their intimate partners also use the latter to control their victims, but they are more focused on getting back at the intimate partner for perceived wrongs than exuding sheer power alone in the relationship. Even in death, the offender believes he still has control over his victim because he successfully defeated the threat or resolved the conflict/confrontation through murder. According to Gerney and Parsons (2014) between 2001 and 2012, 55% of all women killed by an intimate partner or 6410 women were murdered using a gun, making guns the most commonly used murder weapon in intimicide more than any other weapon, including manual strangulation or sharp objects during this period.

Again according to the CDC (2014a), approximately 65% of intimicides were substantiated by an abusive relationship brought forth by the abuser turned intimicide offender. Further, and in cases where the offender is male, a pervasive pattern of victim isolation and intimidation, exuberant displays of masculinity, and the need to be glorified constantly by everyone around him, coupled with his inability to be vulnerable to anyone, might lead him to constantly behave in a neurotic manner because his beliefs about how others should behave around him are unhealthy and unreasonable, which in turn leads to violence because he is typically emotionally primitive and ultrasensitive to threats to his dominance over his victim (Keppel & Walter, 1999). Eke (2007) found that some offenders in her sample reported problems with drugs and alcohol along with having been diagnosed with a mental health–related disorder. Thus, it is arguable that the intimicide offender might abuse drugs and/or alcohol in an attempt to feel or appear more powerful to his victim before or during the murder. Other general characteristics of some intimicide offenders might include a history of antisocial behaviors, having an explosive personality, or being very aggressive.

There is definitely a safe way and an unsafe way to leave a violent relationship. However as mentioned before, the abused victim is at greatest risk for becoming an intimicide victim when he or she leaves the relationship regardless if she took precautions to stay safe or not. When the victim leaves, she is unintentionally creating conflict between her and her abuser. The latter statement does not and should not be taken as the author implying whatsoever that the victim is at fault for the conflict created by her escape, rather that the perception of the offender is the focus, which is that he or she perceives the victim's escape as conflict between him or her and the victim. Thus, the abuser might perceive this act not as victim self-preservation but as pure betrayal, rejection, abandonment, or any other act of defiance toward the abuser. Thus, it is very important to recognize timing in relation to identifying circumstances that can thrust the abuser toward becoming an intimicide offender and possibly then a crime scene stager.

Although no motivational model of intimicide offenders exists at this point in the research, it is not uncommon for them to have underlying issues with antisocial behavior, power, control, and anger. While the motivation for killing the victim normally comes from the need to resolve conflict, the need for power, and/or the need to satisfy anger, there are numerous other micro-reasons why an individual kills his or her intimate partner. Statistically speaking, most intimicide victims are females killed with firearms who are killed by former or current male intimate partners, but to "be on the lookout" for only individuals who carry guns, have access to guns, can borrow a gun, and so on, would be erroneous and overreaching: Ted Anthony Prevatte did not have a gun; he borrowed a gun to overpower, control, and murder Cindy McIntyre; and there is no evidence that supports Scott Peterson using a gun to murder his pregnant wife Laci Peterson, for example. Therefore, when it comes to murder weapon, guns are the most commonly used, but not exclusively used, so being open to alternatives when understanding intimicide and murder weapons is very important in the investigatory process. Never is it best to ever paint oneself into a corner of any kind during the process of developing a criminal profile, building a crime scene reconstruction, or defining any new term or concept too narrowly. And remember that the more research that is conducted and published on staging, the more that the information contained in this book might become more relevant or less relevant over time (definitively a limitation of writing a book based on empirical knowledge gained through a limited number of studies). However, based on the following statistics and published research in combination with the education, training, research, and experience of the author, the following general earmarks of the most common characteristics of the American intimicide offender can be identified toward predicting risk of lethality, intimicide, and in some cases crime scene staging:

- Most offenders are male.
- They are most often between the ages of 18 and 24.
- They are most often Caucasian or African-American.
- They most often have a history of antisocial behavior.
- They have a preceding conflict with the victim (i.e., separation, affair).
- They most often kill behind closed doors.
- They most often kill with firearms.
- They most often have a history of abusing the victim.
- They most often control their victims using threats, emotional, psychological, physical, economic, and/or sexual abuse.
- They often have low self-esteem.
- They often deny their actions and take no responsibility for their behavior.
- Some might threaten to kill the victim and/or commit suicide.
- Some might have attempted to strangle their victims prior to the murder of the victim.
- Some might escalate in force and intensity prior to the murder.

Turvey (2011) argued that certain aspects of physical evidence, such as ransacking and specific factors related to points of entry and exit, do not automatically imply that a crime scene is staged because ransacking and alteration to points of entry/exit are so common in lots of types of crime scene beyond the scope of only staged ones. This concept can be similarly applied to the offender characteristics listed earlier because some are arguably so general that they are not very helpful. Again, while some or all of these offender characteristics could represent the majority of intimicide offenders, it is important to always be open to additional offender characteristics that are identified during an investigation. Successful prosecution begins at the crime scene, and because intimicides are often largely based on circumstantial evidence, they can be difficult to prosecute. Investigating intimicides requires an open mind, objectivity, and an eclectic approach to investigation, coupled with the insight into the dynamics of human behavior (i.e., psychology) of the victim and offender. When approaching any death scene where the last person to see the victim alive was the intimate partner and quite possibly the first person to find the victim's body is the intimate partner as found in Ferguson's (2011) study, no firm conclusions should be drawn at the crime scene especially or early in the investigation for any reason. Intimate partners being last to see the victim alive and/or first to find the body are frequent occurrences in intimicide, and empirical research on crime scene staging has revealed this premise could be applicable to the staging population as well. When this is the case, investigators should heighten their awareness to the possibility that they are investigating an intimicide staged as something else. Unlike uxoricide and mariticide, intimicide encompasses all types of intimate partner relationships including same sex partners, fiancés, spouses, boyfriends/girlfriends, and even biologically related adults engaged in intimate partner relationships. Failing to learn to recognize the earmarks of staging behaviors, assuming the integrity of a crime scene, witness statements especially at the crime scene, and especially suspect statements without extending resources toward verifying the content through scientific inquiry of each can ultimately prove to prevent justice for intimicide victims.

References

ABC News. (2003). Scott Peterson Talks to *ABC News*' Diane Sawyer. Retrieved from http://abcnews.go.com/GMA/story?id = 124563

Black, M. C. (2011). Intimate partner violence and adverse health consequences: Implications for clinicians. *American Journal of Lifestyle Medicine, 5*(5), 428–439.

Center for Disease Control. (2014a). Injury prevention and control. Retrieved from http://www.cdc.gov/violenceprevention/nisvs/infographic.html

Center for Disease Control. (2014b). Intimate partner violence consequences. Retrieved from http://www.cdc.gov/violenceprevention/intimatepartnerviolence/consequences.html

Eke, A. W. (2007). *Staging in cases of homicide: Offender, victim, and offence characteristics* (Doctoral dissertation). Retrieved from ProQuest (1390310091).

Ferguson, C. (2011). *The defects of the situation: A typology of staged crime scenes* (Unpublished doctoral thesis). Bond University, Gold Coast, Queensland, Australia.

Geberth, V. J. (2010). Crime scene staging: An exploratory study of the frequency and characteristics of sexual posing in homicides. *Investigative Sciences Journal, 2*(2), 1–19.

Gerney, A., & Parson, C. (2014). Women under the gun: How gun violence affects women and 4 policy changes to better protect them. Retrieved from https://www.scribd.com/doc/230114462/Women-Under-the-Gun-How-Gun-Violence-Affects-Women-and-4-Policy-Solutions-to-Better-Protect-Them

Hazelwood, R. R., & Burgess, A. N. (1997). *Practical aspects of rape investigation: A multidisciplinary approach*. New York: Elsevier.

Hazelwood, R. R., & Napier, M. R. (2004). Crime scene staging and its detection. *International Journal of Offender Therapy and Comparative Criminology, 48*(6), 744–759. doi: 10.1177/0306624X04268298

Keppel, R. D., & Walter, R. (1999). Profiling killers: A revised classification model for understanding sexual murder. *Interpersonal Journal of Offender Therapy and Comparative Criminology, 43*(4), 417–437.

Keppel, R. D., & Weis, J. G. (2004). The rarity of unusual dispositions of victim bodies: Staging and posing. *Journal of Forensic Science, 49*(6), 1–5.

Maslow, A. H. (1943). A theory of human motivation. *Psychological Review, 50,* 360–396.

National Network to End Domestic Violence. (2104). Guns, domestic violence, and homicide. Retrieved from http://nnedv.org/downloads/Policy/2013AdvConf_GunLegislationBW. pdf

Parker, M. D., & Pettler, L. G. (2009). DV homicide: Hot blooded lovers, cold blooded killers [PowerPoint slides]. *Evidence based domestic violence prosecution course*. Carthage, NC: Authors.

Pettler, L. G. (2011). *Crime scene behaviors of crime scene stagers* (Doctoral dissertation). Retrieved from ProQuest (2251577601).

Ressler, R. K., Burgess, A. W., & Douglas, J. E. (1988). *Sexual homicide: Patterns and motives*. New York: The Free Press.

Roberts, T. A., Auinger, P., & Klein, J. D. (2005). Intimate partner abuse and the reproductive health of sexually active female adolescents. *Journal of Adolescent Health, 36*(5), 380–385.

Safe Haven, Inc. (2014). Statistics and facts. Retrieved from http://www.safehorizon.org/ page/domestic-violence-statistics—facts-52.html

Schlesinger, L. B., Gardenier, A., Jarvis, J., & Sheehan-Cook, J. (2012, April). Crime scene staging in homicide. *Journal of Police and Criminal Psychology, 29*(1), 44–51.

State of North Carolina v. Ted Anthony Prevatte, No. 492A99. (North Carolina, 2002).

Tjaden, P., & Thoennes, N. (2000). *Extent, nature, and consequences of intimate partner violence: Findings from the National Violence Against Women Survey*. Washington, DC: United States Department of Justice, Publication No. NCJ 181867.

Turvey, B. E. (2000, December). Staged crime scenes: A preliminary study of 25 cases. *Journal of Behavioral Profiling, 1*(3).

Turvey, B. E. (2011). *Criminal profiling: An introduction to behavioral evidence analysis* (4th ed.). London, UK: Academic Press.

United States Department of Justice. (2011). Homicide trends in the United States 1980–2008. Retrieved from http://www.bjs.gov/content/pub/pdf/htus8008.pdf

United States Department of Justice. (2014). What is domestic violence? Retrieved from http://www.justice.gov/ovw/domestic-violence

Walter, R., Stein, S., & Adcock, J. M. (2011). Suspect identification using pre-, peri-, and post-offense behaviors. In J. M. Adcock & S. L. Stein (Eds.), *Cold cases: An evaluation model with follow-up strategies for investigators*. Boca Raton, FL: CRC Press/Taylor & Francis Group.

Weinbaum, Z., Stratton, T. T., Chavez, G., Motylewski-Link, C. Barrera, N., & Courtney, J. G. (2011, November). Female victims of physical intimate partner violence (IPP-DV), California 1998. *American Journal of Preventive Medicine, 21*(4), 313–319.

Women Against Abuse. (2014). Types of domestic violence. Retrieved from http://www. womenagainstabuse.org/index.php/learn-about-abuse/types-of-domestic-violence

Types of Staging

8

Introduction

Hans Gross (1924) was the first to address crime scene staging and the responsibilities investigators have to learn how offenders manipulate physical evidence toward simulating something separate and apart from what actually happened. Gross (1924) argued:

> The defects of the situation are just those contradictions, those improbabilities, which occur when one desires to represent the situation as something quite different from what it really is, and this with the very best intentions and the purest belief that one has worked with all the forethought, craft and consideration imaginable. (p. 433)

Staging is the overarching behavioral pattern exhibited by an offender to misdirect an investigation toward self-preservation and avoiding apprehension that can include lying, giving false alibis. Descriptive analysis has revealed that most intimicide offenders are male, that most intimicide victims are female, and that most intimicides are underpinned by a pervasive history of intimate partner violence (United States Department of Justice, 2014). Further, descriptive research on crime scene staging specifically has revealed that most offenders are male, that most victims are female, and that intimate partner homicides are staged more often than murders where the victim and the offender were associated in another way (i.e., neighbor, employee, etc.) (Eke, 2007; Ferguson, 2011; Pettler, 2011). Empirical research has also shown that offenders point their staging efforts toward overall deception, disconnecting association to the victim, misdirecting the investigation, and self-preservation toward avoiding apprehension. Additionally, empirical research on crime scene staging has identified a myriad of staging behaviors exhibited by offenders, and Ferguson (2011) found that staging behaviors appear to be related to the type of scene chosen to simulate by an offender.

Homicides Staged as Suicides

According to Geberth (1996, 2006), staging a crime scene to make it appear as though a victim has committed suicide is one of the most commonly encountered scenarios in the crime scene staging phenomenon. And even nearly 100 years ago, Gross (1924) argued that one of the ways offenders stage poisoning or strangulation homicide is to simulate a suicide death by hanging. Gross (1924) stated:

> It is a fair presumption that a considerable proportion of so-called suicidal deaths by hanging are really caused by another hand. Of course in such cases the murderer will not select a mode of death leaving too distinct traces. One would not hang up, under pretense of suicide, a person killed by a gunshot wound or with a fractured skull; but this is frequently done in cases of poisoning, strangling, or even killing by means of a fine and long stabbing instrument. (p. 430)

Case reviews conducted by Puschel, Holtz, Hildebrand, Naeve, and Brinkman (1984); Ueno et al. (1989); Yamamoto, Hayase, Matsumoto, and Yamamoto (1998); Leth and Vesterby (1996); and Mallach and Pollak (1998) all focused on murder staged as suicide. In all of these cases, victims were strangled or asphyxiated and then hanged by the offender toward simulating suicide by hanging. Additionally, other authors have discussed homicide staged as suicide. O'Connell and Soderman (1936) and then Svensson and Wendel (1974) also discussed how homicidal intent should be uncovered through systematic analysis of crime scenes and how staged suicide can be manipulated to resemble numerous types of death scenes. However, none of these authors supported their ideas with empirical findings. Then, Turvey (2000) found that 4 of 25 staged cases involved sucide with a firearm. In those cases the offenders were intimate partners of the victims who positioned the firearms and the victims' bodies then called police to report that the victims' had committed suicide.

Pettler (2011) found that intimicides are most often staged by offenders who are not connected to any other type of criminal activity otherwise limiting their knowledge about the way crime scenes should look based on the crime scene investigator effect and the media. Intimicide does not happen in a vacuum, and crime scene behavior is based largely on the offender's personality, cognition, behavior, emotionality, and envirosocioculturalism. Emotionality is a dangerous thing, and the author would argue that offenders' emotionality might play a significant role in the way in which they choose to stage intimicides to appear as though something else happened. When the hand of an intimate partner kills the other intimate partner, the offender knows that unless he or she removes the body, the partner's body is going to be found at the death scene location. In most cases, because intimicide is a closed-room murder that most often takes place behind the closed doors of their home, car, boat, or some other private location, the offender feels compelled to detach from the victim and the crime scene and to protect his or her identity, which can largely be driven by raw emotion at that time. But important to remember is emotion-driven behavior can be careless; thus, crime scene stagers are notorious for making errors in the heat of the moment because (1) they really do not know what the details of the evidence should look like and (2) they are consumed with self-preservation, for example (Douglas & Douglas, 2006). When investigators arrive to find that the evidence contradicts the offender's story, the offender can quickly become a suspect, and the investigation can begin to lean toward homicide even if investigators do not reveal that to the suspect. One of the most important things to know about staging is that the elements of the scene that depart from what would be expected in relation to the type of crime scene being investigated can create that *gut* feeling investigators sometimes say they get when stepping into a scene that just does not feel right. It is true that not everything that appears awry in a crime scene means that it is staged; rather, it simply means that suspicious circumstances should lead to greater scientific inquiry, and no conclusions should be drawn as early as during the crime scene investigation.

In a recent study, Schlesinger, Gardenier, Jarvis, and Sheehan-Cook (2012) found that only 6 of the 79 staged homicide cases they studied were staged as suicide. Domestic partners of the victims staged four of these cases, while two of these cases were staged by nonsexual general felony homicide offenders (p. 47). Schlesinger et al., however, did not specify how these cases were staged. Additionally, Ferguson and Petherick (2014) conducted a descriptive study on 16 homicide cases staged as suicide to determine in part (adapted from p. 6) the following:

1. What evidence do offenders most often manipulate, and are their ideas premeditated?
2. What is the victim–offender relationship in these cases?

Ferguson and Petherick found that in all cases, only one offender was involved in staging the homicide simulated as suicide as the result of most often gunshot deaths, followed by ligature strangulation, then multiple weapons. This sample revealed that 15 offenders were male and 1 female, and that 9 victims were male and 7 female. Seven of the victims and offenders were spouses who lived together, but one victim and offender were intimate partners living together. Further, interestingly in this sample, eight of the victims were murdered and staged to have committed suicide by nondomestic family members or friends of the victims, while no victims in this sample were murdered by family members, business associates, or strangers. Additionally, most victims were discovered in their own homes most often in their bedrooms, bathrooms, dens, or living rooms, but one victim was found outside in this sample while one victim was found in the offender's bedroom and one was found in the offender's den or living room (p. 8). See Ferguson and Petherick (2014) for additional details.

Case Example

Cindy was a middle-aged woman who suffered from depression. She was an alcoholic who drank heavily on a regular basis. She recently made arrange-ments to separate from her intimate partner and wrote a suicide note that she left in her desk drawer at work. She went home that evening and drank until her blood alcohol level exceeded 30, which means she had approximately 30 g of alcohol per 100 mL of blood in her bloodstream. At approximately 4:00 A.M., Cindy's boyfriend called 911 to report that Cindy shot herself in the head. Law enforcement officials arrived on scene to find Cindy seated in a recliner in her living room. One of the first responders was a brand-new police officer who picked up the firearm from Cindy's lap, then realizing what he did was incorrect procedure, he put it back in the exact location from where he picked it up and immediately told his supervisor of his mistake. Cindy was holding a small box of fuses in her left hand, which was resting on an end table beside the chair. Cindy's other hand was in her lap, and the gun was sit-ting on her left thigh. One of the first things a savvy detective noticed was that Cindy's feet were crossed as they rested on the floor and that they were show-ing heavy signs of livor mortis. The detective quickly grew suspicious because the boyfriend originally claimed he called police immediately following the fatal shot. The detective knew that more investigation was necessary. The house was in complete disarray. The couple were musicians, and sheet music covered the floor. Cindy's boyfriend appeared distraught over her death. The detective asked to interview the boyfriend and he complied. During the inter-view, information was revealed that continued to raise the suspicion of the detective. The detective contacted the author, who subsequently investigated and processed aspects of the crime scene with negative results. The detective asked the boyfriend to take a polygraph, and they two scheduled the appoint-ment. The boyfriend did not show up for the appointment, and the polygraph was rescheduled. The boyfriend subsequently passed the polygraph, and when confronted about the appearance of the crime scene, the boyfriend admitted to disposing of drugs before police arrived. He also admitted that it took him some time to rid the entire house of paraphernalia and that he did not call police for several hours after Cindy's death.

This case was left open until coworkers discovered the suicide note in Cindy's desk at work a short time later. The medical examiner ruled the gun-shot was self-inflicted, and the case was closed. This is a good example of how a suicide can have earmarks of crime scene staging, but through a persistent detective's dedication to her job, it was ultimately determined that the alteration of the crime scene in this case was not to conceal the identity of the shooter, but to conceal the couple's addiction to heroin and other illegal drugs.

Never assume the integrity of a crime scene because sometimes things are not always the way they look upon first glance. Investigators should learn to recognize that though suspicion does not equate to evidence, it does not mean the case is closed or that the case is over; it means that it is just the beginning. There are times when early detection of crime scene staging is missed altogether, such as in the case of intimicides staged as suicide. Intimicides staged as suicide can be some of the most challenging types of cases to revisit later because the amount of documentation originally generated can be virtually nonexistent, sometimes the body was not sent for autopsy, and no crime scene investigation had taken place. In many cases, upon cursory review, they really do appear to look like suicide, but when one delves deeper, much deeper in some cases, the elements of the mask begin to show themselves, and what started out as death investigation leaning toward suicide has now evolved into a death investigation that warrants further inquiry.

Normally, death investigators have one chance to do it right, so doing it right the first time is innately related to successful prosecution in homicide cases. Homicide investigation is a profession that comes with heavy responsibility to always do the right thing for a victim. It means education, training, and experience; it means being open to alternatives, it means not jumping the gun and drawing conclusions at the crime scene, and it means following up on cases when families come forward arguing against the ruling that their loved one committed suicide. According to Geberth (1996), when families provide information to authorities, it is authorities' responsibility to follow up (p. 96). Further, Geberth (1996) consulted on a case that was clearly a homicide staged as a suicide completely missed by investigators, but authorities never followed up when the family of the victim brought forth pertinent information trying to convince the investigators that the family felt the investigators made a mistake:

> In my professional opinion as an expert in homicide and death investigations, the inquiry into the death of the deceased was perfunctory and inadequate according to the recognized standards of professional death investigation. It was readily apparent that this particular crime scene had been staged and it was a reasonable assumption based upon the above facts that the deceased had not committed suicide. (p. 25)

The facts Geberth was referring to was everything that came out in victimology was inconsistent with any type of suicidal behavior by the deceased.

The author agrees with Geberth that a lack of follow-up in cases where there could be a problem is a cause of professionalism-related concern. Further, homicide investigation is interdisciplinary and should work from the inside out (Walter, Stein & Adcock, 2011). There are many documented cases of crime scene stagers staging the death of their intimate partners as suicide in more ways than one could count. Based on the offender's personality, cognition, behavior, emotionality, and envirossocioculturalism, intelligence and capabilities, and the availability of various methods coupled with the same facets of the victim as aligned with the association the offender has to the victim, he believes staging the crime scene to make it appear as though his intimate partner took her own life is the safest way to conceal his identity as the murderer. Geberth (2006) argued that "the most common type of staging occurs when the perpetrator changes elements of a crime scene to make the death appear to be a suicide or accident in order to cover-up a murder" (p. 23). Adcock and Stein (2011) argued that individuals who are not otherwise involved in any type of criminal activity most often stage crime scenes as accidents, suicide, home invasions, or the victim walking in on a burglar (p. 196). In these cases, crime scene stagers tamper with the physical evidence, moving it around, removing it from the scene, creating various scenarios, until they create what they think is going to be believable to police. Much of their *crime scene* knowledge comes from the media only because these are stagers who have no connection to criminal activity outside of this event. In these cases, the manipulated crime scenes are often consistent with basic staging themes, making them inconsistent with much of the physical and behavioral evidence that can be discovered by investigators who are in tune with early detection.

The investigative reality of staged suicide is this:

1. Victimology should be consistent with the victim being likely to commit suicide.
   a. If the victim had plans to move, start a new job, go out with friends the night before, go to a party, go on vacation, etc., this is not an individual whose behavior is consistent with suicidal behavior.
   b. When those around the victim note that the victim is positive, happy, in good spirits, or just behaving normally for the individual, this is inconsistent with suicidal behavior.
   c. If the individual is engaged in other activities, such as remodeling a house or buying something new, this is inconsistent with suicidal behavior generally speaking.

Suicide and Firearms

Ferguson and Petherick (2014) found that 56.3% of their 16 case samples were staged suicide by gunshot wounds. Special considerations should be taken when approaching a death scene where it initially appears that a victim died of a self-inflicted gunshot wound. Handguns often fall out of the victim's hand upon discharge, but not always like in the case of *cadaveric spasm* or what is sometimes called "instant rigor mortis" (Geberth, 2006). In cases where instant rigor mortis is in question, the victim's hand might be observed tightly clenching the gun in his or her hand. According to Geberth (2006), offenders attempting to make the victim hold the gun when staging a suicide cannot produce a cadaveric spasm by any means. Ferguson and Petherick (2014) again found that elements of staging were monothematic in that the weapon was arranged and the body was positioned. Regardless, at a minimum, an examination of the victim's hands searching for materials consistent with discharging a firearm, such as soot, powder, and blood is first and foremost. Second, it is critically important to investigate whether the victim could have pulled the trigger based on the type of firearm found with the victim (i.e., are the victim's arms long enough to have reached the trigger of a long gun), and whether it was a handgun, long gun, or shotgun, again for materials consistent with operability and biological material, such as body fluids and blood. Third, ballistic testing specific to the situation is also highly recommended.

It is arguable that the most logical locations to shoot oneself would be in the head or chest in an attempt to stop functioning of vital organs. Ferguson and Petherick (2014) found evidence of simulated self-injury in 15 out of 16 cases in their sample and that the locations of these injuries were consistent with suicide, such as in the head (e.g., temple, under the chin) or to the wrist or heart (p. 9). The author would argue that it is illogical, however, to commit suicide by shooting oneself under the left arm into the rib cage, for example, but this type of self-injury was originally suggested by the suspect in the following case.

The Betty "Bea" Lafon Johnson Malone
Flynn Sills Gentry Neumar Case

Acting as the director of Prosecutorial District 20A's former Cold Case Task Force, the author was the lead investigator on behalf of the former district attorney (DA) in *North Carolina v. Betty Lafon Neumar*. This case will be revisited for numerous reasons throughout the remainder of this book; thus, an introduction to the overarching facts of the case is necessary in order to move forward.

In August 2007, the author received several boxes of material regarding the investigation of Harold Gentry's July 1986 death. During the 8 months it took to organize and initially investigate the case, the author discovered that the prime suspect in Harold Gentry's death was his wife Betty Lafon Gentry. Upon a deep dive into Betty Gentry's life, the author discovered that Betty was married five times. Her first husband was Clarence Malone, whom she married in Ironton, Ohio, in the early 1950s and divorced a short time later citing abuse. Clarence Malone was found dead of a gunshot wound to the head in 1970 long after the couple's divorce, but his case was reinvestigated in 2008 because Betty told the author that Clarence Malone died of cancer. Betty and Clarence had one son, Gary, who was subsequently *adopted* by Betty's second husband, James Flynn, and took the last name Flynn. Gary Flynn would later die of an apparent self-inflicted gunshot wound in 1995 at his home in Michigan. During interviews with Betty, Betty or "Bea" as she was called told the author and a former investigator from the sheriff's office at least two different versions of how James Flynn died. The first was that James Flynn froze to death in his truck in New York. The second was that James Flynn was shot to death on a pier. Interestingly, the death of Betty's third husband, Dick Sills, continues to be called into question. During interviews with Betty, she told the author and the former investigator from the sheriff's office that Dick Sills shot himself under his left arm (area of the rib cage beneath the armpit). The author and the investigator were seated across from Betty at her dining room table in her Augusta, Georgia, home, and as she was explaining how Dick Sills committed suicide, Betty pointed to the area on her body where she claimed Dick Sills shot himself. However, during an interview with Betty's daughter who was 13 years old when Dick Sills allegedly took his own life in 1965, Peggy told the author and the former investigator that she heard her mother Betty and Dick Sills come home from a bar arguing late one night in Big Coppit Key, in the Florida Keys. Betty's daughter said the couple had been drinking and that she, Betty's daughter, could hear them arguing. Betty's daughter continued, that from her own bedroom she heard Betty and Dick Sills go into their bedroom and close the door. Then, Betty's daughter said she heard a gunshot. Betty's daughter then said she heard Betty open the bedroom door and exit the room. Betty's daughter left her bedroom and went into her mother's bedroom to find Dick Sills lying on his back at the end of the bed, with his arms more above his head, making gurgling sounds, with a gun lying in his hand. Betty's daughter then said she heard her mother call the police and tell them that her husband just shot himself. Betty's daughter did not see her mother render any type of aid to Dick Sills in between the time of the call and when the police arrived. Her daughter, however, said she liked Dick Sills very much and stayed in the room with Dick Sills until the police arrived, who then hustled her out of the house. She reported that she asked her mother and the officers on the scene many times about Dick Sills's condition, but no one would tell her about it. Betty's daughter recalled Dick Sills being a nice person who was nice to her and her brother, Gary Flynn.

Dick Sills's death was not investigated as a suspicious death in 1965. Police arrived, bought Betty's story, and the case was essentially closed.

Dick Sills was in the navy at the time of his death so necessary paperwork pursuant to his enlistment was necessary, but not much in the way of an investigation into his death … until 2008. Upon investigation, a medical examiner reviewed the case and found that it was noted in the file that Dick Sills not only had one gunshot wound to the rib cage area under his arm, but also had two gunshot wounds to that area, one of which pierced his liver. Betty was never charged with Dick Sills's death.

The following can be observed in this case:

- Betty was the last to see Dick Sills alive and the one to report his self-inflicted injury.
- Betty was not otherwise involved in criminal activity.
- No scientific inquiry was conducted in this case in 1965.
- It appears that investigators assumed the integrity of the crime scene.
- Dick Sills's alleged self-inflicted gunshot wounds were to the rib cage under his arm during the heat of an argument with Betty.

Based on Ferguson and Petherick's (2014) findings, it is arguable that self-inflicted wounds can look similar in nature to wounds observed in homicide cases, and while the number of wounds might be important, it is the lethality of the wounds in cases of suspected suicide and homicide that is of utmost importance during the investigation (Geberth, 2006). Regardless, it does nothing but hinder the case to presume the manner of death in haste.

The ways offenders manipulate a crime scene when staging a suicide are endless, but crime scene staging is often detectable because the physical and behavioral evidence does not match up with the autopsy report, victimology, suspectology, statement analysis, and in some cases reconstructive efforts via the scientific method. Remembering to work the case from the inside out is paramount to success, especially when the intimate partner is the last to see the victim alive and the first to report the victim's death. Do not assume the integrity of crime scenes or statements made by individuals in this position. The upcoming chapters address ways to identify and detect staging behaviors early in an investigation coupled with empirical ways to confirm or refute statements made by suspects, witnesses, and victims.

Case Example 1

Ferguson and Petherick (2014) found that 7 of 16 homicides staged as suicide occurred during the course of an argument/conflict or confrontation between the victim and the offender (p. 9). In the next case example, Joe and Michelle (names changed to protect identities) were intimate partners. One day, Joe walked into the police department to tell them that Michelle just shot herself in their home. An officer asked Joe for his name, and he was reluctant to tell the officer, but the officer drove Joe to their home and found Michelle in their bedroom on a couch lying on her back with blood covering most of her face. The officer saw a wound above her right eye he thought looked like a gunshot wound. Investigators treated the death as suspicious and thought it was curious as to why Michelle's body was cool to the touch and that rigor mortis had begun to set in, in her legs, if she had been dead less than an hour. Investigators noticed that her purse was unzipped, it appeared to have been gone through, and that the entire apartment was cluttered with furniture and the bed was unmade. They found the weapon nowhere near her body that Michelle allegedly shot herself in the head with, but the gun did not have blood on it. However, the investigators did notice blood on the couch, on the end table, and there were several bottles of liquor near her body. Investigators interviewed Joe along with neighbors, the landlord, and friends/family of the couple.

During the interview process, a witness indicated to investigators that Michelle argued with Joe's ex-wife the day before her death. His ex-wife had recently turned Joe in for a parole violation, so Joe was communicating with his ex-wife about that specifically. Because he was talking with his ex-wife, investigators thought there could have been a dispute between Joe and Michelle over him talking to the ex-wife. Interestingly, Joe was a fugitive from a neighboring state and was considered armed and dangerous, and was allegedly planning robberies along his travels.

Based on evidence in the crime scene, investigators determined there was evidence of several staging behaviors in this case:

- Joe positioned Michelle's body from sitting up to lying down on the couch.
- Joe placed the gun at some distance behind Michelle's head, which didn't make sense to investigators when they saw it initially.
- Joe changed his clothes and concealed the clothes he originally had on in the garbage can behind the apartment.
- Joe also threw away a bag of marijuana, his ammunition, and a shell casing from a car window.
- Joe lied to investigators and gave conflicting stories:
  - First, Joe said Michelle killed herself.
  - Second, Joe said he accidently shot Michelle.
  - Joe said they both were drinking, but Michelle tested negative for ethanol at autopsy.
  - Joe said he walked to the police department to report Michelle's death because the phone was broken in their home though he called his ex-wife after shooting Michelle.

In another discovery, Joe left his landlord a note in the apartment saying the gun accidentally discharged killing Michelle. In the end, Joe shot Michelle during a domestic dispute. Joe was charged with first-degree murder, but was convicted of second-degree murder and was sentenced to 16–20 years in prison.

Case Example 2

In this case, Frank and Cindy were intimate partners with a lengthy history of intimate partner violence. The couple was house-sitting for a friend who was out of town for a while. One morning, Frank knocked on a neighbor's door asking him to call 911 because Cindy just shot herself. Friends and family said Cindy had a history of depression and was currently depressed. Regardless, her family was very concerned because Frank was a raging alcoholic, and they knew he physically abused Cindy. Cindy kept calling her family the day before her death telling them he was mistreating her again and that she wanted to leave. Her family called police who conducted two well checks on Cindy in the 24 hours before her death, but she refused to leave even when the officers separated her from Frank and offered to take her back to her family.

In response to the neighbor's 911 call, first responders noticed Frank appeared to have just gotten out of the shower, was very clean, and did not have a speck of blood on him anywhere. When investigators examined the crime scene, they found Cindy, naked in bed with smears of diluted blood on several parts of her body. Cindy had a gunshot wound to the left temple area of her head, and the bullet was found in between the underside of the right side of her head and the pillow beneath her head. Investigators located the gun in a nearby closet.

Investigators suspected it was murder from the beginning based on the couple's long history of intimate partner violence; and interviewed friends, family, and others related to the couple who confirmed the latter. Unfortunately, even though they suspected Frank shot Cindy, they did not have enough evidence to arrest him for murder. The scene was cleared, and the DA's office contacted the author for assistance. The author and law enforcement agency searched the scene a second time specifically to analyze any bloodstain evidence that could be revealed. The author suggested processing the scene with chemical reagents that might help to find latent bloodstains in the scene. Using such reagents, material consistent with latent bloodstains was discovered in the bedroom and bathroom of the house. Discovery of this significant evidence indicated that Frank attempted to clean up the scene after Cindy's death. Additionally, a reconstruction based on crime scene evidence coupled with the results of the autopsy report was consistent with Frank having held Cindy down on the bed, then pressing the barrel of the firearm against her head, and then shooting her. Frank was charged with second-degree murder, but pleaded guilty to involuntary manslaughter and was sentenced to 18 months in prison.

- The position of the victim on the bed was inconsistent with having shot herself.
- The firearm was several feet away from her body, and the medical examiner said Cindy could not have made purposeful movement after the shot.
- Even though Frank said he did not touch Cindy, she had diluted bloodstains on her arms, side, and on other locations indicating she had been moved by someone with wet, bloody, hands, but he did not have bloody hands when observed by first responding officers.
- Frank took a shower and changed his clothes, which were never recovered, but were suspected to have blood on them based on the void patterns within the impact spatter found on the wall where he would have been standing at the time of the shot.
- The chemical reagents revealed areas where Frank had tried to clean up the crime scene before the arrival of police.
- Additionally, Frank gave five differing versions of where he was at the time of shot:
  - In the bathroom
  - In the kitchen
  - In the bedroom
  - Lying on the bed beside Cindy
  - Lying on the bed beside Cindy with his head on her stomach

One of the key points from Cindy's case to recognize is the medical examiner's comment about Cindy not being able to make purposeful movement after being shot in the head. In some cases, a gunshot wound is not incapacitating, but in this case, it was. Therefore, because Frank was the last individual to see Cindy alive and the first to report Cindy's death, investigators worked the case from the inside out. One of the pitfalls of this case for the author was the fact that the crime scene processers specifically did not take high-quality photographs, use scales in the photographs, or retain the sheets from the bed Cindy was lying on. The author would argue that everything that is touching and/or is close to the body should be retained within reason, especially bloodstained sheets in the event bloodstain pattern analysis is relevant later. The second problem in this case with the bedsheets is that the crime scene processors put them in the bathtub after Cindy's body was removed. The third problem the sheets being put in the bathtub created was when the author asked where the sheets were placed after being put in the bathtub, the response was to the effect of in a black, trash bag, which was now in a large landfill. The handling of the bedsheets in this manner negated the ability of author to examine them and the prosecutor to substantiate based on blood found in the shower that Frank bathed after Cindy's death, but with support from first responders, the prosecutor could argue it anyway. Successful prosecution begins at the crime scene, and in this case, had something been done differently in the crime scene, Frank's sentence might have been greater than 18 months.

Arguably, homicides staged as suicide are some of the most commonly staged crime scenes when the offender kills the victim at home and knows the body is going to be discovered there (Ferguson & Petherick, 2014). Although homicides staged as suicide can be monothematic (simple and basic), they can contain other behavioral elements related to

- Destruction of evidence
- Discarding of evidence
- Changing their clothes
- Hiding their clothes
- Bathing or showering
- Fake suicide notes
- Positioning the body
- Positioning the weapon
- Creating an alibi
- Evidence of other cleanup
- Removing drugs and money from the crime scene and/or the victim's body
- Plan aspects of the murder prior to the death of the victim
- More than one account of events, changing stories
- Evidence of argument/conflict and/or verbal or physical confrontation

However, to note, Ferguson and Petherick (2014) found that none of the 16 cases they studied contained any staged points of entry/exit, ransacking, manipulation of bloodstains, or offender self-injury, and all lighting fixtures were found to be intact (p. 11).

Homicides Staged as Botched Robberies, Home Invasions, and Burglaries

Schlesinger et al.'s (2012) study is the most detailed to date in published crime scene staging literature. Pursuant to homicides staged as robberies, home invasions, and burglaries, Schlesinger and colleagues found that 14 of 79 staged homicide cases were staged as burglaries/robberies/breaking and entering (i.e., home invasions). These authors argued that different kinds of homicides appear to have various rates of staging, but the common denominator appears to be the victim–offender relationship (p. 49). Of these 14 staged cases, 10 of them were homicides staged by domestic offenders, nonserial sexual offenders staged 2 of them, and nondomestic general felony homicide offenders staged 2 of them. Schlesinger et al. illustrated an example of a staged home invasion in that a boyfriend stabbed his girlfriend to death. The boyfriend phoned police to report that an intruder robbed his house and killed his girlfriend. It was discovered during the investigation that the offender bought gas and asked for a receipt specifically to try to portray that he was somewhere else at the time of the murder.

Ferguson (2014) found that 47 (40.9%) of 115 in her samples were homicide staged as burglaries, home invasion, or breaking and entering. In these cases, the offender reported that intruders killed the victims and stole property. The offender discovered the victim in almost all of these cases, and the victims were discovered in or around their homes most often shared with the offenders. Additionally, 83% of these 47 cases were domestic related, and most victims were female. These cases tended to have more than one victim more often than other types of staged cases, and nearly 43% of the victims died of injuries sustained from gunshot wounds followed by 27.7% being killed with multiple weapons. Offenders most often brought weapons to the scenes, which could be reflective of premeditation or simply that these offenders carried weapons as part of their normal image. Interestingly, only 10.6% of these cases showed evidence of confrontation prior to the murder, while conflict was not present in 57.4%, and conflict was unknown in 31.9% of these cases. Pursuant to evidence of staging, 34% of these cases contained staged points of entry and/or exit, 51% of these cases had missing valuables, and the crime scenes were ransacked in 40.4% of these cases. Interestingly, 66% of these offenders cleaned up or destroyed evidence, and 32.6% created alibis for themselves, but only 19.1% created self-inflicted injuries as if they were attacked as well. Some offenders also verbally staged by claiming they were unconscious or getting help at the time when the victim was killed. And very few cases included phone line or lighting manipulation (10.6%/6.4%), arson (4.3%), victim mutilation (10.6%), bloodstain manipulation (2.1%), weapon positioning (4.3%), body transportation to dump site (6.4%), positioning of the victim's body or clothing (6.4%), and planting drugs (6.4%). Arguably, while these findings are for a small sample, the information revealed herein by Ferguson in this study is extremely valuable to investigators because to date this is the largest sample of staged cases of this nature descriptively analyzed. To note, these findings align with Turvey's (2000) in that the most commonly staged scenes in his 25 case samples were burglaries.

Crimes and crime scenes reflect the personality of the offender, which is the culmination of who someone is biologically, experientially, and envirossocioculturalistically. While it is true that experts and investigators might subjectively recognize certain crime scene characteristics as red flags of staging when they encounter them in a scene, they still need to be able to scientifically substantiate those opinions in court. In order to understand a crime scene and how it might be staged, one must learn as much as is available about the victim and the offender in relation to the scene. Intimicides, for example, are typically one-on-one crimes where one intimate partner kills another intimate partner. But one of the unique extensions of intimicide compared to other types of murder is that intimicide includes murders solicited by one intimate partner to kill another intimate partner as a homicide staged as a staged robbery, home invasion, or the like. Consider the case of former North Carolina Panthers Football star Rae Carruth. Carruth *had it all* as professional athletes tend to have in the United States including a beautiful girlfriend named Cherica Adams. Cherica told Rae she was pregnant, but Rae was not excited about the idea of a baby because it meant he would have to pay Cherica child support. Several months later, on November 16, 1999, the couple spent an evening out on the town and as they were driving down the road in separate cars, Rae was in his car in front, and Cherica was in her car behind Rae, when another car pulled up alongside of Cherica's car and someone in the car shot Cherica through the door and window striking her four times. Rae pulled off along with the shooter's car leaving Cherica there to die alone. However, Cherica called 911 and was rushed to the hospital where she delivered her son Chancellor Adams by cesarean section, but Cherica remained in critical condition. During her month-long stay in intensive care, when asked who did this to her, Cherica scribbled the name "Rae" on a piece of paper before she died. Along with her 911 call describing to dispatch how Rae was driving in front of her and pulled off after she was shot, Rae Carruth was charged with murder along with the shooter Rae hired to kill Cherica, a man named Van Brett Watkins.

Van Brett Watkins testified for the prosecution that Rae Carruth wanted Watkins to take Cherica's belongings from her car after he shot her making it look like a robbery. Upon hearing he would be charged, Rae fled by hiding in the trunk of a car driven by a female friend, but was arrested a short time later at a motel in Tennessee. To avoid the death penalty, Watkins agreed to testify against Rae Carruth, pled to second-degree murder, and was sentenced to 50 years in prison. Rae Carruth was convicted conspiring to commit murder and was sentenced to 24 years and 4 months in prison.

The Carruth case is an example of how an offender does not actually have to pull the trigger himself to be guilty. Though Rae Carruth was not convicted of murder itself, his actions facilitated, precipitated, and orchestrated the death of intimate partner Cherica Adams along with staging it to appear as though Cherica had fallen victim to a botched robbery, and so on. Evidence of staging in the Carruth case even on a basic monothematic level is as follows:

- Verbal staging
- Physical scene staging
- Concealing evidence

This indicates deception and the need for Rae Carruth to put distance between him and the victim so he is not named a suspect in her shooting death. If someone has done nothing wrong, there is no reason to lie, hide, create, and flee. In addition to the crime scene staging behaviors identified in the Carruth case, there are other ways offenders stage crime scenes as botched robberies, home invasions, or burglaries.

Robberies are profit motivated. Classifying predominate motive is crucial to understanding the crime, the injuries to the victim, and the crime scene. Alert investigators expect to see certain crime scene characteristics that are consistent with the crime of robbery, such as missing belongings and use of some level of force, which vary on the intensity continuum. When a homicide victim is found in what appears to be an interrupted robbery, investigators might find forced entry into a structure, ransacking, and over-arching missing items, but not always. It is true that sometimes individuals rob people for specific items like money and drugs, credit cards, and their cars; in those cases, they might leave jewelry or other types of valuables behind because they have a targeted item to steal, but when it comes to crime scene staging and interrupted robbery, it is important to learn to decipher between an interrupted robbery leading to murder and a murder staged as an interrupted robbery. They are two completely different crime scenes with two completely different sets of identifiers.

Generally speaking, sometimes robbers kill to protect their identities. A robber who has no prior relationship to a victim rarely sticks around to repeatedly stab a victim 50–100 times. Such is the case of the stabbing deaths of a young couple named Samuel and Arica. In this case, both victims were stabbed 70+ times, the house was in disarray, and the only thing missing appeared to be a kitchen drawer. It appeared the victims were killed with their own kitchen knives, and there was a large sum of money recovered in the house during the crime scene search. For years, the investigation proceeded as robbery-gone-bad, but still it went without an arrest. Eventually, two individuals were arrested that were known to have been going around robbing drug dealers in town posing as DEA agents based on statements made by other offenders in the jail. The author became involved with the case a short time later and, upon cursory review, discovered that these murders appeared to be generally consistent with argument/conflict most likely carried out by someone the victims knew. Additionally, the author opined that the attacks were unplanned as the victims appeared to have been killed with their own kitchen knives rather than with a weapon brought to the scene by the offender or offenders. Further, the author opined the offender was male because unidentified male DNA was found mixed with the male victim's DNA in what was consistent with a liquid blood transfer impression (e.g., bloody object touches non-bloody object) on the wall above where the male victim was found. The female victim's DNA was also found on bloody carpet beneath her body with a partial profile of unidentified male DNA, and both victims' DNA were found mixed with the unidentified male DNA in what was consistent with a liquid blood transfer impression found on the edge of the couple's fitted bedsheet. However, the unidentified male DNA did not match either of the defendants in this case. The author opined that it was extremely unlikely that the unidentified male, the male victim, and the female victim were all bleeding simultaneously at any other time besides the time of the victims' murders.

Crime analysis suggested that the male victim was most likely murdered first, followed by the female victim, then the assailant picked up the mattress to look underneath. Regardless, the initial trial proceeded against the two defendants whose DNA did not match the unidentified DNA, but the trial was quickly halted during jury selection *pending further investigation*. In the end, indictments against the two defendants were dismissed because the unidentified male DNA recovered in the crime scene finally hit in CODIS. The unidentified male DNA belonged to a former associate of the male victim named Michael Mosley. Michael Mosley was a former drug runner for the male victim, who was compensated with drugs for his time and effort, but the two stopped doing business together a short time prior to the murders. The author opined that the male victim and the new defendant got into an argument/conflict/confrontation in the victims' kitchen. A fight ensued, and knives from the kitchen drawer came into play. Mosley, who was skilled in martial arts of sorts, overpowered the male victim and proceeded to stab him repeatedly. The female victim sleeping in the bedroom heard the commotion, came out in defense of her boyfriend, and proceeded to fight Mosley until he overpowered her pummeling and stabbing her to death. At least one knife used in the attack was found near the victims' bodies, and it is likely that Mosley then searched for things to steal, which included looking in between the couple's mattresses. Mosley was convicted on two counts of first-degree murder and burglary and was sentenced to life in prison.

Michael Mosley was never identified or interviewed during the 10-year investigation before his DNA hit in CODIS. The male victim's friends and family knew of Mosley in connection to the male victim, but Mosley's name never came up. Again, working homicide cases from the inside out is often paramount to successful prosecution, and in this case, Mosley was on the inside of the male victim's circle.

Most insurance companies will not allow any beneficiary to collect proceeds if the insured has committed suicide. So an intimate partner who knows this, but who is looking to kill his or her intimate partner would be remiss to stage the intimate partner's murder as a suicide. It is possible the offender might choose to stage the murder as an interrupted robbery, natural death, and/or an accidental death, but even still red flags of staging are usually clear and present; recognizing those earmarks is what drives further inquiry. Take, for example, the couple who is struggling financially. The marriage is bad, and one intimate partner has a long history of abusing the other. The abuser knows he or she cannot collect insurance money if his or her spouse commits suicide, but the spouse is found dead under suspicious circumstances that raise investigator suspicion. The death could be the result of whatever the offender thinks will conceal the manner, such as a fall, an illness, poisoning that mimics natural death (e.g., antifreeze, insulin, and arsenic), carbon monoxide poisoning, a drug overdose, a car malfunction, drowning, along with a myriad of other ways that seem feasible to the crime scene stager based on his or her personality, cognition, behavior, emotionality, and envirosocioculturalism.

Theoretically speaking, the offender, predominately motived by profit, might pursue the death certificate with vengeance, discuss the insurance policy at the crime scene and/or contact the insurance company incessantly, get rid of the victim's belongings very soon after the intimate partner's death, change his or her lifestyle, pursue new relations, establish new online identities, move to a new location, move on like the victim never existed, along with telling friends and family numerous stories about how the victim died. In addition to these staging behaviors, because physical evidence can be sparse, virtually nonexistent, or absent completely from cases of this nature, focusing on identifying and substantiating circumstantial evidence can help move the case toward an arrest in some cases (not all cases). For example, staging behaviors are often revealed by comparing the suspect's normal routine, to his or her routine on the day of his or her intimate partner's death, compared to the suspect's normal routine after the victim's death. If the suspect never goes out at night, but goes out on the night of his or her intimate partner's death, then resumes his or her normal routine of never going out at night after his or her intimate partner's death, then at a minimum, special attention should paid, and inquiry should be made as to the what, when, where, why, and how of the suspect's purpose, motive, method, means, and mode on the night in question.

Again, investigators might easily identify the careless or over-ransacking of a house as being consistent with staging behavior (Turvey, 2012). Maybe only particular items have been stolen in an attempt to point to a specific potentially involved party or valuables have only been disrupted but are not missing. Or maybe the death in addition to impending insurance payouts served another purpose, such as revenge, to keep a secret, in addition to countless other reasons. To further illustrate the concept of staged robbery–murder in relation to insurance money, again examining Betty Neumar, the 76-year-old woman, now deceased who had five husbands during her lifetime, one of which was Harold Gentry, who died Sunday, July 7, 1986, is a good case to start with. Betty Neumar was Betty *Gentry* at the time, and she was very angry with husband Harold, a hardworking, very quiet man, for befriending and spending time with a young woman in the area. During the course of the situation, which lasted about 2 years, but then moved to Florida, where her daughter was attending college. Around Christmas 1986, Betty returned to the marital residence accusing Harold of an affair with his female friend. She decided to stay at the marital residence instead of returning to Florida and soon after claimed to Harold that she was dying from leukemia. Concerned for her health, Harold wanted to attend her doctor's appointment, but when checking on the day and time with the doctor's office, Harold discovered that there were no scheduled doctor's appointments, which made Harold very angry. In confronting Betty, Harold learned there was no leukemia and it was another ruse by Betty for attention. Harold started distancing himself even more from Betty, and Betty felt the abandonment coming on. The marriage had been rocky for a long time, and Harold told family members never to trust Betty because she was not an honest person. Betty, who went by "Bea" as mentioned earlier, continued trying to win her husband's affection to no avail. During the early summer months of 1986, through a friend, Bea was alleged to have visited a local store where she allegedly solicited the assistance of the store's owner to kill her husband Harold. The storeowner could not believe what he was hearing and thought Bea was just talking nonsense. On a later date a short time later, Bea returned to the store and allegedly solicited the murder of her husband Harold again to the storeowner, who this time, realized that she was actually serious, so the storeowner went to police. Police investigated the best they could at the time not having much to go from, but found nothing that indicated other than the storeowner's recap of his conversation with Bea that she was trying to find someone to kill her husband. On Saturday, June 6, 1996, Harold asked a few friends if they had seen Bea. Harold said he could not find her and had no idea where she went. Meanwhile, Bea had left town, but not before asking a friend to ride with her to Marietta, Georgia, where she claimed she was scheduled the following Monday to get new tires put on her dually truck.

Harold Gentry was gunned down in his home the evening of July 7, 1986, a Sunday. Harold's body was discovered Monday around 6:30 P.M. by his sister. Harold's sister went to a neighbor's house to ask them to call police. The couple phoned the police, and the first responders arrived on the scene along with investigators who would take charge of the crime scene investigation, and so on. Harold's autopsy indicated that he was struck multiple times in the attack. Coupled with this information, investigators speculated that Harold interrupted a burglary in progress that quickly turned into a robbery–murder. The house was overly ransacked complete with disrupted and missing valuables. Neighbors reached Bea in Georgia and informed her of Harold's death. Bea arrived at the marital residence where the investigation was still going on in full force. Bea stepped out of her truck, and the first thing she said was, "I was in Augusta."

Bea *assisted* investigators by identifying missing items from the home, which included firearms and money from the safe among other things. Interestingly, Betty's jewelry and other belongings were there, but some of Harold's belongings were missing. At no time did Bea cry, display any type of emotion upon, or appear concerned that her husband was dead. Very soon after, Bea visited Harold's place of employment, where he worked for more than 20 years and where was very close to his boss. Distraught by the loss of his friend, Harold's boss could not believe Bea showed up at the factory demanding to have Harold's last paycheck given to her. Additionally, Bea filed for all of Harold's military benefits and was awarded more than $60k in the end. Bea gave numerous statements to police about questionable individuals seen driving through the neighborhood in a yellow Mercedes-Benz in the weeks before the murder. Interestingly, neighbors could not substantiate Bea's claims. No charges were brought against Bea in 1986, and she soon moved from the marital residence to marry fifth husband, John Neumar, a successful businessman from Augusta, Georgia.

Twenty-two years later, Bea was arrested in May 2008 and was charged with solicitation to commit the murder of Harold Gentry based on information gleaned in a new investigation. Although Bea Gentry was never convicted of anything, including soliciting to kill her husband Harold, there are many who believe in her guilt. Regardless, Bea died in June 2011 before her trial. This case is considered closed by all parties due to Bea's death, and the individual suspected of shooting Harold Gentry has never been arrested in this case.

In examining the behavior of ransacking further, according to Turvey (2012), one or more of the following must be eliminated in order to render ransacking of a crime scene connected to the act of staging (p. 270):

1. Ransacking has to depart from the normal way the house looks (cluttered crime scenes in disarray might look ransacked, but are actually normal in that state).
2. Apparent ransacking is not a result of processing the scene.
3. Items and locations of ransacking are inconsistent with searching for a specific item or valuable items.
4. Ransacking occurred due to a fetish held by the offender.
5. Ransacking occurred only because the offender was out of control from a mental health episode or substance-induced situation.

While staging is a possibility in every case, not every murder is staged, but the idea a scene might be staged should not be dismissed before thorough investigation takes place. Further, supporting the argument that a scene is staged simply based on ransacking might be helpful, but it does not get the case to the jury. Even though suspicion is not evidence, suspicious investigators have often motivated investigators willing to continue gathering information that ultimately substantiates the fact that a crime scene is indeed staged. Another key point in regard to ransacking is if the offender was looking for an item, what was the item and why was he looking for it? Value is relative to the individual attributing worth to an item in question, but interestingly, in the case of Harold Gentry's death, missing items were things that Betty only knew where they were, had access to, or would not suffer a loss if they were stolen.

A burglary is committed when an offender steals property from an unoccupied home or business. The difference between burglary and robbery is that property is stolen through violence and intimidation in the act of robbery (Douglas, Burgess, Burgess, & Ressler, 2006). Burglary is a property crime, and robbery is a violent crime against persons. A home invasion can be defined as when an offender enters a home occupied by its residents or others usually by use of force (sometimes through an unlocked door or window) for the purpose of robbery, sexual assault, abduction, murder, or other crimes.

Case Example

A 39-year-old man recently married his new 44-year-old bride. With the union, he gained a 16-year-old stepdaughter. The trio lived in a small rural community in an isolated area. One evening, months later, the new wife and stepdaughter came home and found the man dead in the newlyweds' bed. The wife immediately thought it was a suicide and called police to report a fatal self-inflicted gunshot wound. Upon closer inspection, his wife called back and told dispatch that in looking at him closer, her husband actually had several gunshot wounds and that she discovered that the glass in the backdoor of the house was broken from what looked like a home invasion. When investigators arrived, they too noticed the glass broken from the backdoor, but no signs of forced entry to the front door were present. Then, broken glass was discovered on the front porch around the door on the outside of the house. The broken glass went all the way into the yard several feet from the front door. Investigators noticed that even though the body seemed undisturbed, the victim's wallet was missing.

They quickly ruled out suicide and instead focused on murder. Investigators were suspicious of the home invasion theory and interviewed the family about discovering the body. Additionally, interviews with several friends of the wife and stepdaughter revealed that the new wife and stepdaughter hated the victim. The trio argued constantly about the behavior of the stepdaughter, which caused tremendous unrest for the couple in their marriage. The wife and daughter were developed as suspects in the case, but investigators were certain neither of them actually fired the weapon that killed the victim. When confronted with this idea, the wife and stepdaughter argued that the victim was abusive and would not let them go out of the house. They claimed to live in fear, and the stepdaughter did not want to live with the victim. During the investigation, it was revealed that the wife and the stepdaughter hired an 18-year-old male friend of the stepdaughter to kill the husband and stage it like a home invasion–robbery. On the night of the murder, the wife and stepdaughter drove the killer within close proximity of their home, let him out of the car, then positioned the car, and waited for him to return after killing the victim. The 18-year-old crime scene stager returned with the victim's wallet as proof that he was dead and explained that he kicked out the glass on the door before he left, but didn't disturb anything else in the house. The wife paid the 18-year-old approximately $340 in cash from the victim's wallet for killing him and dropped him off at another location.

First, there was no forced entry because the would-be robber entered the house with a key the wife gave to him prior to the event. Second, the glass on the front porch was on the outside of the house instead of the inside of the house where it should have been if the offender broke into the house. The wife and stepdaughter created a scenario of where they were at the time of the murder and provided alibis for each other. Additional evidence of this murder having been staged was the effort the wife showed by driving the 18-year-old killer to the scene and waiting for him to return. All three offenders were charged and convicted of first-degree murder, conspiracy to commit murder, and were sentenced to life in prison.

Homicides Staged as Accidents

Ferguson (2014) found in 115 staged homicide samples that 16 (13.9%) were homicides staged as accidents, such as firearms-related accidents, household falls, drowning, or death by fire. Red flags of crime scene staging were identified by the way the scenes presented to investigators combined with verbal staging by the offenders and physical manipulation of the evidence, such as making the injury to the victim appear self-inflicted, weapon position, leaving the victim in the crime scene and/or repositioning the victim's body, cleanup, or the destruction of evidence. In a small number of cases, mutilation was evident (12.5%) and in 6.3% of the cases, each respectively, either drugs were planted or the offender created an alibi. Victims were most often female (56.3%), and offenders were most often (75%) domestically related to the victims, while 18.8% of the offenders were friends of the victims and 6.3% of the offenders were business associates of the victims. Offenders most often discovered the victims in 75% of the cases, while 62.5% of the victims were discovered in their own homes with the remaining victims having been discovered in locations, such as their cars, boats, places of work, offender's home, or a firing range.

According to Geberth (1996, 2006), staging a crime scene to make it appear as though a victim had an accident is one of the most commonly encountered scenarios in crime scene staging phenomenon. Schlesinger et al. (2012) found that 11 of 79 staged cases in that sample were homicides staged as accidents of some kind including car accidents and/or falls. Of the 11 cases, domestically related offenders to the victim staged 10 of the cases and a nonsexual general felony homicide offender staged one case. As with suicide, intimicides staged as accidents are commonly seen when a domestic dispute of some kind has led to the death of an intimate partner as in the case of Jack and Jennifer (names changed to protect identities). Jack and Jennifer had been together for years much to the dismay of Jennifer's family. Jack was a vicious abuser, and even though Jennifer had left Jack several times over the years, she always returned to the couple's singlewide trailer along a remote mountainside. Jack was an extremely paranoid and jealous abuser. The couple worked for the postal service, but when out in public, Jack made sure Jennifer remained under lock and key. On days when Jack went out alone, he locked Jennifer in the trailer from the outside using padlocks he had installed on all the doors and windows. Jack ran cameras inside the house that videotaped every move Jennifer made during the time he was away. Jennifer was not allowed to talk to her family. Jennifer did not have any money. Jack would not allow Jennifer to wear shoes except to go to work, and Jack would stomp on her feet so in case she wanted to escape barefooted, her feet were too sore to traverse through the forest. Jennifer was completely isolated without reprieve. Jennifer did not have an available phone to make calls she wanted to make, and the phone she did have was only to talk to Jack when he was away from the home. The trailer sat on approximately 20 acres and was accessible from a back road where a driveway and metal gate were basically installed. The gate remained locked at all times, and even if someone did get through the first gate, there was a second locked gate on the driveway closer to the house. All in all, Jack and Jennifer were a couple with a yearlong history of substance abuse, intimate partner violence, and financial hardship.

One night as Jack and Jennifer slept, a screaming Jack who claimed there were bees all over his body accused Jennifer of having an affair. According to Jack, Jennifer reassured him that she was not having an affair, but he could not go back to sleep, and instead the couple got into an argument. Jennifer offered to get a glass of water for Jack and headed off to the kitchen. Jack sat down in the living room; Jennifer returned handing him a glass of water and then sat down in a recliner across from him professing her love for him and that she was not having an affair. It was impossible for Jennifer to have an affair because she was literally imprisoned by Jack without the ability to make her own life's choices, but Jack refused to listen. Jack said that as he knelt down to retrieve a gun from beneath an end table that was beside the recliner where Jennifer was seated, he waived the gun through the air when it accidently discharged shooting Jennifer in the left side of her head. Jack claimed he called 911 immediately following the shooting, and law enforcement responded to the scene to find Jennifer deceased in the recliner with what appeared to be a single gunshot wound to the head. The investigation revealed that Jack's evidence was consistent with Jack deliberately shooting Jennifer in the head at close range.

Case Example

Not all law enforcement agencies have the funding to send employees to training, which is not anyone's fault, but attending classes taught by individuals who know the empirical literature well and can teach it in theoretical application that would arguably heighten officers' awareness about crime scene staging as it relates to staged suicides, accidents, sexual homicides, and so on, is really important toward avoiding adding to the nearly 200,000 cold cases in the United States today (Hargrove, 2010). However, the following was a case where investigators unfortunately did not have the knowledge necessary to recognize crime scene staging. A woman was found dead in her bathroom, beside her bathtub, wearing a robe. She had an injury to the base of her head where the back of her neck connects to her head. Investigators thought the woman fell out of the tub after showering because of evidence in the scene that led them to believe she was in the shower at the time she fell. The shower had sliding glass doors, and the bottom track that sat on the ledge of the bathtub had what investigators described as a "sharp edge." The victim was married and had children. She enjoyed very simple wholesome things in life, and her death was both untimely and thought to be a tragic accident ... until the medical examiner phoned the lead investigator in the case to tell him that the victim had a bullet in head and what they thought was the result of a fall out of the tub was actually a gunshot wound to the head. The crime scene was not processed as a suspicious death, so with consent, investigators retrieved several items from the scene. During the course of their investigation sparked by the medical examiner's findings, it was revealed that the victim was possibly having an affair. Items collected from the scene included linens and beer cans; however, the victim did not drink. The author was consulted about the nature of the physical evidence and suggested having the cans tested for DNA. A transient individual was identified as potentially having been involved in the shooting death of this victim and staging the scene to appear as though the victim fell from the bathtub. Investigators did not uncover any additional information, and DNA results were inconclusive and the case remains "unsolved" today.

It is most often that law enforcement officers are not forensic pathologists. Thankfully, forensic pathologists are there to help feed the investigation, but like coroners, their summations are largely reliant upon information shared with them by the lead investigating parties. In this case, the victim's body was sent to the medical examiner's office for autopsy because she had health problems investigators thought might have contributed to her apparent fall. At no time, did they suspect they were really looking at a homicide staged as an accident with a gunshot wound to the head. In hindsight, the red flags of staging were there, but premature conclusive opinions drawn by investigators at the scene that this was indeed an accident crippled the investigation and ultimately prevented it from moving forward. In trying to backpedal, they did develop some new information, but the crucial evidence available in the scene on the day of the victim's death was ultimately the most important pieces to solving this murder. Competent death scene investigation is critical. The investigators responsible for this case have been criticized by outside investigators because the overall quality of their work has negatively affected some cases crossing jurisdictional lines on more than one occasion in addition to the numerous cold cases housed by this agency. Without a confession, it is unlikely the victim in the case discussed earlier will ever have justice.

Homicides Staged as Fire-Related Deaths

Schlesinger et al. (2012) found that 20 of 79 cases in their sample were homicides staged as fire-related deaths. Domestic partners of the victims staged six of the cases, nonserial sexual homicide offenders staged seven cases, and general felony homicide offenders staged seven of the cases. Interestingly, arson was the most common staging method that occurred in this sample (n = 79); however, these authors did not specifically discuss staging behaviors in these cases. Offenders might kill their victims and then set fire to a location to destroy evidence of the murder toward making it appear as though a victim died as a result of fire. Death by fire normally results from smoke inhalation/deprivation of oxygen combined with deadly gases created by fire. Forensic pathologists can determine whether a victim was dead or alive before the fire (Geberth, 2006). Some of the evidence forensic pathologists look for when examining burned victims relate to inhalation of smoke stains in and around the nasal passages and lungs, elevated amounts of carbon monoxide, and skin blistering, which might all be present if the victim was alive at the time of the fire (Geberth, 2006, p. 348).

Because arson-related homicides have become more common throughout the past several years, basic knowledge of how fire interacts with a human body is important for investigators working in this modern era of kill and cover-up. The author would argue that while obvious characteristics related to fire investigation might be glaring even to first responders, leaving arson investigation to experts in arson investigation is the most substantial and reliable way of approaching homicide and fire-related deaths.

Case Example

A neighbor called police and the fire department when she saw the house across the street burning. The fire marshal said the house was a complete loss. An adult male's body was found in the charred home later determined to be the homeowner. There was no reason at that time to suspect that the victim died of anything else except injuries related to the fire. The victim was lying on his back in his bedroom doorway. Investigators found the male victim lying on his back in the doorway of his bedroom and upon examination found that he actually had injuries they thought looked like some kind of trauma. The medical examiner determined that the victim died from multiple gunshot wounds and was dead before the fire started. Investigators knew the victim because he recently was accused of a violent crime. Investigators interviewed numerous friends, family, and neighbors, and spoke with the alleged victims of the deceased male victim's recent crimes. The investigation revealed that two male associates of the alleged victim of the deceased male's crimes sought revenge against him for what he supposedly did. They went to his house at night, knocked on the door, claimed car trouble, and asked to use the phone. The male victim allowed the men into his house, they overpowered him, bound him, and shot him to death in the doorway of his bedroom.

These crime scene stagers attempted to conceal their crime in several ways. First, they came up with what they thought was a well-thought-out plan and borrowed a gun from one of their relatives. They drove together in the same car to the victim's house, put socks on their hands, and wrapped the gun in a jacket before approaching the front door. They used a ruse in order to gain entrance to the house, killed the victim, and fled the scene. The duo destroyed related evidence by throwing it out of a moving car window as they fled. They actually went to the center of a bridge and threw additional items including the gun into the river below. Then they went home, bathed, burned their clothes, and threw away their shoes. After all of that, they returned to the victim's house and set it on fire fleeing the scene again. When questioned by their friends, both lied about their whereabouts toward keeping the secret. Both offenders were charged with first-degree murder, first-degree burglary, first-degree arson, and larceny. Offender 3 pleaded guilty to second-degree murder, first-degree arson, and first-degree burglary and was sentenced to 14 years 3 months in prison, and the other offender was convicted on all charges and sentenced to life.

Homicides Staged as Car Accidents

Ferguson (2014) found that 16 cases or 13.9% of the 115 staged homicides she analyzed were homicides staged as car accidents, where the victim–offender relationship was 81.1% domestic partners of the victims, victims were most often female (75%), and victims were recovered by most often strangers or police officers (not the offenders) in either their cars or offenders' cars apparently having died from blunt force injuries (31.1%) sustained from the car accident. Other injuries includes 12.5% gunshot wounds and 12.5% multiple weapons, with 6.3% of the cases where the victims were drowned or died of strangulation (i.e., asphyxia). Interestingly, 31.1% of the offenders made contact with the police claiming to have been involved in the accident with the victims, while 18.8% of these offenders injured themselves toward staging the scene. Further, in 18.8% of these cases, weapons were not brought to the scenes, but rather weapons were opportunistic, and in most cases, the evidence of injury did not align with injuries typically sustained in car accidents alluding to the level of sophistication of the offender. Offenders in 93.8% of these cases made it look as though the car involved had actually crashed where the offender positioned the victim's body in the way in which he or she believed it should present based on what type of car accident he or she was trying to portray. Also interesting about this sample was that in 56.3% of the cases, the offenders mutilated the bodies or burned their victims' postmortem toward making it more believable that the victims died from injuries sustained from the car accidents. In addition, 62.5% of these offenders make cleanup attempts coupled with attempts to destroy evidence; however, only 37.5% created alibis for themselves.

In light of Ferguson's (2014) findings, offenders might theoretically stage car accidents to reflect

1. Drunk driving accidents
2. Car malfunction
3. Offender running the victim off the road and making her appear to have lost control of her car
4. Car fire
5. Victim running off a cliff to commit suicide

Special consideration should be applied to cases involving cars from the investigative and forensic pathological standpoints toward determining mechanical functioning of the car, crash reconstruction, and viability of life during the car-related event (cause of death), in addition to victimological considerations (i.e., did the victim drive, was the victim afraid to drive, did the victim drive at night, etc.).

Homicides Staged as Sexual Homicides

Ferguson (2014) found that 6 of her 115 case samples were staged as sexual homicide, and Schlesinger et al. (2012) found that 1 case out of their 79 case samples was staged as a sexual homicide. According to Geberth (1996,

2006), staging a crime scene to make it appear as though a victim has been abducted, raped, and murdered is one of the most commonly encountered scenarios in crime scene staging phenomenon. However, as discussed in Chapter 1, Geberth (2010) found that in less than 1% of the time do offenders pose victims' bodies in sexually explicit positions toward staging sexual homicide. Physical evidence, some characteristic, or activity that is sexual in nature is a required component when classifying a murder as a sexual homicide. Physical evidence, crime scene characteristics, and sexual activities are individualistic to each offender, making him or her unique in ways that are often recognizable by investigators. Physical evidence might include the medical examiner's discovery of evidence consistent with penal penetration, rape, or with other objects inserted into the victim pre- or postmortem. Forensic reports are critical in cases of sexual homicide, and it is highly recommended to collect as numerous samples and test as many samples as necessary and that is possible.

According to Douglas et al. (2006), the offender attempting to alter the crime scene and the victim's body to make it appear as though the victim was sexually assaulted and murdered rarely leaves the body naked; instead, it is more common to find victims partially clothed (p. 159). Offenders staging scenes in an attempt to obscure the predominant motive of domestic dispute, for example, might also pose the body in a precarious way demeaning to the victim. A partially clothed female victim clad from the waist up might be left with her legs spread apart or the female victim clad from the waist down might have her shirt ripped open or have it gathered up around her neckline. Another staging behavior that can be related to rage in some cases staged or not is that of inserting objects into the vagina and anus. While anything inserted into an orifice of the body could be construed as sexual in nature, the stager who inserts objects into the half-naked victim is trying to send the message that the victim's death was a sexual homicide. On the rage side, offenders who are angry with the victim have been known to insert objects into the vagina or anus of their victims in the heat of the moment toward maximizing the feeling of power and control over the victim even in death.

Theoretically, three key components are important to recognize when investigating the potential staged sexual homicide: point of contact location, the murder scene location, and the disposal site location. In cases where the initial contact is made in a house, for example, offenders might transport the victim in the victim's or the offender's car either dead or alive from the point of contact to the murder scene, then to the disposal location, which is most often familiar to the offender. In other cases, victims might be killed in their homes, in offenders' homes, or in the common home shared by both the victim and the offender, then transported to another location; however, current research does not speak to these points specifically to date.

Weapons used in sexual homicide vary tremendously, but commonly used weapons might include firearms, knives, in combination with multiple weapons, such as restraints, tape, rope, twine, chains, handcuffs, gags, even clothing, and chemicals (Douglas et al., 2006). Sexual homicide victims are found beaten, strangled, mutilated, dismembered, shot, and stabbed among other injuries identified at autopsy. Sexual homicide offenders have a tremendous need to control their victims' every move, so their methods, means, and mode are reflective of planning, organization, and before, during, and after the murder while being very careful to remove any trace of evidence that could be left (Douglas et al., 2006).

Like staged suicide, accidents, and interrupted robberies, the crime scenes of sexual homicide might be staged in an attempt to obscure the predominant motive of the sexual assault and murder (Douglas et al., 2006). Sexual homicide can be challenging to investigate and solve when there is a lack of physical evidence due to the cunning nature of organized offenders who execute well-planned assaults, but with the right tools, distinctive crime scene staging characteristics can be recognizable to the trained eye. In contrast, just as the organized offender whose identity can be cloaked by the organized crime scene, the personality, cognition, behavior, emotionality, and envirosocioculturalism might in fact influence him to embellish the crime scene toward imitating an offender who killed the victim based on an ulterior predominant motive. Schlesinger et al. (2012) discussed minimal, moderate, and elaborate staging efforts by offenders, whereas offenders were found to make little, somewhat, or a lot of effort toward staging their scenes. Though it lacks empirical support, it has been the experience of the author that offenders who are sophisticated and intelligent tend to stage crime scenes in more complex ways than do stagers who are less sophisticated and intelligent. Ferguson (2014) touched on this concept briefly in her discussion of how homicides staged as car accidents were reflective of a lack of sophistication on the part of the offender because the injuries to the victim were misaligned with injuries normally seen in car accident victims. Regardless, the fact remains that offenders sometimes choose rape–murder or abduction–rape–murder as the method for masking to true motive.

Case Example

In this case, Kevin and Beth (names changed to protect identities) had been married for 19 years. Kevin was a pastor at a church, and Beth was a substitute teacher. The couple legally separated in 2001, but they continued to live together for the years leading up to Beth's death in 2004. Kevin did not want to be married anymore and was having an affair with another woman. Beth did not know about Kevin's affair, and Kevin was denied for a divorce because the couple continued to live together after legal separation. Kevin never reported his wife missing after he said she left to go to Wal-Mart on Saturday because it was not uncommon for her to leave on a Friday or Saturday and return on Sunday, but her body was found in the trunk of her car in the next county over on Monday by an officer who was investigating a call about an abandoned vehicle on the side of a rural road. Investigators examined the crime scene and the victim's body and noticed that she was partially clothed, her shirt was pulled up around her neck, and she had a belt around her throat. The first responding officer noted a strong odor of decomposition coming from the car before the trunk was opened. During the investigation, a witness reported seeing a man fitting Kevin's description standing behind the victim's car early Sunday morning. Another witness said that Kevin called her early Sunday morning to ask for a ride from a store that was near to where Beth's car was found. His friend picked him up and noticed he was carrying a black trash bag that appeared to be full. The witness said she dropped Kevin off at a rental car store and left. Kevin rented a car, got a haircut, and went to church. During his sermon, Kevin told the congregation to pray for his wife because she was at home suffering from a toothache. Autopsy results showed Beth died from ligature strangulation, but there was no evidence of sexual assault.

Ironically, Beth suspected Kevin was up to something and called her friend both on Friday and Saturday morning and told her friend that she thought Kevin was going to kill her. Her friend recommended calling police, but never heard from Beth again.

Staging and crime scene staging were evident in this case. Kevin tried to stage that Beth had been abducted along her travels to Wal-Mart or the like and became a victim of sexual homicide. Kevin lied to his congregation about where Beth was on Sunday morning and lied to investigators when they came to his house late Monday night to tell him his wife was dead. Additionally, Kevin took things from the crime scene as reported by the witness who gave him a ride. Kevin was charged with first-degree murder, but pleaded guilty to involuntary manslaughter and was sentenced to 5–7 years in prison.

Homicides Staged as Self-Defense Cases

Ferguson (2014) found that 5 of the 115 homicide cases she studied were homicide staged as self-defense cases. A self-defense theory when posed in cases of homicide case is rarely successful. Self-defense in a homicide case is a legally justified excuse for someone's actions during an assault, but is only justified (Parker & Pettler, 2009)

1. If someone reasonably believes his or her life is in danger, and he or she acts in a manner consistent with protecting himself or herself from bodily injury or offensive contact.
2. If there is reasonable assumption given the circumstances of the event point out that danger was eminent.

3. If the individual claiming self-defense has not used excessive force against the alleged assailant.
4. If the individual claiming self-defense is not the predominant aggressor in the situation.

All of the same applied when a deadly weapon is involved including the necessity of using the weapon to prevent bodily harm. In order to figure out if self-defense is a reasonable defense in a case, investigators must consider several things, such as the size of the victim and the alleged attacker, the ages of both parties, the strength of both parties, the fierceness of the assault, whether or not a weapon was involved, and the victimology and suspectology in the case (Parker & Pettler, 2009).

Determining who the predominate aggressor is in a homicide case is a very important process in the investigation. Characteristics, such as social indicators, if the one claiming self-defense is an abuser, the victim's injuries, and history of strangulation in addition to complete victimology and suspectology, should be evaluated thoroughly. Other factors to consider include (Parker & Pettler, 2009) the following:

1. The explanation the individual gives in relation to the patterns of injury on the deceased party.
2. A comparison of the injuries on the deceased party to the injuries on the injured/alive party.
3. Any evidence of strangulation on either party.
4. Any evidence of forced assault, sexual assault, or otherwise on either party noting that the sexual assault victim is almost always the intimate partner violence victim in these cases.
5. Both parties' offensive and defensive injuries.
6. History of intimate partner violence.

In situations where self-defense is staged in intimicide cases, special consideration should be applied to the entire history of the couple, such as was there a divorce pending and did one party recently separate from the other. Identify any traumatic event that would have prompted negative thinking by the predominant aggressor that eventually led to murder.

Case Example

Carl and Cathy (names changed to protect identities) were a couple with a history of prior violence in their relationship. Cathy's 13-year-old son was only one of several people who tried to help her when Carl strangled her and beat her during their relationship. Cathy finally had enough and decided to leave Carl. Cathy left Carl, but 9 days later, Carl went into a furious rage at their prior common residence and strangled Cathy to death. On the morning of the murder, Cathy's son woke up after a long night before studying with his mom for a social studies test to find Carl in their house and both the kitchen and bathroom sink faucets running and Carl washing a knife. The boy ran back to his room and pretended that he was asleep; Carl looked into the room to confirm the boy was actually asleep and fled the house. Carl called 911 to report that Cathy was dead and then Carl emerged from Cathy's house covered in blood and holding a knife to find emergency crews arriving. He had wounds all over his body, but tried to prevent police from entering the house. They subdued him with a stun gun, entered the house, rescued Cathy's two children, and found her deceased in her basement.

Carl was treated and released from a local hospital for superficial injuries. Carl claimed self-defense, and the author was contacted to consult on the case. The author found nothing consistent with self-defense and instead opined that the totality of evidence was consistent with staged self-defense and intimicide by strangulation based on scientific crime analysis. In the heat of the moment, the author suggested that Carl was driven by emotionality, thus making careless errors when staging the scene as a self-defense case and later with the scenario that came to Cathy's house and found her attacked and murdered. His lawyer later suggested that upon finding his girlfriend in that condition, he was so overwhelmed with grief that he started abusing himself. Prosecutors in the case argued that Carl was a domestic abuser and presented witnesses whom he previously dated and who were allegedly abused by Carl during the time they spent with him. The jury deliberated briefly, and Carl was found guilty of strangling Cathy to death in her home. Carl's injuries were superficial, and it was clear that he was the predominant aggressor, one with a violent history, one with a history of strangling the victim prior to her death, and one who was angry that she had the courage to try to leave their violent relationship.

Homicides Staged as Missing Persons

Hazelwood and Napier (2004) suggested that offenders will sometimes verbally stage crimes by contacting police to report a victim missing after the offender has murdered the victim and disposed of the victim's body. Schlesinger et al. (2012) found in their study that missing persons cases were the most commonly staged cases by domestic offenders and that verbal staging was the most common staging behavior among the sample. These authors argued that reaching out to police to report a victim missing after an offender has murdered and disposed of the body demonstrates tremendous effort on the part of the offender to absolutely and completely misdirect the investigation from its onset.

In light of the empirical findings discussed earlier, the author would argue that sometimes when an offender kills a victim, he or she believes that the best way to protect his or her identity is to cloud the investigation by hiding the victim's body and by contacting the police to report the victim missing. Basically, this means an offender of this nature is trying to portray that no crime occurred by his or her own hand and is by no way responsible for the disappearance of the *missing* victim whom the offender knows is already dead and actually not missing at all. Further, it could be that in these cases, it is likely that victims are murdered in one location and disposed of in another location. It is important to remember that offenders do not move bodies they do not have to move, so if an offender moves a body, he or she feels compelled to do so to protect his identity and to misdirect the investigation. Additionally, it is also possible in these types of cases for offenders to try and point the finger at someone else or imply something else happened altogether, such as the following:

1. The victim ran off with another man
2. The victim ran off to seek a new life
3. The victim ran off with friends
4. The victim was abducted by someone else

Also, in support of Schlesinger et al.'s (2012) findings, Pettler (2011) found that it is very common in these cases that the offender will

1. Report seeing the victim leave
2. Report that he did not see the victim leave
3. Report the victim missing
4. Not report the victim missing
5. Ask someone else to report the victim missing

In addition to these, during the general search for the victim, the offender might

1. Search for the victim
2. Discover the victim's body
3. Not discover the victim's body

According to findings in the author's 2011 study, in these cases, the offender tries to elude capture by removing all evidence from the scene. This could be bedding, clothing, weapons, or anything related to the death of the victim. Offenders will clean with cleaning products, use bleach, air fresheners, and a host of other things to clean blood from the death scene, their method of transport to the dump site, and so on. One important thing to recognize early in an investigation of staged missing people is the extreme importance of the shovel. It should raise immediate suspicion if an intimate partner with a missing intimate partner has purchased a shovel, borrowed a shovel, pulled a shovel out of a storage area, and so on, within the days prior to or days after the victim goes missing. Large heavy-duty contractor bags, tarps, plastic, tape, towels, 55 gallon drums both metal and plastic, boxes, suitcases, and anything else that could be used to conceal a body and transport it to a dump site where the victims are often buried in shallow graves should be investigated thoroughly. Additionally, bagged concrete, mortar, metal chains, and so on, that could be used to weigh down a body should be investigated.

Further, Pettler (2011) found that offenders of this nature will create alibis, accuse someone else of causing the victim to go missing in an attempt to divert attention away from them and onto someone else, and stage not only the crime scene, but also various elements of the crime overall to include lying to family, friends, and associates about the whereabouts of the victim and lying about their whereabouts before the victim's disappearance. These types of cases can be very high profile where the offender might actually paint a sordid tale of the victim implying that the victim was a prostitute, drug user, drug dealer, or criminal, or involved in some other type of questionable activity that would cause him or her to go missing.

Sometimes when confronted when the body of the victim is found, offenders still maintain that they are not responsible (Pettler, 2011). If they do admit involvement at any level, it is often coupled with the argument that the offender acted in self-defense, that the victim and offender were intoxicated at the time of the victim's death and that the offender panicked, but did not mean to kill the victim, or sometimes they actually, when faced with the reality that their time is up, will confess to the murder and justify their behavior by claiming the victim deserved it.

Case Example 1

Ray and Candace (names changed to protect identities) were a married couple with an extremely horrific pattern of intimate partner violence. Ray was the abuser, and Candace suffered tremendously physically, emotionally, and every other way he could think of to abuse her. Candace had been gone for a few days, but Ray had not reported her missing. In speaking with her mother, Ray finally was pressured to report Candace missing even though he kept telling everyone that Candace had done this before and that she would be back. Ray told police that he did not see Candace leave, but she had done this before, and this time he suspected that she ran off to the mountains with another man. Investigators were immediately suspicious of Ray's story, but no one searched the couple's home at that time. Suspicion is not evidence, but investigators worked very hard to find Candace, even though they suspected she was probably already dead.

About 4 months after Candace disappeared, her body washed up onto the bank of a nearby river. Investigators immediately recognized some of the items attached to her body like chains and rope used to weigh her down. The investigation was complicated because the case included numerous crime scenes. The couple's house was searched and processed, Ray's boat and vehicle were searched and processed, and the riverbank where Candace's body washed ashore was processed as well. Investigators discovered the master bedroom of the couple's house had been completely remodeled. Ray did not live in that house any more, but remodeled it after Candace went missing very quickly because he moved out of their house only 3 days after her disappearance and moved in with the girlfriend he had been cheating on Candace with. In comparison, Ray had not remodeled anything else in the home, just the master bedroom. Investigators did not find anything suspicious about Ray's boat, but took samples of rope and paint. Ray's car was completely cluttered, but nothing out of the ordinary struck them about the car. The riverbank was very muddy, but anything of interest was collected that might have been attached to the body. The body was in a severe state of decomposition, but the medical examiner found that Candace died as a result of a gunshot to the back of the head.

Investigators believed Ray wanted out of his marriage in order to live freely with his new girlfriend. Evidence recovered in the master bedroom, even though it had been remodeled, was consistent with Candace having been shot in the back of the head while she slept. After he killed Candace, Ray tried staging the crime and the death scene in several ways. Ray wrapped Candace's body in the bedding of their bed and in plastic in order to transport her to the river. He attached weights to her body, padlocks, and an anchor to weigh her down before throwing her body into the river. Ray cleaned the death scene completely until it was free of blood or any trace that a murder took place. He tried to remodel the bedroom and even asked his girlfriend to pick out new bedroom furniture after having gotten rid of the contents of the entire master bedroom after the murder, including the mattress. Additionally, the offender lied to the victim's mother when she asked him where the victim was while she was missing. When interviewed by law enforcement within days after reporting her missing, Ray stated Candace had not been missing long enough to be a missing person. When Ray was questioned early on in the missing person's investigation, he told police that he was sure that Candace ran off with another man and that he did not care if she was found dead or alive. Ray was charged with and found guilty of first-degree murder and was sentenced to life in prison.

Case Example 2

Amanda's (names changed to protect identities) family could not reach her, and after getting the run around from her boyfriend Joe, Amanda's family called the police and reported Amanda missing. Amanda and Joe were live-in boyfriend and girlfriend with a long history of intimate partner violence. Joe was very controlling and jealous. Joe was angry with Amanda this time because she allegedly had an affair with his best friend and Amanda failed to file financial documents for Joe with his bank. When Joe confronted Amanda about both of these conflicts, Amanda admitted they both were true. When investigators came calling to find out what happened to Amanda, Joe told them he had no idea where she went and that they argued and he went to bed. Investigators asked Joe where they argued, and Joe told them the couple argued outside their house in the backyard. Investigators canvassed the area and talked to the couple's family, friends, and neighbors.

Three days later, a witness called to report that a body was lying on the side of a rural road. Amanda's decomposing body was found wrapped in bedding from the couple's bed covered in black plastic that Joe had secured on both ends with packing tape. Investigators searched the couple's home and found that Joe had worked very hard to clean the entire crime scene and dispose of all the evidence. However, visible bloodstains on the wall appeared to have been missed when someone was trying to remove them. Family and friends confirmed that even though the house was completely cluttered, this was normal for the couple, so investigators moved on from that observation. Based on the information revealed in the investigation, investigators thought that Joe beat Amanda to death outside their house with a piece of wood, then wrapped her up to transport her to the disposal site location.

This case had several earmarks of staging and crime scene staging. First, Frank did not report his girlfriend missing even when she had been gone for a few days. He told police he did not see her leave and that they argued and he went to bed. Further, he lied by telling police they argued over money, when in fact they were arguing over infidelity and her failure to do what he thought she should have done to serve him. Then in a later conversation with police, he told them that he did not see Amanda leave, but he knew Amanda left with another man, but he had no idea who actually killed Amanda. After the murder, Joe carried Amanda's body into the house, undressed her, bathed her, and redressed her in new clothes before wrapping her up in the couple's bedding and plastic and transporting her to the disposal site along the rural road. When Joe returned from dumping Amanda's body, he showered and changed clothes, then reported back to work. Ironically, Joe worked for Amanda's mother, and when she asked Joe where Amanda was that day, Joe lied to Amanda's mother by telling her he did not know where Amanda was at the time. At first, Amanda's mom did not think much of her daughter's absence until Amanda did not show up for Amanda's child's school function. Joe was charged with first-degree murder, but was found guilty of second-degree murder and was sentenced to 19 years and 4 months in prison.

References

Adcock, J. M., & Stein, S. L. (2011). *Cold cases: An evaluation model with follow-up strategies for investigators.* Boca Raton, FL: CRC Press/Taylor & Francis Group.

Douglas, J. E., Burgess, A. W., Burgess, A. G., & Ressler, R. K. (2006). *Crime classification manual: A standard system for investigating and classifying crimes* (2nd ed.). San Francisco, CA: John Wiley & Sons.

Douglas, J., & Douglas, L. (2006) The detection of staging, undoing and personation at the crime scene. In J. Douglas, A. Burgess, A. Burgess, & R. Ressler (Eds.), *Crime Classification Manual* (2nd ed.). San Francisco, CA: Jossey-Bass.

Eke, A. W. (2007). *Staging in cases of homicide: Offender, victim, and offence characteristics* (Doctoral dissertation). Retrieved from ProQuest (1390310091).

Ferguson, C. (2011). *The defects of the situation: A typology of staged crime scenes* (Unpublished doctoral thesis). Bond University, Gold Coast, Queensland, Australia.

Ferguson, C. (2014, July). Staged homicide: An examination of common features of faked burglaries, suicide, accidents and car accidents. *Journal Police Criminal Psychology.* Springer Publishing. doi: 10.1007/s11896-014-9154-1

Ferguson, C., & Petherick, W. (2014, October 13). Getting away with murder: An examination of detected homicide staged as suicide. *Homicide Studies.* doi: 10.1177/1088767914553099

Geberth, V. J. (1996). *Practical homicide investigation: Tactics, procedures, and forensic techniques* (3rd ed.). Boca Raton, FL: CRC Press/Taylor & Francis Group.

Geberth, V. J. (2006). *Practical homicide investigation: Tactics, procedures, and forensic techniques* (4th ed.). Boca Raton, FL: CRC Press/Taylor & Francis Group.

Geberth, V. J. (2010). Crime scene staging: An exploratory study of the frequency and characteristics of sexual posing in homicides. *Investigative Sciences Journal, 2*(2), 1–19.

Gross, H. (1924). *Criminal Investigation.* London, UK: Sweet & Maxwell.

Hargrove, T. (2010, March 23). *Unsolved homicide analysis: A look at what kinds of murders get solved.* New York: Scripps Howard News Service.

Hazelwood, R. R., & Napier, M. R. (2004). Crime scene staging and its detection. *International Journal of Offender Therapy and Comparative Criminology, 48*(6), 744–759. doi: 10.1177/0306624X04268298

Leth, P., & Vesterby, A. (1996). Homicidal hanging masquerading as suicide. *Forensic Science International, 85*, 65–71. doi: 10.1016/S0379–0738(96)02082–8

Mallach, H. J., & Pollak, S. (1998, July–August). Simulated suicide by hanging after homicidal strangulation. *Archiv für Kriminologie, 202*(1–2), 17–28.

O'Connell, J. & Soderman, H. (1936). *Modern criminal investigation.* New York, NY: Funk & Wagnalls.

Parker, M. D., & Pettler, L. G. (2009). DV homicide: Hot blooded lovers, cold blooded killers [PowerPoint slides]. *Evidence based domestic violence prosecution course.* Carthage, NC: Authors.

Pettler, L. G. (2011). *Crime scene behaviors of crime scene stagers* (Doctoral dissertation). Available from ProQuest (2251577601).

Puschel, K., Holtz, W., Hildebrand, E., Naeve, W., & Brinkman, B. (1984, November–December). Hanging: Suicide or homicide? *Archiv für Kriminologie, 174*(5–6), 141–153.

Schlesinger, L. B., Gardenier, A., Jarvis, J., & Sheehan-Cook, J. (2012, April). Crime scene staging in homicide. *Journal of Police and Criminal Psychology, 29*(1), 44–51.

Svensson, A., & Wendel, O. (1974). *Techniques of crime scene investigation* (2nd ed.). New York: American Elsevier.

Turvey, B. E. (2000, December). Staged crime scenes: A preliminary study of 25 cases. *Journal of Behavioral Profiling, 1*(3).

Turvey, B. E. (2012). *Criminal profiling: An introduction to behavioral analysis* (4th ed.). Burlington, MA: Elsevier.

Ueno, Y., Fukanaga, T., Nakagawa, K., Imabayashi, T., Fukiwara, S., Adachi, J., & Mizoi, Y. (1989, February). A homicidal strangulation by ligature, disguised as a suicide. *Nihon Hoigaku Zasshi, 421*(1), 46–51.

United States Department of Justice. (2014). *What is domestic violence?* Retrieved from http://www.justice.gov/ovw/domestic-violence

Walter, R., Stein, S., & Adcock, J. M. (2011). Suspect identification using pre-, peri-, and post-offense behaviors. In J. M. Adcock & S. Stein (Eds.), *Cold cases: An evaluation model with follow-up strategies for investigators.* Boca Raton, FL: CRC Press/Taylor & Francis Group.

Yamamoto, K., Hayase, T., Matsumoto, H., & Yamamoto, Y. (1998, March–April). Suicidal hanging or simulated suicide? Once again a case of Kobue: A spectacular case in the history of Japanese legal medicine. *Archiv für Kriminologie, 201*(3–4), 97–102.

Victim-Centered Death Investigation Methodology

III

Crime has become more and more complicated over time. Once there was a time when homicide investigations were finished quickly and were prosecuted on very little physical evidence if any real evidence at all. Today, the legal bar is high for what gets a case to the jury and the more systematic and in depth a death investigation is, the more likely it results in a successful outcome. Additionally, gone are the days of simplistic crime scene work as well. Today, investigators must approach death investigation and crime scene work by embracing a systematic, scientific, multimodal, interdisciplinary approach. It is important to remember that there are 11 studies on staging in the world thus far, along with all of the anecdotal articles that have been published. The material contained in this book is theoretically substantiated as much as possible by the few studies that can lend credence to each concept. As empirical research continues to populate, the relevance of the aspects of the material contained herein will both wane and gain momentum. Thus far, Section I included possibly the most extensive summary-type literature review of staging to date combined with introducing staging in general and crime scene dynamics. Section II introduced much of what is currently known about offenders, victims, staging purposes and motives for murder, victims, and types of staging. Section III will eclectically draw from the first eight chapters coupled with elements from additional related subdisciplines toward introducing a suggested approach for the identification, comprehension, application, analysis, synthesis, and evaluation of staged crimes.

Crime Identification
Detecting Deception

9

Introduction

Investigating the staged crime is daunting. It is very different from investigating many other types of crimes. Specifically related to homicides staged as something else, investigators are faced with an uphill battle almost every time. Regardless of whether or not an offender has staged a monothematic (i.e., simplistic) or polythematic (i.e., complex) crime, his level of effort even in its smallest measure can create tremendous investigatory obstacles that prove challenging to overcome. But they can be overcome in many instances. Not in every instance, but in many instances they can. It all depends on how those involved in the case choose to view the evidence. Do they make the evidence fit their theories or what they want the case to be or do they allow the evidence to guide the investigation while remaining open to alternatives? The author has seen investigations go both ways many times and is here to proclaim that failing to remain open to alternatives throughout the course of an investigation is the most crippling thing anyone can do throughout the duration. It is ok to say, "I don't know." It is also ok "to be wrong." It is ok to admit one is wrong as well. Sometimes these are hard pills to swallow, but because the issue at hand is capturing the offender, making every effort to evade capture toward justice for the victim of murder and his or her family, investigators must remain focused and remember that these investigations are not about them; they are about the victims. *Victim centered. Victim focused. Grounded by victimology.* This chapter will incite a new journey for some, while others might dismiss it altogether. As a lifelong learner, the author would argue opening one's mind to change or growth is scary, frustrating, and sometimes downright hard, but due to the CSI effect, the fact that research has shown staged crimes are on the rise, and all of the new ways offenders are now trying to get away with murder, changing the way staged crimes are investigated is necessary. And with that, it begins.

Bloom's Taxonomy

"Our system determines out outcome" means that the more structurally sound, systematic, methodical, and comprehensive a system is, the more structurally sound and comprehensive the outcome of the system will be.

According to *Merriam-Webster's* Online Dictionary (2014) taxonomy is "the study of general principles of scientific classification or systematics" (para. 1). Taxonomy takes one thing or many things and shows how they interrelate. Taxonomy differs from typology in that typology groups together like-variables and "calls them something." An example of a taxonomy is how first grade is related to second grade and how third grade is related to second grade and so on. First grade must be completed before second grade begins and second grade must be completed before third grade can start. So each level builds and is interrelated to the one below it. If first grade is not completed or is incomplete, second and third grades will not be as structurally sound, and so on.

Benjamin Bloom created what is known as Bloom's Taxonomy and published his work in 1956 (Bloom, 1956). Bloom's Taxonomy (see Figure 9.1) is comprised of six cognitive domains or levels of higher-level thinking: knowledge, comprehension, application, analysis, synthesis, and evaluation. A cognitive domain is basically an educational activity that helps someone develop intellectual skills (Bloom, 1956). Someone that comprehends something does not understand that thing the same way someone who has analyzed it does. For example, when a baby is born, he or she comes into the world knowing nothing. Then one day someone gives the baby a rattle. The baby does not know what "a rattle" is at first and just holds on to it. The baby gains *knowledge* of the rattle by holding it. Then as time goes on, the rattle moves while in the baby's hand and the baby discovers that the rattle makes a sound. The baby then *comprehends* the meaning of the rattle in that a rattle

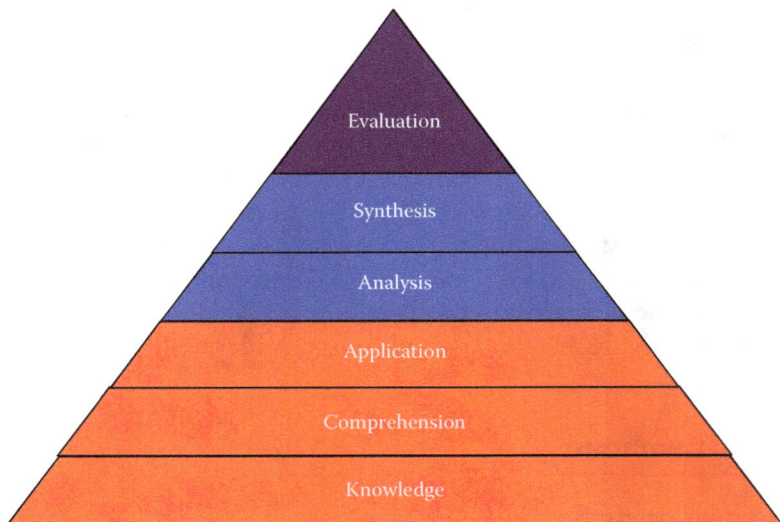

Figure 9.1 Bloom's Taxonomy (From Bloom, B.S., *Taxonomy of educational objectives, Book 1, Cognitive domain*, Longman, White Plains, NY, 1956.)

makes a sound. Further, once the baby has identified what a rattle is and comprehended that the rattle makes a sound the baby then *applies* his or her knowledge and comprehension of the rattle by shaking it for entertainment. The latter is an example of how the first three levels of Bloom's Taxonomy can be understood in a simple way.

The next three levels of Bloom's Taxonomy are a bit more complicated. To note, there are two types of learning: rote learning, which is simply the remembering of facts like on a multiple-choice test, and higher-level learning, such as analysis, synthesis, and evaluation of concepts, principles, procedures, and so forth. Level 4 of Bloom's Taxonomy is *analysis*. Analysis does not mean, "thinking hard." Rather, analysis is defined as breaking something apart, studying each piece to gain new insight about it, then reassembling all of the pieces into a newly understood whole. Take, for example, a plastic milk jug and its lid. Disassembling the jug leaves two parts: the jug, which holds liquid and the lid that prevents the liquid from spilling out of the jug. In studying the jug itself, many attributes can be identified related to size, shape, texture, color, and so on. Next in studying the lid, the same attributes can be identified, but the lid differs from the jug in size, shape, texture, and in some cases color, and so on. The lid is threaded on the inside. Oftentimes lids are ribbed on the outside for grip, for example. So once both pieces are completely analyzed, they can be reassembled toward understanding how they interrelate. The next level of Bloom's Taxonomy is *synthesis*; to synthesize means to combine things to make a newly understood whole. For example, musicians synthesize their instruments when they play together in a band. Each player knows his own instrument. The group wants to play a song. So each of the musicians analyze the song, or break it apart, studying and learning each piece, then assembling those pieces into their whole part of the song. Then when all the musicians come together, the guitar, piano, drums, bass, and so on, all play or synthesize the part of the song they each learned independently with each other to make a new whole, or in this example to create a song. If one musician does not "do his homework" and does not analyze the song properly, guess what happens when he or she goes to synthesize that part with the group. It sounds terrible. Thus, analysis relates to synthesis in that analysis is necessary before something can be synthesized. Likewise, knowledge has to be gained before understanding can happen and understanding must happen before applying what is understood can happen. Thus applying what is understood from the knowledge must happen before analysis can happen and analysis must happen before synthesis can happen. And all of that must happen in order to be then able to *evaluate* something, which is the sixth level of Bloom's Taxonomy. To evaluate something is to attribute worth, value, judgment, or to assign merit for example. It is best never to evaluate anything before gaining knowledge to understand, understanding to apply, applying to underscore analysis, and analyzing to synthesize. Evaluation means to interpret everything presented and to finally draw conclusions. So where do investigations start? At knowledge. But what does one often hear when entering a crime scene? Evaluation. Not good. Not useful. Dangerous and drawing conclusions in a crime scene can prevent murder victims from getting justice. Here is the best example to illustrate this idea. Patrol is starting the crime scene log and securing the scene. Crime scene personnel have been on scene for about 1 hour when the investigators arrive. Upon signing into the scene, a crime scene investigator (CSI) says to an investigator, "Come on in so I can tell you what happened." What level of higher-level thinking *is* this individual operating on? Answer: Evaluation. What level of higher-level thinking *should* this individual be operating on? Answer: Knowledge.

Nothing cripples an investigation faster than failure to consider alternatives and figuring out if a crime scene has been manipulated with criminal intent for the purpose of deception toward misdirecting an investigation. Having an open mind requires submission to the process of learning and growth overriding human nature that wants to jump to conclusions. At no time should anyone involved in a murder scene investigation be evaluating at the crime scene because being presumptuous can lead straight to unfixable critical error. Obviously, a victim killed while standing on a street corner who is shot by someone driving past is a victim of murder and it is ok to proceed under those pretenses. But to walk into the common environment of a victim and offender, such as the bedroom of their home to find the female victim lying on the bed with a gun in her hand dead of injuries sustained from a gunshot wound to the temporal area of her head that was called in by her intimate partner is not automatically suicide. Geberth (2006) argued that when victims' families bring forth information about victims, investigators have an obligation to follow up on that information. In cases where suicide was decided at the crime scene based on the location of the gunshot wound coupled with the victim's intimate partner's statement that they were arguing and she shot herself, sometimes critical errors cannot be undone; sometimes these errors cost victims' justice, families closure, and investigators their jobs.

The latter creates a foundational example for how Bloom's Taxonomy can be used as scaffolding for a scientific, systematic, multimodal, interdisciplinary death investigation approach that incorporates traditional homicide investigation strategy while shifting away from the limiters of such an antiquated suspect-based paradigm. Bloom's Taxonomy provides a conceptual framework that can be divided into three phases for investigating potentially staged crime scenes, analyzing the totality of the evidence, synthesizing all of the analyzed parts, toward eventual evaluation of the totality of circumstances. Bloom's Taxonomy is a system that can be used as a map toward making sure "every i is dotted and t is crossed" without jumping levels that weaken the overall structure. Bloom's is a system that can be applied for how crime scene investigation, analysis, synthesis, and evaluation should occur in rank order in that it exemplifies how each level of learning and thinking interrelates to the category above and beneath it and shows why each is necessary for the other (Bloom, 1956).

Phase 1: Knowledge, Comprehension, and Application

To illustrate using another example, a CSI uses knowledge by identifying items of evidence in a scene and then defines and describes each item by documenting them. CSIs then demonstrate comprehension when by classifying each item by category, such as biological evidence, trace, ballistics, and so forth, all of the evidence is understood and a plan to process it is formed. Then, CSIs apply crime scene processing technology based on their understanding of each type of physical evidence in precise measurement by collecting, preserving, preparing, and reporting the physical evidence also in precise measure using their knowledge, comprehension, and application of crime scene processing procedures, protocols, and report writing skills.

Phase 2: Analysis

Next, in Phase 2, the crime analyst collects everything that is available for analysis in the case and begins the process of breaking apart each piece independently, studying each piece, and reassembling each piece into a newly understood whole.

Phase 3: Synthesis and Evaluation

Finally, in Phase 3, once all of the pieces of the investigation and their subparts have been analyzed completely and the analyst has a new understanding of each of them that he or she did not have when the process began, then the analyst can begin to take each newly assembled whole and synthesize them together with each of the other "newly assembled wholes," for lack of a better word. Then after all of the necessary synthesizing is complete, then and only then can the analyst accurately and dependably evaluate the totality of the crime. "Our system determines our outcome."

Victim-Centered Death Investigation Methodology

Suggested Approach

There is a huge gap between the duties of the detective versus the death investigator. Detectives and investigators are supposed to investigate situations to determine if a crime occurred; that does not make them homicide experts.

Death investigators investigate how an individual died; that does not make them crime experts. The two have totally different skill sets, but are reliant upon each other just the same. This gap presents a problem on both sides of the yellow tape. Again, the paradigm shift from suspect-centered to victim-centered is happening now. The more one learns about the victim, the more one knows about the offender and the crime, which leads to the suggested approach that combines detective/investigator-based homicide investigation with death investigation called "Vic-Dim," that is victim-centered death investigation methodology (VCDIM); see Figure 9.2.

VCDIM is grounded by *the victim*. Components of homicide investigation and death investigation of VCDIM are adhered to the various levels of Bloom's Taxonomy, which as the scaffolding or systematic, organizational infrastructure of VCDIM, serves as a checks and balances system that focuses an investigation and its interrelated parts by level of thinking to minimize the likelihood of skipping steps or jumping to conclusions too far too fast. At first glance, the VCDIM might appear complicated or unrealistic for effective application, but because Bloom's Taxonomy is the core, each category stands independently on its own while being interrelated to the categories above and below it, thus ensuring that each component in the investigatory process is complete before moving to the next level while at the same time relying upon what was completed in the level below. VCDIM is designed for use by investigators, criminologists, and others who investigate a potentially staged crime. As with anything else, VCDIM users experience a learning curve, and practice makes perfect. While no case is perfect, an investigatory methodology should be systematic at a minimum.

Bloom's Taxonomy is the *environment* by which to work a staged case from the inside out. Remember, these are not *normal* murder cases; these are staged cases, so that means physical evidence can be low and circumstantial evidence can be high leaving investigators, both detectives and death scene investigators, scratching their heads as to what to do or where to go next. VCDIM is the solution to that dilemma. Think of Bloom's Taxonomy as a computer operating system like Windows or Snow Leopard. Bloom's is the operating system. Everything that comes in and out of the investigation has to pass through the levels of Bloom's in order to work properly just like a computer operating system. So think of Bloom's Taxonomy as the death investigation operating system and always remember, "Our system determines our outcome."

Overview of the VCDIM Process

The author has combined homicide investigation, forensic criminology, and the hard sciences into one investigatory system. Every part of VCDIM will be fully discussed and analyzed throughout this and the next two chapters

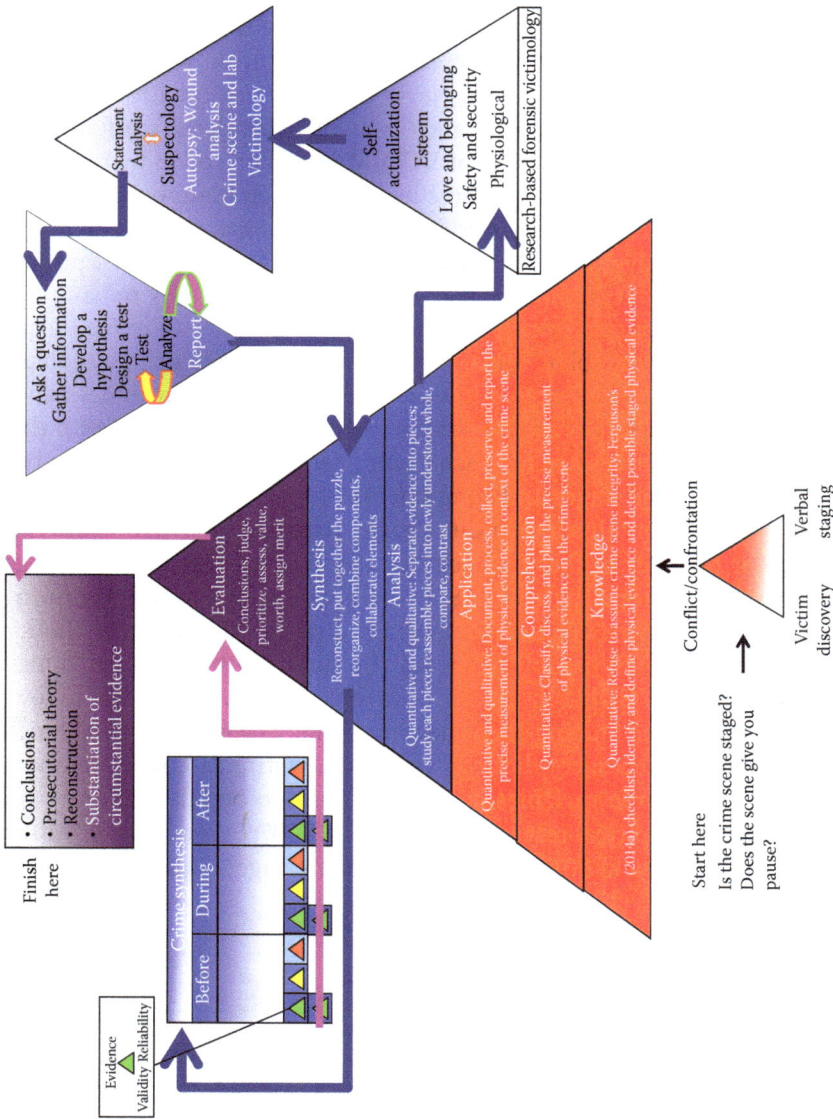

Figure 9.2 Victim-Centered Death Investigation Methodology (VCDIM) Diagram

(Chapters 10 and 11), but in order to provide a road map of where this is going, a brief overview is most helpful. Again the first thing to notice about VCDIM is the large triangle in the middle, which of course, is Bloom's Taxonomy. As mentioned earlier, Bloom's Taxonomy serves as the scaffolding, skeleton, framework, foundation, and/or operating system for the methodology, which means everything flows in and out of its various levels. Bloom's Taxonomy is a bottom-to-top system. Everything starts at the bottom with Knowledge and ends at the top with Evaluation. Never does one begin with evaluation because it is impossible to do it accurately or at all. Second, the scaffolding of Bloom's Taxonomy and other parts of VCDIM are color-coded by red, blue, or purple. Red is the foundational three levels and their components, Stages 1, 2, and 3: Knowledge, Comprehension, and Application are red. Then Stages 4 and 5 are blue: analysis and synthesis. Finally, red and blue make purple, or Stage 6 Evaluation. It is impossible to make purple from only red and it is impossible to make purple from only blue, but it is possible to make purple when combining red and blue. Thus, VCDIM is color-coded using red, blue, and purple to help users perceive it as a checklist of sorts in understanding exactly which stage they are working in, which components go with that stage, what the objectives are for each component, and how those components interrelate to the stages and components beneath and above them.

Next, VCDIM contains lots of directional arrows. These arrows are like road signs for the user in that they tell the user where to start, where to go next, and where to stop. There is a "Start here!" *road* sign at the beginning of VCDIM that contains the most important question to be asked, "Is this crime scene staged?" By simply allowing the question to be asked moves the initial stages of VCDIM in a positive direction upon onset. The following first triangle is the Staging Identification Trilogy (see Figure 9.3), which contains three key pieces: conflict/confrontation, victim discovery, and verbal staging. These three variables have been found to be relevant and supported by staging empirical research to date (Eke, 2007; Ferguson, 2011, 2014; Ferguson and Petherick, 2014; Pettler, 2011; Schlesinger, Gardenier, Jarvis,

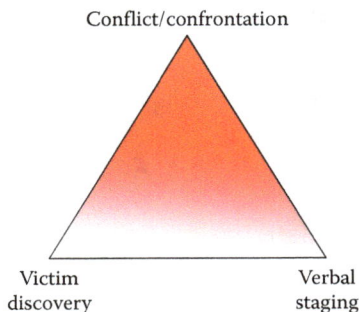

Figure 9.3 Staging Identification Trilogy

& Sheehan-Cook, 2012). Once the information relevant to those key pieces has been established, knowledge is gained about the potential of the crime scene possibly having been staged or not, though the Staging Identification Trilogy is a general guideline and not a tell-all. Regardless, the user begins to understand how to proceed in Stage 1: Crime Scene Knowledge. Here, the CSI or whoever is working the crime scene can utilize Ferguson's (2015) Empirically Derived How-To Checklist to address the issues in the scene related to homicides staged as robberies/home invasions/burglaries, suicides, accidents, or car accidents pursuant to physical evidence identification. Next, in Stage 2: Crime Scene Comprehension, the crime scene personnel classify each type of evidence and develop a plan for crime scene processing. Then, in Stage 3: Application of Crime Scene Technology, the user proceeds in the crime scene by applying various procedures and techniques to process the scene and to precisely measure the physical evidence through notes, photographs, sketches, measurements, and so on, coupled with collecting, preserving, and reporting the precise measurement of the physical evidence. This is the most critical step in the crime scene investigatory process because successful prosecution begins at the crime scene.

Once the first three stages are complete, the user begins Stage 4: Crime Analysis to organize to analyze the evidence (i.e., data) collected at the scene. The goal of analysis is to break apart each piece of the evidence, study it, then prepare it for reassembly into a newly understood whole. In order to do that in a victim-centered approach, the user must first and foremost complete a full victimological study on the victim using the conceptual model of Research-Based Forensic Victimology (see Appendix A), which is a suggested method for studying the victim within the VCDIM approach supported by Maslow's (1943) hierarchy of needs as its "environment," operating system, framework, skeleton, and so forth, like Bloom's is for VCDIM. Once a full victimological study is done on the victim, victimology becomes the foundation for the next piece of the analysis piece of the investigation. Victimology serves as the baseline from which to bounce all other items of evidence off of per se. Included within this part are the crime scene evidence and their corresponding laboratory reports analysis, study of the autopsy and conducting wound analysis with assistance from the forensic pathologist, and suspectology and statement analysis. The last two can be interchanged: suspectology and statement analysis as needed, but the author would argue that victimology always comes first because it is the baseline by which all other evidence is compared.

During this piece of the analytical process, it may become apparent that tests are needed toward answering questions, such as, "Could John have held the rifle along the wound path identified by the forensic pathologist?" In order to figure this out, users must employ the scientific method: ask a question, gather information, develop a hypothesis, design a test, conduct the text, analyze the results, and then either go back to conduct another test or report the results from the first test, generally speaking. Once all of the hypotheses have been tested (and there are normally more than one per case or at least there should be), then the user is adequately prepared to enter into Stage 5: Crime Synthesis.

In this stage, the user implements the author's Crime Synthesis Matrix (see Appendix C) expanded from Walter, Stein, and Adcock's (2011) Crime Matrix that helps to identify pertinent elements of the crime before the death of the victim, during the death of the victim/crime scenes, and after the death of the victim. Each of those elements are then evaluated for their validity and reliability using the author's Modified Triangulation Method (see Figure 5.1) that is based on the crime scene method of triangulating evidence off of two fixed points in a crime scene combined with the research constructs of validity and reliability toward categorizing each element as empirical, quasi-empirical, or nonempirical as discussed in Chapter 5. Once all the empirical elements have been separated from the quasi-empirical, and the nonempirical elements, vectors or one-dimensional lines can be drawn between matching elements or cause and effect–type relationships before the crime, during the crime, and after the crime columns (see Figure 9.4). The same can be done for the *quasi-* and *non-*elements, but they might not be as important in the end as what can be substantiated empirically in the case toward getting the case to the jury. Upon completion, the Crime Synthesis Matrix and vector assignments, the VCDIM user enters Stage 6: Crime Evaluation. At this time, the user has everything he or she needs to evaluate the case accurately, thoroughly, empirically, and correctly because every piece of the investigation has been underpinned by structural soundness of Bloom's Taxonomy as *its system* meaning that the outcome should be as strong the system from which it was derived.

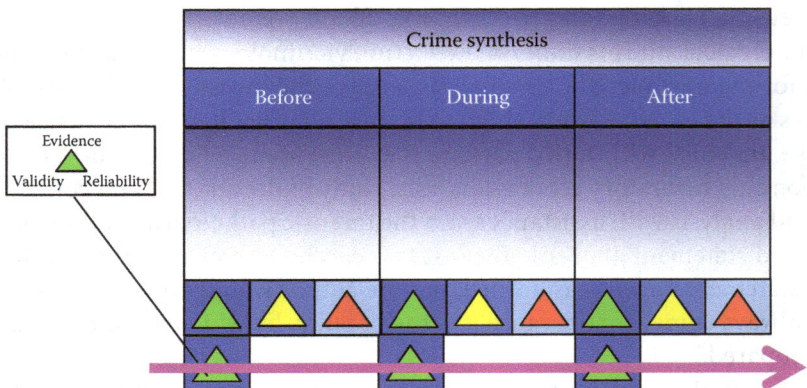

Figure 9.4 Crime Synthesis Vectors (From Walter, R. et al., Suspect identification using pre-, peri-, and postoffense behaviors, in J.M. Adcock and S. Stein (Eds.), *Cold cases: An evaluation model with follow-up strategies for investigators,* CRC Press/Taylor & Francis Group, Boca Raton, FL, 2011.)

During the Evaluation stage, conclusions can finally be drawn *because they can be substantiated,* prosecutorial theory can be made, reconstructions can be planned, and circumstantial evidence might be strengthened and highlighted enough to help move the case toward the courtroom.

One of the benefits of the VCDIM is that although the author built this method toward circumventing the staging offender and his or her kill and cover-up philosophy, this system is applicable in whole or in part to cold case investigation, assault with a deadly weapon cases, attempted murder cases, and other similar situations. One of the limitations of the method is that even though it is a physical map of the author's education, training, and experience spanning more than 20 years and could be useful in many cases, to the author, it is a conceptual model and is theoretical in nature. It is intended for investigatory purposes only; it is not to replace the scientific method or another method that is accepted by the court. VCDIM is emergent or evolutionary in nature and will grow and change over time as more empirical research is published.

The bottom level is always approach every crime scene with an open mind, objectivity, and at the knowledge level. Never draw conclusions at the crime scene and find a system that is acceptable by everyone involved that will help propel investigations in the right direction from the onset. Focus on the identification and detection of staging early in the initial stages of the investigation. Reserve analysis, synthesis, and evaluation for a time when all of the data has been collected for the most part always realizing that investigations are fluid rather than static, they change constantly, have information coming in constantly, and flexibility is a must.

VCDIM: Outline

The process is divided into six stages using Bloom's Taxonomy as scaffolding toward ensuring that each stage is built methodically onto the stage beneath, no stage is jumped, and all substages are completed during each stage.

1. Stage 1: Crime Scene Knowledge
   Type: Quantitative—Precise measurement of physical evidence
   Location: Level 1—Bottom, foundational level of Bloom's Taxonomy.
   a. Is the crime scene staged? Staging Identification Trilogy
      i. Conflict/confrontation
      ii. Victim discovery
      iii. Verbal staging
   b. Ferguson's (2015) empirically derived staging detection how-to.
   c. Refuse to assume the integrity of the crime scene.
   d. Identify and detect the staging behavior and/or staged physical evidence.
   e. Define and describe the physical evidence.

2. Stage 2: Crime Scene Comprehension

Type: Quantitative—Precise measurement of physical evidence

Location: Level 2—One must identify, define, and describe, before one can classify and discuss:

    a. Document the initial observations of the scene.

    b. Classify and discuss physical evidence. This might not be done on paper, but should be discussed with lab personnel and/or experts if needed.

    c. Develop a plan for how to accurately, precisely, and appropriately meet the legal and scientific objectives of crime scene processing procedures and techniques.

    d. Plan needed resources that might not be on hand, such as chemicals or other specialized equipment that could detect staged elements of the scene.

3. Stage 3: Application of Crime Scene Technology

Type: Quantitative and qualitative—Precise measurement of physical evidence in the context of all evidence and crime scene as a whole

Location: Level 3—One can apply knowledge when the knowledge is acquired and understood:

    a. Prepare to execute crime scene processing plan taking careful consideration to process for elements of crime scene staging; this could mean additional photographs of angles not otherwise considered standard.

    b. Precisely measure using multiple points of reference, crime scene search methodology, etc., all items of physical evidence in addition to crime scene measurements. For later reconstructive purposes, be sure to measure everything in three dimensions (L × W × H); the more detailed this section is, the more likely it is for reconstruction to be done.

    c. Collect all physical evidence being sure to document all demographic information related to the evidence. One thing to note: the author has seen countless times bloodstain evidence lost due to inaccurate packaging. Allow wet items to dry, use paper to separate layers, then package so nothing is touching part of any other item (i.e., bedsheet).

    d. Preserve all items of physical evidence and document preservation efforts.

    e. Report all crime scene activity, processing system, include agency protocol, investigative summaries, supplements, crime scene logs, evidence lists and corresponding documents, measurements, photographs, notes, etc., and assemble them into a well-organized system that can be easily reviewed (the author suggests using a binder system to *tab* and organize reports).

The report should be robust in breadth and depth, and contain both quantitative (the what) and qualitative (the how/why descriptive) information in order to help the reader understand all the details about any particular piece of evidence and the crime scene as a whole. Create a Table of Contents and place at the front of the binder. Tab the binder sections.

4. Stage 4: Crime Analysis

Type: Quantitative and qualitative—Studying the precise measurement of physical evidence in context and how it could be interrelated to the victim and other components

Location: Level 4—One can analyze the application once knowledge is acquired and understood:

a. Research-based forensic victimology—Using Maslow's hierarchy of needs as a conceptual framework to use the method and categories discussed in Chapter 5, conduct a full victimological study on all victims then use modified triangulation to determine if select information revealed in the study of the victim are empirical (can be validated and is reliable because it can be proven and substantiated), quasi-empirical (can be partially validated and/or is partially reliable possibly) or nonempirical (cannot be validated or relied upon because there is nothing to substantiate the information). Victimology is then used as a baseline for all other types of analysis, synthesis, and evaluation going forward.

b. Crime scene and laboratory reports—Analyze all crime scene reports contained in the binder from Stages 1, 2, 3 along with interrelating them to the forensic service laboratory reports, such as DNA, serology, ballistics, etc., to compare to victimology.

c. Autopsy and wound pattern analysis—In partnership with the forensic pathologist, medical examiner, coroner, or other relevant parties, break apart each pertinent aspect of the autopsy then focus on studying the wounds to the victim. Complete wound analysis charts, diagrams, and spreadsheets to compare to crime scene, labs, and victimology.

d. Suspectology (or statement analysis)—It is the study of the suspect or suspects. Complete suspectology for each suspect. This substage could be switched with statement analysis. Determine what is empirical, quasi-empirical, and nonempirical then compare with wound analysis, crime scene, lab reports, and victimology.

e. Statement analysis (or suspectology)—For the purpose of this discussion, statement analysis is the breaking apart of statements, studying each piece, then cross-comparing statements given at different times to possibly different individuals to identify, define, discuss, then analyze very specific details related to the crime; this substage could be switched with suspectology. Determine what is empirical, quasi-empirical, and/or nonempirical if necessary then compare with suspectology, wound analysis, crime scene, lab reports, and victimology.

5. Stage 5: Crime synthesis

    Type: Quantitative and qualitative—Putting together all the pieces of the puzzle

    Location: Level 5—One can synthesize all of the pieces of the analysis once the knowledge is understood and applied:

    a. Crime Synthesis Matrix—Place all analyzed pieces in their proper location of one or more of the three columns of the matrix, before, during, or after the crime, then take each piece listed in each column and if not already done during the analysis stage, determine if each piece is empirical, quasi-empirical, or nonempirical; try to enter broad categories first, then underpin with the pieces of each.

6. Stage 6: Crime Evaluation

    Type: Quantitative and qualitative—Drawing conclusions based on substantiation

    Location: Level 6—Only when all other stages are complete, it is time to evaluate toward assigning worth, merit, or value:

    a. In partnership with the district attorney, state attorney, solicitor, prosecutor, or others explain the victim-based death investigation methodology, everything contained in the case, and the system and method by which each piece was analyzed and synthesized, then present all of the information for evaluation.

VCDIM Stage 1: Crime Scene Knowledge

When investigators realize very early in an investigation that the red flags of staging behaviors are present, it saves valuable resources, such as manpower, time, and money. And in contrast, when investigators miss the red flags of staging very early in an investigation, it can waste valuable resources, such as manpower, time, and money because the trajectory of the investigation is cascading in the wrong direction. But, keep in mind that even the most seasoned investigator can miss signs of staging at any point during an investigation. So it is best not to throw stones, but rather approach all investigations using a multimodal, interdisciplinary, systematic approach, such as VCDIM, that speaks to the eventual outcomes rather than the personal agendas, egos, or ranks of the investigating personnel on either side of the yellow tape.

Therefore, instead of going in the wrong direction, the early identification and detection of staging behaviors helps point the investigation in the right direction. "Is this crime scene staged?" and "Does the scene give you pause?" are two of the foremost questions investigators might want to consider asking on the front end instead of the back end because the back end can be "a day late and a dollar short." Most often, crime scene processing is a one-shot-deal. That means investigators only have one shot to get it right. In conjunction, one of the most important things to recognize about offenders pursuant to staging is that if an offender feels it is necessary to stage a crime scene in the first place, the offender outright thinks he is the most logical suspect.

Staging Identification Trilogy

So this begs the question, how does one identify and detect staging? First it is important to note that to "identify" is to first recognize something, which is the first step in building knowledge. Knowledge is the first level of Bloom's Taxonomy and it should be where every investigation starts ... build knowledge first! Research has shown that there are patterns of behavior related to the victim–offender relationship and that are often exhibited by offenders who stage murders, such as conflict and/or confrontation between the victim and offender prior to the murder, victim discovery or notification or the way in which law enforcement finds out the victim is deceased or missing, and verbal staging or the stories or scenarios offenders first try to sell to investigators, friends, family, and so on, about the situation, and the (Ferguson, 2011, 2015; Ferguson & Petherick, 2014; Pettler, 2011; Schlesinger et al., 2012). Plus, investigators often report to the author that "something doesn't look right," for example. By answering these three questions:

1. *Conflict/Confrontation*: Who was in conflict with the victim or was there a confrontation between the victim and offender prior to the death of the victim?
2. *Victim Discovery*: Was the last person to see the victim alive the first person to discover the victim's body?
3. *Verbal Staging*: Did the last person to see the victim alive report the victim dead or missing (via a 911 call, etc.) and/or offer stories to investigators, friends, family, etc.?

Start the investigation where the investigation starts. While it might seem strange to ask what was said on the 911 call when embarking on a crime scene investigation, the 911 call serves as the first baseline for comparison to the physical evidence in the scene. Remember that if an offender stages a crime scene and then calls 911 to report the victim dead or missing, the story that the offender gives to 911 is the story he or she has decided to go with.

A common example is, "He/she shot him/herself while we were having an argument" or "I was in the bathroom/kitchen/bed, etc., when he/she shot him/herself." It is often that this story changes over time because it is not a memory, so really good documentation is a must for everything the offender says to everyone: investigators, friends, family, and so on.

Conflict and Confrontation

Conflict is everywhere: between countries, between political parties, between communities, cultures, families, religious groups, and between individuals. According to Simmel (1950), "conflict is designed to resolve divergent dualisms" (p. 13). Murder is *conflict resolution* for the offender and the crime scene location always meets his or her needs. When really analyzing it, the act of murder creates a sense of unity between the victim and the offender ... they were in conflict before the murder, but because of the conflict of murder, they share that experience, and the conflict is gone. Clearly, the victim does not experience the murder the same way the offender does. There is unity from the standpoint that because the victim is now dead the relationship between him or her and the offender can continue according to the way the offender chooses to perceive the murder. In essence, murder is then the epitome of divergent dualism toward resolving conflict.

But resolving conflict creates more conflict. The concept of conflict and/or confrontation in relation to staging is very important. *Primary conflict* is the conflict between the victim and offender that precedes the death of the victim. *Secondary conflict* is the conflict the death of the victim creates between the offender and investigators pursuant to misdirecting the investigation. Basically, the victim–offender conflict ends and the offender–investigator conflict begins. Staging is how the offender attempts to resolve the offender–investigator conflict that murdering a victim creates. The offender and investigators' goals are in opposition, but it is that very opposition that compels each party to strategically proceed accordingly. For the offender it is a series of lies, concealments, and creations that is the staged crime and its scene. For the investigators it is a series of tests, interviews, and evaluations of the very same thing. In the end, both are working toward a common goal: conflict resolution. Resolution for the offender would be to get away with murder. Resolution for the investigators is to capture the offender.

In addition to all of this, sometimes the media confuses the issue surrounding the true position of law enforcement is when it comes to solving murders; that is, that investigators are information gatherers whose investigative material are there to support or refute as opposed to judge or verify. If the murder investigation was the endgame, there would be no criminal court because investigators would gather information and decide the fate of an offender themselves. But that is not the case at all in the American Criminal Justice System; investigations are handed up to prosecutors, who present investigative material in support and/or refutation of the fact pattern of a case. It is then up to the judge and the jury to decide on the value of the presented information and to render a verdict pursuant to the offender's guilt or his innocence.

Victim Discovery

Like conflict/confrontation, empirical research has also shown that offenders in most staging cases discover the victims' bodies. The importance of identifying the last person to see the victim alive and the first person to discover the victim's body cannot be understated. This type of identification is part of the knowledge-building level of the investigation. Victim discovery could theoretically be a function of the victim–offender relationship, the offender's personality, cognition, behavior, emotionality, and envirosocioculturalism, and quite possibly how much CSI-related television the offender might watch. Although the last part of the last sentence could be taken in jest, it is intended to be fully serious. Consider the following example.

In March 2006, a woman was found beaten to death, wrapped in black plastic secured with clear packing tape on either end and dumped alongside a rural road. The victim was not immediately identified and the case went cold for several months. In October 2006, a woman was found beaten to death, wrapped in a black plastic bag secured with clear packing tape on either end dumped alongside a rural road. The second victim was immediately identified, which led to the identification of the first victim. Additionally, it was quickly ruled out that the cases were connected even when considering the similarities in the two cases. The investigation revealed that both suspects watched CSI-related television programming and implemented ideas they drew from various episodes.

Verbal Staging

Verbal staging is common in staging cases (Ferguson, 2011, 2015; Ferguson & Petherick, 2014; Hazelwood & Napier, 2004; Pettler, 2011; Schlesinger et al., 2012). Hazelwood and Napier (2004) argued that offenders might verbally stage by reporting the victim missing after the offender murders and disposes the body. Additionally, these authors argued that offenders verbally stage in a myriad of other ways as well. Verbal staging interrelates to conflict/confrontation and victim discovery, thus the integrity should not be assumed in statements provided by the discovering or reporting party and instead scientific inquiry should be used toward supporting or refuting verbal statements made by suspects.

The author calls the verbal staging-related unbelievable stories offenders sometimes tell to investigators *fish tales*. "His whole alibi is nothing but a fish tale … ." This means that everything the offender has said is implausible, far-fetched, really "out there," an exaggeration, and a complete lie, all of which departs from the truth and all of which meets the needs of the offender. The best predictor of future behavior is … that's right past behavior, so the fact that Scott Peterson claimed he went fishing on Christmas

Eve, the same day his wife went missing, but never went fishing before with no one even knowing he bought a boat prior to this date is the ultimate "fish tale." Peterson never went fishing, instead he was convicted of murdering his wife and unborn son and disposing of their bodies in the San Francisco Bay where he was "fishing" on Christmas Eve. Peterson sits on California's Death Row today.

Another great example of a fish tale is the story of Betty (Gentry) Neumar, who was charged, but who was never tried in the death of her fourth husband, Harold Gentry. The author was the lead investigator for the District Attorney's Office on this case and this information is straight from the file. Neumar claimed that prior to her husband's death, she saw a yellow Mercedes and that it had actually pulled into the driveway of the Gentry home. This claim was never substantiated and investigators in 1986 found this story to be highly unbelievable for extremely rural and somewhat modest Norwood, North Carolina, 52 miles east of Charlotte, North Carolina. This fish tale was designed to throw investigators off her trail and the trail of the individual she allegedly hired to kill Harold Gentry, a suspect who has never been arrested, but is suspected of being connected to the case.

Suspect Josh Powell's story is another great example of a fish tale. On the night Susan Powell went missing, Josh and Susan had a family friend over for dinner. The friend said Susan felt ill after the meal and lay down on the couch. The friend left soon after to allow Susan to rest. The next day Susan was reported missing and when questioned by police, Josh Powell said he saw his wife that evening before he left to take his two young children on an impromptu camping trip in the subzero degree weather a few hundred miles away. Josh Powell was not a camper or an outdoorsman, and like Scott Peterson's, this story was highly unbelievable. Susan Powell's body has not yet been recovered, but Josh Powell murdered his two boys and committed suicide a few years after Susan's disappearance. They will never grow up to remember and tell what they knew about the night of their impromptu camping trip with only their dad.

Overall, fish tales are unbelievable stories or stories that cannot be reasonably substantiated, corroborated, and so on, those that depart from routine activities, and what would normally be expected from an intimate partner, for example, upon finding their partner's body, being present when the victim allegedly ends his or her own life, has died as the result of an accident, or the claim that the victim ran off with someone else.

Another type of verbal staging are *prescriptive stories*. The author opines that such stories told by the offender to friends and family of the offender, victim, and/or the offender and the victim that keep family and friends at bay, delay action by friends and family, thereby buying time for the offender while trying to keep friends and family from becoming suspicious in general. Prescriptive stories come in all shapes and sizes, but research has shown that they are most often related to the totality of the victim (e.g., personality, cognition, behavior, emotionality, and enviroso-cioculturalism), but are specifically related most often to routine activities (Pettler, 2011). Likewise, prescriptive stories are designed by the offender or prescribed as you will for friends and family by the offender based on his or her relationship with all of them or as individuals in relationship to their relationships to the victim. For example, a young woman goes missing one day, which is immediately noticed by her mom who talks to her daughter several times a day. Her mom phones her daughter's boyfriend who tells the concerned parent that her daughter is out shopping and forgot her phone at home. The woman's mom knows her daughter is a "shopaholic" and her concern is eased ... for a short time. Several hours pass and the woman's mom phones her daughter's home again and again, the woman's boyfriend answers. He tells the mother that her daughter did come home, but left again to go out to dinner and drinks with friends and her phone was dead so she didn't take it. The mother again believes this is reasonable knowing her daughter enjoys frequent dinner dates with friends and is not concerned. The next morning, the mother receives a phone call that her daughter did not show up for work. The mother grows very concerned and phones her daughter's phone, with no answer, and then phones her daughter's boyfriend with no answer. The mother rushes to her daughter's house to find the mattress and bedding missing as well. The mother phones the boyfriend again and he answers this time. The boyfriend tells the mother he spilled paint on the mattress while remodeling the master bedroom as a surprise for his girlfriend who slept over at a friend's house because she had too much to drink and could not drive home and that he's been out shopping for new mattress and bedding to add to the surprise and did not hear his phone ring. In this scenario, the offender bought time by using the victim's routine activities to keep the victim's mother at bay. The mother believed the boyfriend when he told her that the victim was out shopping, eating dinner with friends, and having a few drinks. Meanwhile, what is really going on is that he's scouring every drop of blood from the couple's bedroom resultant from shooting his girlfriend in the head as she slept that previous morning and then burying her body in a shallow grave along a secluded mountainside in the middle of the night 75 miles from the couple's home.

Prescriptive stories meet the needs of the offender. Maybe it is time the offender needs, maybe an alibi, maybe people who can say, "Well he was concerned and calling around looking for his wife?" Whatever the need, the key to understanding the prescriptive story is to ask, "What need for the offender does this story meet?" or "How does the offender benefit from telling this story?" or "What is the payoff for the offender to tell this story?" Asking questions like these help narrow the scope of why an offender says what he or she says to family and friends.

Crime Scene Investigation

Crime scene investigation is a fluid, oftentimes fast-moving phenomenon that requires flexibility in critical thinking, along with keen problem-solving skills and the ability to think outside the box ... a lot. As the next three chapters proceed, it is important to recognize some key points about crime scene investigation and crime reconstruction as they relate to staging behavior in homicide cases.

A sound crime scene investigation is paramount to successful prosecution. Crime scenes come in all shapes and sizes and no two are ever exactly the same. It is arguable that an investigator's instinct is reflective of his or her personal and professional experience, which includes his or her envirosocioculturalism in that it aids in his or her assessment of how a crime scene presents. Any crime scene that departs from what even the novice investigator might recognize as being normal based on his or her experience could raise red flags that the things at a crime scene might not be as they seem. Maybe the crime scene has been tampered with before police arrival. This is an unknown factor upon arrival at the scene of course. And it is critically important to determine that if alterations to the crime scene do exist that they are not the result of emergency medical personnel, first responding officers, and so on, created during an attempt to render aid to a victim. Once aid-rendering and scene security alterations can be ruled out, but suspicion still exists as to the integrity of the scene, it is then time to begin the process of identification, documentation, collection, and preservation by crime scene processing personnel.

Because this is not a crime scene processing book per se, the author will not discuss specific crime scene–related processing methodology except to say that a standard protocol toward processing every crime scene the same way each time with a normal level of flexible variance is recommended toward consistency, accuracy, minimizing investigator bias, and any claim that investigators did something for one victim that they did not do for another. Because like victims and offenders, investigators are also people whose personality, emotionality, cognition, behavior, and envirosocioculturalism influence them as human beings. To argue that every investigator is a replica of the next to exact specifications would be erroneous at a minimum because investigators are individuals, but they are individuals who are charged with the duty of investigating deaths (for the purpose of this discussion) of other individuals while remaining objective, fair, and impartial. All investigations should be grounded in law and should be guided by ethics at all times. However, investigator bias, while safeguards to protect an investigation from it are necessary and appropriate, cannot be entirely removed from the investigative process, but it can be minimized. Simply speaking, investigator bias is the bias applied by an investigator to an investigation toward trying to make the evidence fit his or her theory instead of allowing the theory to emerge from the evidence.

First, as mentioned earlier, experience is extremely important to the investigation of staged scenes. Like in the study of psychology, one must learn what is "normal" before one recognizes the patterns of "abnormal" behavior. However, experience extends only to the brink of the individual's knowledge base, so it is also important to understand where one's experiential knowledge-base ends, thereby understanding the limitations of that organic edge, which then propels an individual to move toward figuring out how to observe new or different phenomena that occurs during the course of a crime scene investigation. One benefit the seasoned investigator has over the first year investigator is experience, but one's individual experience is *qualitative* or in context to that person specifically and is limited in scope by the edge of his or her own knowledge. In the research world, this type of experience is studied using qualitative research design, which means that qualitative researchers often observe study groups by way of open-ended interview questions and observation. This type of research is in sharp contrast to studying something quantitatively, which entails taking something like the total number of homicides reported each year and running statistics to determine how many of them were staged (a very simplistic example). With this said, it is best to combine quantitative data with qualitative data because the quantitative data gives you the "what" (i.e., how many crime scenes were staged) and the qualitative gives you the "how" (i.e., the way in which the crime scene was staged). They are both as important as the other. This is the very essence of the benefit of education, training, and learning about how research and its methodologies are beneficial to all types of investigators in the crime scene world. Education and training opportunities present information via mediums, such as books, conferences, internships, continuing educational courses, college, graduate school, postgraduate study, and during the pursuit of a terminal degree of some kind. This is not to say anyone or everyone requires or should have all of this or any of this, it is only to say that knowledge is power and knowledge is gained many ways. So, with that said, how does experience coupled with education, training, and research, interrelate to the concepts of crime scene staging?

The author has heard time and time again investigators say, "the crime scene appears staged." This is a very good starting point and is an example of the value of an investigator's experience telling him or her that when compared to his or her knowledge base, the crime scene departs from what would be normally expected in a scene of that nature. But what "appears to be staged" does not get a case to a jury. In both the academic and investigatory world, it is not what we think, feel, or believe, but rather it is what we know and can prove that propels a case toward the courtroom. For example, maybe a victim has a gunshot wound to the head right to left, front to back, and upward, but the firearm associated with the immediate area surrounding the victim is being held tightly in the victim's left hand, which might give investigators pause. While the position of the gun does not independently indicate staging or otherwise, what it does indicate is victimology needs to be done, the scene needs examined thoroughly, questions need to be asked, no ruling as to manner of death needs to be rendered at the scene, and lots of follow-up investigation is absolutely necessary ... and that is just for starters.

Assumption of Integrity

Turvey (2002) argued that law enforcement professionals might assume the authenticity of evidence left at a crime scene. Specifically, investigators who are attempting to reconstruct, recreate, or reenact the crime might mistakenly assume that the crime scene was left in a pristine condition upon the suspect's departure. Approaching every scene with caution and objectivity is arguably one safeguard that might help shield law enforcement professionals from assuming anything about the crime scene upon a cursory review. Several high-profile cases illustrate instances of staged crime scenes. So in using VCDIM and specifically the Staging Identification Trilogy, users can see that whether the appearance of the scene gives user pause or not, or whether or not there is a conflict/confrontation, victim discovery, verbal staging issue, the investigation lands in the same place ... Knowledge. And at the Knowledge level, the most important thing a CSI, investigator, detective, and so on, can do is to refuse to assume the integrity of the scene, thereby declining to accept it as it appears because the crime scene's appearance could be staged to meet the needs of the offender toward concealing his or her identity.

Staged crime scenes are those purposely tampered with where critical pieces of physical evidence are altered with criminal intent with the goal to avoid apprehension. These important pieces of evidence can be missed when rushing to process a scene, drawing conclusions about the case in the crime scene, superiors not allocating enough time to CSIs to process the scene properly and with care, CSIs are rushed to another call for service, or a whole host of other reasons.

So, the number one rule of crime scene investigation is to never assume the integrity of a crime scene regardless of resources, regardless of level of experience, regardless of level of education, and so on. That means never walk into a crime scene with the assumption that the way it appears is the way it happened. If the first thing an investigator or CSI does when walking in the door is assumes that he or she is looking at a pristine crime scene, the investigation can be arguably hampered from the beginning. Instead of forming a hypothesis, question, or theory about what happened before, during, and after the event and then searching for ways to affirm what one thinks, form a hypothesis, question, or theory about what happened and then try to disprove it. Behavior is not random and is normally motivated by some type of payoff, which might be gaining, regaining, or maintaining power, satisfying of anger, or countless other payoffs or gains. Therefore, the way the crime scene looks might be or might not be reflective of the particular motive of the murder, but every crime scene meets the needs of the offender. Consider that Turvey (2002) argued that offender characteristics might be inferred by reasoning from the facts developed during an investigation (p. 338). Further, Douglas et al. (2006) discussed how behavior mirrors the personality of the offender. Additionally, Walter et al.'s (2011) Crime Matrix that included a comparison between precrime, crime, and postcrime behaviors supports both arguments because elements of the offender's personality and behavior can be seen interwoven into many areas of countless cases before the murder of the victim, during the murder of the victim, and after the murder of the victim. The VCDIM is an expansion in part of Walter, Stein, and Adcock's Crime Matrix in that it incorporates the before, during, and after of a crime, but classifying those characteristics as empirical, quasi-empirical, or nonempirical for strengthening of circumstantial evidence toward potential prosecution purposes.

Constellation Theory

The conflict murder creates between the offender and investigators can send the investigation into a *tailspin* because the offender is often an incredible *spin*-doctor. Investigators are oftentimes left with a case where they know who the suspect is and why he or she is a viable candidate, but the case is purely circumstantial and the District Attorney's Office is not comfortable proceeding toward an arrest. This scenario is illustrious of too many cases to count. That idea also brings this discussion to constellation theory (see Figure 9.5), which is the author's idea of how circumstantial evidence-based cases can be linked. In relation to astronomy, a constellation is a group of stars that form a pattern in the sky. One star does not make a constellation, but it is several stars located in close proximity to each other that form a recognizable object that are often grouped and named after an animal or mythical creature. This definition sets up the major premise of constellation theory as it applies to circumstantial cases in that one piece of circumstantial evidence does not make a pattern and one piece of circumstantial evidence does not make a case, but several pieces of interrelated empirical (i.e., substantiated) pieces of circumstantial evidence located in close proximity to each other either by chronology/sequence, cause/effect, problem/solution, or by a similar relationship form a recognizable "object" or pattern called a fact pattern that can be grouped together toward organizing the timeline of events, the victim–offender conflict/confrontation, the payoffs the murder created for the offender, how everything about the murder met the needs of the offender, how the murder occurred, and so forth. Just like one bloodstain does not make a bloodstain pattern, one star does not make a constellation,

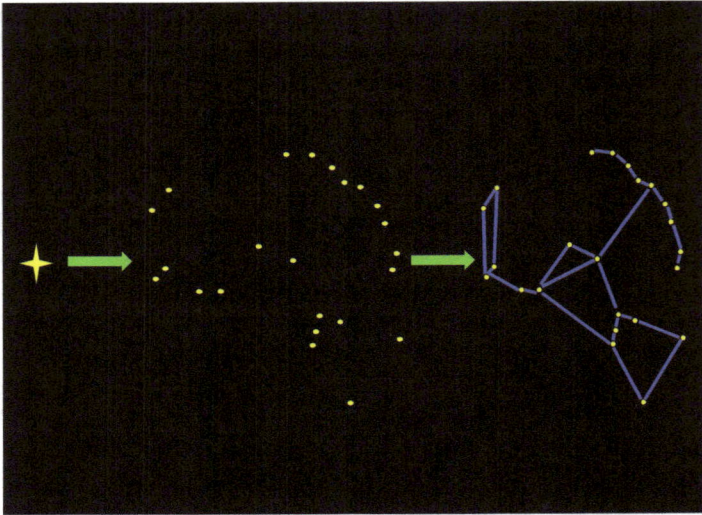

Figure 9.5 Constellation Theory

and one piece of circumstantial evidence does not make a case, but multiple pieces of circumstantial evidence can be analyzed, synthesized, and evaluated toward the establishment of a constellations of circumstantial pieces that might make a case when linked together.

The reason it is important to consider the Constellation Theory in relation to staging behavior is because by and large staged crimes are often circumstantial. As discussed in Chapters 7 and 8, staging is often seen in intimicide cases and various types of staged cases are often circumstantial at best. Therefore, keeping the constellation theory in mind and that "one battle does not win the war" might help drive the investigative process to get creative, really hone in on what *knowledge* truly is, and begin an investigation by striving to identify, define, and describe the precise measurement of the physical evidence while refusing to accept the appearance of the crime scene as pristine in conjunction with choosing not to assume the integrity of the critical evidence.

VCDIM Stage 2: Crime Scene Comprehension

Like the Crime Scene Knowledge stage of the investigation, Stage 2: Crime Scene Comprehension is also primarily quantitative or involves the precise measurement of the physical evidence. Once a CSI, investigator, or detective measures, identifies, and defines the critical evidence, it is time to begin to plan crime scene processing. When it comes to staged scenes, staging could be identified or detected during this phase of the crime scene investigation, but the goal would be to discover it during the initial phases of the investigation.

Normally, a crime scene investigation begins with a call to emergency services where patrol and/or first responders are dispatched. Upon their arrival and depending on what they find, medical aid is rendered to any injured party and then scene security becomes top priority. Obviously, it is completely reasonable and appropriate to put victim aid in front of evidence preservation at this time toward preservation of life. Once aid is rendered, live victims possibly removed, or deceased victims determined to be deceased, crime scenes are normally secured by at least one level of crime scene barrier tape and a crime scene log that captures who enters and exits, times, reasons, and so on, is established. A uniformed officer is normally in charge of maintaining scene security and logging those attending to the scene. Every law enforcement agency is different and handles things in unique ways, but the size of the agency often determines how things proceed from here. Some smaller agencies without in-house crime scene personnel might opt to call in a larger agency like a sheriff's office or the state police. Some sheriff's offices are very small as well and their only option for death investigations is to call in the state police. The state normally has crime scene personnel who will assist the requesting agency in processing the crime scene along with providing field agents who might assist with interviews or running down leads. There are many ways a crime scene investigation proceeds from this point, but one thing is for certain, the quality of the crime scene investigation is a reflection of the education, training, experience, and motivation of the crime scene investigator coupled with extraneous factors, such as allocation of resources, superiors directing crime scene personnel, how long processing may take, and so forth. The author has been part of many crime scene investigations, both good and bad. One of the best agencies the author ever had the pleasure to work with was the Rutherford County, North Carolina Sheriff's Office. The author witnessed on multiple death scenes the administration completely support crime scene personnel by setting up tents, lighting, bringing in food, brining in experts, extra manpower, and so on. This sheriff's office also worked crime scenes using a specific crime scene protocol so that every crime scene was worked the same way, generally speaking, every time. No one was ever rushed. The scenes were planned and processed very thoroughly. The author reconstructed several events with detectives from this sheriff's office who were well educated, well trained, and had tons of experience. While the Rutherford County North Carolina Sheriff's Office is a great example of very intricate, thorough, meticulous, painstakingly long hours of crime scene processing, the author has also seen the worst of the worst crime scene processing, which has stranded some cases without an arrest for years. In some of these cases, the author has witnessed less than 200 photos shot during a death investigation believed to be a homicide, but that was verbally staged as self-defense, evidence packaged in plastic and left for days in places it should never have been left, and very disturbing handling of bloodstain evidence rendering it useless to a bloodstain pattern analyst. Luckily, poor processing is not the norm, it is specific to the crime scene investigator and it is not a problem painted with a broad brush. To reiterate, processing a staged crime scene is tricky, it is complicated, it is not like processing a nonstaged crime scene, and, therefore, beginning to develop a plan for how to process the staged crime scene requires a systematic approach grounded in organizational structure that contains a plan to implement creative means toward capturing as much of the critical evidence as possible, latent or overt.

The crime scene processing plan for the staged crime scene might include several things, such as preparing to use chemical reagents or high-tech equipment that might help reveal latent evidence or calling in experts in specific disciplines to help unravel what investigators are seeing. When in doubt say, "I don't know," and ask; call in resources. The author coined the phrase, "The more I know, the more I know I don't know" to describe how the more one learns, the more one realizes the breadth and depth of the pool of available knowledge on a given subject, and in turn realizes just how much there is left to learn. One would opine that no practitioner is an expert in all areas and those who profess to be an expert and/or to teach in a variety of areas is the master of none. Of course practitioners should be multifaceted and generalists in crime scene investigation, but to claim expert status in too many subdisciplines is a red flag that may indicate overreaching.

As discussed in Chapter 3, crime scenes can be dynamic or passive; that is, they can demonstrate a tremendous amount of force and intensity against the victim or demonstrate virtually none. Crime scene processing and measurement of precise evidence must be reflective of the same dynamic. If a crime scene is static, meaning that there is one victim, in a small room, lying in bed, with a single gunshot wound to the head, crime scene processing might be limited to the entire house, but very specifically targeted to the room in which the victim is found. Likewise, the crime scene where impact blood spatter is found on the walls, ceiling, on the furniture, where a house is ransacked, items are immediately noticeable as being missing, for example, should be processed as dynamically as it occurred. It is important to not confuse the issue that all crime scenes should be processed thoroughly. The author advocates for concentric zone crime scene processing in death scenes, meaning the victim's body and immediate area are processed, then the concentric zone around the target area, then moving out in concentric zones from there. Within a concentric zone approach to processing, everything in each zone is searched, much like a grid search, and so on, but the zones are extended beyond the rectangular or generally square grid of the area immediately surrounding the victim's body. Additionally, crime scenes are three-dimensional and they should be planned to process as such. This means that the ceilings, walls, and floors should be processed and negating the ceiling or the floor or the walls literally leaves out one important part of the scene. The plan should include planning to search everything thoroughly because stagers can be sloppy and discard evidence in garbage cans in the scene thinking investigators are not going to search them. Plan to photograph, document, and search every inch of the crime scene and when everyone thinks that enough measurements have been taken, take more. Nothing is more frustrating later in the process than to have to try to figure out the size of a couch's cushion (e.g., height, depth, width), the size of a table, the size of a wall, and so forth. The author has spent weeks developing estimated crime scene measurements by using objects of standard size, such as playing cards, paper towel rolls, receptacle plates, and so on, toward establishing if reconstruction is possible in specific cases. "Precise measurement of physical evidence" means specific, accurate, and complete measurements of all objects related to the scene. There will be of course items that do not necessarily require inclusion, but it is hard to tell while working the scene what is important at the moment and what might be important later. Best practice is to plan to document the entire scene top to bottom using a standard method of measurement and multiple points of reference. Once all of the evidence has been identified and generally understood, evidence might be then classified by type, such as biological, firearms, impression, tool mark, and so on, which makes it easier to plan what is needed and what resources will be necessary to do it correctly the first time. Another great resource in this area is the crime lab. Crime lab personnel sometimes can be dispatched to aid in specific types of crime scenes, but even when that is not a possibility, phoning the lab to ask about the best ways to process certain types or even unusual types of evidence is critical to success. Again, "our system determines our outcome." Because this is not a crime scene processing book per se, the authors recommend reading a variety of crime scene processing books to glean an eclectic perspective of what published experts opine is useful and correct.

Pursuant to Bloom's Taxonomy's hierarchal arrangement, once initial knowledge is gained from the cursory review of the scene and the critical evidence is basically understood toward the development of an appropriate, accurate, and thorough plan for precise measurement of the physical evidence, types of documentation necessary to capture all relevant data, along with any discussion of the physical evidence among investigators, experts, crime lab personnel, or others who are assisting with the crime scene processing plan, it is then time to apply the crime scene processing plan.

VCDIM Stage 3: Application of the Crime Scene Processing Technology

Jumping from Stage 1: Crime Scene Knowledge to Stage 3: Application of Crime Scene Technology is a slippery slope because information in the Knowledge stage provides such a basic recognition of key crime scene

elements making it impossible to surmise immediately how to prepare, collect, preserve, and report precise measurement of physical evidence ... but
investigators do it all the time. Application is underpinned by Comprehension
and Comprehension is underpinned by Knowledge, so negating the importance of the Comprehension level in the process (i.e., document, planning,
and discussing the physical evidence) decreases the likelihood of achieving
the maximum results from crime scene processing.

Realizing that large law enforcement agencies who are inundated with
calls for service can easily get overwhelmed with multiple death scenes during one shift can benefit from developing a death scene crime scene processing protocol whereby every death scene investigation follows a specific
protocol to minimize bias and maximize opportunity for identified critical evidence recovery. The author advocates for a team approach in crime
scene processing, one that embraces diversity between those involved and
combines the education, training, and experience collectively among law
enforcement personnel, crime laboratory personnel, and experts in a multi-
tude of disciplines ranging anywhere from psychologists and criminologists
to entomologists and anthropologists. Dismissing the value of the assistance
of practitioners who specialize in concentrated areas of homicide, such as
staging, is to dismiss the value of multiple medical specialists consulting on
the same patient's complicated case in a hospital.

The application of a crime scene processing plan should include all elements of crime scene processing relevant to the physical evidence identified and defined during the initial phases of the investigation, which is
then classified and discussed toward the development of a plan for how to
properly process, meaning now the preparation, collection, preservation,
and reporting of the physical evidence. Again, because this is not a crime
scene processing book per se, specific crime scene processing methodology
for various types of specific evidence is recommended as it applies to the
staged crime scene.

Then here is where the twist comes in. During the documentation process of the physical evidence, precise measurement information is captured
thoroughly and accurately toward later potential reconstruction if deemed
appropriate and necessary. Reconstruction is not always ethically possible if gaps exist in the crime scene documentation because to reconstruct
based on incomplete information would be for the reconstructionist to go
out on a thin limb risking ethical practice and professional credibility. In
combination with documenting the "what," that is the quantitative aspects
of the evidence, such as size, shape, weight, and so on, it is now important
to put each piece of physical evidence in context of the scene by documenting the qualitative side of the evidence as well. For example, if there is a
couch in the crime scene, it is best not to just write down that there is a
couch. Instead, measure all aspects of the couch in case the original couch

is not available for reconstruction later and a substitute couch of similar size, shape, and other attributes must be obtained. Next, discuss the couch in great detail. Document the type of couch, color, firmness, fabric, structural soundness, defects, and so on. Assume the reader of the crime scene processing report knows nothing and it is the job of the crime scene investigator to provide a plethora of information about each piece of evidence. Documentation to this degree makes a huge difference in the later stages of the VCDIM.

To recap, knowledge is the foundation of the VCDIM. Within the scope of knowledge, figuring out the answer to key questions related to "is this crime scene staged?" can be instrumental in setting the trajectory of the investigation from onset through fruition. Refusing to assume the integrity of the crime scene is paramount to the identification and detection of just what might be both overt and covert physical evidence tampered with by the offender prior to law enforcement arrival. As the old British Army adage goes, "proper preparation prevents poor performance." So spending enough time in crime scene processing protocol and planning a systematic approach will help facilitate a positive outcome. Finally, applying the crime scene processing plan methodically, systematically, and accurately will have an impact on what can be done with the material during the latter stages of VCDIM (e.g., analysis, synthesis, and evaluation), therefore it is critically important to always do the best job possible with all available resources within reason toward providing every victim who dies under potentially suspicious circumstances the investigation that a human being deserves.

References

Bloom, B. S. (1956). *Taxonomy of educational objectives, Book 1, Cognitive domain.* White Plains, NY: Longman.

Douglas, J. E., Burgess, A. W., Burgess, A. G., & Ressler, R. K. (2006). *Crime classification manual: A standard system for investigating and classifying violent crimes* (2nd ed.). San Francisco, CA: John Wiley & Sons, Inc.

Eke, A. W. (2007). *Staging in cases of homicide: Offender, victim, and offence characteristics* (Doctoral dissertation). Retrieved from ProQuest (1390310091).

Ferguson, C. (2011). *The defects of the situation: A typology of staged crime scenes* (Unpublished doctoral thesis). Bond University, Gold Coast, Queensland, Australia.

Ferguson, C. (2014, July). Staged homicides: An examination of common features of faked burglaries, suicides, accidents and car accidents. *Journal Police Criminal Psychology.* doi: 10.1007/s11896-014-9154-1

Ferguson, C. (2015). Detecting staged crime scenes: An empirically derived "How-To." In W. Petherick (Ed.), *Applied crime analysis: A social science approach to understanding crime, criminals, and victims.* New York: Elsevier.

Ferguson, C., & Petherick, W. (2014, October 13). Getting away with murder: An examination of detected homicides staged as suicides. *Homicide Studies.* doi: 10.1177/1088767914553099.

Geberth, V. J. (2006). *Practical homicide investigation: Tactics, procedures, and forensic techniques* (4th ed.). Boca Raton, FL: CRC Press/Taylor & Francis Group.

Hazelwood, R. R., & Napier, M. R. (2004). Crime scene staging and its detection. *International Journal of Offender Therapy and Comparative Criminology, 48*(6), 744–759. doi: 10.1177/0306624X04268298

Maslow, A. H. (1943). A theory of human motivation. *Psychological Review, 50,* 360–396.

Pettler, L. G. (2011). *Crime scene behaviors of crime scene stagers* (Doctoral dissertation). Available from ProQuest (2251577601).

Schlesinger, L. B., Gardenier, A., Jarvis, J., & Sheehan-Cook, J. (2012, April). Crime scene staging in homicide. *Journal of Police and Criminal Psychology, 29*(1), 44–51.

Simmel, G. (1950). *The sociology of Georg Simmel* [Translated by K. H. Wolff] (pp. 13–17). Glencoe, IL: Free Press.

Taxonomy. (n.d.). In *Merriam-Webster's online dictionary* (11th ed.). Retrieved from http://www.merriam-webster.com/dictionary/taxonomy

Turvey, B. E. (2002). *Criminal profiling: An introduction to behavioral evidence analysis* (2nd ed.). London, UK: Academic Press.

Walter, R., Stein, S., & Adcock, J. M. (2011). Suspect identification using pre-, peri-, and post-offense behaviors. In J. M. Adcock, & S. Stein (Eds.), *Cold cases: An evaluation model with follow-up strategies for investigators.* Boca Raton, FL: CRC Press/Taylor & Francis Group.

Crime Analysis

10

Introduction

Emotionality is a dangerous thing. For example, sometimes rejection breeds blame, blame breeds anger, anger breeds conflict, and for some, that conflict is resolved by murder. Essentially, this chain of synapses can lead an offender to an emotional state where he or she loses control and a death occurs. Keep in mind that every murder has at least two motives: a specific motive and a general motive. According to Parker (2009), the specific motive is always different for every case. The general motive is why the killer murdered the victim; his or her motive is often related to some kind of conflict between the victim and offender, such as jealousy, an affair, unwanted pregnancy, money, intimate partner violence, and argument. However, the general motive is always the same for every case and that is not to get caught. And when an offender is caught, a suspect turns into a defendant and the general motive does not change, but the specific motive can change many times over the course of statements to investigators, family, friends, fellow inmates, jailers, and others, which then becomes the defendant's defense. Some defendants will argue that they were justified in the killing of their victim, while some will point the finger at someone else. Further still, some defendants try "No Crime" as a defense and stand firm that the death of the victim was suicide, accident, natural, or similar. In addition, common defense strategies when staging is present might be

1. Framing by investigators
2. Low-quality investigation
3. No due diligence
4. The CSI effect
5. No evidence of a crime
6. Death was an accident
7. Death was a suicide
8. Defendant did kill the victim, but it was....

All of the aforementioned are commonly heard arguments toward the establishment of reasonable doubt. Again, while there are no statistics on just how many crime scenes are staged each year, it is fair to say that some staged crime scenes are detected where the suspect is tried; some are detected where no arrest is made, but investigators know who the primary suspect is; and then

249

some go undetected being ruled suicide, accident, natural, or undetermined. Of the individuals who are arrested, they become defendants and successful prosecution of a defendant suspected of staging a murder can be very complicated because it often rests on circumstantial evidence. First, this type of prosecution involves developing strong evidence of the general motive, that is, establishing that there was a serious conflict between the defendant and victim that was resolved for the defendant by way of murder. Second, the prosecution must prove the defendant is lying. Third, the prosecution must prove motive two in that the defendant engaged in behaviors consistent with what the specific motive demonstrating consciousness of guilt. This is where the diligent investigator and his or her crime analysis can be helpful in some cases.

Victim-Centered Death Investigation Methodology: Outline

To reiterate from Chapter 9, victim-centered death investigation methodology (VCDIM) is a suggested method that can be used in equivocal death investigations toward establishing if the death of a victim was accident, suicide, homicide, or something else. Moreover, VCDIM is specifically useful when there is very little or no physical evidence in the case that points one manner of death in a case more than another. Further, VCDIM is also very good for cold case investigation and for other types of investigation in full or in part as well. The author recommends research of all of the methodologies published by credible authors on both the criminology side of the house and the law enforcement side of the house and finding something that is agreeable to all investigatory parties. Maybe the best thing to do is to be eclectic and draw from the parts of various methodologies that make sense for that agency. Regardless, "our system determines our outcome" and to not have a standardized death investigation methodology that is flexible and one that can be used in full or in part can lead to disaster on so many levels. Again VCDIM is divided into six stages using Bloom's Taxonomy as systematic scaffolding toward ensuring that each stage builds methodically onto the stage beneath and above while preventing "stage jumping" and toward making sure that all components for each stage are completed for use in the next stage:

1. Stage 1: Crime Scene Knowledge
   Type: Quantitative—Precise measurement of physical evidence
   Location: Level 1—Bottom, foundational level of Bloom's Taxonomy
   a. Is the crime scene staged? Staging Identification Trilogy
      i. Conflict/confrontation
      ii. Victim discovery
      iii. Verbal staging

b. Ferguson's (2015) empirically derived staging detection how-to.
c. Refuse to assume the integrity of the crime scene.
d. Identify and detect the staging behavior and/or staged physical evidence.
e. Define and describe the physical evidence.

2. Stage 2: Crime Scene Comprehension

Type: Quantitative—Precise measurement of physical evidence

Location: Level 2—One must identify, define, and describe, before one can classify and discuss:

a. Document the initial observations of the scene.
b. Classify and discuss physical evidence. This might not be done on paper, but should be discussed with lab personnel and/or experts if needed.
c. Develop plan for how to accurately, precisely, and appropriately meet the legal and scientific objectives of crime scene processing procedures and techniques.
d. Plan needed resources that might not be on hand, such as chemicals or other specialized equipment that could detect staged elements of the scene.

3. Stage 3: Application of Crime Scene Technology

Type: Quantitative and qualitative—Precise measurement of physical evidence in context of all evidence and crime scene as a whole

Location: Level 3—One can apply knowledge when the knowledge is acquired and understood:

a. Prepare to execute crime scene processing plan taking careful consideration to process for elements of crime scene staging; this could be additional photographs of angles not otherwise considered standard.
b. Precisely measure using multiple points of reference, crime scene search methodology, etc., all items of physical evidence in addition to crime scene measurements. For later reconstructive purposes, be sure to measure everything in three dimensions (L × W × H); the more detailed this section is, the more likely reconstruction might be able to be done.
c. Collect all physical evidence being sure to document all demographic information related to the evidence. One thing to note, the author has seen countless times bloodstain evidence lost due to inaccurate packaging. Allow wet items to dry, use paper to separate layers, and then package so nothing is touching another part of the item (i.e., bedsheet).
d. Preserve all items of physical evidence and document preservation efforts.

e. Report all crime scene activity and processing system, including agency protocol, investigative summaries, supplements, crime scene logs, evidence lists and corresponding documents, measurements, photographs, notes, and, and assemble into a well-organized system that can be easily reviewed (the author suggests using a binder system to *tab* and organize reports. The report should be robust in breadth and depth, and contain both quantitative (the what) and qualitative (the how/why descriptive) in order to help the reader understand all the details about any particular piece of evidence and the crime scene as a whole. Create a table of contents and place at the front of the binder. Tab the binder sections.

4. Stage 4: Crime Analysis

Type: Quantitative and qualitative—Studying the precise measurement of physical evidence in context and how it could be interrelated to the victim and other components

Location: Level 4—One can analyze the application once knowledge is acquired and understood:

a. Research-based forensic victimology—Using Maslow's hierarchy of needs as a conceptual framework to use the method and categories discussed in Chapter 5, conduct full victimological study on all victims and then use modified triangulation to determine if select information revealed in the study of the victim are empirical (can be validated and is reliable because it can be proven and substantiated), quasi-empirical (can be partially validated and/or is partially reliable possibly), or nonempirical (cannot be validated or relied upon because there is nothing to substantiate the information). Victimology is then used as a baseline for all other types of analysis, synthesis, and evaluation going forward.

b. Crime scene and laboratory reports—Analyze all crime scene reports contained in the binder from Stages 1, 2, 3 along with interrelating them to the forensic service laboratory reports, such as DNA, serology, and ballistics, to compare to victimology.

c. Autopsy and wound pattern analysis—In partnership with the forensic pathologist, medical examiner, coroner, or other relevant parties, break apart each pertinent aspect of the autopsy and then focus on studying the wounds to the victim. Complete wound analysis charts, diagrams, and spreadsheets to compare to crime scene, labs, and victimology.

d. Suspectology (or statement analysis)—It is the study of the suspect or suspects. Complete suspectology for each suspect. This substage could be switched with statement analysis. Determine what is empirical, quasi-empirical, and nonempirical and then compare to wound analysis, crime scene, lab reports, and victimology.

   e. Statement analysis (or suspectology)—For the purpose of this discussion, statement analysis is the breaking apart of statements, studying each piece, and then cross-comparing statements given at different times to possibly different individuals to identify, define, discuss, and then analyze very specific details related to the crime; this substage could be switched with suspectology. Determine what is empirical, quasi-empirical, and/ or nonempirical if necessary and then compare to suspectology, wound analysis, crime scene, lab reports, and victimology.

5. Stage 5: Crime Synthesis

Type: Quantitative and qualitative—Putting together all the pieces of the puzzle

Location: Level 5—One can synthesize all of the pieces of the analysis once the knowledge is understood and applied:

   a. Crime Synthesis Matrix—Place all analyzed pieces in their proper location of one or more of the three columns of the matrix: before, during, or after the crime; then take each piece listed in each column, and if not already done during the analysis stage, determine if each piece is empirical, quasi-empirical, or nonempirical; try to enter broad categories first and then underpin with the pieces of each.

6. Stage 6: Crime Evaluation

Type: Quantitative and qualitative—Drawing conclusions based on substantiation

Location: Level 6—Only when all other stages are complete, it is time to evaluate toward assigning worth, merit, or value:

   a. In partnership with the district attorney, state attorney, solicitor, prosecutor, or others, explain victim-based death investigation methodology, everything contained in the case, the system and method by which each piece was analyzed and synthesized, and then present all of the information for evaluation.

VCDIM Stage 4: Crime Analysis

Chapter 9 addressed VCDIM Stages 1 through 3: Crime Scene Knowledge, Crime Scene Comprehension, and Application of Crime Scene Technology. The next stage is VCDIM Stage 4: Crime Analysis. *Crime analysis* simply stated is the complete analytical study of a crime. To reiterate, analysis defined is to take the whole, break it apart into pieces, study each piece both quantitatively and qualitatively, and then reassemble the pieces back into a newly understood whole. The quantitative pieces are the "what" it (i.e., the piece) is and the qualitative is the "how/why" that something is. It is like saying, "That is a car." Ok, that is what it is. But it is a red car, large car, loud car, and so on, which is the "how/why" of the car, the context descriptive words. Crime analysis for the purpose of this discussion in regard to deaths that are possibly staged murders means death investigation-, murder investigation-, and homicide investigation-related analysis.

Again, *analysis* is Bloom's Taxonomy level 4, which includes analysis or breaking apart and the complete study of the physical evidence, medical evidence, behavioral evidence, testimonial evidence, victimology, and suspectology, toward gaining full *knowledge and comprehension*. When someone goes to the doctor, the doctor asks the patient for his or her medical history. The doctor uses the patient's medical history as a baseline to figure out what is going on. Sometimes there are things about a person's medical history that facilitate or precipitate an ailment that brought the person in that day. When someone becomes a murder victim, investigators need a baseline or "victim history" just like a medical history or again what is called *victimology* to figure out how and why that person became a victim. The victim–offender relationship is a reflection of the personality, cognition, behavior, emotionality, and envirossocioculturalism of the victim and offender together. It is who they are as individuals and as two people with a common association. And as statistics have shown, someone they know murders most female victims, and generally speaking, most murders occur between people who are associated and the murder is the result of an argument or conflict/confrontation.

To recap, when using VCDIM, the first step always for a user is to raise the question: *"Is the crime scene staged and/or does this scene give you pause?"* Next, the user works to address one to three variables that empirical research has shown, which is common in patterns of staging behavior conflict/confrontation, victim discovery, and verbal staging (Ferguson, 2011, 2014; Ferguson & Petherick, 2014; Pettler, 2011; Schlesinger, Gardenier, Jarvis, & Sheehan-Cook, 2012). Regardless of what is known about those three variables upon the investigation's onset, the case arrives at the same point, Stage 1: Crime Scene Knowledge. The knowledge level of VCDIM includes approaching the crime scene with an objective and open mind that focuses on the identification, documentation, collection, preservation, and the reporting of the precise measurement (quantitative: i.e., car) of the physical evidence in the crime scene. Additionally, crime scene reports must contain descriptive material (qualitative: i.e., a red car) related to the scene, the victim, and the evidence to orient the report reader to the locations and nature of all evidence in context of the crime scene, victim, and to other evidence. In other words, just do not stop at *car*. Reports should contain all relevant and important information related to the scene and the victim.

Once everything from the crime scene has been gathered for analysis, it is then important to gather all forensic service laboratory reports returned on evidence submitted to the lab for testing. Any given case can have an array of evidence that goes to the crime lab and reports are often slow to come back. Once those are gathered, the entire investigatory case file should be gathered as well. Necessary components for crime analysis are as follows, but not limited to:

- The law enforcement file
- The crime scene investigation file
- The crime laboratory files
- The autopsy report and photographs
- Other agencies' files if applicable
- Additional case-specific files and materials

VCDIM Stage 4: Crime Analysis—Component 1 (Victimology)

Victimology is essentially the study of victims. The victim–offender relationship is a reflection of the personality, cognition, behavior, emotionality, and envirosocioculturalism of the victim individually, the offender individually, and the victim–offender together as well. Chapter 5 of this book outlined a suggested approach to victimology called research-based forensic victimology using Maslow's hierarchy of needs as scaffolding (see Appendix A). This conceptual model can be implemented in VCDIM Stage 4: Crime Analysis— Component 1 (Victimology) to analytically study the victim. A review of Chapter 5 is helpful here to set up to study the victim. Much of what is needed might be found in the files attached to the case, but additional information could need to be filled in by family and friends that is not included in the case file. It is important when investigating potentially staged cases to include certain types of investigatory questions that are helpful in pointing the trajectory of the investigation in the right direction:

1. Who is in conflict with the victim?
2. Was there a confrontation of any kind between the victim and someone else prior to the victim's death?
3. Who has the victim rejected?
4. Who was angry with the victim?
5. Who was frustrated with the victim?
6. Who benefits from the victim's death?
7. What is the payoff or what is gained from the victim's death?
8. Whose lifestyle changes with the victim's death?
9. Whose environment was the victim killed in?
10. Is the victim familiar with the scene?

11. Who notified police of the discovery of the victim's body?
12. Is the person who notified police of the death familiar with the scene?
13. Did the person who discovered the victim's body offer "stories" to investigators and/or family/friends that might have sounded "unbelievable" about the victim, the victim's whereabouts, etc.?

This is only a sample of the types of questions that might be asked in relation to conflict/confrontation, victim discovery, and verbal staging with regard to other key elements of establishing if staging really should be considered a strong possibility in a case. Not every case is staged, but some cases are staged either verbally, physically, or both. Triage on the front end always saves time and effort on the back end. To the author, the list of questions provided earlier are like "level 1" type of questions meaning the answers lead to the next level of question. The author looks at this process kind of like an onion with lots of layers. These questions are the top layer of the onion, but the more layers investigators peel off, the more knowledge they will gain about the victim, the offender, and the crime itself. See Chapter 5 for details on conducting research-based forensic victimology as the component of VCDIM Stage 4: Crime Analysis.

VCDIM Stage 4: Crime Analysis—Component 2 (Crime Scene and Lab Reports)

The second component of VCDIM is Stage 4: Crime Analysis is an analysis of the crime scene, physical evidence, crime scene reports, and forensic service laboratory reports. It is helpful to complete victimology before analyzing the crime scene, physical evidence, crime scene reports, and forensic service laboratory reports because all of this information is compared to what the baseline victimology provides. Jumping the step or not completing victimology will leave holes in this phase, which weakens the structurally sound systematic inquiry into a case. The purpose of crime scene staging is ultimately to deceive by misdirecting an investigation in order to avoid apprehension, conceal the offender's identity, and, in the case of death of a victim, get away with murder. In order to analyze the crime scene, one must have working knowledge of crime scene investigation. There are many good books and online sources, professional associations, and the like that can assist one in becoming well versed in crime scene investigation especially as it relates to death scenes.

"Our system determines our outcome" so a systematic, organized, method for organizing and analyzing the crime scene, its evidence, its reports, and the forensic service laboratory reports is best. The author starts a "list of questions" for each component of the crime analysis process so questions do not get lost because it only got jotted down in the margin of an elusive page. The author also uses a series of customizable worksheets to organize and analyze the physical evidence, such as the "Physical Evidence Inventory and Information Worksheet" (see Appendix D) and, if the case does not contain one, the "Crime Scene Photo Log Worksheet" (see Appendix E). The author encourages investigators to create any spreadsheet he or she deems helpful in the organization, sorting, comparison, and analysis of the crime scene, physical evidence, crime scene reports, and forensic service laboratory reports during this stage. The following crime scene and laboratory pieces of information are necessary to dissect toward ensuring that a thorough and complete analysis has been done during VCDIM Stage 4: Crime Analysis—Component 2 (Crime Scene and Lab Reports). To note, there could be many additional pieces not listed which are included in a crime scene file that are very important as well, but some of the more common pieces are listed in Appendix H.

Victim Discovery and Notification

Again, the importance of identifying the last person to see the victim alive and the first person to discover the victim and to notify authorities cannot be understated. As mentioned and discussed in this and in previous chapters, empirical research on staging has shown that the offender discovers the victim's body most often in several types of staging cases (other than car accidents where strangers or police are more likely to discover the victim; see Ferguson, 2011, 2014; Schlesinger et al., 2012). The discovering person is a very important person. This is the person who has the information about what was going on at least right before finding the victim and definitely what was going on after finding the victim. In the case of murder, especially when the last person to see the victim alive is the first person to report finding/discovering the body, reporting the victim deceased meets the offender's needs. Everything about the crime before, during, and after meets the offender's needs somehow some way, so he or she decides that discovering the victim's body and/or reporting finding the victim or that the victim is missing is the method that meets his or her needs the most. For whatever reason, which could be summative theoretically based on the offender's personality, cognition, behavior, emotionality, and envirosocioculturalism combined with the CSI effect or a myriad of other reasons, the offender believes (not *knows*, thinks) that discovering the victim and reporting the victim deceased due to accident, suicide, natural, home invasion, interrupted robbery, burglary, and so on, is the best way to go.

Second, in the case of murder, the offender might be the last person to see the victim alive but chooses not to report finding the victim's body for possibly many of the same reasons discussed earlier as well. This is another reason why it is so important to gather the 911 call information as part of the onset of investigation. Whatever was said by the offender on the 911 call is the beginning of what he or she thinks is going to sell … what is believable. Therefore, the 911 call information can act as a sort of litmus test in the crime scene to test against toward determining if staging is present. This has been empirically found to be uncommon in staged cases at this point in the research, but again, as time goes on and more empirical research is published, information contained in this book could wane or gain strength in support or refutation of what is contained herein (and that is ok by the way; it is the result of moving forward). The point is for the investigators to recognize that not reporting finding the victim's body met the needs of the offender for a reason probably yet to be discovered. Discover the reason. The reason is very important. Behavior is not random and does not happen in a vacuum as discussed in an earlier chapter. Do not simply dismiss conscious decisions, such as notification and its related covert information because there are very clear reasons for why an offender chooses to report or not to report.

Third, an offender in the case of murder who is the last person to see the victim alive might also report the victim missing and/or report seeing the victim leave. There are countless examples of this when analyzing staged case after staged case. Analyze this type of notification by the offender and figure out how reporting being the last person to see the victim alive, being the first person to report the victim missing, and/or reporting to have seen the victim leave, meet the offender's needs.

Another method in which notification can occur is when the offender does not

- Report finding the victim's body
- Report the victim missing
- Report seeing the victim leave

In this case, not reporting any of the aforementioned scenarios meets the needs of the offender. The job of the crime analyst is to compare to victimology to figure out why. Most answers to most crime-analysis-related questions are contained in the victimology. If victimology has been done correctly, expansively, and very thoroughly, bouncing each scenario off the victimology as a baseline can be the very thing that helps the VCDIM user figure out how the notification style of the person of interest, suspect, defendant, and so forth, met the needs of that person. There is always a reason; behavior is purposeful. Remember that behavior is grounded in thinking. That means the offender thought that not reporting finding the body, the victim missing, or that the victim left is a "safer bet" toward concealing his or her involvement in the murder than to do the opposite.

Time, Date, Location, and Number of Crime Scenes
Beginning with the 911 call or notification call (some calls come into non-emergency numbers), any number of crime scenes might be identified. Callers

might be neighbors, victims, suspects, relatives, strangers, or others who have information for authorities. The individual who calls to find a body is very important. The individual who calls to say that he or she just witnessed an abduction is very important. The individual who calls to report a victim missing is very important. Times, dates, and locations are often given in the 911 call. Take, for example, the 911 call made by Cindy Anthony in the *Florida v. Casey Anthony* case. Casey's mother, Cindy, called 911 to report that she found her daughter Casey's car that day and that it smelled like a dead body had been in the trunk. This was a significant event for Cindy Anthony because she had not seen her 2-year-old granddaughter Caylee in about a month. So in this case, investigators immediately know that the car could be a crime scene. Generally speaking, it is important to study the initial contact location where the victim encountered the offender and study the murder scene location.

Initial Contact Location

Pettler's (2011) research revealed two interesting aspects about initial contact locations or the location wherein the victim encountered the offender in 15 of the 18 staged analyzed cases:

1. *Familiarity*: The offender was familiar with the initial contact location.
2. *Risk level*: The offender risked being seen, heard, or both when contact was made with the victim.

It was also interesting that 16 of the homicide case files contained information showing that the victims were also familiar with the initial contact locations, but 7 of the initial contact locations were deserted. Second, 17 of the initial contacts were indoor locations with 14 being single-family dwellings. The conversation of crime analysis for elements of staging is important because many murders motivated by the offender's need to satisfy anger occur in familiar locations to the offender, such as in the offender's residence. To further support this idea, eight of the initial contact locations in Pettler's (2011) study were the common residences of both the victims and the offenders and clearly both parties were familiar with the surroundings. In contrast, only three of the initial contact locations were the residences of the victims alone and only three were the residences of the offenders alone. Regardless, again, the initial contact location where the offender encounters the victim meets the needs of the offender. However, it is interesting to note that two offenders in Pettler's (2011) study were completely unfamiliar with the initial contact location where they met their victims, and likewise, only one victim was unfamiliar with the initial contact location where he or she met his or her attacker. The type of location is also important when conducting crime analysis. Was the initial contact location the home, the place of work, a social location, or something else where the victim first encountered the offender? In three cases analyzed in Pettler's (2011) study, the initial contact locations were the victims' places of employment and only one of those locations was the offender's place of employment as well.

Murder Scene Location

Like initial contact location, the murder scene location is also an important piece of the puzzle when analyzing the crime scene or crime scenes. According to research, crime scene stagers more often kill in familiar locations than unfamiliar locations (Pettler, 2011). Interestingly, many of these murder scene locations are also familiar to the victim. Common familiar locations include single-family dwellings of both parties, the victim, and/or the offender. The type of murder scene location is also very important. These tend not to be random and tend more to be selected by the offender because it meets his or her needs. Research has shown that some murder scene locations are not visible to others, while some are indoor locations or concealed outdoor locations. Again, regardless, the point of the murder scene location is that it meets the needs of the offender. The questions that need to be answered are how and why? The reason the qualitative (how and why) is important here is because it helps establish more timeline events, the sequence of events, and hones in on support for the specific motive in some cases.

Victim Recovery and Disposal Site Location

The body is evidence and is a crime scene itself. In some jurisdictions, the medical examiner is responsible to process the body and immediately surrounding areas while the law enforcement agency is in charge of the rest of the scene. Victims can be recovered from both indoor and outdoor locations. According to Pettler's (2011) study on crime scene staging behaviors of crime scene stagers, the victims in the study's sample were recovered from various locations. Interestingly, 12 victims were recovered from outdoor locations as compared to 6 victims who were recovered from indoor locations. Additionally, 13 locations were virtually deserted, though 10 locations posed a risk for being detected. Further, 12 victims were familiar with the locations as compared to 5 victims who were unfamiliar with the recovery locations. Further still, 11 offenders were familiar with the recovery locations in comparison to 7 offenders who were unfamiliar with the victim recovery locations, yet 10 locations were single-family dwellings, 6 were common residences, 1 was the offender's residence, and 3 were the victims' residences. Finally, 5 victims from the sample in Pettler's study were recovered in wooded locations, 2 from their vehicles on public streets, 1 victim from a vacant field, and 1 victim from a river.

By using even the small number of cases in Pettler's (2011) study, it is observable that recovery location can be just about anywhere. But that does not mean a dump site; hence, recovery location is random. The author would argue against the notion that dump site is random and instead would argue that the dump site/recovery location meets the needs of the offender. Figuring out how and why that particular location meets the offender's needs is part of the crime analysis process.

Victim's Condition at the Time of Recovery   Victim recovery can occur at any time after a victim is murdered or has gone missing; therefore, victims are recovered in all phases of decomposition and in various conditions as well. Exposure to the elements plays a major role in the decomposition process just as water does. Geberth (2006) argued that in his career, he worked staged homicide cases that were staged as sexual homicides. In cases like this, it is common for the victim to be recovered partially clothed. Further, it is also not uncommon if it meets the needs of the offender for victims to be found completely naked and exposed. Victims are also found wrapped in something sometimes, such as tarps, bedding, plastic, or other materials. In support of these ideas, Pettler's (2011) study included six victims of the sample who were found wrapped in bedding or plastic, three victims who were buried completely, one victim who was submerged in water, two victims who were recovered as skeletal remains, three victims who were partially decomposed, six victims who were completely decomposed, one victim who was recovered burned and charred, and five victims who were recovered fully clothed.

Pay close attention to the victim's hair. In many cases, if the victim has longer hair, the position of the hair could indicate movement. Like bloodstain evidence, hair moves when a force is applied to it. So keep in mind that the way in which the hair looks could be important toward the determination if a scene is staged or not. Take, for example, the victim with long hair who is dragged by his or her feet along a carpet by an offender. The author has worked cases where offenders tire during the dragging process and in turn leave the body in a location where it can be dragged no further. Observe the hair. In this case, if the victim is face up, the long hair should be trailing behind the victim. Likewise, if a victim with long hair is thrown down onto the floor lying on his or her back, the victim's hair could splay outward from its roots in somewhat of a circular shape around the head of the victim. Further, a victim who is sleeping in bed on his or her back who is then shot in the head and rolled over with force onto his or her side might have hair that is pointing upward from the roots and in the direction of motion. While there are numerous examples and scenarios that could be discussed herein, the most important thing to remember is that the hair of the victim could lead to information about how the victim was moved around the scene and/or how the victim came to rest in the recovery location.

Additionally, like hair, clothing is important to analyze. Clothing that is bunched up around the victim's chest could indicate that the victim was dragged by his or her feet but could also be a staging behavior to create the appearance of a sexually based homicide. Likewise, pants that are partially pulled down and/or unzipped could indicate deliberate attempts by the offender to stage a sexually based homicide. For many reasons, some offenders believe that a sexually based homicide must present in a certain way in order for investigators to buy it. This is not always the case, but in some cases it is very true. Other considerations as mentioned earlier in relation to Pettler's (2011) study are that clothing can be partially removed or completely removed from a victim for a myriad of reasons. If the clothing is removed from a victim, partially removed, bunched up, rolled up, or otherwise, consider the alternatives during clothing analysis toward identifying how the condition of the clothing met the needs of the offender. Clearly, clothing that is gathered due to dragging is resultant of that behavior, but otherwise, consider alternatives with an open mind.

These are only a few considerations when broaching the subject of victim condition at the time of recovery. Best practice during the analysis phase is to keep an open mind, do plenty of research, contact plenty of experts who have knowledge in specific areas who can help guide the process, and never assume a thing.

Position of the Victim's Body in the Crime Scene   The position of a victim's body is also very important when analyzing a crime scene because an offender can move a body into a certain position to try to make it appear as though the victim was killed in an accident or committed suicide, for example. Paying close attention to the rigor mortis and liver mortis on the body can yield powerful clues as to how the victim might have been positioned prior to being found in its final resting place. Moving a body after death is a slippery slope in some cases and offenders sometimes, as mentioned earlier, give up midway through the process. What makes this so significant is that if the body was positioned one way for a period of time where rigor mortis and liver mortis had an opportunity to set in, disturbing that position by moving the body into a different position can be telling of manipulation of the scene with ill intent.

Sometimes offenders stage crime scenes in the murder scene location, but victims might also be found in car trunks, in fields, and in other locations that meet the needs of the offender. The recovery position of the body does not necessarily mean the body was in that position originally. Pettler's (2011) sample yielded results consistent with 10 victims having been found lying face up in contrast to 3 victims who were lying face down. Another victim's body was recovered curled up in the trunk of her vehicle with her pants unzipped and her shirt pulled up around her neck, while the original body positions of the victims in Pettler's study whose bodies were recovered as skeletal remains were unknown. Additionally, two victims' bodies in Pettler's study were found in the sitting position and one victim's body was recovered lying on her side.

Bloodstains on the body can also help determine if a body has been moved after having stayed in a certain position for at least a while after death.

Once a body dies, blood stops circulating and settles in due to gravity, commonly known as lividity (James, Kish, & Sutton, 2005). Lividity is important to crime analysis and the analysis of the body because areas of compression will appear white while areas that are not compressed will appear reddish or reddish blue (James et al., 2005). After about 24 hours, lividity becomes fixed, or in other words, it does not change any more if the body is moved. For bodies that are moved after a period following death, lividity could be close to becoming fixed and can therefore yield information to investigators about the original position of the body following death. Sometimes offenders require a long period of time to stage a scene in a specific way while the lividity in the body gets closer to becoming fixed. Lividity is also important when in relation to taking the shape of an object that is pressing on the body. If a set of keys, for example, is beneath the body at the time of death, it could be that an impression of the keys might be created as lividity sets in. Then if the offender moves the body and turns it over, investigators might notice what looks like a set of keys on the skin of the victim, but with no keys in sight, such a finding warrants further inquiry. It is important to remember to pay close attention to the lividity in the body because it can sometimes help determine if in fact the body has been moved postdeath. This is critically important information when analyzing a case where the claim of suicide is being made.

First Responders

First responders often hold some of the most valuable information to analyzing a case. First responders might encounter the suspect and/or victim first before anyone else arrives. First responders might help identify *transient evidence*, such as the way the crime scene smells, looks, "tastes," sounds, and feels. While some of this is purely subjective, it cannot be denied that odors can dissipate quickly so documentation of all types of transient evidence, such as odors, is very important. Second, first responders, such as Emergency Medical Services (EMS) and medics, might render aid to a victim in hopes of preserving life. Alteration to the crime scene and the victim can occur when aid is administered, so knowing what was done, how it was done, who did it, why they did it, and so on, is very important toward ruling out criminally motivated alteration of the scene. Gather all emergency service records and study their response to the call, with the victim, and in the scene at a minimum. Break apart each piece and be sure to ask questions about any of the medical treatments administered to gain full understanding of anything that could have altered what investigators encountered in the crime scene.

Crime Scene Logs

The less people in the crime scene the better, or so they say. The author has seen crime scene logs with more than 20 individuals entering and exiting over and over again. While some of that is definitely normal, as mentioned in Chapter 9, processing the scene in concentric zones might be an option toward decreasing the traffic in and out of the crime scene toward preservation and preventing contamination. Contaminated evidence is not good; it will not fly and is rendered useless if any person "walks on it." Less is more in the crime scene log sense, from the standpoint that although it is reasonable to need assistance to process some evidence or the crime scene in general, it is not reasonable to allow 10 people who have nothing to do with processing the scene into the scene "so they can see." Analysis of the crime scene logs is important to crime analysis because it alludes to yet other ways in which the scene could have been altered unintentionally as it could be by medical intervention. Find out what each individual was doing at the scene and in the scene to help narrow the scope for the purpose of overall analysis.

Points of Entry and Exit

When it comes to indoor crime scenes, it is very important for investigators to identify and investigate all points of entry and exit in a crime scene. Some points of entry and exit might be easily accessible from the street, while furniture or other things in the house might normally block other points of entry and exit. During the crime analysis phase, retrieve information that confirms which points of entry and exit could be used, how they are normally used, and what their status was before the event and after the event. It is less likely unless a witness provides such information that a lot of information might be available about the status of points of entry and exit during the event. Analyze each point of entry and exit and record the most important information for each one based on what is contained in the file. Ask crime scene personnel questions to help fill in any blanks. Deductive reasoning could be applied here in that if a particular entry point or exit point is normally blocked by furniture, for example, then it is a most likely and reasonable postulate that the offender did not enter or exit from that particular point.

When it comes to points of entry and exit in outdoor scenes, there could be many more options. Like with indoor scenes, deductive reasoning is helpful here, that is, figure out which ones are the lowest on the totem pole for reasonable access into or out of the crime scene. Rank those lowest. Figure out what is logical, what is illogical, what is easy, what is difficult, and so on. Now that the "what" (quantitative) is established, ask "why" (qualitative) and support or substantiate the rank order. This way, if someone inquires as to which ones are more likely versus less likely, the recorded information provides both the what and the why. It is always very important to not only identify what something is, but also why it is, how it is, and in context to the totality of the crime scene.

It is important to analyze the condition of the crime scene during crime analysis. When something does not appear normal in a crime scene, some investigators might say, "it appears staged." According to Chisum and

Turvey (2011), these types of subjective *feelings* investigators feel might be correct, but what one *thinks, feels,* or *believes* is not what stands up in court; rather, it is what is *known and that can be proven* that stands up in court. Chisum and Turvey argued that forced entry, for example, is not a sign of staging per se because forced entry is seen in both staged and nonstaged crime scenes. Another example might be when investigators notice drawers rummaged through where a search for valuable is apparent. Again, same thing, drawer rummaging is seen in both staged and nonstaged crime scenes, so rummaged drawers alone do not get investigators closer to determining if the scene is staged or not. Third, missing items from a crime scene do not necessarily mean it is staged, but research has shown that often, items, such as bedding, mattresses, furniture, and other items, are missing from staged crime scenes (Pettler, 2011). Interestingly, in contrast, it is important to note that likewise, items like the victim's timepiece, wallet, handbag, and car keys might be recovered in the crime scene even when the victim is reported missing by the last person to see the victim alive.

A certain amount of suspicion is healthy, but only when guarding against investigator bias. At no time should crime scene personnel or those involved in the analysis of the crime in general engage in trying to make the evidence fit a certain theory. No agency *wants* a homicide, but the author has watched a few investigators try really hard to convince themselves that a death is a suicide because they do not want it to be homicide. Clearly the reason no one wants a homicide is because the amount of work a homicide requires differs tremendously from how much work a suicide requires from investigators. It does not make it right, but this has been the observation of the author in a few cases. Sometimes investigators want a case to be a suicide because they do not know what to do. The physical evidence does not reveal a smoking gun and they cannot figure out where to start...VCDIM. Anchor the investigation with a sound crime scene investigation and then start with the victim using a systematic approach. The answers lie there. So remember that the major premise of constellation theory is that one star does not make a constellation, but several stars within close proximity to one another can be grouped together to make a constellation just as one ransacked drawer does not indicate a scene is staged, but several behaviors discovered within in the condition of the crime scene that are interrelated can be grouped together toward establishing a pattern of staging or not in some cases.

Documentation

The importance of crime scene documentation cannot be understated. Without documentation or with incomplete documentation, many times an investigation and especially a reconstruction is halted. No one can do anything without crime scene documentation. It is the core of crime scene investigation. It has been the author's experience that the more tedious, meticulous, detail-oriented, organized an investigator is in his or her own personality and the way he or she normally lives his or her life carries over into making those types of people some of the best crime scene investigators because they take so much time and put so much effort into making sure they document every layer of the onion. On the flip side, individuals who are the opposite forget to write things down, do not measure everything the way things need measured, do not include both quantitative and qualitative information about every item of evidence, and who overall simply do not have the organizational skills to systematically investigate a crime scene are those who are normally like that in life in general as well. The author has analyzed all sorts of crime scene documentation styles and the more systematic and organized, the more it can be analyzed during Stage 4.

Notes

In relation to documentation overall, the crime scene notes provide the narrative in part in addition to the overall crime scene report that illustrates everything that occurred and everything that was done, what was found, and so on in the crime scene. The goal is that all of the pertinent information is contained in the crime scene report, but notes of all kinds can be helpful in filling in any gaps that might exist. Notes come in all shapes and sizes: sticky notes, notebook paper, and scraps of paper, all phone messages, and all kinds. It is critically important to analyze every kind of note from handwritten to notes entered in a word processor by computer. Sometimes it is one name, one comment about a piece of evidence, or one notation about a victim that turns a case on its end. Notes are critically important. For CSIs and investigators, note taking should start when they are notified of the call. From there, the notes should intertwine with the rest of the investigation. Be sure to verify with investigators, first responders, CSIs, and all others that all notes have been recorded and turned over for analysis.

Photographs

"A picture is worth a thousand words" and "if it is not documented or written down it didn't happen" are clichés familiar to investigators. To get straight to the point, a death investigation case file should be saturated with photographs. Those who investigate various types of crime know that both of these clichés appear to be true especially since the dawn of the CSI-related television-programming era. The complete reliance on testimonial evidence alone to meet the burden of proof during a murder trial is now a slippery slope. Once a primary type of evidence presented during court proceedings, testimonial evidence was offered toward asserting the matter asserted (Parker, 2009).

Every crime scene should be photographed systematically macro to micro or large to small. Every crime scene should be photographed overall, in the mid-range, with close-up shots, and some close-up with scale. Every item of evidence should be photographed using four vantage points: overall, midrange, close-up, and close-up with scale. There can never be too many photos. The author has worked cases with 10 or less instant photographs commonly seen in the 1990s to cases with hundreds if not more than 1000 photographs. The number of photographs shot in a crime scene is driven by the crime scene, the number of scenes, the nature of the scene, the processing elements, the number of victims, the number of items of evidence in the scene, and a myriad of other factors. For the purpose of crime analysis, gather every photograph shot by anyone and everyone from cell phone photos to official case photos with an agency-issued camera to bystanders, witnesses, and victims, autopsy photos; all photographs are needed toward ensuring accuracy and thoroughness of the photographic aspects of the analysis. The author suggests categorizing case photos in groups like victim, suspect, crime scene, autopsy, and physical evidence. To be correct, all cases should also contain a photo log, but many cases do not. It is very common to work a murder case without a photo log and the author suggests that the crime analyst make one for all photos if one does not exist.

If a photo log is not included in the crime scene material, the author recommends building a worksheet that can help categorize what the photographs are (see Appendix E). Categorizing the photographs by identification, description of the subject, and the time and date the photograph was taken, coupled with photographer information and/or another important information, makes it easy to go right to the photo needed for any future analysis.

Measurements

The precise measurement of physical evidence both quantitatively and qualitatively is done in Stage 3: Application of Crime Scene Technology when the crime scene processing plan is executed systematically, with accuracy, and with precision. The end result is only going to be as strong as the foundation and the quality of the crime scene investigation is reflective of the crime scene investigator's skill set, so hopefully at this point, the individual conducting the crime analysis will find that the case is saturated with measurements. The author recommends organizing all of the physical evidence on a worksheet that can be used as both an inventory and information database (see Appendix D). It could be helpful to include the precise measurements of the physical evidence, additional diagrams, and CADs toward organizing each piece, studying it, and then plugging it back into the scene. Later in the analysis process, measurements play a key role if needing to reconstruct a bullet's trajectory or bloodstain evidence.

Sketches and Maps

According to Gardner (2012), crime scene sketches and crime scene mapping are very different things. Crime scene sketches are often freehand drawings that illustrate the layout of the crime scene and contain all the fixed items of physical evidence and their corresponding measurements in relation to the scene, while crime scene mapping is the documenting of these measurements (p. 183). Crime scene sketches come by way of various levels of quality, but in addition to the crime scene photographs, the crime scene sketch serves as the graphic documentation of the crime scenes. Crime scene sketches show the interrelationships between the items of physical evidence in their proper orientation and layout as supported, again, by the crime scene photographs. Crime scene sketches are very important to the crime analysis process because these sketches help analysts understand how each piece of physical evidence interrelates to the others. Crime scene sketches are also very important to the reconstructive process because they help in hypothesis development and recreation of the crime scene overall itself. Crime scene sketches in homicide cases or for death scenes should be intricate, meticulous, tedious accounts of the scene representative of all of the aforementioned with the addition of in-depth information about proximities of evidence and precise measurements in a three-dimensional (3D) manner to include, on indoor scenes, the floors, walls, and ceilings and various elevations for outdoor scenes. Sometimes free-hand crime scene sketches are converted using CAD programming later to draw the scene to scale by computer instead of by freehand only. Regardless, all crime scene sketches in death investigations should contain a heading, the area diagramed, a sketch legend, the title of the sketch, the sketch scale, directional areas that orient the sketch and the author opines, the sketcher's name, the time, date, location, and other important case information. The author has found cross-projection sketches or what are sometimes called exploded view sketches to be very helpful because they are overhead views of the crime scene's horizontal surfaces, such as the floors, walls, and ceilings along with elevation sketches, which contain vertical surfaces like walls viewed from the side. Either way, analyzing the crime scene sketches and maps is a very important step of the crime analysis process.

Evidence Lists

The author uses the Physical Evidence Inventory and Information Worksheet (see Appendix D) to list all items of evidence in the crime scene case file. Each item is listed and the corresponding information associated with the item of evidence is recorded in the chart, such as

- Item number
- What report and/or list and page number it can be found on
- Recovery location information
- Recovering CSI, investigator, detective, etc.
- Time and date of recovery
- Type of packaging used to collect item
- Overall photo in file

- Midrange photo in file
- Close-up photo in file
- Close-up scale photo in file
- Item measurements
- Requested laboratory tests
- Pending and/or lab test results
- Notes
- Additional categories as needed on a per case basis

The author has found creating a chart of this nature to be monumentally helpful in understanding what is contained in the case file, but might need follow-up, what is missing from the case file, and so on. Of course, the author prefers to color code the worksheet, as can be seen in Table 10.1.

The worksheet is very easy to make using a spreadsheet database-type computer program and can be customized to meet the users' needs. Items in green in the chart represent the "all clear" for the item, no further inquiry necessary. Items in yellow in the chart represent the "need more info" items. The blocks in red mean that the information is missing from the case file. The items in blue mean lab tests are still pending. Items in gray mean that the information normally recorded in that cell is not necessary or expected for that specific type of item. Once a chart of this nature is complete, for the purpose of reconstruction consideration later, the user can see exactly what he or she has to work with and what might be able to be resolved using a different approach, piece of evidence, and so on.

Reports

Gather and analyze all reports. Contribute to the running list of questions. Be sure to verify that all case file supplements are contained in the case file for analysis and that there are no missing pieces. Analyze the reports by category, sort the information, and enter pertinent information into the Physical Evidence Inventory and Information Worksheet, the Crime

Table 10.1 Physical Evidence Inventory and Information Worksheet Key

	OK, all present and accounted for
	Need follow-up
	Missing
	Lab tests pending
	Item not necessary
ws	Photo with scale
B	Photo is blurry

Scene Photo Log Worksheet, or other spreadsheets customized for the case. Capture as much of the information for later use in the most systematic way possible to keep everything organized and easily understandable for everyone involved.

Many times, evidence is sent to the crime lab for testing. Some of the test results might take a long time to get back. Analyze the reports in relation to the crime scene and its evidence. Compare and contrast against the crime scene and victimology. Note any significant findings and preserve for later comparison to the other components of crime analysis.

Evidence of Staging

This is an introductory book, so there is no possible way it could contain everything intricately necessary to teach every minute step of VCDIM in fine detail. Therefore, the goal is to provide some general guidelines for crime analysis pursuant to some of the most common informational items in death investigation case files. It is important to remember that while the literature on crime scene staging is fairly sparse and lacks substance, the generally accepted definition of staging relates to manipulating evidence for criminal intent rather than including loved ones who find a relative or friend deceased and alter the scene to preserve dignity.

Crime analysis requires the breaking apart of each piece of evidence to study all of its specific parts, how they work, why they work, and the like and then by reassembling them into a newly understood whole; the user then can plug that piece of evidence into the "puzzle" later in the process. Crime analysis requires an intricate system that captures as much macro to micro data about each piece of evidence as possible. Beginning with a full victimological study using research-based forensic victimology underpinned by Maslow's hierarchy of needs as conceptual framework is very helpful in this process (see Burgess, Regehr, & Roberts, 2010; Petherick 2015; Turvey, 2014 for more examples of victimology). The VCDIM user can immediately understand where the victim is strong, where the victim is weak, how the victim might have become a victim, who was in conflict with the victim, and other important related facts. Second, the VCDIM user then analyzing everything contained in the crime scene case file and when finished can compare and contrast the crime scene information to the baseline victimology toward gaining more understanding about how the victim behaved in the crime scene and how a suspect might have behaved toward the victim in the crime scene, along with other critical information about the victim and a potential offender.

Once the basics are taken care of, victimology and crime scene information data analysis, the next step is to analyze the crime scene by possibly using laboratory reports, photographs, sketches, and other resources to ascertain if staging appears to be present and if so how can it be substantiated. Several key points are relevant to this part of the analysis, such as but not limited to the notification to authorizes that the victim was deceased, injured, missing, and so on, the number of crime scenes discovered and processed by investigators, the initial contact location of the event, the murder location, and the body recovery location.

Svensson and Wendel (1974) argued, "a clever murderer may very well arrange an accident, or make the death appear to be due to a suicide" (p. 439). Since then, while very little resources have been dedicated in the scholarly world to studying crime scene staging, experts appear to agree that crime scene staging is criminally driven by the intent to misdirect the criminal justice process. However, like Hans Gross in 1924, Svensson and Wendel (1974) were most concerned with how suspicious deaths were handled by investigators. For more than 100 years, the core of the methodology has remained the same when discussing how to properly investigate a potentially staged crime scene, that is, in a well-planned, well-organized, systematic, and analytical manner while assuming nothing and meticulously comparing every forensic piece of evidence to the other pieces of the crime toward supporting or refuting the act of staging (Chisum & Turvey, 2011; Eke, 2007; Ferguson, 2011; Geberth, 2006; Gross, 1924; Pettler, 2011; Svensson & Wendel, 1974). The power of method helps accomplish numerous objectives, such as defining technique, processes, and routines along with organization of thought, ending aimless wandering, while helping ideas to take shape. Method gives us a route to new knowledge and keeps the analysis on track by avoiding haphazard guesses, wasted time and energy, confusion, mistakes, or misdirection due to incorrect analysis.

"A major part of the crime scene analysis depends on the analyst's insight into the dynamics of human behavior, speech patterns, writing style, verbal and non-verbal gestures, and other traits and patterns compose human behavior" (Douglas et al., 2006, p. 32). When investigators realize very early in an investigation that the earmarks of staging might be present, it saves valuable resources, such as manpower, time, and money. Instead of going in the wrong direction, the detection of crime scene staging behaviors helps point the investigation in the right direction. There are five manners of death: natural, accident, suicide, homicide, and undermined. Natural deaths are those that occur by the organic consequences of old age, for example. Accidental deaths can be just about anything, such as drowning and car accidents. Suicide is a death that occurs by purposeful self-infliction with the intent of ending one's own life. Individuals commit suicide in many different ways from shooting oneself to asphyxiation and everything in between. Homicide does not mean murder, it simply means that one individual killed another individual; however, murder means that the death occurred with criminal intent. When everything in a case has been compared to the criteria for natural, accidental, suicide, and homicide and there are still lingering questions for at least more than one of the latter, sometimes medical examiners, coroners, forensic pathologists, or others will rule a death *undetermined*, which generally means that a manner of death could not be concluded at that time. This is not to say that the investigation into the death of the individual does not continue; it very well might in some cases, but in others, manpower, lack of training, lack of resources, or a whole host of other blockades often prevent undetermined cases from really moving forward with vigor.

When a murderer stages a crime scene to make it look like an accident, suicide, homicide that he or she had nothing to do with, or even a natural death, there are many ways in which they manipulate the scene with criminal intent toward obscuring the truth. This is why it is so important to assume nothing and to question everything when investigating an unexpected death and not to rush to judgment at the crime scene that any individual has died as the result of natural causes, by accident, or as the result of suicide or homicide with criminal intent. As discussed in previous chapters and illustrated by numerous cases, there are countless ways a crime scene stager tampers with a crime scene to send the investigation of course.

Again revisiting constellation theory is worth mention here too because the prosecution of numerous murders where staged crime scenes are part of the case is largely based on circumstantial evidence. Constellation theory's primary idea is that one star does not make a constellation, but a group of stars does just like one piece of evidence does not make a case, but numerous interrelated pieces of evidence might.

It is important to reiterate that the empirical research on staging has not supported the practical application of effective use of crime scene staging typologies at this point because no typology empirically tried was found to be mutually exclusive of the others (Ferguson, 2011; Pettler, 2011). To note, Pettler (2011) found that thematic analysis or categorization of 18 staged homicide case offenders was basically useless because of the sheer overlap and Ferguson's (2011) findings were similar, based on a totally different typological set. Thousands of cases are needed toward developing typologies if any were to ever be developed, but that is not to say those who are working in that direction are remiss. They are not. Because resources have not been adequately dedicated to this topic in general, everyone's contributions to the pool of literature are important even if and especially if they are all very different. Critics abound will pick and pry at pieces of each contribution, but the truth remains that each contribution is important, each researcher dedicating himself or herself to heightening awareness of this very important category of crime scenes is appreciated, and every research-based investigation on crime scene staging is warranted and justified. So although typologies do not work yet generally speaking, understanding types of crime scene staging, such as the difference between a staged suicide and a staged car accident, behavioral patterns of stagers without classifying any crime scene as one thing or the other can be helpful. Crime scene staging behaviors include cleaning, hiding, creating, destroying, removing, and a host of other types of broad category behaviors. This does not mean that classifying a crime as a "cleaner"-type category is helpful at all because undoubtedly unless it is a strictly monothematic staged crime scene, there could be overlap into other types of staging behaviors somewhere (i.e., verbal staging).

Cleaning the Crime Scene

The previous chapters of this book illustrated examples of staged crime scenes manipulated by cleaning up the scene in order to conceal the offender's identity. According to Pettler's (2011) research, cleaning up a crime scene is a patterned behavior, and offenders who clean the crime scene are attempting to strip the scene of evidence of the crime; their ultimate goal is to avoid apprehension, and evidence of clean up might mean they might argue "no crime." They could also argue something else by only cleaning up evidence in part. Cleanup can involve the cleaning of almost anything but often involves removing traces of blood or other biological evidence with either readily available household chemicals or solvents purchased before or after the crime. It also includes washing walls, floors, ceilings, clothing, and/or the murder weapon, such as knives, tools, firearms, wood, their own fists, and other types of weapons. It is important to mention at this time that crime scenes are 3D and should be processed as such. This means that when using chemical reagents or other types of equipment to search for evidence of cleanup, all floors, all walls, and all ceilings should be processed the same way. The author has encountered numerous crime scenes where the ceiling was never processed. Cleanup is not limited to just interior crime scenes and/or to clothing and weapons. Cleanup can be evident by the offender who in the middle of the night or on a day when it is markedly *odd* to wash a car is vigorously outside scouring his or her vehicle. The list of what stagers might clean or clean with is endless; however, bleach is a very common household chemical often readily available and one of which stagers might employ.

Hiding and Removing Evidence

Hiding evidence or concealing it is also another very commonly observed crime scene staging behavior. Analyze the case file for evidence of hiding evidence. The hiding of weapons, clothing, belongings of the victim, and so on are often revealed. Search laundry receptacles or even bags for stagers who have taken off their bloody clothes, for example, and hid them somewhere before police arrive. Concealing this type of evidence includes hiding evidence in secret places in locations only known to him or her. If not overtly visible, some of the items that could be hidden are weapons, the body of the victim, and other evidence from the crime scene in an attempt to prevent investigators from discovering the truth.

Another commonly observed pattern of staging behavior is that of removing evidence from a crime scene. This might mean removing the victim's body from the murder scene location. Familiarity and risk level are two key factors related to crime scene staging that should be considered. Murder is about what the offender needs, not what the victim needs, so if it meets the offender's needs to remove evidence and the victim's body from the crime scene, then he or she might opt to do that. Likewise, if it meets the offender's needs to leave the body in the crime scene especially in order to stage a scene as a home-based accident or suicide, they might opt to do that instead. One of the primary questions to always continue to ask when analyzing each piece of evidence during the crime analysis process is, "How does this meet the offender's needs?"

Creating Evidence

Some stagers bring evidence into the crime scene to make the death look like it was natural, accident, suicide, or otherwise. Some of these cases could be staged this way for profit specifically but are of course staged to deceive and misdirect the investigation one way or the other. Creating evidence includes building fake evidence into the crime scene by moving the victim, weapon, or other items to make it appear as though something else happened. Obviously, when reviewing what cleaning the crime scene and hiding evidence includes, it is not difficult to imagine that many of these behaviors could overlap, thus making typologies useless. For example, a stager could clean up the scene, then hide the body by dumping it in a remote location, hide the weapon by throwing it in a lake, then paint the murder scene location and bring in new furniture therefore creating a remodeled crime scene thinking all of the evidence of staging is removed. The author once had a scene where a man was beaten to death in a bathroom of a singlewide trailer, very small quarters. The offenders ripped up the bathroom floor, removed the toilet, cleaned up the walls and ceiling, bought a new toilet and new flooring, and installed it all to cover-up the murder. The body of the victim was found in a shallow grave several miles away on a later date and the remodeled bathroom was top on the list for the prosecutor toward proving what happened (not to mention the victim's blood was found absorbed into the subfloor of the bathroom).

Moving a bloody victim can arguably create drag marks. Drag marks are sometimes found in the scene or cleaned up by the stager, but regardless, examination of the victim, and especially the victim's hair, can help clue investigators into the fact that a victim might have been dragged. This type of staging behavior might set up the scene to look like an accident, suicide, or sexual-assault homicide (Geberth, 2006). Another way stagers create evidence is by putting blood in locations where does not belong and/or where it does not make sense with the rest of the crime scene. Additionally, offenders might stage a home invasion, burglary, or interrupted robbery by breaking a window, creating tool marks on a door, or creating other evidence of forced entry and a subsequent violent attack as well.

Pursuant to ransacked crime scenes, Chisum and Turvey (2011) argued that several objectives must be met toward the establishment that the ransacking is resultant of crime scene staging, such as the following:

1. The ransacking is inconsistent with what would be considered the normal appearance of a crime scene of that nature.
2. The ransacked appearance of the crime scene was not resultant of investigator or offender searches, investigators during crime scene processing, and offender in search of items of value or interest (p. 219).

By establishing the validity and reliability of the aforementioned objectives, the crime analysis could reveal that the ransacked condition of the crime scene was indeed due to offender crime scene staging (empirical), could possibly be due to offender crime scene staging (quasi-empirical), or was not due to offender crime scene staging behaviors (nonempirical) (Figure 10.1). It is however important to note that even if a piece of evidence does not have anything to validate it or make it reliable, it does not mean that the item of evidence is untrue; it only means that it cannot be substantiated to prove truth.

Again, the Sam Sheppard case (*Estate of Sam Sheppard v. Ohio*) is a controversial case where some opine Dr. Sheppard did not stage the scene and some argue that he did. One of the things investigators claimed did not add up in Sam Sheppard's story was that a robber killed his wife, Marilyn Sheppard. One of the reasons investigators thought this statement was untrue was because no valuables were missing from the house, and specifically, a timepiece (i.e., wristwatch) was found on the first floor of the house undisturbed. Investigators surmised in this case that Sam Sheppard killed his wife

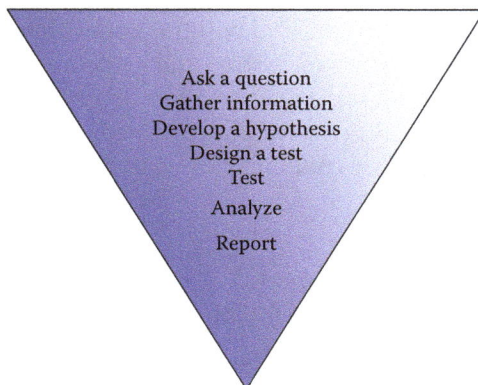

Figure 10.1 The Scientific Method

and tried to stage the scene but forgot to remove the valuables from the scene in accordance with the robbery motive. If this scene was staged, this is an example of how crime scene stagers might forget what they are doing in the heat of the moment and, therefore, focus too much on staging a break-in or similar while forgetting to remove valuables or only remove a few items from the scene, which might give investigators pause (Chisum & Turvey, 2011). Again it is important to remember the constellation theory when it comes to crime scene staging: one missing piece of jewelry does independently indicate a robber stole the jewelry or an offender removed the piece of jewelry to make it look like there was a robbery.

Destroying Evidence

There are so many ways to destroy evidence. Obviously, water and fire are probably the first that come to mind for any investigator with any amount of experience. Water and fire are actually probably two of the more common ways to destroy evidence. The first thing to realize is that if something is destroyed it was important and destroying it met the needs of the offender. If something is cleaned up, it is important and cleaning it up met the needs of the offender. If something is hidden, it is important, and so on. One of the more common things stagers do sometimes is discarding weapons in bodies of water. Pettler (2011) found that when discarding weapons or other items of evidenced in water, stagers more often than not discard the evidence from the very center of a bridge, in what they perceive is the deepest part of the body of water, or in numerous locations in the water. Some offenders even travel to several bodies of water to discard evidence in more than one place or to dump a car under water.

Fire is another way to destroy evidence. It is fairly common for offenders to burn clothes, weapons, letters, cars, or other materials connected to the crime toward *concealing* the evidence, but in turn they destroy it. Some crime scenes are found ablaze when authorities arrive. Upon inspection, victims are found inside burned-out cars and buildings after they were shot, beaten, stabbed, or strangled in order to destroy the evidence and further conceal the crime. There are lots of ways offenders can destroy evidence. The author would argue that criminal behavior does not depart far from noncriminal behavior and that familiarity could play a role in how an offender chooses to destroy evidence.

VCDIM Stage 4: Crime Analysis—Component 3 (Autopsy: Wound Pattern Analysis)

The essence of crime analysis is to discover new interrelationships between pieces of evidence toward eventual synthesis of all the pieces together. Again, all stages and substages of crime analysis are systematic and methodical to minimize and guard against chance. Analysis means critical thinking (i.e., not "thinking hard," but *critical* thinking) as opposed to regular thinking, and this type of critical thinking should be applied to all aspects of the analysis. It is this type of thinking that is applied to wound pattern analysis.

It is fair to say that the majority of those investigating suspicious death cases from law enforcement agencies are not medical professionals who hold medical degrees. While it is quite common for paramedics to also work in law enforcement or former military medical personnel, it is a fact that forensic pathology differs tremendously from regular emergency services work. The autopsy is a highly important piece of the analytical puzzle for accurate crime analysis. There are times, however, for whatever reason, a decision maker opted against doing an autopsy in an unexpected yet suspicious death, which can cause a mountain of problems plus cost a *mountain of money*. This problem can be avoided by putting only those highly trained individuals in the field who have experience in forensics, medicine, and death investigation and are competent in ruling the manner of death while not jumping to conclusions at the scene under suspicious circumstances, so errors of this nature are less likely to occur. Take, for example, the couple who has a history of domestic violence. One day, the husband calls 911 to report his wife shot herself during an argument. An investigator is dispatched to the scene from the Medical Examiner's Office and rules the woman's death a suicide within an hour after arriving on scene. The woman's family confronts the medical examiner himself or herself about the handing of the case; a new investigation is brought forth based on victimological information revealed by the family. The investigator did not send the body for autopsy because the investigator thought, "it looked like suicide." Herein lies the problem. Just because something "looks like something" on the outside does not mean that is what it truly is. Never assume the integrity of the crime scene nor the integrity of the statements coming from the individual who discovered the body. For that matter, it is best to be skeptical about all statements from everyone until verification is obtained.

The medical examiner or forensic pathologist deals with the victim's bodily injuries, the victim's cause of death, and the victim's manner of death. The cause of death is what caused the victim to die, such as injuries sustained as the result of a gunshot wound. And the manner is the way in which the victim died, such as naturally, by accident, by suicide, or by homicide, and in some cases where the manner of death cannot be determined, the death is ruled *undetermined* or *unclassified* (Spitz, 2006). If a forensic pathologist is telling investigators that he or she is "checking pending further investigation" when investigators brought the body in thinking it was suicide, this is the forensic pathologist waving a red flag that autopsy results do not overwhelmingly support suicide as manner of death.

When an individual dies, the body might be first taken to the hospital for cursory evaluation before being transported to the medical examiner's office for autopsy by a forensic pathologist. The author has seen in some cases where hospital pathologists conducted autopsies in traumatic death, but it has been the author's experience more often than not that hospital pathologists do not include the level of detail that forensic pathologists do in their reports. An autopsy consists of an external examination, evidence of injury examination, internal examination, microscopic examination, toxicology testing, and other tests as ordered by the forensic pathologist generally speaking. The pathologist renders his or her opinion as to the cause and manner of death based on many factors. Sometimes the forensic pathologist can provide investigators with a window for the time of death, what type of weapon might have been used, and other important things about the victim. This is why the autopsy is so incredibly important to analyze during crime analysis.

Toxicology reports are supplemental reports based on samples most often taken at the time of autopsy. The toxicologist studies the adverse effects some chemicals can have on the human body generally speaking. It is common for victims to be screened for all kinds of drugs, alcohol, and anything specific that is warranted. In cases where carbon monoxide poisoning is suspected, for example, the toxicology report is critical to the crime analysis phase of VCDIM because it could mean it was related to the cause of death. During the course of crime analysis, it is critical to incorporate not only the laboratory reports generated from the testing of the physical evidence but also to include as well all medically related laboratory results. The author fully relies on experts of all kinds to interpret DNA, toxicology, ballistics, fingerprints, and other subdisciplines of forensic science when analyzing a crime because again, as mentioned earlier, it is very important to practice within the scope of one's expertise only.

The time of death is a very important marker when investigating a suspicious death. In some cases, after the murder of a victim, the offender takes hours if not days to stage the crime and the corresponding crime scenes and all of this while the body begins the process of decomposition. It is critically important for those investigating death cases, such as coroners, death investigators, CSIs, and others, to not lock down on a specific time of death but instead to use a reasonable range if a range can be determined. One of the things to keep in mind is the scope of one's expertise. It is not a good idea to document medical information about the victim if one is not qualified to do so. Investigators should not be estimating the time of death in the scene unless the medical personnel who are trained to render such opinions are in agreement. Overreaching in reports can create credibility issues on the witness stand; thus, this situation should be avoided altogether.

So what to do with the information contained in the autopsy report? There are several things nonmedically trained investigating personnel can do to analyze the autopsy material that does not overstep a medical boundary for which the investigator is not qualified to do. In partnership with the forensic pathologist and medical professionals involved in the case, investigators can analyze the traumatic injury or wounds of the victim toward gleaning important information about his or her death. Wound pattern analysis is the critical examination and analysis of every wound the victim has pursuant to their recognition, preservation, documentation, examination, and reconstruction. Wound pattern analysis is not an autopsy, but instead, the information for the analysis is gathered from the forensic pathologist's autopsy report. The VCDIM user can create a Wound Pattern Analysis Worksheet (see Appendix F) that contains four columns of information:

1. Evidence of injury
2. *Quantitative measurement*: length
3. *Quantitative measurement*: width
4. Forensic pathologist remarks and/or investigator questions

To note, some forensic pathologists provide more levels of detail than others, so it is best to work in partnership with the forensic pathologist so he or she can explain his or her findings. Another way to analyze the wounds is by using the autopsy report and corresponding autopsy photos along with the Wound Pattern Analysis Worksheet to map the wounds on the autopsy photos. The author has found that using PowerPoint is very helpful for doing this. Most often the forensic pathologist will draw wounds on body diagrams, but having the actual photographs, hopefully in color, sometimes makes learning about each wound and understanding the nature of each wound a little easier. Insert the photo onto a blank slide in PowerPoint, and then based on the autopsy report, use circles and other markers to diagram on the photo what the forensic pathologist has diagramed in his or her drawings in the autopsy report. Label and compile the slides and print. Take to meetings with the forensic pathologist to learn more about each wound recognizing that during this process, identifying where the wounds are located on the body is as important as where they are not.

Yet another way to analyze the perforating or even the penetrating gunshot wound to the head, for example, is by way of a Styrofoam head. Take a Styrofoam head and a dowel rod to the forensic pathologist and ask the forensic pathologist to mark the entrance and exit wound if there is one on the head. Insert the dowel rod along the two points of reference and confirm with the forensic pathologist that this is an approximate estimated location of the wound track. The author always asks the forensic pathologist to initial the bottom of the apparatus in case the district attorney wishes to use the apparatus in court at some point. The same procedure can be done using a forensic mannequin, though the author does not ask the forensic pathologist to initial the mannequin because the mannequin is very expensive and is used over and over again. To note, sometimes two Styrofoam heads are made, one for investigatory purposes and then one at a later date for court purposes.

Once an apparatus has been made, such as a Styrofoam head with dowels or a forensic mannequin with dowels inserted in it, investigators now have a 3D tool that could shed some light on what could be possible and what might be impossible when compared to victimology, the crime scene and lab reports, and other aspects of the autopsy. Styrofoam heads and forensic mannequins can be used during the scientific method part of this stage as well.

According to DiMaio and Dana (2007), violent deaths include accidents, suicides, and homicides from the medicolegal perspective and suspicious and unexpected deaths are those that might be due to violence as well. Even if a body is not sent for autopsy, the details of the death should be thoroughly investigated, documented, and retained. A medicolegal investigation is used to determine the cause of death and manner of death and to document the details of both (p. 1). Further, medical examiners or forensic pathologists determine factors that might have contributed to the death of an individual along with collecting evidence from bodies brought to the morgue. Forensic pathologists and medical examiners work in tandem with coroners and law enforcement agencies on death cases and forensic pathologists could be called to testify in court.

The cause of death is the reason someone died. It is basically the reason why the body ceased to continue functioning that sustains life. The manner of death is how the person died, such as naturally, by accident, by suicide, by homicide, which does not necessarily mean murder, or by way of something undetermined or unclassified (DiMaio & Dana, 2007).

Physical Evidence on the Body

The body is a crime scene that can contain physical evidence that requires identification, documentation, collection, preservation, sometimes testing, and definitely reporting. Several different types of physical evidence can be found on the body, such as biological evidence like blood or semen, and even nonbiological evidence, such as paint, soil, and glass (DiMaio & Dana, 2007). One of the ways to help preserve this evidence that might be on the body is by way of a clean, white sheet. Before placing the body in a body bag, wrap the body in a clean, white sheet and then place the body in a body bag. Investigators cannot collect evidence that is lost in transport inside the body bag or in another way, so it is critically important toward preservation of evidence that the body is wrapped in a body bag, placed in the body bag, and then transported to its destination. It is common to see the hands and feet of a victim wrapped in brown paper bags secured by tape. This is done to preserve evidence that could be on the hands. But why not wrap the rest of the body as well for the same reason? Based on Locard's exchange principle, it is very clear that evidence is transferred when two items touch, so assuming that there is only potential evidence on the hands and feet is remiss. Therefore, during crime analysis, it is important to study how the body was transported, what evidence might have been recovered or lost, or otherwise toward knowing exactly what is available in the case.

Time of Death

A forensic pathologist, not a medical examiner, not a coroner, not an investigator, can determine the exact time of death unless witness to the event or under other specific circumstances. Time of death is a very important landmark in a suspicious death investigation for many reasons. Timelines are a huge part of victimology, so knowing when the victim was last alive is one marker, knowing when the victim was found deceased is another marker, and there is only so much that can occur in between those marks for the body to be recovered in any particular condition. Of course this general guideline varies tremendously and by every case, but overall, timestamp-type markers are very important in victimological study and the autopsy findings toward the establishment of time of death are part of that process.

According to DiMaio and Dana (2007), forensic pathologists use several factors to help determine time of death, such as livor mortis, rigor mortis, temperature, vitreous potassium levels, the contents of the stomach, and some environmental factors (DiMaio & Dana, 2007, p. 23). Again, livor mortis is not only important to the movement of the body postmortem, but in this case, livor mortis is also important when trying to determine time of death because it begins to set in within about 30 minutes after death occurs and becomes more visible as time passes. Therefore, the more livor mortis generally speaking, the more time has passed. Likewise, as mentioned earlier, rigor mortis is the stiffening of the muscles of the body. Rigor mortis begins to set in as the muscles lose adenosine triphosphate (ATP) within approximately 2 hours after death and take about 6 to 12 hours to set in (p. 25). Rigor begins in the head, specifically the jaw, and then the face begins to follow until it works its way throughout the body. Then, in reverse it dissipates in the same order due to the decomposition of the body (p. 25). Rigor mortis is important in crime analysis because if investigators respond to a call to find a body in full rigor, but the caller says he or she called 911 as soon as the victim shot himself or herself, inquiry is definitely warranted in partnership with the forensic pathologist. Further, the forensic pathologist uses body temperature to help determine cause of death, which is important to learn about during crime analysis for the same reason that rigor mortis is important, that is, how much time has passed. Furthermore, the vitreous fluid potassium level and environmental factors like insect activity are also useful for the establishment of time of death. Regardless of what the forensic pathologist uses to establish time of death, VCDIM users should ensure full understanding of how those pieces interrelate to the whole systematically and methodically.

Evidence of Injury

Because this is simply a general overview of the crime analysis process of information that could be contained in the autopsy report, in-depth discussion about evidence of injury is not included here. The author recommends reading and referencing forensic pathology books and articles to broaden knowledge of core concepts for deeper understanding of the material when explained by the forensic pathologist. Although there are many ways offenders kill their victims, too many to identify, define, and discuss here, a brief overview of four of the more common types of injury follows: blunt force trauma, sharp force trauma, injury by gunfire, and asphyxia.

"Blunt force is probably the single most common type of trauma" wrote Werner U. Spitz in Spitz and Fisher's (2006) *Medicolegal Investigation of Death Guidelines for the Application of Forensic Pathology to Crime Scene Investigation*, Fourth Edition. Blunt force injury might cause the traumatized area to bleed, become crushed, tear, or to become sheared (p. 460). It is critical to accurate crime analysis to work with the forensic pathologist toward understanding the nature of the evidence of injury. While blunt force trauma might be the most common type of trauma, sharp force trauma or injury created by way of a knife, piece of glass, piece of sharp metal or anything else that is sharp and can cut human skin is also common. Various areas of the body respond to trauma caused by blunt force or sharp force differently, so it is best to ask lots of questions and record on the Wound Pattern Analysis Worksheet and corresponding diagramed photos that identify which wound is which. A full analysis of each wound is absolutely necessary for comparison to victimology, the crime scene, and lab reports, and later to suspectology and statement analysis. A partnership with the forensic pathologist is required for this step.

Injury by gunfire is also a way an offender might kill a victim. As discussed earlier in this book, firearms are the most commonly used weapons by murderers to kill their victims in the United States. Gunshot wound injuries are created from being shot with handguns, rifles, and shotguns, although the latter two are less common (Spitz, 2006). Part of the medicolegal process is for forensic pathologists to conduct external examinations of bodies. According to Spitz (2006), the range of fire and direction of fire can both be determined upon external examination of a gunshot wound on a victim's body (p. 607). Gunshot wounds should always be completely examined by a forensic pathologist for thorough and precise evaluation for many reasons, such as toward determining what type of firearm might have been used. Remember that not all offenders leave the weapon at the crime scene. Some crime scenes of murders staged as home invasions or interrupted robberies might indeed not include weapons. Also, it is not unheard of that an offender kills a victim with one firearm and then actually stages another firearm in its place. According to Spitz (2006), handguns and rifle gunshot wounds can present very similarly, even more reason to send a body for autopsy and not make a mistake that costs everyone a lot of time and money later. Again to reiterate, the author recommends autopsy in all unexpected and/or deaths where the last person to see the victim alive is the first person to report the victim dead, missing, or having left a particular location. Another important note about murders staged as suicides where the last person to see the victim alive is the first person to report the victim's suicide. It has been the author's experience that many of these stagers are very clean when first responders arrive at the crime scene as in having just showered or cleaned up in some way. Second, pursuant to gunshot wounds and staged suicides, it has also been the experience of the author that many offenders have claimed something to the effect of the following:

1. "I was in the bathroom at the time of shot."
2. "I was getting a drink in the kitchen at the time of the shot."
3. "I was in standing in front of him or her at the time of the shot."
4. "I was coming out of the bathroom at the time of the shot."
5. "I was asleep at the time of the shot."
6. "I was outside at the time of the shot."
7. "I was standing on the other side of the room."
8. "I was watching TV."

And the list goes on. Prosecution of staged cases where an offender has staged a murder as a suicide requires the prosecution to put the firearm in the hand of the offender. There are many ways prosecutors present this type of evidence in the courtroom, but one thing is for sure: prosecutors might not have as much to work with if an autopsy is not done in cases of suspicious death that involves a firearm. Always do the autopsy because one never knows what could be discovered.

Death by asphyxia can occur in several ways including the neck or chest become compressed, when the airway becomes obstructed, or when oxygen is depleted from the body because another gas is taking its place (Spitz, 2006). Strangulation can cause death because it compresses the neck. Hanging can also compress the neck and cause death. Likewise, smothering can cause death because an object covering the face obstructs the airway. Asphyxiation can also occur when a victim inhales carbon monoxide from a car, for example, which replaces the victim's oxygen with the poisonous gas. It is interesting to note that many victims of intimicide have been victims of incomplete strangulation on dates prior to their deaths. In a case the author had several years ago, a victim was badly beaten upon cursory review in the crime scene, but when autopsied, it was discovered that she actually died of asphyxiation due to a shower curtain rod being pressed against her neck.

There are many, many ways people die; too many to discuss within the scope of this book. Wound pattern analysis works best when the individual conducting the crime analysis partners with the medical team who are responsible for processing the body. The medical skill set is invaluable to the investigator in so many ways, but specifically because the body being as complex as it is behaves in many ways under various circumstances that can only be explained scientifically, systematically, medically, and methodically by a forensic pathologist or other individual so highly skilled in such topics.

VCDIM Stage 4: Crime Analysis—Component 5 (Suspectology)

The point of a suspicious death investigation is to determine several things, one of which is if another person is criminally responsible for the death of the victim. However, this can be a daunting task. As discussed in a previous chapter, there is clearly a paradigm shift from sole focus on the suspect of more focus on the victim in homicide investigation. That is not to say that all homicide investigation practitioners agree or partake in that shift, but overall, the shift has occurred and is continuing to occur. Like victimology being the analytical study of victims, suspectology is the analytical study of suspects. Suspectology is focused on learning everything possible about a suspect or suspects just like in learning about the victim because there is a relationship in most cases between the victim and offender. Sometimes, there is more than one suspect in a case. When this happens, suspectology should be conducted on each suspect individually for later comparison. Normally, at some point in the analysis, there will be factors that do not match up to the victimology, crime scene, and/or wound analysis, rendering certain suspects less viable than possibly another. Sometimes, there is no suspect in a case at all. These cases are often referred to in a slang way as a "whodunnit," that is, "who did it?" type of case. In this situation, several suspect characteristics, such as his or her personality, cognition, behavior, emotionality, and enviro-socioculturalism, are reflected in the other components of the case.

Again in order to conduct suspectology correctly, one must be systematic, methodical, and meticulous just like in victimology. Sometimes it is the smallest detail that changes the whole course of the crime analysis and the investigation. One of the ways to conduct a systematic suspectology is to attempt to collect and learn all of the informational categories studied about the victim in research-based forensic victimology in turn as they apply to the suspect. Simply speaking, this means taking the victimology packet and applying it as a framework for the most part for suspectology as well. Granted, there will be some categories that might not be applicable and some categories that must be added, but generally speaking, all of the main categories required for victimology are necessary for suspectology as well. In essence, the more one knows about the victim, the more one knows about the suspect, and the closer to positive resolution the case becomes. One of the things to keep in mind is that suspects sometimes offer statements as to what happened to a victim and sometimes they never even admit to having every encountered the victim. Some die taking their murderous information straight to the grave with them often leaving questions unanswered for families and investigators. So, conducting suspectology will help narrow the scope of which suspects are most viable and which might not be as viable. Remembering the "rules of conflict" is helpful when analyzing suspects because one of the first questions asked in research-based forensic victimology is, "Who is conflict with the victim?" When answering this question, it is important to recognize that the conflict could be long standing or immediately preceding the murder. So keeping an open mind and really doing a "deep dive" into the suspect's history, prior relationships, family, health occupation, envirosocioculturalism (ESC), routine activities, and everything else captured during victimology are relevant to the study of the suspect.

Again, it is important when investigating potentially staged cases to include certain types of investigatory pursuant to both research-based forensic victimology and suspectology, such as but not limited to

1. Was this suspect in conflict with this victim?
2. Was there a confrontation of any kind between the victim and this suspect prior to this victim's death?
3. Did this victim reject this suspect?
4. Was this suspect angry with this victim?
5. Was this suspect frustrated with this victim?
6. Did this suspect benefit from this victim's death?
7. Did this suspect gain some kind of payoff from the death of this victim?
8. Did this suspect's lifestyle change with the death of this victim?
9. Was this victim found dead in this suspect's familiar environment?
10. Is this suspect familiar with the murder scene and/or victim discovery location?
11. Did this suspect notify police after having discovered this victim's body?
12. Did this suspect offer "stories" to investigators and/or family/friends about the victim, the victim's whereabouts, etc.?

This is a sample list of questions that might be included in suspectology. Some of these questions might be answered during the course of victimology and/or the crime scene and lab report analysis. If there are known suspects in a case, suspectology is critically important for being cross-compared against the victimology, crime scene and lab reports, and the wound pattern analysis. Next, another way suspectology can be useful in narrowing the pool of suspects down to one is by way of applying what is learned about the suspect to statement analysis. It is important to note that suspectology might work better as component 5 and statement analysis might work better as component 4 in some cases. Flexibility is vital to success.

VCDIM Stage 4: Crime Analysis—Component 5 (Statement Analysis)

Everything the offender tells investigators and in the order he or she says it with the words he or she selects with the affect he or she demonstrates means something and meets his or her needs. Statement analysis is an extremely useful tool in the process of crime analysis for many reasons. Investigators can learn to use statement analysis along with taking continuing educational courses in it and so on. First, statement analysis is grounded in the words of the English language (McClish, 2001). This means statement analysis or what is sometimes referred to as *discourse analysis* is focused on analyzing the linguistic patterns of the speaker toward verification of the facts in pursuit of the truth, but in turn identifying gaps that could indicate deception. Statement analysis is the same as the qualitative research method called *scientific content analysis*. Social scientists, such as criminologists, psychologists, and other researchers use scientific content analysis to scientifically and systematically analyze data spoken, written, and contained in statements in various settings. The author conducted scientific content analysis or statement analysis as an analytical method for examining the content of witness statements in 18 staged homicide case files, which contained countless statements by witnesses, victims, and suspects. The overarching concept of statement analysis is that words mean things and people generally say what they mean (McClish, 2001). The catch is when their actions, body language, and verbal discourse are misaligned. Emotions are conveyed through both body language and verbal conversation; if someone is claiming to be devastated but is demonstrating body language inconsistent with that statement, further inquiry might be warranted. When verbal and nonverbal signals are in conflict, it is best practice to ask the qualitative question of why.

Polygraph examinations are based in biological responses because for normal people telling a lie most often generates some amount of anxiety that could be detected in biological measurement like a polygraph machine. Statement analysis is much different. Instead of relying on biological cues to signal deception, statement analysis is reliant upon nonverbal and verbal cues to signal deception instead. McClish (2001) wrote a phenomenal book entitled *I Know You Are Lying*, which introduces readers to the scientific practice of statement analysis. The author highly recommends this book, as it has proven useful in countless cases worked by the author. One of McClish's key points about observing behavior is that in his experience, when an individual lies, his or her hands will subconsciously gravitate toward the individual's mouth in some way. McClish argued that this is a form of deceptive behavior and investigators should be aware of this gesture because it alludes of an attempt to mask the information being said. Most people have witnessed a child tell a lie where the child immediately covers his or her mouth following telling the lie. In adulthood, people have more self-control, but some cannot resist the urge to touch one's face during the commencement of lying, but they might more often touch their noses instead of their mouths in adulthood (McClish, 2001). While some opponents of statement analysis or scientific content analysis argue its irrelevance to homicide investigation, the author has found resounding success both during her terminal degree academic study and in practice working various types of homicide cases.

An individual's language is the primary focus of statement analysis during a suspicious death investigation, homicide investigation, and/or during crime analysis. While nonverbal gestures, such as touching one's nose, might be embedded in the conversation, the crux of the matter is what is being said by the person overall. It is difficult to recognize deception regardless how much education, training, or experience one might have because there might not be overt signs of deception. Individuals might offer information about what they did or what they saw, but they will not offer information that incriminates them. If they do begin to encroach on what would incriminate them, they never tell investigators everything. The author always says, "there is always a thread of truth of in the fabric of the lie" so to speak because it has been her experience that it is up to the savvy investigator to figure out which threads of the fabric are lies and which are the truth.

Sometimes a suspect will lie regardless of what he or she thinks the investigator knows or not. Take, for example, a situation where there is a video or audio recording of a suspect abusing a victim prior to the victim's death, but the suspect is unaware that such a tape exists. The suspect in this case might believe he or she is in the clear and that his or her abuse prior to the victim's death is completely concealed thus alleviating the suspect from culpability. Investigators can use their knowledge of the case as a litmus test to see if the suspect will tell the truth. If the video or audio tape clearly shows a victim being physically, verbally, or emotionally abused, in some other way, asking the suspect to tell investigators about the nature of the relationship between him or her and the victim might yield results consistent with the suspect's willingness to avoid discussion about their relationship or by telling investigators that there was never a problem in their relationship.

"How-To": Organize to Multiple Statements

Like all stages of VCDIM, statement analysis is also time consuming, but well worth the time invested. As mentioned several times before, the system determines the outcome of any situation; thus, a systematic approach for analyzing words or discourse is necessary too. Again, it is important to note that statement analysis could follow wound pattern analysis in some cases and therefore be switched in order with suspectology. While VCDIM is structured in a way toward ensuring soundness, every methodology requires the ability for flexion based on the case under investigation. It is important to arrange the components of VCDIM in accordance with the way in which a case flows and always using Bloom's Taxonomy as the framework for ensuring every step is completed systematically combined with using research-based forensic victimology as the foundation for everything in the crime analysis phase. Jumping stages or omitting components increases the chance for error and decreases the opportunity to have conducted a complete evaluation of a case accurately.

Transcripts are a must have. Take, for example, a case where a suspect has given three statements to police. In order to analyze each statement, written transcripts are necessary. It is very interesting to watch or listen to a statement, but even more interesting to see it written on paper. While one can clearly hear or see moments of hesitation like "I, I, I…I don't know where she was when I left," to see it actually written on paper is truly another experience. Therefore, the first step when dealing with audio and video recordings of statements is to always transcribe them as close to verbatim as possible. Again, the author recommends using a Statement Analysis Worksheet (Appendix G) for this step that can be customized based. Enter one sentence or sentence fragment per cell in the first column of the spreadsheet. The author found with practice that the analyst learns what to record and what might be able to be left out. Best practice is to transcribe all sentences putting one sentence into one cell at a time until the entire statement can be read cell by cell. If all the sentences are entered in the first column for statement #1, skip a row and enter the next set of sentences from statement #2. Do the same for statement #3 *all in the first column*. Then label the second, third, and fourth columns with the statement number, such as statements #1, #2, and #3. Go through the sentences and enter an X or notate in some way that each sentence was said in which statement. Begin to notice the pattern. Some sentences will appear in all three statements. Some sentences will only appear in one statement. Some will appear in both. The more the suspect statements, the merrier. Not only does the Statement Analysis Worksheet cross-compare the statements, but it makes a great courtroom demonstrative that can be customized to reflect only the pieces that a prosecutor wants to present. To note, all worksheets can be used in this same manner, as courtroom demonstratives customized to meet the need of the prosecuting attorney.

Detecting Deception

According to Rabon (1994) statement analysis can be compared to crime scene processing in that for a rookie who is not educated in crime scene investigation, he or she might walk through a scene not being able yet to identifying anything of value. The same concept applies to those unfamiliar with statement analysis and might not see the value in analyzing narratives given by witnesses, victims, and suspects. Investigators can learn how to conduct accurate statement analysis. The author would argue that just as it is important to process a crime scene as part of a case, analyzing what the witnesses, victims, and suspects say is of equal value. Clearly, one short segment in this book cannot begin to include or explain all of the nuances of statement analysis, how it should be done, how one should "pick up" on words and phrases, or how it can be used, so the author recommends continuing education on all components of all types of analysis. This book is an introductory book designed to introduce some of the concepts of crime scene staging and to suggest a unique, systematic, interdisciplinary methodology for investigating suspicious deaths where staging could be present. VCDIM can be applied to both staged and nonstaged cases; however, toward strengthening the ever so common completely circumstantial staged murder case, VCDIM has proven to be very useful when applied even in pieces or in concept only to a variety of cases.

There are many ways to detect deception in both verbal and written statements. McClish (2001) argued that the first and foremost thing to do is to pay close attention to the language being used by the speaker therefore; the analyst must be a good listener. For example, if a speaker says, "You know, I'm really trying to be honest here." What is the speaker really saying? The speaker could have said, "You know, I'm being honest here." Noticeable difference. The point is to really listen to what people are saying. In this example, is the speaker trying to be honest or is the speaker being honest? Most of what is said is really only given cursory thought by most people. During statement analysis, really break apart the whole statement into pieces and study each individual piece of the whole.

Listening to the way in which a pronoun is used or listening for grammatical rules in a sentence is another way to detect potential deception (Rabon, 1994). Pronouns identify who (i.e., he, she) and allude to possession (i.e., ours). If a speaker says "I," then he or she is implying himself or herself. If the speaker says "we," he or she is implying himself or herself in addition to at least one other individual. If a speaker says, "I left my wallet on the table at the restaurant," the speaker is admitting the wallet is his or hers. If the speaker says, "I left the wallet on the table at the restaurant," the speaker is not taking ownership of the wallet. When it comes to suspect statements, there can be many reasons for this. One such reason is to create distance between him or her and the object in question, individual in question, time, location, or whatever it is that is in question. Watch for possessive pronouns that imply ownership versus words that do not imply ownership. If the reason for this type of discourse is to create distance (i.e., the what/quantitative), the next logical question then is *why*, or the qualitative. All questions have a quantitative and qualitative answer and should be answered using that format. Knowing "the what" or knowing "the why" is only identifying half of the whole. Knowing "the what" and knowing "the why" is identifying the whole. According to McClish (2001), another way to use pronouns to detect deception is to analyze the speaker's statements to assess whether or not he or she is taking responsibility for his or her behavior and actions. Listen for when a speaker uses the word "I" or uses the word "my." Does the speaker say, "No one thinks I killed my wife. That's crazy. No one believes in my guilt." Whose guilt is it? The speaker's guilt: "my guilt." It is quite possible an innocent person might have said something to the effect of "No one thinks I killed my wife. That's crazy. No one thinks I am guilty." Consider the possibilities with an open, objective mind toward analyzing each piece of the whole.

According to McClish (2001), verb tense is also a way words are signs. Once words are understood to be signs, much more direction can be taken from them. People generally say what they mean, but that does not mean it is always the truth. When the sky grays over and becomes cloudy and/or dark, it is a sign that it is about to rain. This same principle goes for statement analysis. As one becomes more familiar with what words are actually signs and what direction they imply to take, what was once just a bunch of words written on paper become a road map straight to the truth. Word signs symbolize an idea, they mean something, and to the alert investigator, it will guide him or her to where the heart of the matter really is (Rabon, 1994). So, for example, Jane is the name of a woman, but not the actual woman herself. The word "knife" symbolizes an object intended for cutting, but is not the actual knife itself. Therefore, "Jane threw the knife on the floor and ran out" describes the relationship between Jane and the knife and convey meaning and action.

Another thing to watch for in a narrative is a suspect's usage of the words: *think, feel*, and *believe*. In comparison to the word *know*, which means affirmative cognition, *think* means to have an opinion of something or suppose, *feel* is an experiential emotion, and *believe* means to have an opinion toward the truth of a matter. If an investigator poses the question, "Where was Julie when you left?" and the suspect says (long pause then), "Where was Julie when I left? (short pause) As far as I can recall, I think Julie was asleep in her bed." The first thing that should red flag this sentence is the long pause. The second thing that should red flag this sentence is the suspect repeating the question. The third thing that should red flag this sentence is the second short pause. The fourth thing that should red flag this sentence is *as far as I can recall*. And the fifth thing that should red flag this sentence is the usage of the word *think* in relation to where Julie was when the suspect left. In this small two-sentence scenario, the suspect's words have signaled several key points:

1. That there was no preplanned answer to this question.
   a. *Signals*: Long pause and repeating the question, both to buy time.
2. That the suspect is not sure where the best place is for Julie to be when the suspect left toward meeting the suspect's needs. In other words, where does the suspect need Julie to be? That's where the suspect puts Julie.

If the suspect killed Julie as she stood washing dishes in the sink by shooting her in the back of the head and then reported coming home to find Julie dead on the kitchen floor, the suspect knows that is where Julie was when he left, but he has to put her somewhere else in order to meet his or her needs. The suspect does not need to use the word *think* if the suspect knows.

Similar to an investigation method like VCDIM that is grounded by "our system determines our outcome" philosophy, people build language and sentences in much the same way. A sentence is nothing more than a system of selected words that are strung together by the speaker toward conveying meaning to the listener (Rabon, 1994). Pay close attention to verb tense to be sure the speaker is using the past tense to speak about the past and the present tense to speak about the present. If a suspect is asked a question, listen analytically to the answer. And no matter what interview style one might choose to employ, never finish the sentence of a suspect, witness, or victim during an interview. It is not the investigators predicate to the sentence that is of value; it is the suspect predicate that is relevant. Silence after a question where as a pause occurs before the suspect answers is a tremendously underused interviewing tool. Let there be silence because what follows to break the silence might *break the case.* Allow the suspect to say what he or she has to say without interference by finishing his or her sentences.

Types of Narratives
Remember small lies can turn into big problems for the suspect. It is the experience of the author that crime scene stagers often forget the minute details when staging a crime scene. Their emotionality drives the process, thus, they end up faltering badly in some area for which it makes it hard to recover. Although finding that hole can be precarious, it is not impossible to say the least. As discussed earlier, notification is critically important when conducting crime analysis because the last person to see the victim alive who is the first person to discover the victim's body and to report the victim dead often has the answers that the investigators are searching for. Despite the fact that offenders intend to take investigators on a *wild goose chase* toward self-preservation and because the staged crime scene is their *wonderland*, it is imperative for investigators to arm themselves in a multimodal, interdisciplinary manner that works toward cumulative outcomes.

Toward those goals, there could be several types of narratives or statements available for analysis in any given case. Sometimes there are and sometimes there are not. The following are types of statements that can yield valuable information that set up an offender for what is to follow. It is the experience of the author that offenders have tremendous difficultly keeping up with everything they say. The truth does not change and the only constant in this situation is the ever-changing lie.

911 Calls and Emergency Services   The 911 call is a statement. The information in the order in which it was received should be entered in the Statement Analysis Worksheet. Deaths are reported to authorities in many different ways. One of the most common is when a caller phones 911. Typically, a dispatcher receives the call that triages the situation for the type of emergency and what type of response is needed. The importance of analyzing any 911, emergency services, or even calls that come in on nonemergency lines is critical for many reasons. One reason is that if the caller is the last person to see the victim alive and the first person to report the victim dead, he or she normally tells the dispatcher that the victim is either deceased or injured in some way. Sometimes these callers provide explanations for why they are with the deceased or injured person and sometimes they offer explanations for how the victim became injured or died. Analysis of the 911 call serves as a baseline in the scene for comparison and later for Statement Analysis, so having this informaiton readily available during Stage 1 and Stage 4 is critically important. Another reason these calls are important is that oftentimes when listening for chorology or the order in which something occurs, an individual guilty of foul play might begin the call by explaining what happened. *What happened* might change ten times, but by analyzing what the caller says happened the first time, his or her other statements can then be compared.

Additional Types of Statements   There are several other types of narratives that are worth analyzing when conducting statement analysis. The following are some other examples, but not a complete list of what could be analyzed:

- Text messages
- E-mails
- Social media posts and private messages
- Jail calls
- Letters and notes
- Journals and diaries
- Flower notes
- The entire law enforcement case file statements from
  - Family
  - Friends
  - Neighbors
  - Victim(s) and past
  - Employers and coworkers
  - Prior cases statements
  - Medical records
  - EMS, police, probation, and DSS reports

This list contains samples of what could be analyzed; each case is different so flexibility is a must. Regardless, the amount of critical information that could be contained in narratives of this nature cannot be understated.

Statement analysis is a great tool that can aid in the examination and analysis of victimology, suspectology, witness statements, suspect statements, victim statements, and in a host of other ways. Taking the time to analyze statements takes practice, just like learning to process a crime scene takes practice. Investigators who choose to use crime analysis and its embedded components of victimology, crime scene and laboratory report analysis, investigatory wound pattern analysis, suspectology, and/or statement analysis in a systematic and interrelated manner can only benefit from its use. As mentioned earlier, it might behoove the investigator to conduct statement analysis first before suspectology or the other way around for reasons specific to a case. Regardless, the suspectology will help identify personal attributes about the suspect's *internal dictionary* as well or the words he or she normally uses when speaking to others. Everyone's internal dictionaries are unique. Learning as much about the suspect's personality, cognition, behavior, emotionality, and ESC will help identify the signals in what he or she is saying, but it will help identify why he or she is saying it.

VCDIM Stage 4: Crime Analysis—Component 6 (The Scientific Method)

Sometimes during crime analysis, investigators notice that the way in which the suspect claims the victim died does not match up with the victimology, crime scene and lab reports, and investigatory wound pattern analysis in whole or in part. As discussed earlier, wound pattern analysis is the analytical process by which wounds on the victim are studied. In order to support or refute the suspect's statement or statements about what happened, investigators must scientifically create a test based on what is confirmed about the case, such as the following:

1. Results from victimology and information about the victim and the way in which he or she most likely would have behaved during an attack
2. Results of crime scene processing, measurements, etc., in combination with results from crime lab testing
3. Results of autopsy, toxicology, other ordered tests, and investigatory wound pattern analysis
4. Results of suspectology
5. Results of statement analysis

In order to be scientific at its most basic level, the method of testing must be systematic and replicable at a minimum. There are many parameters and guidelines that constitute scientific testing, but one of the easiest and most applicable ways to test a suspect's claim is using the scientific method. The reason the scientific method testing comes after victimology, crime scene and lab reports, investigatory wound pattern analysis, suspectology, and statement analysis is because the results of all of those components are required for accuracy. The process by which the scientific method is used toward supporting or refuting the claims of suspects, witnesses, or even victims is commonly called *crime scene reconstruction* or something similar. Many experts have developed methodologies like VCDIM that contain various components organized in various ways, but when it all comes down to it, the scientific method is usually the common thread. The author would encourage readers to read and learn about every method available.

According to James and Nordby (2005), crime scene reconstruction is "the process of determining or eliminating the events that occurred at the crime scene by analysis of the crime scene appearance, the locations and positions of the physical evidence, and the forensic laboratory examination of the physical evidence" (pp. 179–180). Saferstein (2007) offered a definition of crime scene reconstruction as well, "the method used to support a likely sequence of events by observing and evaluating physical evidence and statements made by those involved with the incident" (p. 83). In both of these definitions, words such as *process, analysis, physical evidence, laboratory*, and *statements* signal that crime scene reconstruction is a process that uses victimology, crime scene and lab reports, autopsy results, suspectology, and statement analysis to support scientific testing.

In order to safely and ethically reconstruct, several components of the case must be fleshed out and verified before moving forward toward the development of a plan:

1. The crime scene must be well documented:
   a. Accurate notes
   b. Accurate photographs
   c. Accurate sketches
   d. Accurate and abundant measurements
   e. Accurate interrelationships of physical evidence in the scene

The author does not recommend attempting to reconstruct anything that is not well documented because doing so puts everyone involved out on *an ethical thin limb*. The author recommends analyzing all components under the umbrella of crime analysis toward verification of the validity and reliability of the information before proceeding. In some cases, gaps in the case can be filled by way of other information, reinvestigation, or other methods readily available. Also, be sure the case file does not contradict itself and that all of the information is congealed. The entire case file must be analyzed and reviewed, and the author highly recommends using a Pre-Reconstruction Checklist (see Appendix H) toward determining if a crime scene reconstruction is the way to go.

Crime scene reconstruction, such as bullet trajectory reconstruction and/or bloodstain pattern reconstruction, will only give a glimpse of what occurred during the incident at best. Crime scene reconstruction is an approximate estimate and should never replace traditional homicide investigation or any other part of the process. Some of the ways crime scene reconstruction can be helpful is by identifying the following:

1. Is the scene staged or has it been manipulated with criminal intent?
2. The estimated positions of the parties involved.
3. The number of individuals involved in the incident.
4. How the victim was killed.
5. The sequence of events.
6. Prosecutorial theory.

And more specifically related to staged crime scenes in suspicious death cases

1. Was it homicide, specifically murder?
2. Was it suicide?
3. Was it an accident?

And what were both the victim's and suspect's approximate estimated actions or behaviors before, during, and after the incident grounded by the physical evidence in comparison to their statements? It is very important to be ultra-conservative when conducting crime scene reconstruction because it is limited by several factors, such as

1. Being an approximate estimate at best
2. Having no clear standard to compare to
3. Results that do not reveal the answer
4. Results yielding more than one way an incident occurred

This type of reconstruction is based on the precise measurement of the physical evidence or static features of the crime scene specifically, but the qualitative or interpretive value interplays to a degree. Furthermore, it is important to recognize and avoid formulating conclusions early in the process.

Again, before embarking on a reconstruction using the scientific method, be sure to have analyzed the entire case file to include, but not limited to, the law enforcement case file (i.e., crime scene, statements), the medical examiner's/forensic pathologist's case file (i.e., autopsy report, toxicology report), the laboratory reports (i.e., DNA, ballistics), other agency case files, and other documentation related to the case. All of the latter most likely were already analyzed during the earlier stages of crime analysis (see Appendix H).

One of the benefits of using the scientific method for reconstructive purposes is that it enhances the validity and reliability of the reconstruction and minimizes investigator bias. Simply speaking, the scientific method contains a series of steps that are designed to incorporate all of the ways people think in a slow process toward coming to the substantiated end result. The value of the scientific method is found in its aim, which is to guide thinking in a purposeful and decisive manner. For this discussion, after identifying the problem that needs to be addressed, the scientific method has been pared down to seven steps (Figure 10.1):

1. Ask a question
2. Gather information
3. Develop a hypothesis
4. Design a test
5. Test
6. Analyze
7. Report the results or design another test and analyze again

For example, a man called 911 to report that his wife shot herself while cleaning a gun in the couple's master bedroom suite. The initial results of the crime scene investigation were unclear as to if her death was accidental, suicide, or homicide and the forensic pathologist could not be sure either based on the evidence of injury. The prosecutor asks investigators, "Was the victim standing at the time she was shot?" Investigators decide to use VCDIM to analyze the case. Investigators gather information and conduct victimology, crime scene and lab report analysis, wound pattern analysis, suspectology, and statement analysis toward developing a hypothesis. Based on the totality of information, investigators hypothesized that the victim was actually sitting at her vanity chair in the bathroom when she was shot. Next, the investigators designed a test that included the information from the crime scene analysis and in partnership with the forensic pathologist from the autopsy report and investigatory wound pattern analysis. The test included short-range shooting incident trajectory reconstruction using a several reference points:

1. *Point 1*: The entrance wound on the victim
2. *Point 2*: The exit wound on the victim
3. *Point 3*: Defect entry location scientifically found to be consistent with a bullet having created it
4. *Point 4*: Defect exit location scientifically found to be consistent with a bullet having created it

When a dowel rod and laser were used to reconstruct location and orientation of the path this bullet took coupled with the bloodstain evidence recovered at the scene, investigators determined that the victim in this case was indeed sitting and not standing when she was shot. Investigators analyzed and interpreted their results and reported them.

Again, this in an introductory book that could not possibly cover all of the necessary micro skill sets, such as bloodstain pattern analysis and shooting incident trajectory reconstruction. The author recommends a well-rounded skill set in order to gain an eclectic perspective from the generalist's standpoint on victimology, crime scene and lab report analysis, wound pattern analysis, suspectology, and statement analysis; however, bloodstain pattern analysis and shooting incident reconstruction are worth mention in the next paragraph.

Bloodstain Pattern Analysis

According to James et al. (2005), bloodstain pattern analysis or "BPA focuses on the analysis of the size, shape, and distribution of bloodstains resulting from bloodshed events as a means of determining the types of activities and mechanisms that produced them" (p. 1). This means bloodstain pattern analysis is the analysis of bloodstains and their observable characteristics. It is very common to find blood in death scenes. Dating back to ancient times, bloodstains have been used to help understand what might have occurred during an individual's death or for other reasons (e.g., Story of Quintilian). The identification of bloodstains in crime scenes is very important and their documentation is no less important. Even if a bloodstain pattern expert is not available to help process the scene, thorough documentation can dramatically help bloodstain experts later analyze events that might have taken place at the crime scene.

Bloodstain pattern analysis is very important to crime scene staging because empirical research has shown that offenders go to great lengths to clean up and destroy bloodstain evidence (Ferguson, 2011; Pettler, 2011). Stagers have been found to clean flooring, walls, weapons, victims, clothing, bedding, their person, and so on. Blood behaves by specific scientific principles, such as certain laws of physics and is expressed in the language of mathematics so a fundamental understanding of those principles is paramount to accuracy and success (MacDonell, 2005). Bloodstain pattern analysis should always remain objective and grounded in scientific principle. When conducted correctly, the interpretation of bloodstain patterns can help determine an approximate estimation of

1. Where the victim was at the time of the assault
2. Where the assailant was at the time of the assault
3. What type of weapon was used

4. To locate evidence
5. The direction from which the blood originated
6. The area from which the blood originated
7. The number of offenders
8. Movements made during and after the assault by both the victim and offender

This is a limited list of the information bloodstain patterns can yield, but in relation to crime scene staging, it is very important to mention the use of bloodstain pattern analysis as a scientific tool toward unraveling the staged crime scene because one of the most important things bloodstain pattern analysis can do is to help support or refute statements made by witnesses, victims, and suspects. A suspect might say one thing, but proper analysis of the bloodstain evidence might reveal something else. In other words, bloodstain evidence analysis is very important to the processing efforts and then to reconstructive efforts because it can not only help explain in part what did happen but it can also help explain in part what could not or did not happen in accordance with direct statements given in a case. Pursuant to this fact, bloodstain pattern analysis is also used to help determine what occurred and in what order the events occurred. And again, as everything throughout the entire crime analysis process has been, bloodstain pattern evidence analysis helps investigators learn more about how each piece of the physical evidence interrelates under the arch of the totality of evidence as a whole. Understanding each individual part is just as important as understanding the whole.

Ferguson (2011) found that the majority of offenders who staged suicides moved bodies and weapons in the primary crime scene. Bloodstain pattern analysis can often be very helpful in situations like this toward determining the original position of the body versus the discovered position and likewise for weapons or other objects. In cases like these is where the scientific method comes in, which, as discussed earlier, is not a complex methodology only performed by scientists but rather a process method of which can be used to solve complex problems (Bevel & Gardner, 2008). There are limitless questions that could be asked to initiate the process that is the scientific method, but it is important to realize that the scientific method is used to answer one small question at a time, not big, overarching questions. Trying to use the scientific method to answer the question, "What happened in the crime scene?" is much too broad. Instead, one must narrow the scope of the problem and start out by identifying the problem. Again, each piece of the crime scene interrelates to the others so that is why breaking apart the problems in the case that require solving on the individual level is paramount to success of the whole. For example, maybe the problem is, "Was the victim lying down when he/she was beaten?" This is a very focused, direct question that can be tested using the scientific method in relation to the bloodstain evidence. The next step would be to gather as much information from the victimology, crime scene and lab reports, the autopsy report, suspectology, and statement analysis in order to understand the problem as a whole and what information can be used to design a test. Next, develop a hypothesis or what is expected. In this case, the hypothesis might be, "the victim was lying down at the time he/she was beaten." Using the principles of bloodstain pattern analysis, a bloodstain pattern analyst can then design a test to determine if yes the victim was lying down or no the victim was not lying down based using the bloodstain evidence in the case. Not every case had bloodstain evidence, but in cases that do, sometimes using it for this purpose is possible. After conducting the test, the analyst should interpret the results, which will lead to the results that indicate the position of the victim. In actual application, it is precise and requires a lot of education in this area in order to be accurate, but it is totally reasonable that the scientific method can be used to help address issues related to the bloodstain evidence in cases where crime scene staging is in question.

Shooting Incident Reconstruction
A potentially staged case that is a murder is very serious business. It is the opinion of the author that because a life was lost potentially at the ill will by the hand of another, it is the responsibility of the investigating party to exhaust all efforts in gathering information about the incident at hand. As discussed in a previous chapter, firearms are the most commonly used weapons in American homicides today. Interestingly, Ferguson (2011), Pettler (2011), and Schlesinger et al. (2012) found that firearms were also the most commonly used weapons in staged homicide cases. Therefore, like bloodstain pattern analysis, a brief mention about shooting incident reconstruction is warranted as well. According to Haag and Haag (2011), there are many considerations when discussing shooting incident reconstruction, such as the following:

1. How evidence is collected from the scene
2. Ammunition
3. Projectile penetration and perforation
4. The differences between firearms
5. Determination of actual bullet holes or defects in crime scenes
6. Trace evidence and gunshot residue in relation to distance and orientation of firearms
7. Ricochets
8. Trajectory reconstruction
9. Wound track reconstruction
10. Falling bullets in long-range shootings
11. Cartridge case ejection patterns

Like bloodstain pattern analysis, this is not an exhaustive list, but a sample of what shooting reconstruction experts commonly analyze. Two of particular interest are bullet trajectory and wound track trajectory. According to Hueske (2006), "fired cartridge cases missing or out of place and bullet trajectories inconsistent with stated shooter positions" are two ways that can signal a crime scene could be staged (p. 251). In addition to the fact that weapons are frequently positioned during staging attempts in some types of staged crime scenes, the importance of working with practitioners skilled in shooting incident reconstruction is essential toward resolving these types of issues (Ferguson, 2011; Pettler, 2011). One issue to commonly arise from the potentially staged shooting crime scene is, "Could the victim have shot himself or herself?" There are some, for example, who when encountering a victim with a bullet hole to the back of the head immediately think murder because one cannot shoot oneself in the back of the head. The author would argue that by turning the head all the way to the left or the right, that indeed one can shoot oneself nearly in the back of the head and thus, a shot to the back of the head does not automatically indicate murder, nor does it indicate staging. However, whether it is an unusual circumstance or not is not important to debate here, but what is important is the mention of how shooting incident reconstruction via the implementation of the scientific method can be instrumental in working toward resolving one small issue at a time in a case. Working in partnership always with the forensic pathologist and forensic laboratory analysts is paramount to success during this stage because in order to contemplate conducting a bullet trajectory and/or wound track trajectory analysis requires intricate levels of detail that can only be reported by those directly involved in testing the totality of the evidence submitted to the crime lab in compilation with the autopsy report results. Of course, the incorporation of victimology as the litmus test is the core of VCDIM, so using elements of the victim's information is critical to understanding the whole situation and all of the evidence in totality. This is not to say the implementation of the scientific method should be qualitative in any way; in fact the author recommends strict quantitative testing exclusively during this stage; however, it is important to always realize that when there's a "what," there is always a "why" and to minimize the importance of either is to limit the investigation to only one side of the coin so to speak.

Kaleidoscope System

Pursuant to the scientific investigations, the CSI effect, and the necessity of grounding in traditional methodology, in 2008, partnered with Lt. Detective Billy Scoggins and Lt. Detective Kelly Aldridge from the Rutherford County, North Carolina Sheriff's Office, the author invented what is known as tubular dowel crime scene reconstruction as seen in Figure 10.2.

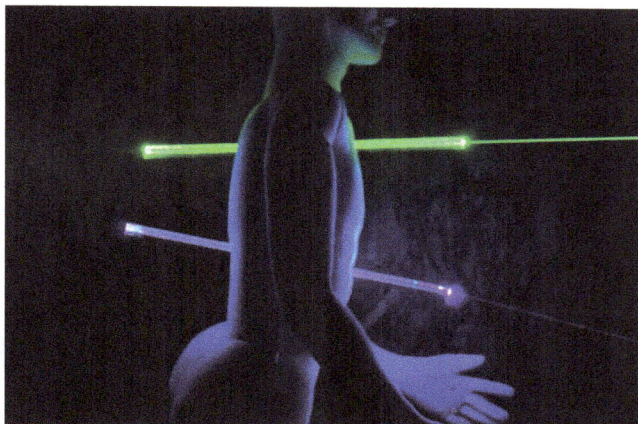

Figure 10.2 Example 1: Tubular Dowel Crime Scene Reconstruction

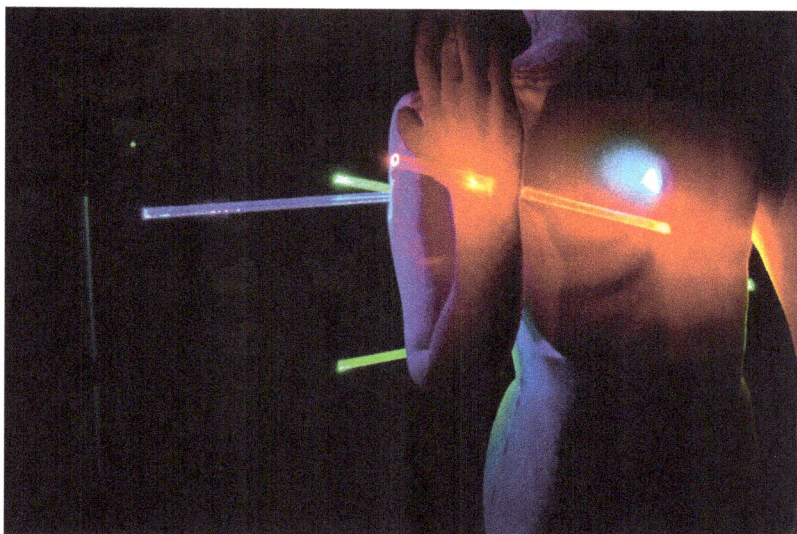

Figure 10.3 Example 2: Tubular Dowel Crime Scene Reconstruction

On the heels of a very complicated trajectory reconstruction conducted by the author and the detectives, it became obvious that using hollow dowel rods with lasers was the future of this type of reconstruction as seen in Figure 10.3.

After a tremendous amount of research and testing, tubular dowel crime scene reconstruction kits hit the market and were used successfully by agencies around the world who were looking to advance field-based traditional-type methods that met the objectives of not only the scientific requirements of trajectory reconstruction but the expectations of jurors because of the CSI effect as seen in Figure 10.4.

After 4 years of additional research, testing, trial and error, and working to improve the original concept and components of the tubular dowel crime scene reconstruction system, the author and her team, to include colleagues Dr. Galen Collins, Harold W. Ruslander, and other contributors, created the next-generation crime scene reconstruction, the Kaleidoscope System as depicted in Figure 10.5.

Figure 10.4 Example 3: Tubular Dowel Crime Scene Reconstruction

Figure 10.5 The Kaleidoscope System—Photo of an Original System

The Kaleidoscope System is the most comprehensive and versatile field-based crime scene reconstruction system in the world for those who wish to integrate both the reconstructive components of the blood-stain evidence and bullet trajectory evidence simultaneously. Most of its components are interchangeable with other reconstruction systems most commonly found in the field. While both components can be used independently as well, the integration of these two components is unique because both reconstructions are done completely by way of lasers, therefore eliminating strings, tape, and wooden dowel rods. Users of the Kaleidoscope System have many options, including the choice to use fiberglass dowel rods, as seen in Figure 10.6; or hollow dowel rods, as seen in Figure 10.7; whereas lasers, as seen in Figure 10.8, can be attached to

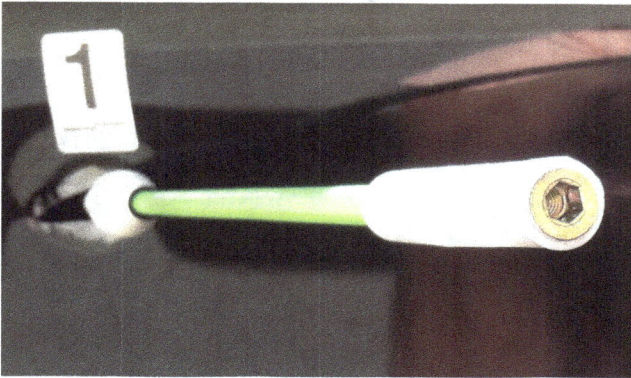

Figure 10.6 A Kaleidoscope System—Fiberglass Dowel Rod

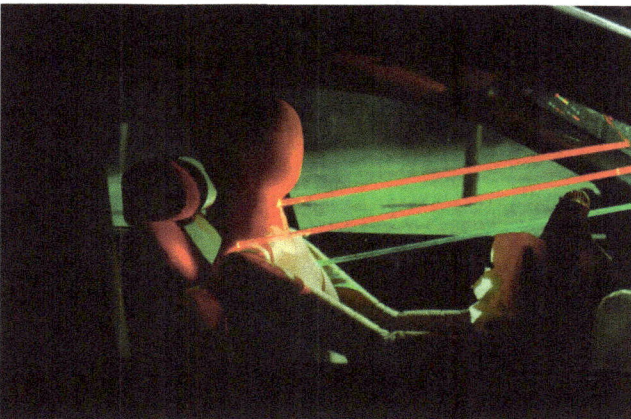

Figure 10.7 A Kaleidoscope System—Hollow Dowel Rod

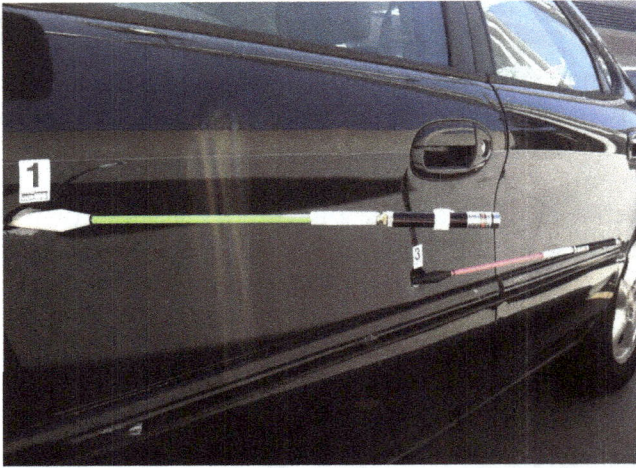

Figure 10.8 A Kaleidoscope System—Dowel Rod with Laser Attached

Figure 10.9 Lasers Attached to a Tripod for Forward Projection of Bullet Paths

tripods; as seen in Figure 10.9, for forward projection or attached to either the fiberglass or hollow dowels; as seen in Figure 10.10, for back extrapolation of bullet trajectories. On the bloodstain side of the Kaleidoscope System, users can reconstruct impact spatter bloodstain distributions on both the 2D using flatline lasers and on the 3D planes using dot beam lasers as seen in Figure 10.11.

The Kaleidoscope System has been met with resounding success and is currently carried by 18 forensic product distributors where it is sold in more than 30 countries worldwide. The Kaleidoscope System was born

Figure 10.10 Lasers Attached to Dowel for Back Extrapolation

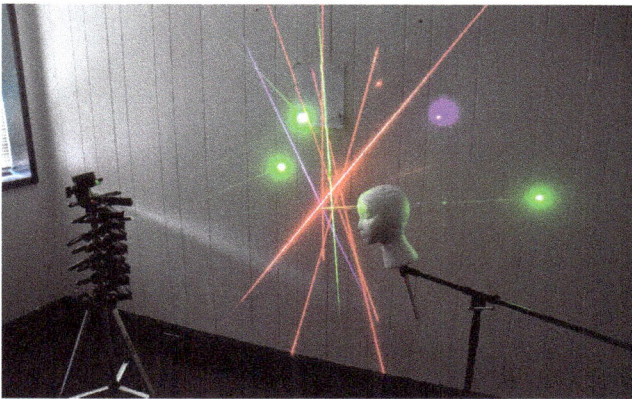

Figure 10.11 A Kaleidoscope System—3D Bloodstain Impact Distribution Reconstruction Using Flatline Lasers on the 2D Plane and Dot Beam Lasers on the 3D Plane as Seen in Figure 10.12

from the author's education, training, and experience in homicide investigation and specifically in staged cases where accident, suicide, or homicide is the question. The Kaleidoscope System is the only available reconstruction product on the market; thus, the author would encourage investigators to learn more about all reconstructive products on the market toward flexibility in the field.

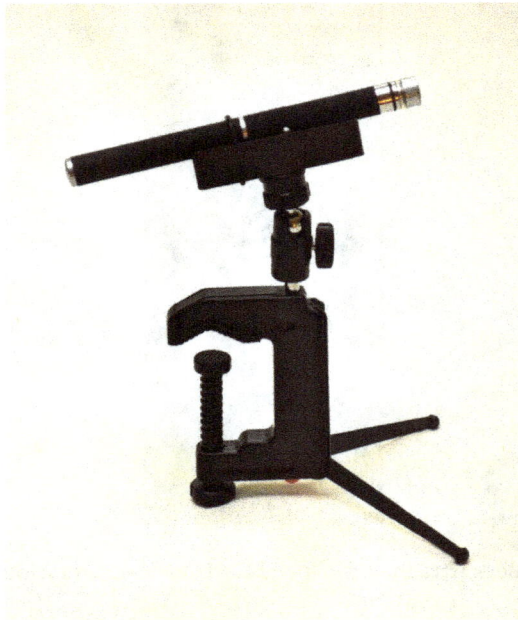

Figure 10.12 Tripod with Flatline Laser

References

Bevel, T., & Gardner, R. M. (2008). *Bloodstain pattern analysis* (3rd ed.). Boca Raton, FL: CRC Press/Taylor & Francis Group.

Chisum, W. J., & Turvey, B. E. (2011). *Crime reconstruction.* Waltham, MA: Academic Press.

DiMaio, V. J. M., & Dana, S. E. (2007). *Handbook of forensic pathology* (2nd ed.). Boca Raton, FL: CRC Press/Taylor & Francis Group.

Douglas, J. E., Burgess, A. W., Burgess, A. G., & Ressler, R. K. (2006). *Crime classification manual: A standard system for investigating and classifying violent crimes* (2nd ed.). San Francisco, CA: John Wiley & Sons, Inc.

Eke, A. W. (2007). *Staging in cases of homicide: Offender, victim, and offence characteristics* (Doctoral dissertation). Retrieved from ProQuest (1390310091).

Estate of Samuel Sheppard v. Ohio. (1995). CR64571, Case No. 3123322, October 19, 1995.

Ferguson, C. (2011). *The defects of the situation: A typology of staged crime scenes* (Unpublished doctoral thesis). Bond University, Gold Coast, Queensland, Australia.

Ferguson, C. (2014, July). Staged homicides: An examination of common features of faked burglaries, suicides, accidents and car accidents. *Journal Police Criminal Psychology.* Springer Publishing. doi: 10.1007/s11896-014-9154-1

Ferguson, C. (2015). Detecting staged crime scenes: An empirically derived "How-To." In W. Petherick (Ed.), *Applied crime analysis: A social science approach to understanding crime, criminals, and victims.* Waltham, MA: Elsevier.

Ferguson, C., & Petherick, W. (2014, October 13). Getting away with murder: An examination of detected homicides staged as suicides. *Homicide Studies.* doi: 10.1177/1088767914553099

Gardner, R. M. (2012). *Practical crime scene processing and investigation* (2nd ed.). Boca Raton, FL: CRC Press/Taylor & Francis Group.

Geberth, V. J. (2006). *Practical homicide investigation: Tactics, procedures, and forensic techniques* (4th ed.). Boca Raton, FL: CRC Press/Taylor & Francis Group.

Gross, H. (1924). *Criminal investigation.* London, UK: Sweet & Maxwell.

Haag, M. G., & Haag, L. C. (2006). *Shooting incident reconstruction* (2nd ed.). Burlington, MA: Academic Press.

Hueske, E. E. (2006). *Practical analysis and reconstruction of shooting incidents.* Boca Raton, FL: CRC Press/Taylor & Francis Group.

James, S. H., Kish, P. E., & Sutton, T. P. (2005). *Principles of bloodstain pattern analysis: Theory and practice.* Boca Raton, FL: CRC Press/Taylor & Francis Group.

James, S. H., & Nordby, J. (2005). *Forensic science: An introduction to scientific and investigative techniques* (2nd ed.). Boca Raton, FL: CRC Press/Taylor & Francis Group.

MacDonell, H. L. (2005). *Bloodstain patterns* (2nd rev. ed.). Corning, NY: Laboratory of Forensic Science.

Maslow, A. H. (1943). A theory of human motivation. *Psychological Review, 50,* 360–396.

McClish, M. (2001). *I know you are lying.* Wintersville, NC: The Marpa Group.

Parker, M. D. (2009). DV homicide: Hot blooded lovers, cold blooded killers [PowerPoint slides]. Vass, NC: Author.

Pettler, L. G. (2011). *Crime scene behaviors of crime scene stagers* (Doctoral dissertation). Retrieved from ProQuest (2251577601).

Rabon, D. (1994). *Investigative discourse analysis.* Durham, NC: Carolina Academic Press.

Saferstein, R. (2007). *Criminalistics: An introduction to forensic science* (9th ed.). Upper Saddle River, NJ: Pearson.

Schlesinger, L. B., Gardenier, A., Jarvis, J., & Sheehan-Cook, J. (2012, April). Crime scene staging in homicide. *Journal of Police and Criminal Psychology, 29*(1), 44–51.

Spitz. W. U. (2006). *Medicolegal investigation of death guidelines for the application of forensic pathology to crime scene investigation* (4th ed.). Springfield, IL: Charles C. Thomas.

Svensson, A., & Wendel, O. (1974). *Techniques of crime scene investigation* (2nd ed.). New York: Elsevier.

Turvey, B. E. (2011). *Criminal profiling: An introduction to behavioral evidence analysis* (4th ed.). London, UK: Academic Press.

Turvey, B. E. (2014). *Forensic victimology: Examining violent crimes in investigative and legal contexts* (2nd ed.). London, UK: Academic Press.

Crime Synthesis and Evaluation

11

Introduction

There are five truths in almost every murder case (Parker, 2009):

1. The killer is usually the last person to see the victim alive.
2. The killer is in control of the crime scene until either he or she leaves and/or someone else, including law enforcement, arrives.
3. The killer has a reason why he or she killed the victim.
4. The killer always has at least two motives for every murder.
5. The killer is lying.

It is arguable that when embarking on an investigation, it pays off to be the skeptic. It makes a difference to be the investigator who does not "buy" the crime scene as it is presented, the one who hungers to solve the problem, and the one who is willing to do whatever it takes to gather all of the necessary information in copious amounts if need be toward resolving every issue in the case. These are the types of investigators who do the very best with staged crime scenes (and cold cases). These are the investigators who consider everyone a suspect until the investigation reveals otherwise. It is important to recognize that those without a lot of homicide experience might not be as prone to recognize the signs of a staged homicide because stranger-to-victim homicides present much differently in many ways than staged stranger-to-victim homicides. This is why it is so very important to study the literature on the topic from both the policing and criminological scientific perspectives. Both are very valuable, but while advise can be offered based on anecdotal experience or opinions can be suggested, the author recommends a systematic, scientific methodology of one's choosing for conducting investigations into the potentially staged crime scene because it needs to hold up in court.

It is very important to recognize the significance of the last individual who sees the victim alive and/or the first person to discover the victim's body (Ferguson, 2011; Pettler, 2011). Further, it is always proactive to presume everyone involved is lying, and only through deductive reasoning and substantiation of events, eliminate (1) the last individual to see the victim alive, (2) the first person to discover the victim's body, and (3) all of those closely related to the victim before expanding to outside the victim's circle. Work the case from the inside out. A colleague of mine once said, "Look at the in-laws before you look at the outlaws." In the context of staged murder cases, the last person to see the victim alive and the first person to discover the victim's body and/or report the victim missing are more often one in the same than the opposite (Ferguson, 2011; Pettler, 2011).

Summary of Crime Scene Staging Behaviors and Characteristics

According to Eke (2007), Ferguson (2011), and Pettler (2011), empirical research has demonstrated that crime scene stagers in homicide cases most often have a current or former relationship of some kind with the victim. The current or former relationship with the victim is most likely an intimate partner, such as a spouse, ex-spouse, boyfriend, ex-boyfriend, girlfriend, and ex-girlfriend. In addition to staging the physical evidence in a crime scene, they will cross the line, and on top of manipulating just the physical evidence in the crime scene, they manipulate the entire crime itself by verbally staging or lying to investigators, friends, family, strangers, and others. Research has shown that stagers will clean up a crime scene and destroy the evidence, they will conceal and hide the evidence, and they will create and fabricate the evidence into the scene toward making the scene appear to be a completely different scenario as far from the truth as possible.

According to the literature published on crime scene staging, most of which has been primarily anecdotal, crime scenes are staged in ways that have not yet been supported by the empirical studies conducted on this topic. Most of the literature on crime scene staging is obsolete as well, especially due to the fact that the empirical research alludes to the fact that specific patterns of behavior are learned via the media and the Crime Scene Investigation effect (Podlas, 2006). It is also apparent that many crime scene stagers are not involved in criminal activity otherwise and have no idea how to stage a fatal car accident, train wreck, suicide, accident, sexual homicide, interrupted robbery home invasion, burglary, and so on, and therefore investigators must be alert to recognize the red flags (Ferguson, 2011; Pettler, 2011). Investigators must guard against moving toward using the evidence to endorse their own theory of the case and instead allow the evidence to lead the way. In doing so, the red flags can turn into signals that can create a road map to the truth.

Further, both Ferguson (2011) and Pettler (2011) found that empirical research does not support the use of crime scene staging typology or typologies at this time, and further research is needed in this area toward establishing if crime scene staging typologies could be useful in the field some day.

Conservative approach: steer clear from categorizing crime scene staging scenes, behavioral patterns, and so on, because it cannot be backed up in court at this time by the 11 empirical studies published on staging to date none of which support any typology tried to date for effective use in the field at this point. This is not to say that typologies could be useful at some point, but offering something based solely on experience or one's interpretive opinion is again not helpful to the scientific investigation of staging behaviors. Thus, unfortunately like many other typologies on homicide offenders, crime scene staging typologies are subjective and speculative at best. So, at this point, while some staging red flags have been discovered in the research, anything could really indicate staging that is why it is so important to examine every piece of physical evidence from every angle. It is very unfortunate that, while both those from the policing community and those from the scientific community/forensic criminology communities mention staging almost in passing in many books and articles and even claim that the number of staged cases could be increasing, still adequate resources have not been dedicated to the empirical study of crime scene staging and the criminal justice community needs to find more productive ways to move forward.

In tandem, two studies by Ferguson (2011) and Pettler (2011) have revealed the following about staging offenders and their characteristics:

1. Offenders are most often male.
2. There is most often one offender and one victim per case.
3. In more than 90% of the cases, the victim and offender have a previous relationship (Ferguson, 2011, p. 125).
4. In most cases, there is a conflict or confrontation preceding the murder.
5. Weapons used are most often firearms.
6. Weapons are second most often sharp objects like knives.
7. Offenders most often discover the body or report the victim missing.
8. Some offenders will reposition the body in the crime scene, but not as often transport the body away from the crime scene, especially in cases of staged suicide.
9. Home invasions, botched robberies, burglaries gone wrong, and suicides are staged more often than other accidents, car accidents, or sexual homicides.
10. Offenders most often clean and destroy the evidence, followed by removing it, hiding it, or bringing it into the scene.
11. Victims are most often found in their environment, such as in their homes and most often in their bedrooms, living rooms, and rarely in the offender's environment, unless the environment is a shared space between the victim and offender (Ferguson, 2011).

One of the interesting points found in Ferguson's (2011) study was that in cases of home invasion, offenders did not appear completely committed to staging the crime scene and did not stage points of entry and exit in the scenes; they had no evidence of injury although they brought the weapon to the scene, no alibi for the suspect, and personal items were not removed, but only ransacked through. In light of Ferguson's findings, Pettler (2011) found that an offender did stage points of entry and exit in at least one case where information was contained in the case file.

Staged suicides can be considered the second most common form of crime scene staging when assessing Ferguson's 2011 sample. In that sample of 18 cases, Ferguson (2011, p. 137) found the following facts:

1. 94% simulated self-injury
2. 56% of the offenders used firearms to kill their victims
3. 44% of the offenders "discovered" the victims' bodies
4. 83% positioned the weapon in the primary crime scene (movement not related to medical aid)
5. 66% positioned the body in the primary crime scene
6. 44.3% victim–offender were intimate partners or friends
7. 39.9% victim–offender were spouses
8. 5.5% victim–offender were strangers to each other before the murder

These findings support Pettler's (2011) findings in that the intimate partner victim–offender relationship and potentially intimate partner violence are compelling factors of which to base the decision as whether to stage a crime scene or not because it does not make sense to an offender to stage a crime scene if he or she would not be considered a suspect in the first place due to not having known the victim (Ferguson, 2011, p. 162). Additionally, the fact that an offender even debates whether or not to stage a crime scene is illustrious of the fact that the offender recognizes that what he or she did is inherently wrong and that there are organic consequences for such behavior, so lying to investigators coupled with the attempt to disguise the crime scene as something else is simply an admission of guilt. Further, these factors also appear to influence the offender's decision to be the one to discover the body when there is an effort to stage the scene as a legitimate death, therefore simulating it as though no crime occurred. Thus, the sequence seems to follow a pattern of conflict–murder–conflict, then clean up, destroy, reposition, discover, or some version of those variables. Following this was Ferguson's (2011) finding that in 75% of murders staged like accidents, the offender there is to opt to discover the victim's body (p. 137). At this point in the research, findings such as these and of course those not included in this book based on the date of publication are those which should be seen as red flags for investigators in the field that limits speculation and drawing conclusions based on intuition.

It is important to remember that the crime scene, the weapon, the location, and the evidence meet the needs of the offender. If the offender chooses a particular weapon, whether it be a firearm or a knife, for example, the reason he or she chose that weapon was because it met his or her needs down to accessibility, convenience, and opportunity. If the offender chooses to tell investigators anything, it is because it meets his needs. If the offender cleans, destroys, and hides the evidence, it is because it meets his or her needs. Always answer every question with "because it meets the needs of the offender" then peel back that first layer and ask "what need does it meet," peel again, and ask "why." There is a great place to start peeling away the layers of how what the offender did in the crime scene to stage the scene met his or her needs, what those needs were, and why.

VCDIM Outline

Again, to assist the reader in not having to look back in a previous chapter to recall the stages of victim-centered death investigation methodology (VCDIM) and its associated components, mentioned in the succeeding text is the VCDIM process outline for quick reference (see Appendix B). To reiterate, VCDIM is a systematic, multimodal, interdisciplinary approach that integrates homicide investigation, hard sciences, behavioral science, and forensic criminology into one investigatory approach.

1. Stage 1: Crime Scene Knowledge
   Type: Quantitative—Precise measurement of physical evidence
   Location: Level 1—Bottom, foundational level of Bloom's Taxonomy
   a. Is the crime scene staged? Staging Identification Trilogy
      i. Conflict/confrontation
      ii. Victim discovery
      iii. Verbal staging
   b. Ferguson's (2015) empirically derived staging detection how-to.
   c. Refuse to assume the integrity of the crime scene.
   d. Identify and detect the staging behavior and/or staged physical evidence.
   e. Define and describe the physical evidence.
2. Stage 2: Crime Scene Comprehension
   Type: Quantitative—Precise measurement of physical evidence
   Location: Level 2—One must identify, define, and describe, before one can classify and discuss:
   a. Document the initial observations of the scene.
   b. Classify and discuss physical evidence. This might not be done on paper but should be discussed with lab personnel and/or experts if needed.

    c. Develop plan for how to accurately, precisely, and appropriately meet the legal and scientific objectives of crime scene processing procedures and techniques.

    d. Plan needed resources that might not be on hand, such as chemicals or other specialized equipment that could detect staged elements of the scene.

3. Stage 3: Application of Crime Scene Technology

Type: Quantitative and qualitative—Precise measurement of physical evidence in the context of all evidence and crime scene as a whole

Location: Level 3—One can apply knowledge when the knowledge is acquired and understood:

    a. Prepare to execute crime scene processing plan taking careful consideration to process for elements of crime scene staging; this could mean additional photographs of angles not otherwise considered standard.

    b. Precisely measure using multiple points of reference, crime scene search methodology, etc., all items of physical evidence in addition to crime scene measurements. For later reconstructive purposes, be sure to measure everything in three dimensions (L × W × H); the more detailed this section is, the more likely reconstruction might be able to be done.

    c. Collect all physical evidence being sure to document all demographic information related to the evidence. One thing to note, the author has seen countless times bloodstain evidence lost due to inaccurate packaging. Allow wet items to dry, use paper to separate layers, then package so nothing is touching another part of the item (i.e., bedsheet).

    d. Preserve all items of physical evidence and document preservation efforts.

    e. Report all crime scene activity and processing system; include agency protocol, investigative summaries, supplements, crime scene logs, evidence lists and corresponding documents, measurements, photographs, notes, etc.; and assemble into a well-organized system that can be easily reviewed (the author suggests using a binder system to *tab* and organize reports). The report should be robust in breadth and depth, and contain both quantitative (the what) and qualitative (the how/why descriptive) in order to help the reader understand all the details about any particular piece of evidence and the crime scene as a whole. Create a table of contents and place at the front of the binder. Tab the binder sections.

4. Stage 4: Crime Analysis
   Type: Quantitative and qualitative—Studying the precise measurement of physical evidence in context and how it could be interrelated to the victim and other components
   Location: Level 4—One can analyze the application once knowledge is acquired and understood:
   a. Research-based forensic victimology—Using Maslow's hierarchy of needs as a conceptual framework to use the method and categories discussed in Chapter 5, conduct full victimological study on all victims, then use modified triangulation to determine if select information revealed in the study of the victim is empirical (can be validated and is reliable because it can be proven and substantiated), quasi-empirical (can be partially validated and/or is partially reliable possibly), or nonempirical (cannot be validated or relied upon because there is nothing to substantiate the information). Victimology is then used as a baseline for all other types of analysis, synthesis, and evaluation going forward.
   b. Crime scene and laboratory reports—Analyze all crime scene reports contained in the binder from stages 1, 2, and 3 along with interrelating them to the forensic service laboratory reports, such as DNA, serology, and ballistics to compare to victimology.
   c. Autopsy and wound pattern analysis—In partnership with the forensic pathologist, medical examiner, coroner, or other relevant parties, break apart each pertinent aspect of the autopsy then focus on studying the wounds to the victim. Complete wound analysis charts, diagrams, and spreadsheets to compare to crime scene, labs, and victimology.
   d. Suspectology (or statement analysis)—It is the study of the suspect or suspects. Complete suspectology for each suspect. This substage could be switched with statement analysis. Determine what is empirical, quasi-empirical, and nonempirical, then compare to wound analysis, crime scene, lab reports, and victimology.
   e. Statement analysis (or suspectology)—For the purpose of this discussion, statement analysis is the breaking apart of statements, studying each piece, then cross comparing statements given at different times to possibly different individuals to identify, define, discuss, then analyze very specific details related to the crime; this substage could be switched with suspectology. Determine what is empirical, quasi-empirical, and/or nonempirical if necessary, then compare to suspectology, wound analysis, crime scene, lab reports, and victimology.

5. Stage 5: Crime Synthesis

Type: Quantitative and qualitative—Putting together all the pieces of the puzzle

Location: Level 5—One can synthesize all of the pieces of the analysis once the knowledge is understood and applied:

   a. Crime Synthesis Matrix—Place all analyzed pieces in their proper location of one or more of the three columns of the matrix: before, during, or after the crime. Then take each piece listed in each column and if not already done during the analysis stage, determine if each piece is empirical, quasi-empirical, or nonempirical. Try to enter broad categories first, then underpin with the pieces of each.

6. Stage 6: Crime Evaluation

Type: Quantitative and qualitative—Drawing conclusions based on substantiation

Location: Level 6—Only when all other stages are complete, it is time to evaluate toward assigning worth, merit, or value:

   a. In partnership with the district attorney, state attorney, solicitor, prosecutor, or others, explain victim-based death investigation methodology, everything contained in the case, and the system and method by which each piece was analyzed and synthesized, then present all of the information for evaluation.

VCDIM Stage 5: Crime Synthesis

Crime Synthesis is level 5 of Bloom's Taxonomy, or as it applies to VCDIM as a conceptual investigative model, synthesis is Stage 5. Synthesis means to put parts together to make a new whole. Synthesizing is a creative experience, where parts of something are united toward forming something like a piece of music, for example. When a band comes together, the guitarist plays his or her part, the drummer his or her part, the bassist his or her part, the keyboard player his or her part, and the vocalist his or her part; together they synthesize their individual parts of the music to create a song. Based on this example, synthesis in relation to investigation means to synthesize the relevant components of victimology, the crime scene and laboratory investigation and reports, the autopsy results and investigatory wound pattern analysis, suspectology, and statement analysis and morph them into "the case." Within this context, investigators should be able to identify new patterns and interrelationships in both the physical and behavioral (i.e., victimology, suspectology) evidences, along with being able to formulate new ways to solve the ultimate problems related to potentially staged suspicious death case: was this crime scene staged; was this death an accident, suicide, or murder; and if it is a murder, who is the primary suspect?

Crime Synthesis Matrix: Keppel and Walter (1999) published an article about their four motivational typologies for rape–murder. Keppel and Walter began with two major types of offenders: power-based offenders and anger-based offenders. These researchers developed two subtypes for each major category: power assertive, power reassurance, anger retaliatory, and anger excitation. Each of these subtypes was defined by dynamics, homicidal pattern, and suspect profile based on nearly 22,000 offenders collectively interviewed throughout Keppel and Walter's careers. Keppel and Walter argued that most typologies are actually useless in practical application, but these four subtypes could be reasonably used to classify the type of crime scene first, followed by the dynamics and suspect profile characteristics. Keppel and Walter admitted in the abstract of the article that these typologies were based on their combined experience and were extensions of the already established rape motivational typologies.

In Adcock and Stein's (2011) book, they included a chapter written by Walter, Stein, and Adcock about identifying suspects using precrime (i.e., before), pericrime (i.e., during), and postcrime (i.e., after) behaviors. Their proposed method included using the crime scene data to identify the subtype of the offender as one of the latter (e.g., power assertive, power reassurance, anger retaliatory, or anger excitation) and build the three column matrix out from there. Once the subtype is identified and crime scene aspects are listed, then users are to identify the precrime behaviors and then the postcrime behaviors, then to draw vectors that connect the precrime, pericrime, and postcrime behaviors, which will identify the primary suspect based on what he or she did before the crime, during the crime, and after the crime. Walter et al. recommended building a crime matrix for each suspect because at some point the precrime, pericrime, and postcrime behaviors will not align and that suspect can be eliminated leaving in the end a schematic diagram of the primary suspect interconnected by vectors.

The major objective of VCDIM Stage 5, Crime Synthesis, is to be able to build a new structure or "build a case" from all of the pieces analyzed in VCDIM Stages 1–4: Crime Scene Identification, Crime Scene Comprehension, Crime Scene Application, and Crime Analysis, respectively. Therefore, the author would argue that while crime matrix of Walter et al. is very useful in the field, it can be expanded to meet both its originally intended objectives coupled with additional objectives on a case-specific basis. Thus, the author's expansion of crime matrix of Walter et al., called the "Crime Synthesis Matrix" (see Appendix C), is the working plan for how all of the important pieces come together in an empirically substantiated, systematic manner.

Before, During, and After the Death of the Victim

Like Keppel and Walter (1999) who expanded on existing typologies, the author's crime synthesis matrix is an expansion of Walter, Stein, and Adcock's (2011) crime matrix in several ways. The author recommends building this matrix in a spreadsheet-type computer program. First, the author's crime synthesis matrix retains the three-column approach but titles each column, respectively,

1. Before the death (precrime)
2. During the death (at the crime scene) (pericrime)
3. After the death (postcrime)

In each of the columns, there should be several bold level 1 headings: conflict/confrontation, verbal staging, victimology, crime scene and laboratory reports, autopsy (wound pattern analysis), suspectology, and statement analysis. The first column should include "last person to see the victim alive" and the third column should include "victim's body discovered by and/or victim reported missing by." The most critical information that was determined to be relevant to the case for each of the respective columns should be entered into the matrix in the appropriate column and under the appropriate level 1 heading as having occurred before the death, during the death/at the crime scene, or after the death. Additional level 1 broad headings should be added to flesh out each case-specific investigatory component. For example, in suspectology, it is determined that the suspect bought an insurance policy on his wife 3 months prior to her unexpected death (before the death), then mentioned the policy at the crime scene to investigators (during the death), then called the insurance company the next day to find out how to make a claim (after the death). There is a chain of behaviors that link together or interrelate that can be synthesized as having occurred before, during, and after the death of the victim. But based on the constellation theory, an insurance policy purchase, mentioning it at the crime scene, or even cashing it in the very next day, does not constitute that the death of the victim was a murder or that it was staged, so it is important to keep going at this point. The case begins to take shape a bit after categorizing all of the physical and behavioral evidence into one of the three columns (note that maybe a behavior is recurrent and thus is entered into more than one column). In cases of murder, when organizing the material in this way, it becomes much clearer what the conflict was between the victim and offender that precipitated the murder, how the murder resolved that conflict for the offender, and how the offender benefited from the victim's death whether it be emotionally, financially, or psychologically. But it does not stop there. Even though there is a tremendous amount of information that can be entered into the crime synthesis matrix under the categories listed earlier, it is then important to calculate which pieces listed in each column are empirical, which are quasi-empirical, and which are non-empirical (see Figure 9.4).

Victim-Centered Modified Triangulation: Empirical, Quasi-Empirical, and Nonempirical

To reiterate from the previous chapters, all evidence is not equal. That means that some evidence holds more weight than other pieces generally speaking. It is important to recognize that it is not the job of the investigators to determine which piece of evidence is more valuable to the case or not, but rather, it is the prosecutor's job to determine which pieces of evidence will get the case to the jury, and then it is ultimately the jury's decision as to just how much value a piece of evidence might hold. However, it is extremely helpful in the crime synthesis process to categorize the evidence by empirical, quasi-empirical, and nonempirical, because then when prosecutors ask "How do you know that for sure?" investigators can respond with what evidence they have that substantiates that piece-specific piece of evidence the prosecutor's asking about, therefore making it valid and reliable and in turn making the prosecutor more comfortable with the case. The process by which a piece of evidence is substantiated is called victim-centered modified triangulation as seen in Figure 9.4.

The idea is based on the crime scene mapping method of triangulating physical evidence in a crime scene. In this sense, when investigators find a piece of evidence, one way of mapping it in the crime scene is to triangulate the item at multiple points of reference from two fixed points, such as the corners of a room, for example, to document the item's orientation and how it interrelates to other items of evidence. By triangulating the item at multiple points of reference, it can then be placed in nearly the exact same position during reconstructive efforts. Likewise, the triangulation crime scene mapping method can be applied to every piece of evidence in the case whether physical or behavioral. There are three types of victim-centered modified triangulation to help categorize the evidence by how well it can be substantiated. *Empirical evidence* is evidence that can be triangulated by placing the piece of evidence at the top of the triangle just like in the crime scene, then listing at one fixed point what validates that piece of evidence and on the other fixed point listing what verifies the validation and/or the piece of evidence as is marked by a green triangle (see Chapter 5 for details). Then maybe an item under suspectology can only be validated, but the validation is weak and it is therefore not very reliable. This would be a *quasi-empirical* item of evidence as indicated by the yellow triangle in Figure 9.4. Additionally, there could be items brought over into the crime synthesis matrix from the crime analysis stage that cannot be validated or were not found to be reliable. These would be *nonempirical* items of evidence as denoted by the red triangles that symbolize that they might be illustrious, based on opinion, observation only, hearsay, and so on. The crime synthesis matrix like all other parts of any good investigation takes time, but once the entire matrix is fleshed out, the case really comes together in the next step.

Tying It All Together

Once each item listed in each of the three columns has been categorized as empirical (i.e., can be validated and is reliable), quasi-empirical (i.e., can be partially validated and/or is somewhat reliable), or nonempirical (i.e., cannot be validated or relied upon because nothing in the case substantiates it), at that point, all of the empirical evidence can be grouped together in the before column, the quasi-empirical can be grouped in the before column, nonempirical can be grouped under the before column, and the rest of the items can then be grouped in the same way under the during and after columns. The empirical items grouped together in the before, during, and after columns are the strongest items of evidence in the case because they can be validated and are reliable. The quasi-empirical items grouped together in the before, during, and after columns are also strong, but only moderately strong, because they can only be partially validated or are partially reliable. The nonempirical items grouped together under the before, during, and after columns are the weakest parts of the case, but should not be discounted completely, because they cannot be validated or were found to be reliable because prosecutors sometimes can use this type of material as illustrious evidence in opening and/or closing. It is important to focus on the empirical evidence as it will help develop the fact pattern of the case, the timeline, the sequence of events, and so on. Sometimes, the nonempirical items are not very helpful at all as well.

At this point, the empirical, quasi-empirical, and nonempirical evidence under the before, during, and after columns can be cross compared to each other in many different ways, and some will "jump off the page" as running concurrent in the before, during, and after columns in the matrix. These are very strong points of the case as well. All of the items should be cross compared and synthesized, as they interrelate as appropriate by drawing lines between them like matching vocabulary words to their appropriate definitions. Again, it is important to note that while nonempirical evidence is unsubstantiated evidence or evidence that cannot be validated or is relied upon, that does not mean that it is useless by any means. It only means that there is nothing known to investigators *at that time* that validates the evidence or its reliability. Cases are fluid all the time.

New information continually comes in many instances; therefore, a piece of nonempirical evidence on Monday could turn into an empirical item of evidence on Friday hypothetically speaking. Being open to alternatives always is the name of the game.

VCDIM Stage 6: Crime Evaluation

At this point, the investigation has come a long, long way: Beginning with VCDIM Stage 1, crime scene knowledge, and moving through all of the stages and their various components to finally reach the pinnacle, VCDIM Stage 6, crime evaluation. After reading the last two chapters and the first part of this chapter, it is probably much easier to understand now why it is impossible to draw conclusions at the crime scene. It has been the author's experience in teaching Bloom's Taxonomy to law enforcement as an investigative scaffolding that what investigators think at the beginning of the workshop is not often what they think at the end. One of the most common themes among them is that they know others who definitely draw conclusions too early and that Bloom's Taxonomy levels of thinking really illustrate how that can happen and why it should not happen.

VCDIM is not only an investigatory method, but it is also a journey. It is a journey with a case from beginning to end where investigators might be surprised how well they know their victims and even their suspects in the end. Out of all the homicide cases the author has been involved in, there are a few where through VCDIM the author ended up feeling as though "she knew" the victim even though there was no meeting before the victim died. As investigators, the author is sure that there are victims that "stick with you" long after the case is over. This is the truth about doing this job.

In the final stages of VCDIM, just like in the scientific method, after all of the steps are completed thoroughly and completely, the case can finally be evaluated. This means each item of evidence can be discussed scientifically with decision makers, such as police administrators, district attorneys, and coroners. Each piece of evidence is unique and special and should therefore be considered independent yet interrelated to the other items as well as its assigned investigatory and/or prosecutorial merit, value, and worth, but the jury ultimately decides the credence of evidence in the end. Pursuant to the investigatory purpose during Stage 6, investigators can also attribute investigatory worth or merit and so can the prosecutor. Having lots of experience working in a District Attorney's Office, the author can assure readers that prosecutors prefer to assign their own amount of value or worth to every item of evidence regardless of its investigative value to investigators. That is just the way it is. Prosecutors have a different skill set than investigators or even forensic criminologists like the author, and because they are the ones left holding the bag and presenting what they receive in the case file, giving them the strongest case possible is always the best course of action.

Now, if investigators *thought, felt,* or *believed* the case was a staged murder from the beginning, upon the completion of crime synthesis matrix, investigators *know* if it was a staged murder and can present their scientifically sound and substantiated circumstantial case to the prosecutor for his or her review and potential decision to prosecute. It is quite possible that the case really does not come together until Stage 5, crime synthesis, when all of the components are brought together in their interrelationships and in substantiating the facts but then really become a reality once having met with the prosecutor who adds his or her skill set and evaluation to the mix. One of the greatest strengths of the crime synthesis matrix is that when investigators explain to the prosecutor "this is what we got" based on the green triangles of empirically validated and reliable evidence and the prosecutor responds "ok, well how do you *know* that for sure?" Investigators can refer back to the two underpinning points of the green triangle and offer the prosecutor what they believe validates it and makes it reliable information then it is up to the prosecutor to interpret the prosecutorial value from there.

Regardless, now it is appropriate, possible, and desirable to draw conclusions; develop fact patterns, sequence of events, and timelines; develop prosecutorial theory; develop plans for prosecutorial reconstructions and courtroom demonstratives; employ the concept of constellation theory, which all stems from the VCDIM and its interrelated components that systematically allow investigators to gain knowledge of the situation; comprehend the situation; apply necessary constructs to the situation; analyze everything in the case completely; synthesize all of the analyzed parts; and then finally draw conclusions based on empirical findings. This is *VCDIM*-centered scientific and systematic, multimodal, interdisciplinary death investigation that redirects the misdirected crime staged by the offender for the sole purpose of deception.

Using Bloom's Taxonomy as a conceptual framework for organizing material at every level of thinking to ensure that no step is missed and no stone is left unturned is the heart of the VCDIM. The author recommends the study of Bloom's Taxonomy because the more one learns about the foundation, the better the pieces will fall into place. The importance of scientific, systematic, crime investigation methodology in applicable practice cannot be understated. And there is no doubt that after learning how to use VCDIM as scaffolding for organizing an investigation whether it is a staged intimicide or a stranger murder, the user is sure to discover that "Our system determines our outcome."

References

Adcock, J. M., & Stein, S. (2011). *Cold cases: An evaluation model with follow-up strategies for investigators.* Boca Raton, FL: CRC Press/Taylor & Francis Group.

Eke, A. W. (2007). *Staging in cases of homicide: Offender, victim, and offence characteristics* (Doctoral dissertation). Retrieved from ProQuest (1390310091).

Ferguson, C. (2011). *The defects of the situation: A typology of staged crime scenes* (Unpublished doctoral thesis). Bond University, Gold Coast, Queensland, Australia.

Ferguson, C. (2015). Detecting staged crime scenes: An empirically derived "How-To." In W. Petherick (Ed.), *Applied crime analysis: A social science approach to understanding crime, criminals, and victims.* Waltham, MA: Elsevier.

Keppel, R. D., & Walter, R. (1999). Profiling killers: A revised classification model for understanding sexual murder. *Interpersonal Journal of Offender Therapy and Comparative Criminology, 43*(4), 417–437.

Parker, M. D. (2009). DV homicide: Hot blooded lovers, cold blooded killers [PowerPoint slides]. *Evidence based domestic violence prosecution course.* Carthage, NC: Author.

Pettler, L. G. (2011). Crime scene behaviors of crime scene stagers (Doctoral dissertation). Retrieved from ProQuest (2251577601).

Podlas, K. (2006, December 1). The CSI effect and other forensic fictions. *Loyola of Los Angeles Entertainment Law Review, 27*(2), 87–125.

Walter, R. Stein, S., & Adcock, J. M. (2011). Suspect identification using pre-, peri-, and post-offense behaviors. In J. M. Adcock & S. Stein (Eds.), *Cold cases: An evaluation model with follow-up strategies for investigators.* Boca Raton, FL: CRC Press/Taylor & Francis Group.

The Future
12

Introduction

Any deliberate effort made by an offender before police arrive to manipulate the pristine condition of a crime scene to purposely misdirect and thwart the investigation and with the criminal intention to frustrate the overall criminal justice process is the essence of crime scene staging. Empirical research has shown that crime scene staging is on the rise, which could be due to public fascination with crime scene-related media, enhanced awareness of forensic science application, and/or offenders' belief in their understanding of how crime scenes should look (Ferguson, 2011, 2014; Schlesinger, Gardenier, Jarvis, & Sheehan-Cook, 2012). This book has explored what is empirically known about crime scene staging and has introduced an empirically derived how-to (i.e., victim-centered death investigation methodology [VCDIM]) for field use toward the early identification and detection, crime analysis, synthesis, and evaluation of potentially staged crime scenes. Further, VCDIM integrates the precise measurement and critical documentation techniques used to create a permanent record of the physical evidence in a crime scene, such as bloodstain pattern evidence and/or firearms-related incident evidence for the purpose of a systematic, scientific, comprehensive, multidisciplinary reconstructive process toward supporting or refuting claims made by an offender in relation to all other aspects of the evidence in totality.

Crime Scene Staging Awareness Initiative (Figure 12.1)

It is difficult to believe that of all the literature published on crime scene investigation (CSI), offenders, victims, intimate partner violence, and so on, only a handful of empirical studies exist specifically dedicated to the study of crime scene staging. This has to change. Resources must be allocated for the study of staging because it is an important public safety issue. The necessity for available education of crime scene staging dynamics in homicide cases cannot be understated. Therefore, upon the completion of the author's 2011 dissertation, "Crime Scene Behaviors of Crime Scene Stagers," the author launched the Crime Scene Staging Awareness Initiative housed at http://www.crimescenestaging.com and in 2014 highlighted by

Figure 12.1 Crime Scene Staging Awareness Initiative Ribbon

an awareness Facebook page, *The Crime Scene Staging Awareness Initiative* (Carolina Forensics, LLC, 2014; Pettler, 2014). These two web resources contain information about crime scene staging, historical references lists on crime scene staging, the author's articles on crime scene staging, published literature on the topic, along with other information. The goal of these resources is to help heighten awareness of the societal problem crime scene staging creates. For investigators and those in the criminal justice profession that are charged with the duty of investigating staged crime scenes, the goal of the initiative is to house resources in one easy-to-find location. For students, the author hopes it helps with their literature reviews so they do not go through what the author went through toward locating much of the literature on the topic. The author always welcomes contributions from anyone who wishes to contribute and hopes this outreach is helpful.

Recommendations for Future Research

Maybe not the most detailed, but definitely one of the most extensive summative literature reviews on crime scene staging to date could be comprised in this book. This book is the first book dedicated to the topic of crime scene staging in both theory and concept substantiated by the empirical research findings published on the topic to date. The goal of this book was to use case examples to illustrate behavioral patterns, but relying only upon the empirical evidence to underpin the theory and concepts presented herein. Although very few empirical studies exist on crime scene staging with the exception of Eke (2011), Ferguson (2011), Ferguson and Petherick (2014), Geberth (2010), Hazelwood and Napier (2004), Keppel and Weis (2004), Pettler (2011; in press 2015), Schlesinger et al. (2012), and Turvey (2000), several characteristics have been confirmed about staging, such as the following:

1. Offenders are most often male.
2. Victims are most often female.
3. Victims and offenders almost always have a prior relationship.
4. Conflict between the victim and offender precedes the murder.
5. Victims are most often discovered by offenders or reported missing by offenders.
6. Weapons are most often firearms.
7. Scenes are most often staged as burglary/home invasion/robbery types and suicides more than accidents or sexual homicides.
8. Offenders will verbally stage or lie toward facilitating the staged physical evidence and/or crime scene.
9. Typologies have not been found to be mutually exclusive limiting or negating their effective use in the field at this point.
10. An abundance of resources must be dedicated to update and continue the empirical research of crime scene staging.

Clearly, this short list does not do justice to the tremendous efforts of all of the authors cited in this book toward contributing to the gap in the literature on crime scene staging, their findings, ideas, and suggestions both empirically and anecdotally throughout the literature, but it does capture some of the key points that might act as a springboard toward future research.

Expanded Sample Sizes

Based on her 2014 findings, Ferguson recommends continued research in several areas that begin with expanding sample sizes toward broad-brush application of results across the general target population. It is important to remember that while the *what* is certainly important, the *why* is also very important, so selecting larger case samples is paramount to forward movement in filling the gap of empirical literature on crime scene staging, but coupling the quantitative research with supporting qualitative research so descriptive studies can be put in context would also be helpful in the future as well (Ferguson, 2014; Pettler, 2011). To date, sample sizes have remained rather small. In order to gain knowledge that is applicable to the broader population of offenders, sample sizes must be expanded.

Staging Prevalence and Frequency

Another area of future research that is necessary toward understanding the phenomenon of staging is in the area of prevalence and frequency.

Ferguson (2011, 2014) found that crime scene staging increased 104% in support of Geberth's (2006), Hazelwood and Napier's (2004), Pettler's (2011), Schlesinger et al.'s (2012), and Turvey's (2000) suggestions that crime scene staging is on the rise due to crime scene-related media and "forensic education" via crime scene-related television programming and the like. Various types of longitudinal studies focusing on specific time spans using sophisticated methodologies for data analysis are warranted as underpinning for the separation of specific types of overlapping behavioral patterns observed in staged crime scenes (e.g., burglaries/home invasions/robberies, suicides, accidents, sexual homicides) over time to be studied independently (Ferguson, 2014).

Again, pursuant to context of why offenders stage, further research should be dedicated to the area of studying why some offenders choose to stage and some do not, when ultimately most offenders aim to not get caught (Schlesinger et al., 2012). Here qualitative research design using sophisticated methods for data analysis studying homogeneous samples of offenders toward understanding their intrinsic motivations (i.e., personal reasons) for staging their particular crime scenes could and possibly even expand this research into examining why certain offenders choose the specific type of staging they chose, which could yield thematic analysis results that could aid in a greater understanding of the quantitative data published to date and in the future. Although qualitative research design focuses primarily on small sample sizes with results that cannot be applied generally with a broad brush, the author recommends purposive samples delineated by focused parameters toward inclusion of only the most relevant cases using expanded sample sizes.

Staging and the CSI Effect

The societal problems brought on by crime scene staging have not been thoroughly researched or well documented. As Hollywood continues to saturate American television with crime scene-related programs, additional empirical research with regard to crime scene staging and the CSI effect (i.e., the CSI effect is the effect fictional and nonfictional crime scene-related media, movies, and television in various forms has on the American public) is necessary and warranted (Douglas & Munn, 1992; Ferguson, 2011, 2014; Geberth, 1996; Pettler, 2011). In light of studying offenders themselves, research is necessary toward measuring the CSI effect in relation to crime scene staging and if it correlates to influence, effect, impact, and/or predict offender motivation and decision making in both general and specific terms to stage a murder. Empirical findings have shown that offenders range on a level-of-effort or sophistication-type continuum from simplistically staged scenes (i.e., monothematic) through elaborately staged scenes (i.e., polythematic), notwithstanding the notion that most offenders who stage crime scenes are assumed to have no other connection to criminal activity; thus they have no idea how a staged burglary/home invasion/robbery, suicide, or accident is supposed to look (Ferguson, 2011; Pettler, 2011; Schlesinger et al., 2012). Dedicating resources toward studying offenders and what they actually believe they know about forensic science, crime scene investigation, and related concepts is warranted.

Offender Characteristics and Behaviors

To reiterate, approximately 340 staging offenders have been studied to date (see Chapter 4). Again, Douglas and Munn (1992) argued that crime analysis requires in-depth insight into the dynamics of human behavior (p. 249). Further, these authors argued the combination of an individual's speech patterns, writing styles, verbal and nonverbal gestures, and other traits shape their behavior and that it is this very combination that causes individuals to behave in specific ways. Additionally, Douglas and Munn posited, "this individualistic behavior usually remains consistent, whether it concerns keeping house, selecting a wardrobe, or raping and murdering" (p. 249). Douglas and Munn's argument has credence. Petherick and Ferguson (2009) supported Douglas and Munn with their concept of *behavioral consistency* or the notion that an offender's behavior will be consistent across the board between his or her criminal and noncriminal behaviors, which is based on the concept of *interpersonal coherence* (Canter, 1994).

Throughout this book, the author has theoretically argued that the totality of personality, cognition, behavior, emotionality, and envirosocioculturalism is the driving force behind both staging and nonstaging behavior. Currently, empirical findings about offenders who stage are limited to primarily descriptive findings, which are critically important toward building quality research designs to adequately study those subcategories of findings and others. With the exception of Ferguson's (2011) international sample of staged cases, at this point in the literature, the author's concept of envirosocioculturalism or the aggregate of environmental, social, and cultural conditions that influence the life of an individual combined with the circumstances by which one is surrounded as part of a community distinguishable by particular ways of living within the social construct and its unique identity as seen in its beliefs, customs, religion, lifestyle, professions, interpersonal relationships, and routine activities has not been addressed. Thus, the author would recommend future research centered on identifying commonalities, types, frequency, and so on, of offenders' characteristics and behaviors from not only various cultural pockets throughout the United States but cross-culturally from around the world.

Victim Characteristics: Victimological Studies

Not much information is available about the victims of staging offenders yet in the empirical literature. While victimological information is plentiful in other areas of homicide studies, the handful of empirical studies on staging thus far have been mostly descriptive with some other types of analysis included in a few of them. The author opines that one of the most critical areas that warrants further research is on the victims of staging offenders. Research has shown that most victims are female. Research has also shown that someone they know murders most female victims. Research has shown victims are most often killed with firearms. But who are these victims? What are these victims' thematic similarities, commonalities, characteristics, and so on? All of which is so vital to understanding who the offenders are of crime scene staging in relation. Knowing that they are female and that either intimate partners or someone else who they are associated with kills them most often with a firearm is too broad to be much help.

Victim–Offender Relationship

Eke (2007) argued that crime scene staging could be a function of the relationship and the experience of the offender and the victim. Ferguson (2011, 2014) and Schlesinger et al. (2012) supported Eke's argument with the results of their studies. While Pettler's (2011) study yielded victim–offender-related results that modestly supported staging as a function of victim–offender relationship (e.g., in six homicide cases, offenders were boyfriends of the victims, three offenders were spouses of their victims, and two offenders were the son of their victims), these findings are believed only to be an outcrop of the broad definition Pettler used in that study specifically in relation to the parameters set for the purposive sample in this study. The results of more recent studies confirm the linkage between victim–offender relationship and crime scene staging; thus more research in this area is necessary. What is most interesting about victim–offender relationship again is that if an offender feels he or she is going to be thought of as the most logical suspect in the death of the victim, it often compels him or her to stage the scene theoretically speaking. Research has shown that intimate partners are more likely to murder than stage more; thus, further inquiry about the nature of those intimate relationships and recurrent themes, commonalities, frequencies, and so on would move the ball forward as well.

Conflict and Confrontation

The concepts of primary conflict and secondary conflict as they relate to crime scene staging have been discussed in this book. To reiterate, primary conflict is the conflict between the victim and offender that precedes the murder, while secondary conflict is the conflict between the offender and investigators that is created by the murder of the victim. The author agrees with Ferguson's (2011, 2014) argument that confrontation (i.e., conflict) is a core, exacerbating factor in relation to crime scene staging, especially in intimicide cases. Future research on the types, commonalities, characteristics of, and other concepts related to the issue of conflict in crime scene staging could yield results that are significant for early identification and detection of staged crime scenes and for crime analysis purposes.

Victim Discovery

The author argued that the last person (i.e., the offender) to see the victim alive is most often the first person (i.e., the offender) to discover the victim's body or report the victim missing as confirmed by current empirical research conducted by Ferguson (2011, 2014). Therefore, research that examines offenders, specifically in regard to how they discovered the victim, when they discovered the victim, why they claimed to have discovered the victim, what they were doing when they discovered the victim, where they discovered the victim, and related ideas via quantitative descriptive analysis would shed some light on this virtually uncharted territory of crime scene staging research.

Weapons

In her doctoral dissertation, the author (2011) found that firearms were the most commonly used weapons in her sample of staged homicide cases. Pettler found that 12 offenders used firearms, 4 offenders bludgeoned their victims, 1 offender used ligature strangulation, and 1 victim's cause of death could not be determined. Likewise, Ferguson (2011, 2014) and Schlesinger et al. (2012) reported similar findings; thus toward understanding murder weapon selection in greater detail, future research is necessary. Related to weaponry but not discussed herein is that of the weapon of poison. Thus far, the published literature has not included much on the use of poison as a murder weapon, but because poison could also be used as a murder weapon, it justifies its inclusion.

Verbal Staging

Verbal staging or lying is the act connected to either the offender falsely supporting the physical evidence staged in a crime scene by way of verbal discourse or the offender verbally falsifying that the victim is missing after the offender has disposed of the victim's body (Ferguson, 2011; Hazelwood & Napier, 2004; Pettler, 2011; Schlesinger et al., 2012). Within the scope of this research, the author would also recommend focusing resources on studying the initial stories that are told to investigators at the onset and how those stories change and/or remain consistent across time, all of which should be analyzed using statement analysis. Second, along the same strain, research in the area of what offenders tell family and friends of the victim (and/or offender) and how those stories change and/or remain consistent across time might aid in the establishment of behavioral patterns when it comes to verbal staging among offenders before, during, and after the death of the victim. For example, based solely on the author's experience, this idea stems from the numerous cases where offenders who staged murders as suicides claimed they were coming out of the bathroom at the "time of the shot" or when the victim allegedly committed suicide with a firearm during an argument in the presence of the offender. While this idea is purely anecdotal, empirical research could lend credibility or refute this author's experience.

Behavioral Taxonomy

Both Ferguson (2011) and Pettler (2011) found that the effectiveness that crime scene staging typologies could have in practical application at this point is greatly reduced by the sheer overlap between behavioral patterns exhibited by offenders as examined in both studies. Ferguson and Pettler's independent studies are the only studies to date that have attempted to classify staged crime scenes using proposed typologies that are mutually exclusive of each other, because neither typological set was successful. Thus, again the author cautions others from utilizing any proposed typologies related to crime scene staging because at this point, no typological system is supported by the empirical literature (Ferguson, 2011; Pettler, 2011). In order to be applicable in practical crime scene field application, any proposed typology would have to be substantiated by a very large sample size.

Crime Scene Staging and Law Enforcement Professionals

Former city of Monroe, North Carolina, police officer, Josh Griffin was convicted in 1998 for the murder of a Kim Medlin (*North Carolina v. Joshua Patrick Griffin*, 1998). Medlin was on her way home one late night in March 1997 when, while on duty driving his patrol car, former officer Griffin ran his blue lights and stopped Medlin to allegedly make a sexual advance toward her. Medlin never arrived home from work and her body was recovered 36 h later partially concealed under a pallet and other debris. While laboratory tests revealed negative results for biological or trace evidence connecting

Griffin or his vehicle to Medlin or the crime scene, circumstantial evidence led a jury to convict Griffin of first-degree murder and first-degree kidnapping, thus sentencing him to life in prison.

In 2004, Kathleen Savio's body was recovered in a bathtub in her home. The medical examiner ruled her death accidental. Upon a second look in 2008, autopsy results were changed to homicide. Savio's former husband and father of her children, former police officer, Drew Peterson was convicted in 2012 of killing Savio and sentenced to 38 years in Illinois State Prison. However, prior to these events in 2007, Drew Peterson reported that his fourth wife, Stacey, had gone missing. Peterson claimed Stacy *ran off with another man* to flee from life's obligations. Peterson is the only suspect in the missing person case of Stacy Peterson. Because of cases like Kathleen Savio, where red flags were missed that the scene was staged by the offender in this case, additional research is necessary toward assisting law enforcement in recognizing the red flags early in investigations. Considering that Geberth (2006) argued that homicide investigators are very highly trained and well-educated law enforcement professionals and their training and experience would indicate that they would most likely be proficient in areas like crime scene investigation, the manner in which offenders with law enforcement experience is of particular interest. In light of Turvey's (2000) study of 25 staged homicide cases, which contained 5 offenders who were law enforcement professionals combined with offenders with prior law enforcement experience having been represented in more recent studies, further research in this area might help to identify the connection between the two variables toward shedding light on this concentrated target population (Ferguson, 2011, 2014; Schlesinger et al., 2012).

American Cold Case Epidemic

According to Hargrove (2010), "more than one-third of America's killers are getting away with murder," and homicide clearance rates have dropped significantly from around 90% in the 1960s to roughly around 65% in the 1990s (Hargrove, 2010, p. 1). Cold case homicides and missing persons cases are cases that have remained unsolved for some period or a specific time or a case ruled homicide by a forensic pathologist, medical examiner, or coroner that has gone without an arrest (Walton, 2006). Cases go cold for many reasons, but one of the main reasons is because many cold cases lack the evidence to make an arrest. Sometimes, a case can be factually strong but legally weak. And many times, circumstances like these are completely out of investigator control. According to Walton (2006), it is important to remember that law enforcement has no control over factors, such as (p. 21)

1. Lack of physical evidence in a case
2. Witnesses refusing to talk
3. Inability to identify the victim
4. Inability to determine the murder weapon
5. Inability to locate the primary crime scene

Beyond these reasons, there are several police agency organizational reasons why cases might go cold related primarily to leadership, politics, budget, personnel, management, and allocation of resources. The bottom line is many agencies are short handed, underfunded, and overworked leaving no one completely committed to take on the cold case work. These circumstances leave detectives with no time to work the *hot* cases adequately that keep happening every day let alone having time to focus on the cold cases piling up. Additional challenges are brought by detectives retiring, leaving the job due to transfer, being promoted or sometimes individuals leave the field of law enforcement altogether, which leaves cases in limbo waiting to be assigned to other detectives when possible.

According to Walton (2006), cases that most often go cold are gang- and drug-related street crimes, missing persons, or cases involving immigrants, transients, or the homeless (p. 21). Hargrove (2010) reported similar findings that substantiated Walton's (2006) claim. Following those types are unidentified victim cases, potentially staged cases as some type of accident or a suicide (Ferguson, 2011; Walton, 2006). According to Hargrove (2010), the American murder problem became more violent, senseless, and random with the increase of stranger-to-stranger homicides and the exacerbation of America's illegal drug trade during the 1980s through the 1990s, which bred more gangs and more drug- and gang-related murders. This blurred the lines between the victim and offender, and the link between them became more challenging to identify along with motives remaining cloaked and physical evidence remaining bleak. The sheer number of homicides that were occurring during this period brought about new challenges for law enforcement, and insufficient investigations became more commonplace leaving violent offenders to roam free with the opportunity to offend again. Although proven ineffective, the homicide investigatory paradigm remained seated on suspect and motive rather than the shift seen today toward the victim and physical evidence. All of this combined with a lack of training, education, and experience of some law enforcement personnel continued to contribute to the backlog.

The most accurate and relevant American cold case statistics known today come from the analysis of case details contained in the files housed by the Federal Bureau of Investigation of nearly one-half million homicides and nonnegligent manslaughter cases (525, 572) that occurred between 1980 and 2008 in the United States (Hargrove, 2010). Although this analysis conducted by Scripps Howard News Service (i.e., Hargrove) published in 2010 revealed the very clear pattern, which was that most of America's 185,000 cold case homicide victims are young, minority males, the second most significant pattern it revealed was that the majority of female cold case homicide victims are those suspected to have been murdered by someone they knew, such as a close associate like a spouse, boyfriend, or other type of intimate partner (Hargrove, 2010). This finding is remarkable in that it supports the victim–offender relationship link identified in empirical crime scene staging studies conducted by Eke (2010), Ferguson (2011), and Pettler (2011), which found that the female victims are most often killed by someone they know and whose killers are more often likely to stage the scene of the murder in some way in an attempt to simulate a legitimate death because these offenders automatically know they will be considered a suspect immediately. This finding is also significant because it is reflective of the likelihood that suspects are known to investigators in many intimicide cases, but most likely these cases are largely circumstantial possibly due to the initial response, documentation, identified evidence, and overall investigation where the earmarks of staging were missed, supported by the fact that if investigators revealed that these victims are potential victims of intimicide, crime scene staging might be occurring more often than the previously published literature predicted (Keppel & Weis, 2004). But what about all the cases that were actually murders that were ruled suicide, accident, and so on? Those "cold cases" are not included in any of these numbers because they are not considered unsolved "homicides." The manners of death in these cases were not ruled homicide, and therefore, the author would argue that the actual number of unsolved murder cases in the United States far exceeds findings of Hargrove (2010).

The days of lone-detective homicide investigation are over (Adcock & Stein, 2011; Ferguson, 2011; Pettler, 2011; Turvey, 2002; Walton, 2006). Gone are the days where speculation, intuition, and instinct bring cases to fruition. The homicide investigations of the 1980s and 1990s clearly demonstrated the dire need for the development of a new investigative technique that responds appropriately to the ever-changing ways homicides occur in America today. Interdisciplinary teams consisting of all types of investigators, crime laboratory personnel, various types of medical professionals, attorneys and legal professionals, and a wide array of experts in criminology, psychology, biology, chemistry, anthropology, entomology, and physics, coupled with tremendous new technological advancements are the here and now and the future of scientific homicide investigation today. It must become the norm that this interdisciplinary team come with extensive homicide experience, proficient quantitative and qualitative interview techniques, strong deductive reasoning skills, creativity and innovation, motivated and enthusiastic, yet patient and analytical, but with the hunger to go to the ends of the earth to catch a killer (Walton, 2006). In addition to these attributes, experts in bloodstain pattern analysis, shooting incident reconstruction, linguistic analysis, forensic criminologists and psychologists specializing in victimology and suspectology all grounded by the scientific method are a must-have too. Pursuant to this shift, in order to address America's cold case homicide problem, the author would argue that an interdisciplinary, scientific, systematic review of many of the 185,000 cold cases is warranted, which might yield new information for investigators to use to reopen and reinvestigate the case toward making the arrest.

American Investigative Society of Cold Cases (Figure 12.2)

Kenneth L. Mains, cold case detective for the Williamsport, Pennsylvania, District Attorney's Office, was assigned a very challenging cold case where a young woman and her school-age daughter had been brutally murdered in their home. The case had been cold for more than a decade when Mains was assigned and in no time at all did he realize that a scientific, interdisciplinary approach was needed to help move the case forward. This revelation sparked Detective Mains' idea to create a society where experts from every discipline and beyond banded together as volunteers to provide scientific, interdisciplinary, and professional case review for law enforcement agencies afflicted with part of the backlog of America's cold cases. In May 2013, Detective Mains reached out to some of the top practitioners in the United States inviting them to sit on the newly founded American Investigative Society of Cold Cases (AISOCC) Honorary Review Board. Within no time,

AISOCC
THE AMERICAN INVESTIGATIVE
SOCIETY OF COLD CASES

A PROFESSIONAL REVIEW OF THE UNSOLVED

Figure 12.2 American Investigative Society of Cold Cases

many of the practitioners accepted Mains invitation and "AISOCC's" first year (2013–2014) Honorary Review Board was seated. Members included, Dr. Henry Lee, Dr. Cyril Wecht, Dr. Werner Spitz, Dr. Katherine Ramsland, Dr. Robert Keppel, Dr. John Liebert, Dr. Mary Ellen O'Toole, Dr. Thomas Young, Dr. John Liebert, Dr. Laura Pettler, Lt. Joe Kenda, B.S., Mark Safarik, M.S., Susanna Ryan, M.S., James Clemente, Esq., and W. Jerry Chisum, B.S. The author was honored to sit on a board of such prestige and diversity whose distinguished contributions to the criminal justice community had in many ways changed the world. From the Review Board grew AISOCC's Consulting Committee chaired by Dr. Chris Kunkle comprised of exemplary practitioners seated on one of the subcommittees: legal, investigatory, forensic science, behavioral science, medicolegal, and academic. Together, President Kenneth L. Mains and Vice President Dr. Laura Pettler, and Director of Development, Angela Clemente AISOCC provides scientific, interdisciplinary cold case review completely free of charge to requesting agencies. AISOCC's Board of Directors, Review Board Members, and Consulting Committee Members, coupled with its General and Student Members, and empower and uplift AISOCC's mission by also serving on AISOCC's Cold Case Awareness Initiative Committees: membership, cold case intake, social media, media, academic journal, educational outreach, and victim and family. AISOCC is as strong as its membership, and its membership is made up of extremely strong world-class practitioners whose impeccable character, desire to give back, and dedication to AISOCC's mission are unparalleled.

Cold Cases and Crime Scene Staging

As mentioned earlier, it is quite possible that more crime scenes than previously predicted are actually staged and are going undetected (Ferguson, 2011; Keppel & Weis, 2004). Throughout this book, the author has identified, defined, discussed, analyzed, synthesized, and evaluated many of the substantiated and unsubstantiated ideas regarding staging, but one book is not nearly enough space to capture every intricate detail revealed in the empirical literature on crime scene staging dynamics in homicide cases to date. This book might be the first log on the fire. The importance of becoming well educated in what is known about crime scene staging dynamics in homicide cases thus far is critical to public safety in that when the staging efforts by offenders go undetected, it leaves a victim and family without justice and a violent offender in society with the opportunity to reoffend. Second, staged cases do not have to go cold because there are modern investigatory tools, such as the author's VCDIM presented in this book; Gardner and Bevel's (2009) event analysis method; Chisum and Turvey's (2011) crime reconstruction method; Walter, Adcock, and Stein's (2011) crime matrix method;

and other scientifically based methodologies that help investigators organize and solve even the most complex problems many murder cases contain.

With the results of Scripps Howard News Service's study (Hargrove, 2010) that revealed that the suspects in the majority of the female victim cases of the 185,000 homicides and nonnegligent manslaughter cases that have gone unsolved from 1990 to 2008 in America today are the intimate partners and associates of the female victim, but where no arrest has been made, it is indicative that some of these cases might have been staged and are probably circumstantial at best at this point. This prediction, though speculative in and of itself, is supported by the empirical literature and what is known about crime scenes staging dynamics in homicide cases today coupled about what is known about intimicide and intimate partner violence and is enough to warrant support that crime scene staging is a threat to public safety and one that needs to be addressed (Chisum & Turvey, 2011; Eke, 2010; Ferguson, 2011; Gross, 1924; Pettler, 2011; Turvey, 1999, 2002, 2012).

Conclusion

Crime scene staging in homicide cases is the purposeful and deliberate acts of an offender to misdirect the investigation of the death of a human being who the offender murdered regardless of the circumstances or events that exacerbated the situation between them. Therefore, it is important not to lose sight of the fact that staging is about people's lives. It is about families who have lost loved ones to violence and victims who deserve justice. Investigators must take heed and invest in their profession by learning everything there is empirically to know about staging toward capturing those who wish to evade capture. Every dead victim is someone's daughter, someone's son, someone's grandchild, sister, brother, friend, and so on, who deserves a thorough death investigation. Crime scene staging is a problem for victims, families, investigators, prosecutors, judges, communities, and for society. Regardless of whether or not the number is right, even 185,000 on the low side of the spectrum is too many cold cases to ever have at any time. Scientific, systematic inquiry and examination can help. The time has come and the time is now.

...Aspire to inspire.

References

Adcock, J. M., & Stein, S. (2011). *Cold case: An evaluation model with follow-up strategies for investigators*. Boca Raton, FL: CRC Press/Taylor & Francis Group.

Canter, D. (1994). *Criminal shadows: Inside the mind of a serial killer*. London: HarperCollins.

Carolina Forensics, LLC. (2014). *Crime scene staging awareness initiative*. Retrieved from http://www.crimescenestaging.com

Chisum, W. J., & Turvey, B. E. (2011). *Crime reconstruction*. Waltham, MA: Academic Press.

Douglas, J. E., & Munn, C. (1992, February). Violent crime scene analysis: Modus operandi, signature, and staging. *FBI Law Enforcement Bulletin, 61*(2), 1–10.

Eke, A. W. (2007). *Staging in cases of homicide: Offender, victim, and offence characteristics* (Doctoral dissertation). Retrieved from ProQuest (1390310091).

Ferguson, C. (2011). *The defects of the situation: A typology of staged crime scenes* (Unpublished doctoral thesis). Bond University, Gold Coast, Queensland, Australia.

Ferguson, C. (2014, July). Staged homicides: An examination of common features of faked burglaries, suicides, accidents and car accidents. *Journal Police Criminal Psychology*. Springer Publishing. doi: 10.1007/s11896-014-9154-1.

Ferguson, C., & Petherick, W. (2014, October 13). Getting away with murder: An examination of detected homicides staged as suicides. *Homicide Studies*. doi: 10.1177/1088767914553099.

Geberth, V. J. (1996). *Practical homicide investigation: Tactics, procedures, and forensic techniques* (3rd ed.). Boca Raton, FL: CRC Press/Taylor & Francis Group.

Geberth, V. J. (2006). *Practical homicide investigation: Tactics, procedures, and forensic techniques* (4th ed.). Boca Raton, FL: CRC Press/Taylor & Francis Group.

Geberth, V. J. (2010). Crime scene staging: An exploratory study of the frequency and characteristics of sexual posing in homicides. *Investigative Sciences Journal, 2*(2), 1–19.

Gardner, R. M., & Bevel, T. (2009). *Practical crime scene analysis and reconstruction*. Boca Raton, FL: CRC Press/Taylor & Francis Group.

Gross, H. (1924). *Criminal investigation*. London, UK: Sweet & Maxwell.

Hargrove, T. (2010, March 23). *Unsolved homicide analysis: A look at what kinds of murders get solved*. New York: Scripps Howard News Service.

Hazelwood, R. R., & Napier, M. R. (2004). Crime scene staging and its detection. *International Journal of Offender Therapy and Comparative Criminology, 48*(6), 744–759. doi: 10.1177/0306624X04268298

Keppel, R. D., & Weis, J. G. (2004). The rarity of unusual dispositions of victim bodies: Staging and posing. *Journal of Forensic Science, 49*(6), 1–5.

North Carolina v. Joshua Patrick Griffin, Case No. CRS98000401 (1998).

Petherick, W., & Ferguson, C. (2009). Behavioral consistency, the homology assumption, and the problems of induction. In W. Petherick (Ed.), *Serial crime: Theoretical and practical issues in behavioral profiling* (2nd ed.). London, UK: Academic Press.

Pettler, L. G. (2011). *Crime scene behaviors of crime scene stagers* (Doctoral dissertation). Retrieved from ProQuest (2251577601).

Pettler, L. (2014). Crime scene staging awareness initiative: Public figure. Retrieved from https://www.facebook.com/crimescenestaging

Schlesinger, L. B., Gardenier, A., Jarvis, J., & Sheehan-Cook, J. (2012, April). Crime scene staging in homicide. *Journal of Police and Criminal Psychology, 29*(1), 44–51.

Turvey, B. E. (1999). *Criminal profiling: An introduction to behavioral evidence analysis* (1st ed.). London, UK: Academic Press.

Turvey, B. E. (2000, December). Staged crime scenes: A preliminary study of 25 cases. *Journal of Behavioral Profiling, 1*(3).

Turvey, B. E. (2002). *Criminal profiling: An introduction to behavioral evidence analysis* (2nd ed.). London, UK: Academic Press.

Turvey, B. E. (2012). *Criminal profiling: An introduction to behavioral evidence analysis* (4th ed.). London, UK: Academic Press.

Walton, R. H. (2006). *Cold case homicides: Practical investigative techniques*. Boca Raton, FL: CRC Press/Taylor & Francis Group.

Appendix A: Research-Based Forensic Victimology

Table of Contents

V. Self-Actualization: Victim in Relation to Relative Adoption of Worldly Concepts
    a. Envirosocioculturalism
        i. Environment
        ii. Society
        iii. Culture
    b. Victim risk
    c. Victim's daily routine
VI. Appendices
    a. Live photos of the victim
    b. Family and friends organizational chart
    c. Timelines and calendars

Certificate of Victimology Completion

Victimology completed by _____

Title/Agency_____Date_____

Signature_____Date_____

Adapt Research-Based Forensic Victimology on a Case-to-Case Basis

Section I
Physiological: Victim's Physical Demographics and Attributes

Victim Demographics

Victim name:_____

Date of birth:_____ **Date of death:**_____ **Sex:**_____

Race:_____

Height:__'__" **Weight:**_____lb

Hair color:_____ **Hair type:**_____**Hair length:**_____

Eye color:_____ **Jewelry:**_____

Identifying characteristic(s):_____

Tatoos:_____

Country of origin:_____

Religion:_____

Other important demographic information:

_____

_____

Home/Residence

Present address(es):

_____

_____

Prior address(es):

_____

_____

Transportation and Vehicle Information
Present: _____
Other prior vehicles and/or other transportation-related information:

_____

_____

Heath and Medical Information
Identify and describe macro to micro any physical health conditions or impairments (include medications and/or treatments):

_____

_____

Identify and describe macro to micro mental health history and/or diagnosis(es) (include medications and/or treatments):

_____

_____

Section II
Safety: Victim in Relation to Personal, Familial, Financial,
and Occupational Safety

Personal Safety
Did the victim feel safe? _____
Was the victim aware of his or her personal safety? _____How so?

_____

Other important factors related to personal safety:

_____

_____

Was the victim paranoid or fearful of violent crime?

_____

_____

Was the victim a "victim of violent crime" previous to the event (i.e., domestic violence [physical abuse, economic abuse, sexual abuse, verbal, and/or emotional abuse]; sexual assault, rape [acquaintance rape, date rape, drug-induced rape, gang rape, rape]; child abuse [sexual abuse, physical abuse, physical neglect]; hate crime, terrorism)?

_____

_____

Was the victim security conscious and/or felt uncomfortable leaving doors and windows unlocked?

_____

_____

Did the victim take precautions to avoid victimization of any kind on his or her person, at home, in the car, and/or at his or her place of business?

_____

_____

Identify and describe any functioning or nonfunctioning security systems and note if they were functioning at home, in the car, and/or at a place of business at the time of the event.

_____

_____

Did the victim discuss defense mechanisms if he or she were to be attacked?

_____

_____

Familial Safety
Members at the time of the event:

_____

_____

Former members, estranged, etc. (if necessary):

_____

_____

Did the victim feel secure in his or her family?_____

Financial Situation and Socioeconomic Status
Did the victim feel safe in his or her financial situation/were there money problems? _____
Impact of socioeconomic status: _____ How so? _____
Other important factors related to financial situation:

_____

_____

Occupational Safety
Occupation: _____
Present employer: _____
Did the victim feel secure in his or her job? _____
Prior employers:

_____

_____

Other important factors related to employment and occupation:

_____

_____

Section III
Love and Belonging: Victim in Relation to Relationships

Intimate Partners, Marriages, and Intimate Relationships

Marital status: _____

Present:

_____

_____

Prior:

_____

_____

Interpersonal Relationships and Friendships

Present:

_____

_____

Prior:

_____

_____

Significant Acquaintances That the Victim Knew from Work and/or Other Activity(ies)

Present:

_____

_____

Prior:

_____

_____

Strangers

Did the victim meet any individual(s) who were noticeable to family, intimate partners, and/or friends/acquaintances or whom the victim mentioned?

_____

Why was the individual noticeable? _____

If yes, gather macro to micro detail on "stranger(s)" encounter(s) (i.e., gender, age, physical description, other demographic info, location of encounter, any and all information [**if necessary complete suspectology to record all pertinent information in any case where a stranger might be involved]):

_____

_____

Sexual encounters between the victim and "stranger," stalking, police reports, etc., anything related to stranger encounter that was out of the ordinary:

_____

_____

Enemies

Present:

_____

_____

Prior:

_____

_____

Problems and Conflicts

Who was in conflict with the victim? Known confrontations.

_____

_____

Was the victim conflicted by any recent court decisions, acquittals, convictions, and/or failures by law enforcement to apprehend suspects in an alleged crime against the victim?

_____

_____

Identify and describe any known enemies:

_____

_____

Identify and describe any individual(s) known to be angry with the victim, jealous of the victim, or who were frustrated with the victim. (Note significant jealousy or frustration, maliciousness, etc.) Who has the victim rejected?:

_____

_____

Was the victim a known obstacle to another individual? Why?

_____

_____

Who benefits from the victim's death? What is the payoff or what is gained from the victim's death? Was the victim's death or the event a resolution to a known problem or conflict? How?

_____

_____

Whose lifestyle improves with the victim's death?

_____

_____

Whose environment was the victim killed in?

_____

_____

Is the victim familiar with the scene?

_____

_____

Who notified police of the victim's death?

_____

Is the person who notified police of the death familiar with the scene?

_____

Victim/Offender Relationship, Initial Contact, and Location
Relationship of victim to offender (suspect):

_____

Victim was familiar with offender (suspect):

_____

Victim was specifically selected by offender (suspect):

_____

Offender (suspect) encountered victim by:

_____

Murder Scene and Crime Scene
Victim's death was opportunistic and/or circumstantial:

_____

Victim's location increased the level of risk to the offender (suspect):

_____

Victim's lifestyle placed him or her in a position of physical threat:

_____

How did the victim's behavior affect the crime scene (qualitative domains)?

_____

Case Linkage Analysis
Crimes, cases, missing persons, suspects, others ideas, leads, and interesting features that might link to this case:

_____

Computers
*Note about media and computers: It is crucial to keep this section extremely broad in the beginning. It is fair to narrow the scope as the investigation progresses, but begin at the broadest, widest part of the top of the funnel first.

Did the victim use a computer (i.e., desktop, laptop)? _____

If so, type(s), brand(s), location(s) most often used, location(s) infrequently used, activities, web sites, video games, what did the victim do on the computer, details macro to micro, etc.

Present:

_____

_____

Prior:

_____

_____

E-mails written by the victim to others or by others to the victim (identify senders and recipients and macro to micro content ideas):

_____

_____

Instant messages written by the victim to others or by others to the victim (identify senders and recipients and macro to micro content ideas):

_____

_____

Identify and describe all social networking sites, screen names, logins, and passwords. Include attachments from actual sites if possible:

_____

_____

Telephones

Did the victim use a landline telephone? _____

Carrier(s) and phone numbers:

_____

_____

Did the victim use a cellular telephone? _____

Carrier(s) and phone numbers:

_____

_____

If so, (either landline, cellular, or both) specify type(s), location(s), activities, details macro to micro, etc.

Regular calls to and from whom, times, dates, and/or reason for call(s) (specify to which phone [i.e., cell, land home, land work]):

_____

_____

Unusual calls to and from whom, times, dates, and/or reason for call(s) (specify to which phone [i.e., cell, land home, land work]):

_____

_____

Present messages or messages left within the determined time frame related to the event from whom, times, dates, and/or reason for call(s)/messages (specify if landline answering machine, left on digital cell phone voicemail, etc.):

_____

_____

Text messages victim texted to others or that were texted to victim (identify senders and recipients):

_____

_____

Books, Journals, and Other Written Media
Did the victim keep a journal, notebook, scrapbook, datebook, and/or something that he or she recorded daily, weekly, and/or monthly information?

_____

If so, is this media available for content analysis? _____
Notes that the victim left for others or left for victim (identify writers and recipients):

_____

_____

Did the victim read books? _____ If so, what kind of books and who were the victims favorite authors?

_____

_____

Television and/or Video Games
Did the victim watch television? _____
Did the victim play video games? _____
If so, what programs did the victim watch and/or what kinds of games did the victim play?

_____

_____

Music and Movies
Did the victim play any instruments? _____ If so, what and for how long? _____
What type(s) of music did the victim listen to? Who are the victim's favorite artists?

_____

_____

Did the victim watch movies? _____ If so, what type(s) of movies did the victim watch?

_____

_____

Section IV
Esteem: Victim in Relation to Personality, Cognition, Emotionality, Behavior, and Achievements

Personality

Check or select any personality traits relevant to the victim. Gather traits information from valid, credible longitudinal sources.

	Respects authority		Rebels against authority
	Loyal, devoted		Insincere, dishonest
	Work ethic		Distant, cold, aloof
	Motivated		Unmotivated
	Caring		Uncaring, unfeeling, callous
	Affectionate		Rude, impolite
	Decisive		Indecisive, unsure
	Self-satisfied		Closed, guarded, secretive
	Cheerful		Rejects change
	Courteous		Cheerless, gloomy, sour, grumpy
	Considerate, thoughtful		Discourteous, inconsiderate
	Brave		Inconsiderate
	Cooperative		Cowering, fearful
	Courageous		Uncooperative, unhelpful
	Devoted		Thoughtless
	Does what is necessary, right		Relies on others for everything
	Perseveres, endures		Combative, hostile
	Enthusiastic		Involved with dominant female
	Unselfish		Dependent on a dominant female
	Trusting		Unenthusiastic, apathetic, indifferent
	Thoughtful toward others		Relents, gives up
	Flexible		Dishonest, deceiving, lying
	Forgiving		Does what is convenient
	Focused		Inflexible, rigid, unbending, stubborn
	Freedom given to others		Unforgiving, resentful, spiteful
	Authoritarian, controlling		Unfocused, scattered
	Friendly		Unfriendly, distant, aloof
	Frugal, thrifty		Wasteful
	Generous		Stingy, miserly
	Involved		Ill will, malice, hatred
	Interested		Ungrateful, unappreciative
	Hardworking		Selfish
	Honest		Lazy
	Self-disciplined		Arrogant, conceited, egocentric

	High self-esteem		Indifferent, uncaring
	Kind		Jealous
	Not jealous, envious, covetous		Unkind, uncaring, cruel, mean
	Mature		Immature
	Modest		Vain
	Persistent, sustaining		Narrow, close, small-minded, intolerant
	Open-minded, tolerant		Pessimistic
	Perfectionist/OCD		Negative
	Optimistic		Unreliable, undependable
	Positive		Disrespectful, rude, impolite
	Practical		Blames others
	Punctual		Lack of self confidence, insecure
	Realistic		Suspicious, mistrusting
	Reliable		Insensitive, indifferent
	Respectful		Directed by others
	Responsible		Unresponsive, unreceptive
	Confident		Silly, trivial, petty
	Independent		Undisciplined, unrestrained, indulgent
	Selfless		Low/no self-esteem
	Sensitive/sympathetic		Self-centered
	Serious		Impulsive
	Sincere		Social approval required
	Social independence		Unsympathetic, unfeeling
	Systematic		Unsystematic, disorganized, random
			Insists on own view
			Wants to be the star
			Selfish

(Posner, 2010)

Cognition *(notable ideas, opinions, etc.)*

_____

_____

Emotionality *(emotionality stable, unstable, etc.)*

_____

_____

Behavior *(types of behaviors that were normal and any unusual behavior)*

_____

_____

Formal Education and Achievements

Elementary school and location: _____

Middle school and location: _____

High school and location: _____

College, location, major, minor, degree, date awarded:

_____

Graduate school, location, major, track, concentration, internships, thesis/ graduate research paper/dissertation, degree, date awarded:

_____

Doctoral school (if separate from graduate school), location, major, track, concentration, internships, thesis/graduate research paper/dissertation, degree, date awarded:

_____

Identify and describe the victim's former and/or socioeconomic status:

_____

_____

Section V
Self-Actualization: Victim in Relation to Relative Adoption of Worldly Concepts
(Envirosocioculturalism)

Environment, Society, and Culture
Describe the overall lifestyle of the victim:

_____

Describe the overall environment of the victim:

_____

Describe the overall social structure of the victim:

_____

Check or select any personality traits relevant to the victim. Gather traits information from valid, credible longitudinal sources.

	Family was affectionate.
	Family was hostile and/or indifferent.
	Family has high mental abilities.
	Family has poor mental abilities.
	Parents graduated from high school.
	Parents have low social status.
	Parents were motivated and gave direction.
	Parents sat around and failed to instruct.

	Parents strived for success and achieved success.
	Parents stagnated and remained in the same place for years.
	Individual is attractive.
	Individual is unattractive.
	Individual is successful in school, work, and life.
	Individual is unsuccessful in school, work, and life.
	Family was prosperous during the individual's upbringing.
	Family lived in poverty during the individual's upbringing.
	Individual has psychological problems.

Describe the overall culture of the victim:

_____

Describe the victim's normal and regular actions and any notable recent changes:

_____

Describe the victim's normal and regular clothing and any notable recent changes:

_____

Identify and describe any recent notable changes to the victim's lifestyle (i.e., clothing, friends, frequented locations, protection from abuse orders, separation agreements, divorces, breakups)

_____

Identify and describe the victim's interests, hobbies, extracurricular activities, clubs, sports, etc.

_____

Identify and describe the victim's high-risk behaviors if any, such as alcohol or drug abuse, prostitution, gambling, gang activity, domestic violence, extramarital affairs and/or promiscuity, criminal enterprise, and/or other high-risk behaviors or criminal activity. Create attachments if needed.

_____

Victim Risk
*It is important to recognize that this section is not reflective of offender motive, excuses, defense, etc.; this section is investigatory in nature only.

Identify and describe the victim's *participation* if any (i.e., domestic violence, slapping, hitting, gang activity, drug dealing, offensive behavior, aggressive, and/or provocative behaviors) that could have played a role in the event:

Identify and describe the victim's *participation* if any (i.e., A well-dressed woman driving an expensive car; woman to takes the same routine every day) that might or could have played a role in the event:

The victim engaged or witnessed in a high-risk activity, such as contributed funds to a scam without reporting it to authorities, hangs out in the street with drug users, witnesses assaults or murders, or creates situations that facilitate becoming a victim.

Was the victim a vigilante? If so, what was he or she avenging?

Was it necessary for the victim to die or for the event to occur pursuant to financial constraints (i.e., insurance fraud), extramarital affairs, etc.?

Identify and describe any compensation by an insurance policy or funding from another source before the event (i.e., car accident, restitution, settlement). Was there anyone who would have benefited from the victim's death?

Did the victim suffer from "battered women's syndrome" (*State v. Kelly*, 478 A2d 364,1985) (i.e., feminist theory)? :_____

Victim's Daily Routine

*Note any locations frequented at the time relevant to the event (i.e., 72 hours before or sooner; in some cases, a broader window might be necessary).
For all of the succeeding text, specify day of the week.
Victim's morning routine macro to micro:

Victim's morning travel to work routine macro to micro (specify intermediate and final destinations; include any significant individuals or events that regularly occur):

Victim's morning work routine macro to micro:

_____

_____

Victim's lunch break routine macro to micro:

_____

_____

Victim's afternoon routine macro to micro:

_____

_____

Victim's after-work travel routine (specify intermediate and final destinations; include any significant individuals or events that regularly occur):

_____

_____

Victim's pre-evening meal routine:

_____

_____

Victim's evening meal routine:

_____

_____

Victim's post-evening meal routine:

_____

_____

Victim's nighttime and bedtime routine:

_____

_____

*Complete additional sheets if different routines on different days; create routine labels (i.e., routine 1) and map on chart.
Were there any recent and notable changes to the victim's routine?

_____

_____

Were there any other locations previously significant to the victim that he or she did not visit anymore (i.e., bar, gym, school)? _____
If so, describe macro to micro and reasons why the victim no longer frequents those locations.

_____

_____

Appendices

Appendix A. Live Photos of the Victim
Attach to victimology.
Appendix B. Family and Friends Organization Charts
Build in PowerPoint or similar program and attach to victimology.

Appendix C. Timelines and Calendars
Create attachment with broader timeline (i.e., week, month) if needed.
Victim's 72, 48, 24 Hours before Death
72 hours before the event in 1-hour increments (create spreadsheet):
48 hours before the event (create spreadsheet):
24 hours before the event (create spreadsheet):
Attach spreadsheets to victimology.

References

Maslow, A. H. (1943). A theory of human motivation. *Psychological Review, 50*, 360–396.

Pettler, L. G. (2011). *Crime scene behaviors of crime scene stagers* (Doctoral dissertation). Retrieved from ProQuest (2251577601).

Posner, R. (2010). *The miraculous phenomenon of life response* (1st ed.). CA: Author.

Walton, R. (2006). *Cold case homicides: Practical investigative techniques.* Boca Raton, FL: CRC Press/Taylor & Francis Group.

Appendix B:
Victim-Centered
Death Investigation
Methodology Outline

Victim-centered death investigation methodology is designed for use by investigators, criminologists, and others who investigate the very daunting task of the staged crime scene. The methodology is a systematic interrelated structure, but with the available flexion needed for adaption on a per-case basis. The method looks complicated in whole, but in pieces each piece is clear, concise, and field-applicable. With anything, there is a learning curve, but a process well worth it in the end.

1. Stage 1: Crime Scene Knowledge
   Type: Quantitative—Precise measurement of physical evidence
   Location: Level 1—Bottom, foundational level of Bloom's Taxonomy:
   a. Is the crime scene staged? Staging Identification Trilogy
      i. Conflict/confrontation
      ii. Victim discovery
      iii. Verbal staging
   b. Ferguson's (2015) empirically derived staging detection how-to.
   c. Refuse to assume the integrity of the crime scene.
   d. Identify and detect the staging behavior and/or staged physical evidence.
   e. Define and describe the physical evidence.
2. Stage 2: Crime Scene Comprehension
   Type: Quantitative—Precise measurement of physical evidence
   Location: Level 2—One must identify, define, and describe, before one can classify and discuss:
   a. Document the initial observations of the scene.
   b. Classify and discuss physical evidence. This might not be done on paper, but should be discussed with lab personnel and/or experts if needed.
   c. Develop plan for how to accurately, precisely, and appropriately meet the legal and scientific objectives of crime scene processing procedures and techniques.

   d. Plan needed resources that might not be on hand, such as chemicals or other specialized equipment that could detect staged elements of the scene.
 3. Stage 3: Application of Crime Scene Technology
    Type: Quantitative and qualitative—Precise measurement of physical evidence in context of all evidence and crime scene as a whole
    Location: Level 3—One can apply knowledge when the knowledge is acquired and understood:
   a. Prepare to execute crime scene processing plan taking careful consideration to process for elements of crime scene staging; this could be additional photographs of angles not otherwise considered standard.
   b. Precisely measure using multiple points of reference, crime scene search methodology, etc., all items of physical evidence in addition to crime scene measurements. For later reconstructive purposes; be sure to measure everything in three dimensions (L × W × H); the more detailed this section is, the more likely reconstruction might be able to be done.
   c. Collect all physical evidence being sure to document all demographic information related to the evidence. One thing to note, the author has seen countless times bloodstain evidence lost due to inaccurate packaging. Allow wet items to dry, use paper to separate layers, and then package so nothing is touching another part of the item (i.e., bedsheet).
   d. Preserve all items of physical evidence and document preservation efforts.
   e. Report all crime scene activity and processing system, including agency protocol, investigative summaries, supplements, crime scene logs, evidence lists, and corresponding documents, measurements, photographs, notes, etc., and assemble into a well-organized system that can be easily reviewed (the author suggests using a binder system to *tab* and organize reports. The report should be robust in breadth and depth, and contain both quantitative (the what) and qualitative data (the how/why descriptive) in order to help the reader understand all the details about any particular piece of evidence and the crime scene as a whole. Create a Table of Contents and place at the front of the binder. Tab the binder sections.
 4. Stage 4: Crime Analysis
    Type: Quantitative and qualitative—Studying the precise measurement of physical evidence in context and how it could be interrelated to the victim and other components

Location: Level 4—One can analyze the application once knowledge is acquired and understood:

a. Research-based forensic victimology—Using Maslow's hierarchy of needs as a conceptual framework to use the method and categories discussed in Chapter 5, conduct full victimological study on all victims and then use modified triangulation to determine if select information revealed in the study of the victim are empirical (can be validated and are reliable because it can be proven and substantiated), quasi-empirical (can be partially validated and/or are partially reliable possibly), or nonempirical (cannot be validated or relied upon because there is nothing to substantiate the information). Victimology is then used as a baseline for all other types of analysis, synthesis, and evaluation going forward.

b. Crime scene and laboratory reports—Analyze all crime scene reports contained in the binder from Stages 1, 2, and 3 along with interrelating them to the forensic service laboratory reports, such as DNA, serology, and ballistics, to compare to victimology.

c. Autopsy and wound pattern analysis—In partnership with the forensic pathologist, medical examiner, coroner, or other relevant parties, break apart each pertinent aspect of the autopsy and then focus on studying the wounds to the victim. Complete wound analysis charts, diagrams, and spreadsheets to compare to crime scene, labs, and victimology.

d. Suspectology (or statement analysis)—It is the study of the suspect or suspects. Complete suspectology for each suspect. This substage could be switched with statement analysis. Determine what is empirical, quasi-empirical, and nonempirical and then compare to wound analysis, crime scene, lab reports, and victimology.

e. Statement analysis (or suspectology)—For the purpose of this discussion, statement analysis is the breaking apart of statements, studying each piece, and then cross comparing statements given at different times to possibly different individuals to identify, define, discuss, and then analyze very specific details related to the crime; this substage could be switched with suspectology. Determine what is empirical, quasi-empirical, and/or nonempirical if necessary and then compare to suspectology, wound analysis, crime scene, lab reports, and victimology.

5. Stage 5: Crime Synthesis
Type: Quantitative and qualitative—Putting together all the pieces of the puzzle

Location: Level 5—One can synthesize all of the pieces of the analysis once the knowledge is understood and applied:

a. Crime Synthesis Matrix—Place all analyzed pieces in their proper location of one or more of the three columns of the matrix: before, during, or after the crime. Then take each piece listed in each column, and if not already done during the analysis stage, determine if each piece is empirical, quasi-empirical, or nonempirical. Try to enter broad categories first and then underpin with the pieces of each.

6. Stage 6: Crime Evaluation

Type: Quantitative and qualitative—Drawing conclusions based on substantiation

Location: Level 6—Only when all other stages are complete, it is time to evaluate toward assigning worth, merit, or value:

a. In partnership with the district attorney, state attorney, solicitor, prosecutor, or others, explain victim-based death investigation methodology, everything contained in the case, the system, and method by which each piece was analyzed and synthesized, and then present all of the information for evaluation.

Appendix C: Crime Synthesis Matrix

Before the Death	During the Death	After the Death
Victimology	*Victimology*	*Victimology*
Relevant items here	Relevant items here	Relevant items here
Crime scene and lab reports	*Crime scene and lab reports*	*Crime scene and lab reports*
Relevant items here	Relevant items here	Relevant items here
Wound pattern analysis	*Wound pattern analysis*	*Wound pattern analysis*
Relevant items here	Relevant items here	Relevant items here
Suspectology	*Suspectology*	*Suspectology*
Relevant items here	Relevant items here	Relevant items here
Statement analysis	*Statement analysis*	*Statement analysis*
Relevant items here	Relevant items here	Relevant items here
Other relevant information	*Other relevant information*	*Other relevant information*
Relevant items here	Relevant items here	Relevant items here

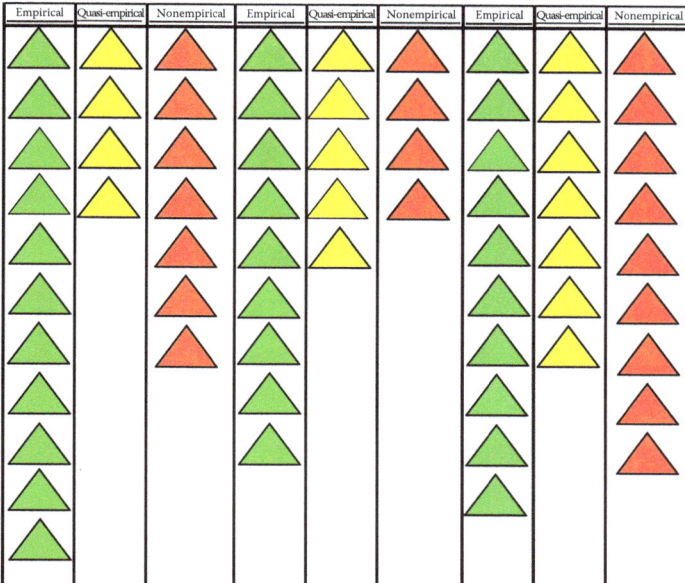

Appendix D: Physical Evidence Inventory and Information Worksheet (Example)

Key:

	OK, all present and accounted for
	Need follow-up
	Missing
	Lab tests pending
	Item not necessary
ws	Photo with scale
B	Photo is blurry

Item #	Report and Page #	Item	Recovery Location and Info	CSI/Inv.	Time/Date	Packaging	Overall Photo	Midrange Photo	Close-Up Photo	Close-Up w/Scale	Measurements	Requested Lab Tests	Lab or Pending Lab Results	Notes
1	224	Plaza pawn and gun bill of sale	$219.40, AIT, debit card receipt	Kimbrough	5/13/2011 1813	Plastic						Fingerprints/ touch		
2		GSR kit—John Doe	Sheriff's office	Hale	5/13/2011	Plastic						GSR	Negative	
3		Clothing—James Doe	Gray shirt, khaki shorts, white socks, Boulder Creek shoes,	Cannon	5/13/2011 1730	Paper						GSR/ serology		Check on packaging of #3 for BPA purposes
4		Clothing—Jane Doe	Taken from patrol officers	Cannon	5/13/2011							None	N/A	
5		Bullet fragment	Bullet fragment 39" from master bedroom door in ceiling on north wall	Fair		Plastic		234, 238 ws			39" from door? Wall?	?		Need follow-up on measurements; unclear what the 39" means
6		Bullet fragment	North wall at entry to master bedroom	Deese	5/13/2011	Plastic	162	163				DNA/ ballistics	Female victim/ pending	No notes for this item of evidence. Deese took notes for everyone, but her notes do not include this item. More inforamtion needed.
7		Shell casing	On north wall between female victim's waist and wall	Fair		Plastic		231, 232 ws				DNA/ ballistics	Male victim/ pending	
8		Shell casing	Stomach of female victim	Deese	5/13/2011	Plastic	147 Blurry	154 Blurry, 161, 166	165			DNA/ ballistics	Male victim/ pending	
9	289	Broken glass	From bedroom area	Halsac	5/16/2011 1400							None	N/A	
10		Hi-point .40 Cal S&W rifle	On floor at built-in dresser in master bedroom	Halsac	5/13/2011	Paper		175	178, 179	181, 180		DNA/ fingerprints/ ballistics		

Appendix E: Crime Scene Photo Log Worksheet

(Example)

Photo #	Type	Item/Subject	Time/Date	Photographer
DS_00001	Overall	Street view of house	0845/1-2-13	Parker
DS_00002	Midrange	Yard view of house	0846/1-2-13	Parker
DS_00003	Close-up	House	0848/1-2-13	Parker
DS_00004	Overall	House front door closed	0849/1-2-13	Parker
DS_00005	Midrange	House front door closed	0900/1-2-13	Parker
DS_00006	Close-up	House front door closed	0902/1-2-13	Parker
DS_00007	Overall	Bullet hole in front door	0905/1-2-13	Parker
DS_00008	Midrange	Bullet hole in front door	0912/1-2-13	Parker
DS_00009	Close-up	Bullet hole in front door	0914/1-2-13	Parker
DS_00010	Close-up ws	Bullet hole in front door	0915/1-2-13	Parker

Appendix F: Wound Pattern Analysis Worksheet

Case: _____

Case Number: _____

	Location	Length	Width	Description	Notes
Evidence of Injury					

Appendix G: Statement Analysis Worksheet

Case: _____

Case Number: _____

Item from Statement	Statement 1	Statement 2	Statement 3	Statement 4	Comparison to Crime Analysis Components

Appendix H: Prereconstruction Checklist

Adapt on a Case-by-Case Basis

**Name of Individual Completing
Checklist:**_____

Date Checklist Completed:_____

Indicate Which Files Are Included for Review:
- ☐ Police department
- ☐ Sheriff's office
- ☐ State investigative agency
- ☐ State crime lab
- ☐ Federal investigative agency
- ☐ District Attorney's Office file

Victim Information:
- ☐ Live photos (digital preferred)
- ☐ Autopsy report
- ☐ Autopsy photos (digital preferred)
- ☐ Interviews/statements from victim(s)
- ☐ Medical history, mental health history, alcohol and drug history, and/or high-risk lifestyle history

Suspect(s)/Defendant(s) Information:
- ☐ Live photos (digital preferred)
- ☐ Interviews/statements from suspect(s)/defendant(s)
- ☐ Medical history, mental health history, alcohol and drug history, and/or high-risk lifestyle history

Crime Scene Information:
- ☐ Agency's standard crime scene processing protocol and/or standard operating procedure (Every agency should have a standard crime scene processing protocol/checklist that they use. This is very helpful to us to understand their work so we are all on the same page and helps us understand why they might do something in a particular manner per their agency's directive.)

☐ Crime scene entry log
   ☐ Photos and video (CD and DVD)
☐ Notes
   ☐ Diagrams, sketches, and measurements
   ☐ Neighborhood canvass (should be included with Law Enforcement [LE] file)
      ☐ Physical evidence
         ☐ List of evidence and evidence log.
         ☐ Dispositions, chain of custody, etc.
         ☐ Photos of all evidence collected (CD/DVD).
         ☐ Evidence is available for review and testing.
         ☐ List of any known missing evidence.
Crime Lab Reports (Not Every Type of Evidence Is Collected in Every Case):
       ☐ Serology/biology
       ☐ Firearms
       ☐ Fingerprints
       ☐ Trace
       ☐ Other_____
Interviews/Statements (Paper):
   ☐ First responders, emergency medical service, first responding officer, hospital personnel, social workers, etc.
   ☐ Friends, family, employer(s), coworker(s), and associates
   ☐ Victim(s)
   ☐ Suspect(s)/defendant(s)
   ☐ Cell phone, landline phone, and text message records (paper)
   ☐ Victim(s)
   ☐ Suspect(s)/defendant(s)
   ☐ E-mails, instant messenger, etc. (paper)
   ☐ ☐☐ Victim(s)
   ☐ ☐☐ Suspect(s)/defendant(s)
   ☐ Diaries
   ☐ Notes
   ☐ Documents
   ☐ ☐ Geographical map(s) of the crime scene, traffic patterns related to the crime scene
   ☐ Weather reports
   ☐ Obituary and/or other media

Index

For Product Safety Concerns and Information please contact our EU
representative GPSR@taylorandfrancis.com
Taylor & Francis Verlag GmbH, Kaufingerstraße 24, 80331 München, Germany